READING ASSESSMENT TO PROMOTE EQUITABLE LEARNING

Also Available

Collaborative Coaching for Disciplinary Literacy: Strategies to Support Teachers in Grades 6–12
Laurie Elish-Piper, Susan K. L'Allier, Michael Manderino, and Paula Di Domenico

The Common Core Coaching Book: Strategies to Help Teachers Address the K–5 ELA Standards
Laurie Elish-Piper and Susan K. L'Allier

Reading Assessment to Promote Equitable Learning

An Empowering Approach for Grades K–5

Laurie Elish-Piper
Mona W. Matthews
Victoria J. Risko

Foreword by H. Richard Milner IV

THE GUILFORD PRESS
New York London

A Division of Guilford Publications, Inc.
370 Seventh Avenue, Suite 1200, New York, NY 10001
www.guilford.com

Printed in the United States of America

This book is printed on acid-free paper.

Last digit is print number: 9 8 7 6 5 4 3 2 1

Library of Congress Cataloging-in-Publication Data

Names: Elish-Piper, Laurie, author. | Matthews, Mona W., author. | Risko, Victoria, author.
Title: Reading assessment to promote equitable learning : an empowering approach for grades K-5 / Laurie Elish-Piper, Mona W. Matthews, Victoria J. Risko ; foreword by H. Richard Milner IV.
Description: New York : The Guilford Press, 2022. | Includes bibliographical references and index.
Identifiers: LCCN 2022016195 | ISBN 9781462549979 (paperback) | ISBN 9781462549986 (hardcover)
Subjects: LCSH: Reading (Elementary)—Evaluation. | Reading comprehension—Evaluation. | BISAC: EDUCATION / Teaching / Subjects / Language Arts | EDUCATION / Evaluation & Assessment
Classification: LCC LB1573 .E44 2022 | DDC 372.48—dc23/eng/20220506
LC record available at *https://lccn.loc.gov/2022016195*

About the Authors

Laurie Elish-Piper, PhD, is Dean of the College of Education at Northern Illinois University, where she also holds the titles of Distinguished Engagement Professor and Distinguished Teaching Professor. Dr. Elish-Piper is a past director of the Jerry L. Johns Literacy Clinic. Her scholarship addresses literacy assessment, literacy coaching, family engagement, and supporting struggling readers. She has coauthored 13 books and more than 80 articles and chapters. Dr. Elish-Piper has served in leadership roles in the Association of Literacy Educators and Researchers, the International Literacy Association, and the Illinois Reading Council. Previously she worked as an elementary teacher, a middle school language arts and reading teacher, and an educational therapist.

Mona W. Matthews, PhD, is Professor Emerita in the Department of Early Childhood and Elementary Education at Georgia State University. Dr. Matthews's scholarship, which merges research and theories related to young children's social, literacy, and individual development, addresses how young children's social resources (e.g., classmates, teachers, family) influence their literacy development. She has coauthored one previous book and 47 articles and chapters. Dr. Matthews is a past president of the Association of Literacy Educators and Researchers. She previously worked as a preschool teacher, a first-grade teacher, and an educational consultant working with teachers to support their literacy teaching.

Victoria J. Risko, EdD, is Professor Emerita at Vanderbilt University, where she taught in the language, literacy, and culture program within the Department of Teaching and Learning. Her research focuses on teacher education and professional development, teacher reflection, and equity-based multimedia environments that support English learners and readers who are experiencing difficulties. Dr. Risko is a past president of the International Literacy Association and the Association of Literacy Educators and Researchers. She is coauthor of several books and numerous articles and chapters. A recipient of several national and international awards for contributions to research and literacy education, Dr. Risko is a member of the Reading Hall of Fame. She began her career as a first- and fourth-grade teacher.

Foreword

I recently had a conversation with a Black high school student in his last year of school. This student attended a mostly White, rural, scarcely resourced school in the South. As we talked, this young person revealed how "stressed" he was that the majority of his junior year of high school was virtual and that he was "really anxious" about impending college entrance examinations that would play a role in his college selection opportunities and also potential scholarships that he hoped to receive to cover his tuition, room, and board. This was not a student with exorbitant means. Instead, the student had moved to the community to live with his grandparents from a neighboring state after both his parents died—first his mother, then his father—fewer than 6 months apart.

This student's grandfather was ill, with medical bills "out of control," according to the student. This student believed that his "only way out" to help his family—his younger sister who lived with an aunt, an aging grandmother, and his seriously ill grandfather—was through education. And when I probed about his anxieties, this student pointed to an assessment that would have some predictive bearing on his college admissions and moreover on his ability to earn an academic scholarship, which he had hoped to secure. The student would likely receive other forms of financial support, but the grants and such would not cover the full range of expenses about which he worried. As a young person, he did not want to accrue student loans that would deepen his family's financial burdens. This interaction reminded me how assessments can be used as a tool to psychologically and emotionally abuse young people.

In *Reading Assessment to Promote Equitable Learning: An Empowering Approach for Grades K–5*, Laurie Elish-Piper, Mona W. Matthews, and Victoria J. Risko have produced an extraordinarily important text about how obsession with testing in education can limit what educational assessments have the potential to provide. While their book focuses on the role and impact of reading assessments in elementary schools, the underlying issues they address and many of the strategies they propose are relevant and applicable at any grade level. To be sure, this book provides a level of context and nuance essential to any serious conversation about reading assessment practices designed to humanize learning and development processes. But the book has insightful implications beyond literacy. Understanding and centralizing context, both within and outside the walls of schools and classrooms, are necessarily essential in discourses about assessment. This book about assessment is timely.

This book is being published at a time when we are living through global pandemics. These pandemics are not singular to COVID-19. For instance, young people have had to draw meaning from the killings of Breonna Taylor, Ahmaud Arbery, Rekia Boyd, Antwon Rose Jr., George Floyd, and many others. Especially for minoritized bodies, and Black bodies in particular, attempting to make sense of the killing of unarmed individuals in the name of justice means that while young people and their families are working through COVID-19, they are concurrently working through anxieties related to the death of bodies like theirs by the state vis-à-vis police. Accordingly, to be potentially transformative, equitable, and thus useful, assessment mechanisms cannot be constructed and/or enacted as neutral tools. Assessments must be understood as context-specific (Milner, 2020) if we are to have a fighting chance of improving educational opportunities in reading for those most marginalized by, in, and through educational systems.

In his groundbreaking work, Robert Moses (*https://algebra.org/wp/bob-moses*) identified algebra within the field of mathematics as the gatekeeper for students' academic success, higher-level math learning, and potential for college access and achievement. In the field of literacy, reading comprehension, I would argue, carries a similar gatekeeping function. Although students' processing speed, their capacity to decode, and/or their skill to draw inferences are certainly essential elements to students' successful profiles in reading, reading comprehension remains perhaps the most important aspect of students' capacity to succeed across disciplines in schools and classrooms. In PreK–12 schools, a student's capacity to read and comprehend an informational text in science is perhaps just as important as their ability to read a graphic novel in an English language arts class. This book shows us that educators must understand how assessments can and should be used, when, by what means, and on whose behalf. For instance, educators' capacity to codesign formative assessments and/or summative assessments with students necessitates that teacher education programs and professional development opportunities help teachers view assessments as more than mere tools designed by others. Educators are invited to conceptualize and enact assessments as potential data points to help educators identify how to co-construct with students learning opportunities that are restorative, relevant, responsive, and opportunity centered. In other words, assessments should tell educators more about what the educators are (and are not) doing rather than identify deficits and shortcomings of students' reading skills, knowledge, and abilities. Thus, Elish-Piper, Matthews, and Risko remind us that assessment design, development, and practices require a focus on inputs—powerful pedagogy; robust, deep curriculum practices; and the building and sustaining of relationships with students, families, and communities. Outputs identified through assessments are consequences of inputs.

Moving away from an ethos of invisibility where educators and young people alike are viewed as unseen and unheard, this book centralizes the importance of using student talk and diverse assets to assess students' reading development. A call to recognize and value a rich repository of educators in our fight for equity through assessment, this book powerfully engages and merges the conceptual with the practical.

H. RICHARD MILNER IV, PhD
Cornelius Vanderbilt Distinguished Professor of Education
Vanderbilt University

Reference

Milner, H. R. (2020). *Start where you are but don't stay there: Understanding diversity, opportunity gaps, and teaching in today's classrooms* (2nd ed.). Cambridge, MA: Harvard Education Press.

Acknowledgments

We are grateful to the many teachers and students we have worked with over the years who informed the content and strategies in this book. Their passion for teaching and learning and deep commitment to equity inspired us to write this book.

Laurie: I wish to thank my parents, George and Lois Elish, for teaching me the power of literacy, education, and kindness to change the world. While they are gone now, their legacy lives on in me and in the words and ideas in this book. (laurieep@niu.edu)

Mona: I am filled with gratitude for my husband, Jim Matthews. For 48 years, Jim encouraged and supported me in each of my professional endeavors. Although he is not here to witness the book's publication, he was there during the years of research and writing that led to that publication. I continue to be sustained by memories of his love and the richness of our life together. (rmatthews@gsu.edu)

Vicki: I am thankful for the special people in my life. My parents taught me that if we want to make a difference for others we must speak up for equity and that everyone has special talents. I am grateful for my husband, Marino Alvarez, our son and daughter-in-law, Christopher and Heather Alvarez, and our two granddaughters, Elliana and Abigail, for their support and encouragement to live life fully. They demonstrate the power of literacy and of taking the lead in one's own learning. (victoria.j.risko@vanderbilt.edu)

Special thanks to Craig Thomas, Senior Editor at The Guilford Press, for believing in this book and its goal of making teachers and students visible through equitable literacy assessments. We also offer sincere gratitude to Anna Nelson, Senior Production Editor, whose care and attention to detail helped transform our manuscript into this book.

An invitation to our readers: Our previous collaborations with students, teachers, and parents inspired us to write this book. We would love to hear from you as you examine and implement the assessment strategies that we recommend. We would appreciate your comments and feedback, and we will be happy to answer any questions that you might have. Please email us at Victoria.j.risko@vanderbilt.edu.

Contents

Purchasers of this book can download and print the reproducible forms at *www.guilford.com/elish-piper3-forms* for personal use or use with students (see copyright page for details).

1

The Urgency of Now

Addressing Assessment Inequities

We live in challenging times. Recently we have faced a global pandemic, increased calls for equity and racial justice, extreme political divisiveness, assaults on the integrity of our democracy, and even questions about what science and facts are. And on top of these challenges, we are in the midst of an assessment craze in education. High-stakes testing and mandated state-level testing reign in schools across the United States, with the assessment of students' reading progress a primary focus. In this book, we use the construct of *invisibility*, feeling unseen and unheard, to describe the repercussions to teachers and their students of this obsession with testing. Teachers find their role in deciding how, when, and for what purposes reading is taught and assessed in their classrooms diminished and feel pressured to march through the curriculum fixated on raising test scores. Students encounter instruction that bears minimal or no evidence of their histories or lived experiences and conclude their teachers do not care about them. Both see themselves as inconsequential—that is, *invisible* to the instruction and the assessment that occurs in their classrooms.

Further, this obsession exacts huge costs on teachers and students (Koretz, 2017). When increased test scores become the marker for students' reading achievement, promotion, and/or placement into special programs, teachers spend inordinate amounts of time preparing their students for these tests, and students spend far too much time taking tests. When their role as instructional decision makers is diminished, teachers come to discount their literacy instructional knowledge and their capability to assess their students' reading ability. As a result, they come to believe that the content they are mandated to assess (and told how to assess) becomes more important and valuable than what is assessed during the formative, in-the-moment, ongoing assessment they do as part of their instruction. Students fare no better. Koretz (2017) recounted multiple stories of students experiencing physical responses, stomachaches, headaches, and the like brought on by anxiety about upcoming tests. No doubt, these costs harm teachers, and students, but there is a more insidious cost paid by too many students who attend U.S. schools.

The Testing Obsession Fuels Existing Inequities in Our Educational Institutions

This obsession with testing exacerbates the systemic and pervasive inequities present in the U.S. educational system. Standardized and mandated testing fuel many of those inequities. First and foremost, standardized tests are products of the dominant, White middle-class culture. This reflection of that culture takes place in subtle ways, such as in the words used, the topics selected to contextualize the questions, and the allusions made. These biases disadvantage students not socialized within a White middle-class culture, specifically students of color and those who are linguistically diverse, culturally diverse, and from underresourced communities (Koretz, 2017). Unfortunately, students of color who attend schools in underresourced communities are more likely to experience standardized and mandated tests scores as the primary measure of students' reading performance (Darling-Hammond, 2010; Koretz, 2017). And such tests typically use a multiple-choice format, which by default requires the assessment of small bits of information, such as knowledge of basic reading skills (International Literacy Association [ILA], 2019a; Shepard, Penul, & Davidson, 2017). Testing bits and pieces of language denies students the enriched curriculum they need to develop the dispositions needed, such as toward collaboration and problem solving; and the skills required for the twenty-first century, such as the ability to read critically and make informed decisions (Brady, 2012). Poor children, children of color, and linguistically and culturally diverse learners disproportionately bear the negative ramifications of these inequities. The irony here is that improving educational equity is often a justification given for employing such testing practices (Koretz, 2017).

Linguistically and culturally diverse learners experience additional ramifications when test scores become the marker for student success. Too often assessment content is prioritized over a curriculum that values their home language. Instead, many linguistically diverse learners receive reading instruction framed by a narrow, Eurocentric view of language based on monolingualism that often dissuades or even requires students not to use their home language at school (ILA, 2019b). Students are thus denied the opportunity to become fully bilingual and further develop their home language's linguistic knowledge (e.g., language structure, word knowledge, how language sounds) needed to leverage their reading growth.

Such inequities begin and are sustained by what Angela Valenzuela (1999) referenced as the process of *subtractive schooling*. Even though she used this term to describe the schooling experiences of Mexican American students in a Texas high school, similar processes are well documented in the schooling of younger students and students of color (Nieto & Bode, 2018), in explanations of critical race theory (Delgado & Stefancisc, 2017), and in the rationale for enacting culturally relevant pedagogy (Ladson-Billings, 2014). The verb *subtracted* means to strip, to take away. Thus, this is not a passive problem of representation, but an active erasure of the lived experiences of linguistically and culturally diverse learners. What is subtracted is what makes each student unique—their lives outside of the classroom, the interests that motivate their attention, the culture that informs their life's meaning, and the linguistic gifts appropriated from their families. Essentially, what is subtracted, stripped, or taken away is what makes them visible to others.

Not only does this process of subtraction fuel educational inequities and dehumanize learners, it is also bad instructional practice. Marie Clay (2001) helps us understand the substantial and foundational role students' personal and lived experiences play in their reading development. When children arrive at school, they bring already developed systems for processing information. Those most relevant to their reading growth include a grasp of the syntax of the language they speak; the meanings of the words they speak; the rituals and routines that help them make sense of their daily lives; the visual forms of objects, pictures, scenes that populate their world; and the understanding of the structure of stories told by significant people. Clay calls these *working systems* and views these processing systems as an essential foundation upon which more formal reading instruction must be built. Furthermore, children develop these processing systems via interactions with those closest to them—members of their family and community. Thus, subtracting what students learned in the laps and by the sides of others leaves them unmoored, without a foundation—essentially invisible.

In this book, we work to provide an alternative to these assessment practices that lead to teachers and students becoming invisible and that feed existing educational inequities by creating literacy assessments that do just the opposite. Teachers become visible when they, not those outside of their classrooms, determine the how, when, and for what purpose reading is taught and assessed. Students become visible when their teachers honor their dignity and unique histories and backgrounds, and they use those insights as the vital foundation upon which reading instruction and assessment are built. Therefore, we view visibility as an antidote to counteract the educational inequities fed by the current testing practices and the personal costs exacted on teachers and students by the current testing obsession.

To highlight the contrast between the assessments described in this book and those which contribute to the assessment craze, we look at the example of a 1-minute assessment for reading fluency. We chose this assessment because we have observed it in many classrooms. It may be required by your school district or it may be that you use it because you are uncertain about how to choose the best means to assess fluency. Teachers have shared with us that when required to give assessments such as this 1-minute fluency assessment, they feel compelled to have their students participate in drills to increase the number of words their students can read per minute so they will score higher on the test. Moreover, the power of required assessments becomes magnified when their students' performance plays a role in determining their students' placement in special programs or evaluating if they meet, exceed, or do not meet standards. That is a lot of power given to an assessment performed in 1 minute!

Not only does it garner outsized power, this 1-minute fluency assessment takes on a degree of importance that far outweighs the amount of useful information it offers. It provides only a tiny bit of data (how quickly and accurately a student can read a short passage), collected during 1 minute on one day of a school year while using just one text. This assessment does not offer information about the student's ability to comprehend the text, generate inferences, or understand important vocabulary words. Neither does it provide information about the students' phonics knowledge or other foundational skills, nor does it account for students' personal interests or motivation to read. In short, this assessment provides a small piece of what constitutes a very complex reading process, and as in the case of the 1-minute fluency assessment, leads students to think that the purpose of reading is to do it fast!

Moreover, how many words a student reads in 1 minute even undersamples the ability it purports to assess—a student's ability to read fluently. This 1-minute assessment accounts for only one of three dimensions that comprise reading fluency—rate (how many words a student can read in a minute), while it ignores the other two—accuracy (recognizing and decoding words correctly) and prosody (reading with expression and appropriate phrasing) (Hudson, Lane, & Pullen, 2005). Ignoring the dimensions of accuracy and prosody when assessing reading fluency ignores valuable information related to students' comprehension of the text read (Rasinski, Reutzel, Chard, & Linan-Thompson, 2011).

Further, not only is this 1-minute assessment inadequate in its assessment of reading fluency, but its delivery ensures teachers and students remain detached, invisible. Instead of teachers playing the role of an empowered professional, they perform the assessment as a technician giving it when and in the ways others decide. Students fare no better, for they, too, are invisible in this assessment event. Aside from the confined act of reading the text, students play no part in the assessment. They were not asked to reflect on what a fluent reader does. Nor were they asked to reflect on themselves as fluent readers or consider how their reading fluency had changed over time. Given the inadequacies of this 1-minute fluency assessment, we must wonder, "What do the teacher and student give up when preparing for the test?" and "What is omitted, obscured, or downplayed when teaching in order to prepare students for this test?" These seem like questions worth exploring.

Literacy Assessment as a Catalyst for Making Visible the Capabilities of Teachers *and* Students

Let us return to the construct of *invisibility*. As a teacher, what does it mean to you as a professional to be in **your** classroom with **your** students, yet you feel unseen or unheard by your school or district administrators? What about your students? What does it mean to your students when they feel unseen or unheard by you because they see no evidence of their knowledge, their cultural histories, their diverse languages, their lived experiences, or their reading strengths and needs in the instruction they receive? From a series of studies we conducted, we began to grasp what it means to both teachers and students when they feel invisible within their reading instruction. And we learned the role testing pressures played in the development of those feelings.

Over several years, we conducted a set of studies to learn about teachers, students, and parents' views about the reading instruction and reading experiences that occurred in schools (Bass, Dasinger, Elish-Piper, Matthews, & Risko, 2008). To understand their views, we surveyed 399 teachers, 350 students, and 120 family members and interviewed a subset of each group. We learned firsthand that both teachers and students felt they were inconsequential to the teaching and learning enactments in their classrooms—enactments often based on top-down directives accompanied by mandated testing. Teachers shared concerns about the intransigent force assessment played in their classrooms, a force they considered unrelenting. Teachers lamented about the intrusion of the pressures of testing on their decisions about what and how they taught. Respondents described the experience as intrusive and one that significantly reduced the power their students wielded over their instructional decisions. Teachers told us that their inability to push back on the demands of standardized and mandated tests disempowered them. Heather, a first-grade teacher, shared comments that typify the disempowerment and exhaustion felt by many teachers across grade levels:

> These first weeks of school are the worse. I have a class full of children [28] whom I have to individually test. Four of the five tests I must give have to be read aloud. I have little time to teach, and I must complete these tests within a given time-period. Please, my students are only six!! I'm beyond stressed and exhausted. I have many valuable ways to assess my young readers that are more useful to me. Why can't I be trusted to use my own assessments? I'm a professional!!!

In fewer than 100 words, Heather's comments capture the essence of what many teachers in our studies shared with us. Like Heather, they complained about how preparing their students for tests and administering tests left *little time to teach*. Like Heather they wondered why they must give tests under strict time constraints, that use decontextualized or contrived texts, and for the effort they received nothing but snapshots of what their students know and can do as readers. And like Heather, they wondered why as professionals *they were not trusted to use the valuable ways they know to assess their readers*. Consequently, many teachers spoke of how the demands wrought by standardized and mandated testing not only left them feeling disempowered and exhausted but extinguished the joy they once experienced from teaching.

Unfortunately, the students' comments revealed they sensed their teachers' lack of joy in teaching. Students described rigid classrooms in which their teachers strayed little from lesson plans that evidenced little awareness of students' knowledge, their cultural histories, their diverse languages, their lived experiences, or their reading strengths and needs. One student shared that he felt his teacher "was on autopilot"—teaching one lesson after another, suggesting their teacher was more concerned about covering than about teaching the material to the students in the class. Many students said their teachers' inability to engage them in lessons led them to believe their teachers did not care enough to take the time to learn about them as individuals. The following comments from Trae, a fifth grader, typify the sentiments expressed by many of the students in our studies:

> When I walk into my language arts class, the teacher doesn't even look at me. I'm not sure he even knows who I am. In fact, I wonder if he saw me outside of class, would he recognize me. When class starts, he stands in front of the room and teaches us from the book—boring!!! It's hard for me to pay attention.

Like Trae, many students felt their teachers did not know or care about them. Many like Trae wondered, if her teacher saw her outside of class, *"would he recognize me?"* Like Trae they felt disconnected from their teachers and the instruction they experienced in their classrooms. And like Trae when students viewed themselves as absent from the instruction, they spoke of being bored and disengaged. As implied in Trae's comments but voiced by many students, they yearned to be seen and heard by their teachers. They wanted their teachers to care enough to seek a close personal relationship with them.

As we analyzed the responses of the teachers and the students, we searched for a word to capture their meaning and that expressed the personal experiences teachers and students reported. We chose the word *invisibility* because it accomplished both. As a concept, invisibility, can be thought of in different ways. First, its literal definition captures the experience of being unseen or unheard. Teachers spoke of district and school administrators who rarely sought their opinions when designing policies that influenced what they taught or how they taught. And students shared that their strengths, needs, or interests were absent from the instruction they received. Second, the word *invisibility* captures the consequence when individuals feel invisible—they feel disempowered and therefore lack the agency to change their circumstances. Teachers spoke of wanting professional development to increase their knowledge of the best ways to assess their students' literacy growth but were told by their administrators that the professional development calendar was set for the year. Teachers complained that even when they possessed knowledge of assessments they viewed as more humane and student-centered, they were stymied in their efforts to use them because of the constraints in time and preparation required for the mandated assessments. Students spoke of becoming bored and disengaged when their interests and needs were absent from the instruction in their classrooms and attributed this absence as a sign their teachers did not care about them as learners. Teachers and students were clear about the antidote to their invisibility in their classrooms. Teachers wanted to be respected as professionals by their district and school administrators, and learners wanted to know that their teachers cared enough to take the time to learn about their interests, backgrounds, and literacy strengths and needs.

As we thought about the ramifications of the testing practices that resulted in many teachers and students feeling invisible and the inequities, such as ignoring student differences and using test scores as markers for promotion, associated with standardized assessments, we knew reading assessment must be grounded in a different paradigm. A paradigm that diverges from those that result in teachers and students being inconsequential within the assessment process, and a paradigm that is more equitable, just, and humane. In this book, we propose a view of reading assessment as a humanizing, empowering process that proceeds through an equity mindset. As a humanizing process, assessment honors the dignity of each student and is guided by the belief that all humans deserve the opportunity to fulfill their human potential. Being able to read provides a necessary tool for fulfilling one's potential (UNESCO, 2020). For teachers this means using assessments that provide an expansive, not a restrictive, look at students' reading potential. For students this means assessments that account for their knowledge, cultural histories, diverse languages, lived experiences, and reading strengths and needs. As an empowering process, assessment becomes an agentive space for both teachers and students. For teachers, this means they hold the assessment reins. Thus, assessment as an empowering process places a high value on teachers' knowledge, their ability to collect and analyze authentic data, and their use of such data to make instructional judgments. For students, this means they become active partners not passive participants during the assessment process. Students engage in self-analysis, reflect on their reading preferences, and become aware of the perspectives they hold of themselves as readers. Finally, the assessment process proceeds through an equity mindset, so teachers use assessments to understand and to provide all students the instruction they need to become fully engaged readers. For teachers, this means they need the support of school and district administrators to acquire the knowledge of and access to a wide range of reading assessments. For students, this means they receive the instruction they need when they need it and aligned with their strengths and needs, thereby increasing their opportunity for continuous reading growth. These opportunities exist for **all** students regardless of race, ethnicity, gender and gender expression, language, disability, background, or income (Aspen Education and Society Program and the Council of Chief State School Officers (2017).

In the next section, we provide more description of this view of assessment as a humanizing, empowering process that proceeds through an equity mindset. First, we explain why we limit our focus to reading assessments as opposed to literacy assessments broadly writ. Then, we further define this view of assessment by presenting how the assessments we support foreground teachers and students and account for reading's complexity.

The Reading Assessments We Champion

Literacy comprises multiple processes, including reading, writing, listening, and speaking. In this book, however, we focus primarily on the assessment of reading. We chose this focus for three reasons:

1. *Students' scores on reading assessments garner an outsized importance in defining their academic abilities.* Too often, these scores serve as a proxy for a district's, school's, or teacher's success. And they often carry high-stakes implications for students—such as determining whether they progress to the next grade level or will be graduated from high school.

2. *A single score or composite score on a standardized test cannot validly capture the complexity of students' reading.* Consider the complexity implied in Alexander's (2020) description of reading. "Reading is an expansive activity that occurs whenever a person and written language interact" (p. 594). Think about the complexity of the reader and the need to account for not only the reader's grasp and application of reading's cognitive aspects but also the personal, social, and cultural influences that weigh on their reading. Now think about the breadth of the written language in which readers interact. They engage with written language in almost infinite forms—books, digital devices, online, street signs, grocery aisles.

3. Perhaps most important, *standardized tests are products of the dominant, White middle-class culture and reflect that culture, while disadvantaging students not socialized within that culture*—students of color, linguistically and culturally diverse learners, and students from underresourced communities (Koretz, 2017). Therefore, these tests are inherently biased for many of the students who attend our schools. Unfortunately, the ways in which this bias appears, such as in the words used, the topics chosen to contextualize the questions asked, and the structure of the sentences, makes the bias less obvious, and thereby more pernicious (Kim & Zabelina, 2015). That bias leads to such tests being inherently unfair to many students in our schools and, therefore, antithetical to assessment as a humanizing, empowering process that proceeds through an equity mindset. For these reasons, we promote reading assessments that *foreground teachers and students* and assessments that are *attuned to reading's complexity*.

Reading Assessments That Foreground Teachers and Students

We began this chapter by describing the corruption to teaching and learning that results from the emphasis placed on raising test scores and the costs this emphasis exacts on teachers and students. To counter these costs, we promote a more humane and just approach to assessment; one we described as a humanizing, empowering process that proceeds through an equity mindset. This perspective prioritizes formative assessment over summative assessment. Summative assessments, which include standardized tests, end of course tests, and quarterly or benchmark tests, assess the cumulative progress students have made toward learning specific standards or content (International Reading Association, 2013). In contrast, formative assessment is not a specific type of assessment but describes a process interwoven within daily classroom instruction and thus that is part of the instruction. Formative assessment becomes an agentive space for teachers and students. Teachers observe and engage with their students as they apply their literacy knowledge and monitor their students' responses to the instruction. Teachers' presence during instruction enables them to offer timely advice in a manner responsive to the students' actions. Students engage in self-analysis, reflect on their preferences as readers, and attend to the perspectives they hold of themselves as readers. Students, through sustained engagement in the assessment process, become partners in their own learning (International Literacy Association, 2014). Moreover, given the nature of formative assessment, teachers gain more accessible and actionable feedback they can share with their students who then can use this feedback to set personal learning goals and to gain important insights about themselves as readers (International Literacy Association, 2013). Collectively, these features create an assessment process that provides teachers and students with information that is instructionally situated, practical, timely, and sensitive to the nuances of students' actions.

In addition, data gathered during the formative assessment process provide teachers the information they need to create high-quality reading instruction. Teachers need such data to design and implement instruction that enables students to make continuous progress in their reading ability. Essentially, information gained from formative assessments provides teachers a roadmap to follow when they plan, design, and implement reading instruction (International Reading Association, 2013). To illustrate the essential role formative assessment plays in delivering such instruction, we use the analogy of a ship's navigator. Informed by their[1] knowledge and experience, a ship's navigator uses maps and instruments to chart a ship's destination. Once a path is charted, the navigator monitors the ship's progress and stays alert to potential challenges, those expected, such as guiding the ship through a familiar waterway, and those unexpected, such as an approaching unmarked iceberg. Thus, the navigator's success in safely guiding the ship though these challenges and arriving at its destination hinges not only on their background and experience, but on the accuracy of the maps and instruments that inform their decision making.

When using this analogy to describe the role formative assessment plays in providing reading instruction attuned to students' backgrounds, strengths, and needs, the

---

[1] We freely use *they* (and *them* and *their*) as a singular pronoun throughout this book to avoid the need for binary and gendered pronouns, except where appropriate in specific examples.

teacher assumes the role of navigator. The assessments serve as the teacher's maps and instruments. And ensuring each student makes continuous progress toward becoming an effective, independent reader serves as the destination (i.e., goal). Like the ship's navigator, the teacher, informed by their knowledge and experience, uses data gathered from assessments to monitor the student's progress toward meeting the goal and stays alert to potential challenges. To monitor their students' progress and to stay alert to challenges that might impede that progress, teachers, like the ship's navigator, assume tremendous responsibilities. At a minimum those responsibilities include being vigilant data collectors, performing probing data analysis, keeping consistent records, and using what they learn from their assessments to inform their instruction. These occur while all along being alert to challenges that might impede student progress—challenges expected, such as those that occur when introducing a student to an unfamiliar text genre, and those unexpected, such as recognizing that a student fails to connect information read at the beginning of a text with information read in subsequent parts of the text. And finally, like the ship's navigator, the teacher's success in guiding their students through these challenges hinges on their knowledge and experience, as well as the accuracy of their assessments (i.e., their maps and instruments). Thus, the teacher, like a ship's navigator, must know where they are going, must know how to get there, must base their plans on their ongoing analysis of the data gathered, and must be willing to adjust their plans as needed.

Reading Assessments That Account for Reading's Complexity

Reading's complexity stems from its cognitive processes as well as the personal, social, and cultural influences that bear on its development. As a cognitive process, the enactment of reading varies by purpose (e.g., reading for pleasure, reading to learn about a topic) and by text (e.g., reading a fictional text for pleasure, reading a procedural text to learn how to do something). Reading's complexity also varies by strategy possession and use (e.g., rereading a portion of a text to solidify its meaning) and by motivation (e.g., reading a text about a topic of interest, versus reading an assigned text about a topic of little interest). This complexity includes not only recognizing what students know and can do but also recognizing their ability to call forth this knowledge when needed. So, a student not only knows that previewing a nonfiction text improves text comprehension but also knows when to apply this strategy. To assess adequately reading's cognitive complexity, teachers need diverse and dynamic ways to collect information, such as observation and interviews, gathered as students read in different contexts, read different types of texts, and read for different purposes. Further, because reading develops across time, teachers must gather information about their students' reading progress throughout the school year as they engage in authentic reading and writing experiences.

In addition, reading's complexity accounts for the influence a student's personal, social, and cultural experiences exact on their interpretations of texts read, their responses to the instruction received, their disposition toward literacy, and the meaning they ascribe to a text's purpose and use. Therefore, these influences must be considered when collecting, analyzing, and interpreting assessment data.

To account for these influences, Penul and Watkins (2019, p. 202) found promise in using a sociocultural model to guide views about teaching and learning and the nature of the assessments used. By using such models, teachers become intentional in their efforts to create learning experiences that account for their students' personal, social, and cultural experiences. Accordingly, teachers who embrace a sociocultural model of learning expand their assessment focus beyond the students' acquisition of the content that contextualizes the assessments to include what they know about how their students' knowledge, cultural histories, lived experiences, and reading strengths and needs shape their responses to the content. Hence, teachers' assessments must consider how students' identities as members of particular families and communities shape learning outcomes (Penul & Watkins, 2019, p. 202). Moreover, assessments must account for students' perceptions of themselves as agents in their own learning, and teachers must consider how the students' relationships with peers can enhance or detract from their learning outcomes. Further, Penul and Watkins (2019) maintained connecting students' classroom learning and assessment experiences with their experiences outside of school creates a more just and humanistic educational experience, and by doing so, offers students the opportunity to put their best learning foot forward. So how do teachers account for personal, social, and cultural influences during their assessment of student learning? Table 1.1 offers some ideas. It lists each

TABLE 1.1. Influences, Example Questions, and Sample Assessment Strategies in This Book

Influence	Examples of questions addressed by this influence	Sample assessment strategies
Personal	• What does the student do when out of school? • What interests does the student possess? • Which instructional experiences engage the student? • What makes reading hard for the student? Easy? • What type of assistance does the student need when engaged in literacy activities? • What assistance do other students seek from the student?	*Initial Student Conversation* (2.2) *Conferencing with Care* (3.1) *Student Self-Assessment* (7.3) *Goal Setting* (7.4) *Photo Elicitation Interview* (8.5)
Social	• How does the student describe themselves as a reader? • How do others respond to their classmates' reading behavior, for example, interpretations offered by the student during book discussions? • Whose ideas in the classroom are valued and whose ideas are discounted?	*I Am Who I Am as a Reader* (2.4) *The Blob Tree* (3.3)
Cultural	• What do I know about the communities in which my students live? • What objects, activities, routines are common in the students' homes? • How is reading used in the students' homes and communities? • If students are immigrants: What do I know about their home country or why they left to come to the United States? What family members remain in their home country? How do their families stay in touch with family in their home country?	*Initial Parent Conversation* (2.1) *Celebrating Identities with Students and Their Families* (2.3) *Literacy Provision Inventory* (8.4)

influence, provides sample questions related to each influence, and displays assessments useful in answering such questions. Please note that even though we present each influence separately to emphasize its distinctiveness, in reality they entwine.

To account for students' **personal influences,** literacy instruction and assessment must build on students' backgrounds, strengths, interests, and needs. These inform instruction in substantive, not incidental, ways (Penul & Watkins, 2019). Teachers identify topics students find interesting and relevant to their lives and then uses their questions to guide their learning. So, a teacher learns that students want to decrease litter in their community and uses this concern to initiate a unit of study on the environment. The teacher uses questions generated by students about this issue (e.g., "Why do people throw trash on the ground?") to structure learning events. Questions teachers might ask related to this influence include "What does the student do when out of school?" "What interests does the student possess?" "Which instructional experiences engage the student?" "What makes reading hard for the student? Easy?" "What type of assistance does the student need when engaged in literacy activities and what assistance do other students seek from the student?" Assessment strategies in this book that are useful in addressing these questions include *Initial Student Conversation* (2.2), *Conferencing with Care* (3.1), *Student Self-Assessment* (7.3), *Goal Setting* (7.4), and the *Photo Elicitation Interview* (8.5).

To consider students' **social influences,** literacy instruction and assessment must account for how students view themselves as literacy users and how other students view their peers' literacy behavior. Questions teachers might ask related to this influence include: "How does the student describe themselves as a reader?" "How do others respond to their classmates' reading behavior, for example an interpretation offered during a book discussion?" "Whose ideas in the classroom are valued and whose ideas are discounted?" Assessment strategies useful in addressing these questions include *I Am Who I Am as a Reader* (2.4) and *The Blob Tree* (3.3).

To account for students' **cultural influences,** teachers must learn about their students' families and communities and seek to recognize how these influences shape their students' beliefs and predispositions toward literacy. Questions teachers might ask related to this influence include: "What do I know about the communities in which my students live?" "What objects, activities, and routines are common in their homes?" "How is reading used in the students' homes and communities?" If students are immigrants, they ask questions like "What do I know about their home country or why they left to come to the United States?" "What family members remain in their home country?" "How do their families stay in touch with family and friends in their home country?" Assessment strategies useful in addressing these questions include *Initial Parent Conversation* (2.1), *Celebrating Identities with Students and Their Families* (2.3), and *Literacy Provision Inventory* (8.4).

Assessment must account for reading's complexity. Too often reading assessments limit their range to a partial assessment of students' reading ability, such as assessing basic reading skills (e.g., phonics knowledge) with worksheets, assessing comprehension with prescribed questions, or assessing some but not all dimensions of a multidimensional process (e.g., reading fluency). To assess reading's complexity necessitates that teachers have access to an expanded, not a restrictive, cache of assessment tools. Teachers need that expanded assessment toolbox if all students, not just those socialized within the dominant culture, are to make continuous progress toward becoming effective and engaged readers.

Principles That Guide Our Approach to Reading Assessment

The following principles make explicit the beliefs just outlined in this chapter and that guide our thinking about reading assessment. These beliefs align with our central desire to represent reading assessment as a humanizing, empowering process that proceeds through an equity mindset. Those beliefs bring visibility to teachers and students. Teachers become visible when they, not those outside of their classrooms, determine the how, when, and for what purposes reading is taught and assessed. Students become visible when their teachers believe their students' knowledge, cultural histories, diverse languages, lived experiences, and reading strengths and needs provide the linchpin, the vital foundation, upon which reading instruction and assessment is built. Importantly, we view visibility as an antidote to counteract the personal costs exacted on teachers and students by the current testing obsession.

Each principle offers a distinctive variable to consider when creating, selecting, or conducting reading assessment. However, as a collective, they provide guardrails that keep us from veering away or from selecting literacy assessments that place teachers in the role of technician and treat students as a monolithic group. As guardrails, they offer us explicitly stated parameters to inform our choices of the assessments to include in this book. As guardrails, they offer you an explicated framework to guide your choice of assessments to use in your classroom.

We group our beliefs into four broad principles, with each principle achieving further definition by the central ideas subsumed under it (see Figure 1.1).

Principle One: Reading assessments must occur through an equity lens/mindset

Three components constitute this principle:
- Promotes respectful teacher–student relationships
- Embraces students as active partners
- Builds on students' strengths

Principle Two: Reading assessment must ensure the visibility of teachers and students in the assessment process

Two components constitute this principle
- Is guided by thoughtful teachers
- Leverages students' reading histories and lived experiences

Assessment as a humanizing and empowering process that proceeds through an equity mindset

Principle Three: Reading assessment must be embedded in daily instructional and learning activities

Two components constitute this principle:
- Is planned along with instruction
- Offers timely and thus useful data

Principle Four: Reading assessment must account for reading's complexity

Two components constitute this principle:
- Accounts for the whole child
- Takes multiple forms and serves multiple functions

FIGURE 1.1. Principles that guide the selection of assessment methods and processes.

Principle 1: *Reading Assessment Must Occur through an Equity Mindset*

The assessments presented in this book are grounded in the belief that all students deserve to be treated with dignity and to have the chance to fulfill their human potential; learning to read provides substantial support for those efforts. Teachers control the assessment reins, so they choose what to assess, when to assess, and how to assess their students' reading development and performance. Students are empowered because they become active, not passive participants in the assessment process. Teachers who work through an equity mindset see that reading assessment plays an essential role in their efforts to provide each student the instruction needed to fulfill their human potential. To that end, the three central ideas subsumed under Principle 1 include selecting assessments that (1) promote respectful teacher–student relationships, (2) embrace students as active partners, and (3) build on students' strengths (see Figure 1.1).

1. *Promote respectful teacher–student relationships.* A humanizing, empowering assessment process that works to achieve equity necessitates positive teacher–student relationships. We have known for decades from research that positive teacher–student relationships increase students' academic success and satisfaction with school (Gershoff & Aber, 2006). What is less discussed is the unique role such relationships play when conducting reading assessments. Students must trust their teachers if they are to engage in self-analysis, reflect on their preferences as readers, and become aware of the perspectives they hold of themselves as readers. A positive teacher–student relationship supplies the psychological context students need to develop that trust, so they feel comfortable in sharing such personal information (Gershoff & Aber, 2006). Throughout this book the assessments presented support your efforts to promote respectful teacher–student relationships, but we offer additional support with the inclusion of Chapter 3, "Building Trusting Relationships: The Linchpin of Productive and Effective Reading Assessment." Chapter 3 describes the significant role such relationships play when conducting assessment and illustrates how these relationships inform the development and implementation of reading assessments.

2. *Embrace students as active partners.* The assessments in this book engage students to become agents in their own learning and as such they become full partners in the assessment of themselves as readers. To ensure students become agents in their own learning, teachers set as an assessment goal to support their students' efforts to self-assess and to reflect on themselves as readers. Further, teachers and students reverse roles. Instead of playing the typical roles of the teacher talks and the students listen, it is students who talk and the teacher who listens. Throughout this book we support your efforts to embrace students as full partners in the assessment process. We provide additional support with the inclusion of Chapters 4, 5, and 7. Chapter 4, "Using Student Talk to Assess Students' Reading Comprehension," and Chapter 5, "Assessing Readers' Text Comprehension," discuss how making students aware of their reading processes promotes their role as an active assessment partner. The chapters then illustrate how that awareness informs the development and implementation of reading assessments. Chapter 7, "Using Assessment to Support Students' Development of Agency," explains why students must be active partners in their reading assessment and illustrates how that partnership informs the development and implementation of reading assessments.

3. *Build on students' strengths.* The assessments in this book originate from a belief that each student is a unique and competent individual capable of continuous reading growth. Teachers who work from this belief see differences among their students as assets not deficits. Teachers position themselves as keen observers who watch and listen to their students as they engage in reading practices. They build on what students know, and to help them learn what they do not know. Throughout this book the assessments presented support your efforts to build on students' strengths. Chapter 8, "Starting with Student Strengths," provides additional support in those efforts and illustrates how students' strengths inform the development and implementation of reading assessments.

Principle 2: *Reading Assessment Must Ensure the Visibility of Teachers and Students in the Assessment Process*

In this book, we offer a fresh and timely perspective on reading assessment—moving from technical and top-down decision making to thoughtful assessments that engage teachers and students. We promote assessments where teachers become more visible. Teachers are viewed as professional educators who make decisions rather than technicians who conduct assessments for the sake of getting them done. Students are made visible because they serve as the purpose, the north star, in the assessment process. It is all about them—not about the tests, the standards, or the mandates. To that end, the two central ideas subsumed under Principle 2 are that assessments must (1) be guided by thoughtful teachers and (2) leverage students' histories and lived experiences (see Figure 1.1).

1. *Be guided by thoughtful teachers.* To be thoughtful when conducting assessments means to give attention to and be intentional about the literacy assessments one chooses to use in their classroom. Hence, teachers conduct literacy assessment as thoughtful actions embedded in rich teaching and learning opportunities (Dennis, 2017). And importantly, those actions are informed by variables at the core of what makes us human—our identity, our personal relationships, and our life experiences. Throughout this book, we support teachers' efforts to conduct literacy assessments as thoughtful actions. This chapter offers additional support by providing research, an expanded definition of what comprises reading, and principles to inform teachers' selection and use of reading assessments.

2. *Leverage students' histories and lived experiences.* The assessments in this book stem from a belief that students' lives outside of school serve as substantive instead of incidental contributors to how students make sense of their world. Students' sense-making includes but is not limited to preferences for how to learn, the values they hold, and the disposition they possess. For assistance in creating reading instruction students find meaningful, teachers learn about their students' cultural and experiential histories and lived experiences and then use what they learn to leverage their students' reading instruction. Throughout this book we support teachers' efforts to understand the importance of learning about their students' histories and lived experiences. Chapter 2, "Understanding Students' Funds of Identity," offers additional support in those efforts by explaining why it is important for teachers to prioritize learning about their students' histories, identities, and lived experiences. The chapter then illustrates how leveraging students' histories and lived experiences informs the development and use of reading assessment.

Principle 3: *Reading Assessment Must Be Embedded in Daily Instructional and Learning Activities*

Reading assessment must activate and reveal the capabilities of both teachers and their students; a key way to accomplish this is to embed assessment within instruction. Assessment must be at the heart of instruction. Thus, teachers embrace the use of a formative assessment process embedded within daily teaching and learning events that enables teachers to observe their students as they apply reading processes in real time. Such opportunities allow teachers to manage their time efficiently while providing their students in-the-moment support, and when needed, to recast their instruction. To that end, the two central ideas subsumed under Principle 3 are that assessments must (1) be planned along with instruction and (2) offer timely and thus useful data (see Figure 1.1).

1. *Be planned with instruction.* Assessment is not something done at the end of learning but occurs throughout the learning process (International Reading Association, 2013). Therefore, the assessments promoted in this book become part of, not separate from, instruction. As such, teachers plan their assessment as they plan their instruction, and they conduct assessments in the context of their daily literacy instruction and routines. That planning ensures assessment becomes a forethought not an afterthought, thereby ensuring opportunities exist for data collection. To capitalize on assessments' potential, teachers must create literacy events that make literacy learning visible and audible (Johnston & Costello, 2005). Throughout this book we support teachers' efforts to embed assessment within their instruction, for example we use vignettes situated in classroom settings, called implementation examples, to demonstrate how teachers can use the assessment strategies within their literacy instruction and routines. Chapter 6, "Assessing Constrained Skills within the Big Picture of Reading," offers additional support in those efforts. This chapter discusses the value of assessing constrained reading skills as students engage with authentic text. The chapter then illustrates how the use of authentic text can inform the development and use of reading assessment.

2. *Offer timely and useful data.* The most opportune time to assess students' literacy abilities is when they use reading for authentic purposes. Observing and talking with students in the process of reading offers an immediate context for learning about how students apply what they learned during formal reading instruction. Furthermore, observing students in the process of engaging in reading enables teachers to provide in-the-moment support to students and, if necessary, to alter instruction. Throughout this book, we support teachers' efforts to enact assessments to gain timely and thus useful information, by providing examples of assessments as well as data collection strategies aligned with those assessments. In addition, in each chapter, we complement the detailed descriptions of the assessments with vignettes that demonstrate how to use the assessment strategy during instruction.

Principle 4: *Reading Assessment Must Account for Reading's Complexity*

Reading is a complex process comprised of both cognitive processes and personal, social, and cultural influences. Cookie-cutter one-size-fits all assessment approaches cannot accommodate that complexity. Although we do offer assessments that assess students' knowledge of skills—for example, Chapter 6, "Assessing Constrained Skills within the Big Picture of Reading"—we balance such assessments with assessments that extend beyond skills and strategies. To that end, the two central ideas subsumed under Principle 4 include selecting assessments that (1) account for the whole child and (2) take multiple forms and that serve multiple functions (see Figure 1.1).

1. *Account for the whole child.* The assessments in this book consider what students know, what they think about what they know, the history of how and where they learned what they know, and their interest in what they know. To support those efforts, reading assessments must extend beyond assessing skill and strategy knowledge; we find support for an expanded range of assessments from the field of developmental science, the study of how humans grow and develop. "Cognition, emotion, and social behavior develop in an integrative, mutually influential way" (Sroufe, Egeland, Carlson, & Collins, 2005, p. 30). Hence, learners cannot and thus do not compartmentalize learning experiences into cognitive, emotional, cultural, and social compartments. Rather, they experience learning holistically, with all their human systems working dynamically and in an integrative fashion (Sroufe et al., 2005). Therefore, students experience reading events in the same way, wherein cognition, emotion, and cultural and social responses interact holistically. To that end, throughout this book the assessments presented support teachers' efforts to extend assessments beyond the assessment of students' knowledge of skills and strategies. In Chapter 7, "Using Assessment to Support Students' Development of Agency," we describe assessment strategies that bolster students' knowledge of self as a literate being. Chapter 2, "Understanding Students' Funds of Identity," describes and demonstrates the use of family and parent interviews to learn about students' family and community as well as their life outside of school.

2. *Take multiple forms and serve multiple functions.* The complexity of the reading process means that no single assessment can provide adequate information about a student's reading ability. In this book, we promote assessments that recognize that students engage in reading differently, such as when they read for different purposes or read in a different context. For an accurate understanding of students as readers, we must account for those differences. Collectively the assessments described in this book come in multiple forms, for example, observations, interviews, and conferences. They also serve different purposes, for example, using interviews to gather information about students' lives outside of school and using observation to determine students' knowledge of basic reading skills. The implementation example that accompanies each assessment strategy supports teachers' efforts to use different forms of assessment and to use assessments for multiple purposes.

Teachers will find support for implementing this approach to assessment in Chapter 9, "Literacy Assessment as Oeuvre: Teachers and Students Building a Visible Body of Work." This concluding chapter presents the concept of *oeuvre,* which describes a substantial body of work that represents an artist's creative expressions. We discuss how a student's *literacy oeuvre* represents their mental and creative efforts in reading through assessments and work products compiled over time. We also explore the notion that teachers who use this approach to assessment build their own body of work, or *teaching oeuvre,* which makes visible their knowledge and professional growth related to teaching, learning, assessment, literacy, and supporting all of their students over time. This chapter also addresses frequently asked questions about this approach to assessment, including how teachers can get started, how to manage implementation by embedding assessment into daily instructional activities and routines, and how to discuss this approach to assessment with key stakeholders like students, families, administrators, and colleagues.

Why Another Book about Reading Assessment?

Books related to reading assessment abound. So, you may wonder, why add another? Our examination of the multitude of available literacy assessment books laid bare a glaring omission. Although many acknowledge the influence that variables such as a literate identity, student agency, and the role a positive teacher–student relationship play in assessment, we go beyond touting their value. We devote a full chapter to each. As a collective, these topics—along with those covered in the other chapters—create a more humane, just, and empowering approach to literacy assessment.

In Chapters 2–9 we present a total of 28 assessment strategies that you can use to make your students' literacies, identities, interests, goals, skills, strengths, and areas of need visible so you can use that data to plan and deliver meaningful instruction to support all of your students. Figure 1.2 provides a matrix of all the assessment strategies in this book and shows what areas of literacy and learning they each address.

Conclusion

We hope that by reading the chapters in this book, you can begin to see assessment as a tool for teaching, learning, and equity. As you learn how to tweak assessments you may currently use and discover new assessments, you will be able to assume your role as a professional who determines how, when, and for what purposes reading is taught and assessed in your classroom. In turn, your students will feel valued because they see evidence of their histories, identities, funds of knowledge, and lived experiences in how reading is taught and assessed in your classroom. To that end, assessment becomes a humanizing, empowering process that is your partner in achieving equity. As such, assessment, guided by your thoughtful actions, embraces differences and builds on student assets. Most importantly, the reading assessment approach promoted in this book moves teachers and students from invisible no ones to visible someones!

Area of assessment →	Comprehension	Vocabulary	Fluency	Word identification	Phonemic awareness	Student interests	Student background and assets	Strategy use and reading behaviors	Metacognition	Student engagement and agency
Strategy ↓										
2.1 *Initial Parent Conversation*						X	X			
2.2 *Initial Student Conversation*						X	X			X
2.3 *Celebrating Identities with Students and Their Families*						X	X			X
2.4 *I Am Who I Am as a Reader*						X	X	X	X	X
3.1 *Conferencing with Care*						X	X	X	X	X
3.2 *Conferencing with Retrospective Miscue Analysis*	X	X					X	X	X	X
3.3 *The Blob Tree*						X	X			X
4.1 *Vocabulary Knowledge Assessment*	X	X					X	X		
4.2 *Language Detective*	X							X	X	X
4.3 *T-Chart*	X	X					X	X	X	X
5.1 *Retellings*	X	X						X	X	

5.2 *Think-Alouds*	X	X					X	X	X	
5.3 *Questioning of Text Comprehension*	X	X					X	X	X	
5.4 *Semantic Word Sorts*	X	X								
6.1 *What Can You Show Us?*				X	X		X	X	X	X
6.2 *Running Records*			X	X				X		
6.3 *Oral Reading Analysis*			X	X				X		
6.4 *Elkonin Sound Boxes*					X					
6.5 *Developmental Spelling Assessment*				X						
7.1 *Teacher Self-Evaluation of Opportunities for Student Agency*										X
7.2 *Student Agency Questionnaire*							X	X	X	X
7.3 *Student Self-Assessment*							X	X	X	X
7.4 *Goal Setting*							X	X	X	X
8.1 *Kidwatching*	X	X	X	X	X	X	X	X	X	X
8.2 *Portfolios*	X	X	X	X	X	X	X	X	X	X
8.3 *Can You Help Me Understand?*	X	X	X	X	X	X	X	X	X	X
8.4 *Literacy Provision Inventory*						X	X	X	X	X
8.5 *Photo Elicitation Interview*						X	X	X	X	X

FIGURE 1.2. Assessment strategy matrix.

2

Understanding Students' Funds of Identity

Funds of identity . . . when people actively internalize family and community resources to make meaning and to describe themselves.
—ESTEBAN-GUITART AND MOLL (2014, p. 33)

Who cares about some dumb little Chinese girl who's always off alone by herself?
—SHARED BY HAI, A FIFTH-GRADE STUDENT, DESCRIBING HER CLASSROOM IDENTITY

Assessments need to go far beyond measuring students' knowledge, skills, and strategies to foster equitable learning opportunities for all students. Assessments also need to capture how students and teachers view themselves and the identities they have acquired. Knowledge of identities informs how we respond to and connect with our students during instruction. It helps us make our instruction *personable.* And understanding students' identities, especially as literacy learners, provides important information about what influences their responses to reading and their dispositions toward our reading instruction. Thus, our assessments should be "expansive" and inclusive of multiple sources of information. As such they provide opportunities for educators to "revise and refine their practices" and respond to students' diverse histories and capabilities (Milner, 2018, p. 88). Milner asserts that assessments for equity "should help us learn about students—not sort them" (p. 88).

Our identities as children, adolescents, and adults are informed by our histories, our experiences, and the multiple interactions we have with our family members, peers, and those around us. Children as young as four have a sense of who they are and can be heard declaring how they perceive themselves, such as "I am the fastest runner" or "I am smart." Raburu (2015) and Siroj-Blatchford (2009), for example, learned that preschool children begin to identify early with significant others around them, such as their teachers, and act out those roles during play with their newly claimed "identities" as teachers, doctors, or nurses. And, starting at a young age, children begin to adopt multiple identities (e.g., I am a girl, a football player, Daddy's daughter; Paechter & Clark, 2007).

This sense of "who we are" continues to develop through adolescence and adulthood, impacted by the norms, values, and customs of those around us. Adolescents identify themselves with an array of identities, including those associated with academic, sports, musical pursuits, popular culture, everyday literacy practices, and community literacy practices (Enright, Wong, & Sanchez, 2021). Typically striving for independence and autonomy as part of their identities, adolescents sometimes feel the pressure of competing identities, such as identifying with values and norms of their parents (e.g., being a serious student is important) and taking on values and norms of peers (e.g., setting aspirations as a musician and holding jam sessions to write and perform music). These identities can be positive and bolster our views of competence, or as Hai's words illustrate at the beginning of this chapter, these identities may reflect an internalization—how she perceives others are evaluating her (e.g., as "dumb" and that "Chinese girl"). Identities are dynamic; they continue to develop across experiences, interactions with others, and perceived expectations of others. Similarly, adults, and in particular, teachers adopt multiple identities (e.g., mentor, instructional leader, data analyst) as they strive to be nurturers of their students' academic development while responding to increasing demands and expectations for their identities as teachers and roles as data collectors and masters of juggling multiple curricular demands.

Children's views of themselves as successful literate learners are especially powerful. How students view their identities as readers and writers shape their literacy actions and their engagement in literate activity. Students who identify themselves as successful readers and writers are more likely to hold interest and engage in literacy activities and achieve academic success. Often these students set goals for themselves and believe they can achieve those goals. For example, a first-grade student might share that they want to "read and read and read so that soon I can read the thick books that are on my mother's bedside table." Conversely, students who regard themselves as unsuccessful often develop identities of low self-esteem and low expectations that can have devastating effects on their literacy development.

Students' identities as successful readers and writers begin early in school (Brown, 2011), often the result of how they are positioned in the classroom, through their interactions with others, and how they are viewed by others. Positive identities develop in supportive relationships in which teachers honor and praise students for their efforts and when students are viewed as "capable" or "good readers and writers." Teacher language can position students as belonging in categories of successful or failing readers. For example, a teacher might call a small group of students together and say "let's work on your reading problems" instead of saying "let's learn some new comprehension strategies." The identities that frame students as "having problems" versus "learning new strategies" [like everyone else is learning] begin to take hold and gain strength across the school years for the students themselves and how they are viewed by their peers (Wortham, 2010).

We need to be concerned, then, about how students view their literate identities and ensure that our formative assessments make visible these identities throughout the school year. As students acquire new literacy practices (e.g., use of comprehension strategies for analyzing texts, use of multiple sources of information for word learning) and receive feedback about their literacy work from teachers and peers, we need to determine how these practices and feedback affect their feelings of competence and confidence as literacy learners.

As you learn about students' identities, especially those associated with failure (e.g., as reflected in Hai's comment about feeling dumb), it is important to reinforce positive identities (e.g., "yes, you are a great word learner") and to know that negative identities can be "disrupted, reinforced and/or reshaped" (Alsup, 2005). For example, extremely important is instruction that encourages students to take risks in applying newly learned knowledge and skills to texts they are reading and that praise students' efforts for those attempts, or instruction that advocates students' agency, such as encouraging students' choice of reading material. With such opportunities, readers reinvent themselves as successful and avid readers, moving students from negative views or an avoidance of reading to self-descriptions of "I used my prior knowledge about engines to help me understand that illustration" or "I am becoming a bookworm" (e.g., Ivey and Johnston, 2017; Martens & Adamson, 2001).

The formative assessments we describe in this chapter support teachers' abilities to be keen observers of students' capabilities. They are useful for making visible students' prior knowledge and experiences, cultural and language resources, and preferences and interests so that teachers can develop what Luis Moll (2015) called "resource-based" pedagogy, a subject that we will address more specifically in Chapter 8. Students identify themselves according to histories or traditions, for example, when they share that their "family is from Mexico" or "my mother speaks Portuguese," "we celebrate Eid" or "my family likes to camp with tents in our state parks." These multiple and culturally developed identities that each teacher and student brings to teaching and learning is referred to as funds of identity, identities that people use to define themselves (Esteban-Guitart & Moll, 2014). Instruction that is equity-based and responsive makes connections to students' cultural practices, beliefs, ideas, and knowledge, all funds of identity, while engaging them academically—it finds places where such connections to learning are made explicit and celebratory.

Students' cultural identities are too often overlooked yet they are fundamental to instruction that successfully engages students' interest and knowledge building and for promoting literacy (Maitra, 2017). Making connections to students' ethnicity, language, out-of-school practices, and family customs is important for facilitating students' engagement, their sense of belonging in the academic setting, and their beliefs about their capabilities as learners. And when their out-of-school literate behaviors are honored in the classroom and made relevant to the in-school practices and activities of the classroom, their engagement and achievement soars. As we demonstrate in the example below, students learn best when their prior knowledge and experiences, such as their heritage languages and ethnicities, are integral to classroom literacy activities and books that are read (Campano & Carpenter, 2005).

As teachers, it is not as difficult to teach students whose histories and experiences are similar to our own, but it can be much more challenging to teach students' whose histories and experiences are widely different. Without purposeful assessments, these histories and experiences remain invisible and assumptions about students and their families can lead to misunderstandings, intruding negatively on opportunities for meaningful dialogue among teachers, their students, and their students' families. Moje (2004) advised that teachers should be deliberate in making visible at least four sources of information about their students' lives: family, community, popular culture, and peer groups. We would add students' language history, including the language practices they use in everyday communication and whether they are literate in their home language(s).

Pacheco, Daniel, Pray, and Jimenez (2019) provided a powerful example of how one third-grade teacher, Ms. Gardner, whose language history was different from some of her students, was deliberate in making visible their heritage language histories and identities to co-construct meaning making during a text discussion. While discussing the three pumpkins in the text they are reading, Miguel offers, "Um, *crecen.*" Alan follows up by explaining to Ms. Gardner the meaning of *crecen:* "they grow." Later during the discussion, Ms. Gardner asks what the author is saying about the pumpkins. Miguel answers by saying "*Estan grandes . . . pesatas?*" (They are big . . . heavy?). Alan asks, "*Pesadas?*" (asking if they are heavy). Miguel answers, "*Como tres, que va a llevar*" (explaining there are three; they would weigh as much as three). Frank agrees that they would be heavy. Miguel goes on to ask, "*Pesa, pesadas?*" (which word would we use, *weighs* or *heavy*). Ms. Gardner is unsure of which word should be used, *pesa* or *pesada*. She then asks Miguel, "When do you say *pesadas?*" Miguel responds by saying "My mom just say *pesa,* Ms. Gardner. It's *pesa.*" Ms. Gardner accepts this as a meaningful response (Pacheco et al., 2019, p. 84).

The above conversation provides a wealth of information and makes visible the language histories and identities of Miguel, Alan, and Frank. Further, when Ms. Gardner accepts Miguel's conclusion (i.e., it's *pesa*), she is acknowledging the importance of making visible bilinguals' academic language and use of prior knowledge to make sense of texts and to contribute meaningfully to text discussions. Ms. Gardner demonstrates that she views students as meaningful sources of information that she is seeking. To engage in such conversations, teachers need to affirm students' everyday language identities as meaningful vehicles for their participation in the classroom community. Denying the value of these identities also denies students' identities and use of their own language/thinking to "support meaning making" that is necessary for acquiring new knowledge (Pacheco Daniel, & Pray, 2017, p. 64).

To support your efforts to make your students' identities visible, we share four formative strategies in the next part of this chapter. These assessment strategies are designed to engage your students and their parents in ways that make visible their identities and how these identities may influence their views of literacy. As you consider how you can use these assessment strategies in your practice, these questions may be helpful for guiding your thinking.

- What can you learn about your students' identities by using these assessment strategies? How can you use what you have learned to plan instruction that is personable?
- How do these assessments help you revise teaching practices in ways that support equitable learning opportunities for your students?
- How does engaging in conversations with students and parents make their identities visible and enhance your assessment practices? Compare these assessments with ones you may have used previously, such as an interest inventory. What are the value-added qualities of these conversations with parents and students?

ASSESSMENT STRATEGIES: UNDERSTANDING STUDENTS' FUNDS OF IDENTITY

In this part of the chapter, we offer four strategies for making visible the identities of students and their parents. These strategies are:

2.1. *Initial Parent Conversation: What Can You Tell Me That Will Help Me Be a Good Teacher for Your Child?*

2.2. *Initial Student Conversation: What Can You Tell Me That Will Help Me Be a Good Teacher for YOU?*

2.3. *Celebrating Identities with Students and Their Families*

2.4. *I Am Who I Am as a Reader*

We begin our presentation of these strategies with a discussion about the benefits of holding conversations with parents.

Power of Conversations with Parents as an Assessment Strategy

Building relationships with parents is central to learning about your students' identities and establishing a partnership for developing shared goals and methods for reaching those goals. Of equal value is the message these conversations send to the parents and your students. You are acknowledging explicitly how much you value them and their experiences and that you value them as partners to support your teaching and their children's learning. Learning from parents takes us beyond assumptions, that are often misinformed, and provides opportunities to see students through the eyes of those who have "bathed their children in love, culture, and traditions" (Morrell, 2020).

It has been our experience that often parents are "waiting to be asked in." For example, a few years ago, our research team was supporting teachers of bilingual students who had recently moved to this school district. One mother brought her second-grade daughter to school each morning and then sat on the bench outside the school office for at least an hour before leaving. Finally, one of our team members joined this mother on the bench, engaging her in a conversation. The mother explained that she was "waiting to be invited into the classrooms to help the teachers with the English learners." She had been a volunteer teachers' aide supporting English learners at their former school and she was hoping to be helpful in this new school. Here was information that would have been lost if that conversation had not occurred. Thus, holding conversations can be at the heart of building mutual understandings and shared goals.

ASSESSMENT STRATEGY 2.1.

Initial Parent Conversation: What Can You Tell Me That Will Help Me Be a Good Teacher for Your Child?

Purpose

An initial parent conversation that focuses on student and family identity should occur early in the school year. The goal is to begin a two-way communication that continues throughout the school year and beyond. There is so much to learn during these conversations, including understanding parents' hopes and goals for their children, their worries and concerns, and the out-of-school activities and cultural traditions that are the most meaningful to them. Teachers can learn about students' interests, activities, goals, attitudes toward self and others, heritage language, and how literacy activities occur at home or in the community. And students can learn about their teachers' identities when they share their goals, worries, activities, and cultural traditions.

Value

Parent conversations provide a wealth of information that can inform your teaching and enhance support of your students as well as strengthen communication with families. For example, you can make connections between students' out-of-school interests and the texts that are read in class. You might invite family members to come to your class and share experiences or community projects that are related to the students' curriculum. When teachers share information about their own identities with parents, they build parents' trust and understandings that they share common histories, traditions, goals, and concerns. Additionally, as teachers share information, they are modeling for parents the many sources of information that can be shared with each other.

Procedures

1. **Preparation** for the conversation requires clarity about expectations and setting explicit boundaries. Identify what you want to learn from this interview and who will be invited (both parents or one, or a grandmother or aunt or guardian). If appropriate, ask parents if a translator should be invited. Having students present during the interviews may be valuable at times and can achieve a three-way communication affording different perspectives on issues and concerns. Identify a time and place for your meeting. Plan for ways that you will follow up after the visit. These might include a thank-you text message or a note sent via e-mail or regular mail. Plan also for frequency of follow-up meetings (e.g., 20 to 30 minutes three times during the year) and share these expectations.

2. **Preview** the process you will initiate and sustain during the conversation. There are at least three key parts to previewing.

   - First, plan for an opening greeting that will be a conversation starter. For example, you may want to refer to times you have met previously in the community or during school events that were more informal. This opener should help parents/family members feel comfortable while expressing your desire to build a partnership with them. We offer some examples of conversation openers in Figure 2.1.
   - Next, plan to share information about yourself that might include your goals, hobbies, traditions, and history as a teacher, and why teaching is so important to you. Typically, this sharing is informal and will not come all at once (as in a formal presentation), but instead is distributed throughout the conversation. You might preview your teaching goals and a brief description of your planned instruction.
   - Third, identify questions that will help you accomplish your goal of learning about your students' interests and talents. We provide some examples of questions, also in Figure 2.1. Throughout the conversation, use straightforward, conversational language, avoiding jargon or use of acronyms commonly used by educators but unknown to parents.

Conversation starters
Thank you for meeting with me. I have looked forward to this opportunity to partner with you so that I can understand your hopes and goals for your child this year. I want to learn about your child so that I can be the best teacher possible for them. I was so pleased that we met at your restaurant (or at our school Open House) and you shared some goals that you have for your child this year. Your goals are very similar to mine. I want to learn more about your child and you so that I can be a good teacher for them. I have been a teacher for many years, and I have learned that knowing my students–such as their out of school interests or how they feel about themselves in school–and communicating with their families strengthens my ability to connect with them and make visible their attributes while teaching. [This is a good time to share briefly your beliefs about making connections between your instruction and your students' identities, culture, and experiences.]
Examples of questions focusing on parents' funds of identities
What is a typical evening like in your home? A typical weekend? Describe these times together. Are there hobbies that you share with your children? Tell me about them. I know that you work as (e.g., a gardener, accountant, cook). Tell me about your job(s). Are you involved in the community? Tell me about these activities. Who helps you take care of your children? (if appropriate) Who lives in your home? What holidays do you celebrate each year? How do you celebrate each of these? I was so excited to see you at your restaurant and to see your child helping with the table settings. What does your child do when they are in the restaurant? Your child has been telling me about their soccer games. Tell me about these games and what you have observed. I want to know more about the community work of my students' parents, and you told me that you volunteer for the Habitat Foundation. Would you be willing to come to our class and describe what you do when helping to build houses? Are you willing to come to our class and tell us about your special skills and/or interests?
Examples of questions/statements focusing on students' funds of identities
Does your child like to read? To write? Do they see themselves as a reader and writer? If so, what do they read? Write? Tell me about their interests. What does your child like to do after school? In the evenings? On the weekend? Tell me about what they enjoy.

FIGURE 2.1. Initiating and engaging parents during conversations: Examples.

3. **Engaging parents** during the meeting requires flexibility. Even though you prepared and previewed what you might say, recognize the need to be flexible with how you proceed. As you know, conversations can take on their own life and may go in directions that are not fully anticipated. Thus, it is important to keep your plan in mind and draw on some of your original questions as appropriate for the context, but you can also learn a great deal by sitting back, listening, and following the lead of the parents.

Collecting, Analyzing, and Using Data

1. One method for recording information is notetaking. For example, you can take notes, using an abbreviated format that will not intrude too much on your ongoing conversation. A few words can signal main ideas that will prompt your recall after you leave the meeting. At that time, you can fill in additional details. We provide an example of questions you might ask during notetaking in Form 2.1[1] and illustrate notes taken during the implementation example in Figure 2.2.
2. Another method for recording information is setting up a chart or checklist prior to the conversation, such as shown in Figure 2.3. Prior to your meeting, anticipate categories of information that will be addressed, leaving multiple spaces to create new categories as you gain additional information.
3. Prior to your conversations, you may want to conduct a practice session with a colleague, taking notes as you talk. With a little practice, you will find that notetaking is quite doable. We recommend that you avoid tape recording this conversation, as that can move the conversation to a much more formal exchange and/or be uncomfortable for parents.
4. Shortly after completing your conversation, review your notes and add information that may be missing or not fully explained.
5. Analyze the information by identifying categories related to identities (e.g., I have two siblings, I am a good writer) and interests (e.g., books that are science fiction) and possible directions for follow-up conversations and/or providing answers to parent questions that were not addressed.

Making Students and Teachers Visible

Our goal for parent conversations is to make visible information that will help teachers understand the perspectives, dreams, and lives of their students and their families. Taking time to ask open-ended questions, starting perhaps with the name of our strategy, *Initial Parent Conversation: What Can You Tell Me That Will Help Me Be a Good Teacher for Your Child?*, signals to parents that you hope to collaborate with them as you work closely to support the learning of your students. Additionally, it is a time for teachers to make visible their perspectives and history, and their goal for building a partnership with the parents/family. It provides a time for making connections, as families and teachers often find that they share common interests and goals.

---

[1] All forms are at the ends of the respective chapters.

Questions focusing on parents' funds of knowledge/ identities	**Notes taken during conversations**	**Teacher reflections**
What is a typical evening like in your home? A typical weekend? Describe these times together.	Eat together at kitchen table. Grandfather tells stories, **reads to children during quiet time after dinner.** Children asked to tell about their day, sometimes repeat each other, **not knowing what to share or with little to say** TV after dinner—**but limited** Quiet time for homework, reading, about one hour	I need to learn more about Grandfather's stories. Also, how does Carlos feel about quiet time after dinner.
Do you and your children have special interests, things you like to do together?	Interested in what we see in sky—astronomy **Bought himself a telescope** **He goes to museum website with grandfather – Museum of Science and Astronomy in Canary Islands.**	Interesting. I need to ask Carlos about this. Learn more about the museum and its website.
Are there other special interests or activities that your child enjoys?	Writes in diary Loves *Wimpy Kid* and *Diary* Read and reread *Wimpy* books Loves to write, draws and tells funny stories	Perhaps Carlos will share his journal with me, our class.
How many family members live in your home?	Mother, father, grandfather, and three children – Diego (13), Carlos (10), and Josie (8) **Grandfather is dad's father**	

FIGURE 2.2. Questions to guide open-ended notetaking during parent conversations, with responses added. (**Bold** indicates additional notes added after the conversation.)

Who attended meeting?
____ mother
____ father
____ children (add names)
____ grandparent(s)
____ guardian
____ other ________________________
Literacy activities at home
____ quiet time for reading
____ siblings reading to each other
____ parents reading to children
____ family songs and plays initiated by siblings
____ journals for writing and drawing
____ keeping lists of activities and things to do
____ notes to family
____ other ________________________
Activities at home in evening
____ TV
____ eating dinner
____ games
____ family songs
____ reading
____ other ________________________
Activities on weekends/holidays
____ sports, soccer, basketball
____ church
____ family games, story telling
____ activities with grandparents
____ TV
____ other ________________________

FIGURE 2.3. Checklist example for notetaking during parent conversations.

Implementation Example

Ms. Margret is a fourth-grade English language arts teacher who teaches three sections of fourth- grade students, with 22 students in each section. She starts each year using the *Initial Parent Conversation: What Can You Tell Me That Will Help Me Be a Good Teacher for Your Child?* strategy by inviting parents of her students to meet with her individually for about 20 to 30 minutes. This is Ms. Margret's fifth year of teaching fourth grade. She began inviting parents/families to meet with her at the beginning of the year since her first year of teaching, and she notices that each year there are more parents who accept her invitation. This year 100% of her students' parents are meeting with her.

Today Ms. Margret's **preparation** focuses on a meeting planned with Carlos's parents. Both parents will meet with her at the neighborhood coffee shop at 4 P.M. Carlos's parents are managers of the coffee shop where both English and Spanish is spoken, and churros are served in addition to muffins and bagels. This coffee shop is independently owned and is located in a low- to middle-income neighborhood with families representing multiple ethnicities. Carlos's dad works the late afternoon/evening shift and Carlos's mom works the day shift. His mom is able to be at home after school and in the evenings. They asked for a meeting at their shop so as not to disrupt their work schedules.

Ms. Margret is **previewing** the process she will follow by first thinking about a possible conversation opener and questions she will ask. She has met Carlos's parents several times at the coffee shop, but those meetings have typically been quick without opportunities to learn about Carlos or his parents. She plans to open the conversation acknowledging their previous meetings and describing her favorite coffee drinks and pastries from the coffee shop.

Ms. Margret then conducted the conversation and we present highlights of the conversation she had with Carlos's parents to share some of what she learned about them and Carlos.

MS. MARGRET: Thank you for meeting with me! I love coming to your coffee shop and especially like the vanilla lattes and the churros served with the chocolate syrup! I have looked forward to getting to know you so that you can help me be the best teacher possible for Carlos. This is my fifth-year teaching language arts, after graduating from college. I always wanted to be a teacher like my dad. I love to read and write and love sharing my favorite books and what I write with my students.

Carlos told me that he has a brother and sister. Will you please tell me about them and your family?

CARLOS'S MOTHER: Yes, we have three children. Carlos is 10, his brother, Diego, is 13, and his sister, Josie, is 8. Most of the time they are happy children and are nice to each other. Their grandfather, my husband's dad, lives with us and he watches the children when we are not home. Sometimes I need to stay later at the coffee shop to help my husband in the early evening, but mostly I am home in the evenings.

MS. MARGRET: What is a typical evening like in your home, especially when you are there?

CARLOS'S MOTHER: We always eat together at the kitchen table. The children's grandfather insists on us all being together for dinner. He usually has a story to tell the children and he asks each child to tell us something that happened to them that day. Sometimes the children have very little to say and just repeat what the first one said, such as "I saw my friends today." After dinner, the children watch television but I try to limit that. And every night there is a quiet time for about an hour when we all do something important—the children may do homework, their grandfather or I will read or we will read to them.

MS. MARGRET: Your story about the children's grandfather telling stories reminds me of visiting my grandmother in the summers when I was young. She lived in another state and we would go there for a week each summer. She and I would sit on her front steps and she told me stories about growing up as an only child. What are the stories shared by your children's grandfather?

CARLOS'S DAD: My father has many different stories. Some are about living in Kansas when he was small. His parents and grandparents were farm workers there and that is where they settled when they came to the United States from Spain. He sometimes speaks in Spanish and teaches us some Spanish words, but he thinks we should talk in English most of the time.

My father's favorite story and one that he tells most often is about how he was in the U.S. Air Force and stationed on the Canary Islands. He visited the Museum of Science and Astronomy there and went back many times. When he came home to Kansas, he brought some pictures from the museum that we still talk about, and my dad shares the stories about what we can see in the sky.

MS. MARGRET: Wow! How interesting. We will be reading about objects in the sky this year. Do you think your father would come to our class and share his stories with us? Maybe Carlos will join in and share what he has learned from his grandfather!

CARLOS'S MOTHER: Yes, Carlos is very interested in astronomy and last summer he saved his birthday money and bought a little telescope for himself. He talks with his grandfather about what he sees in the sky and sometimes he draws pictures of these objects in his diary.

MS. MARGRET: Carlos writes in a diary! Please tell me more about this.

CARLOS'S MOTHER: In third grade, Carlos's teacher got them excited about the *Diary of a Wimpy Kid* books. Carlos has read each one over and over. He brings them home from the school library and this summer he brought them home from our neighborhood community center. His teacher last year suggested that he might want to start a diary, just like the one he was reading about. Carlos writes in his diary almost every day, and he draws pictures in it, too. It looks just like the pages in the book. Sometimes he writes about things in the sky, sometimes he writes about something that happened with his brother or sister, or something from school.

Sometimes he writes funny stories and laughs as he writes these.

MS. MARGRET: I know that diaries can be very personal and some people don't like to share theirs with others. I respect that but I will ask him if there are pages that he might like to share with me and/or the class. Sharing will be his choice.

Are there special events or holidays or traditions that you enjoy as a family? For example, my favorite family tradition was cooking with my relatives before a holiday. This was the time when my aunts and uncles would share their favorite stories about growing up in a small coal-mining community in West Virginia.

CARLOS'S DAD: We celebrate the holidays of Thanksgiving and Christmas but I think our favorite tradition is listening to grandfather's stories about Spain and his remembrance of how holidays were celebrated by his grandparents. For example, on Christmas they would open gifts from Papa Noel and then go out on the plaza to meet with neighbors and share stories and songs.

MS. MARGRET: That is so interesting and helps me think about all the different ways that students in my class may celebrate their own holidays. That could lead to family nights of sharing how holidays are shared in our homes.

What else can you tell me about Carlos that will help me be a good teacher for Carlos?

CARLOS'S DAD AND MOTHER: (*in unison*) Carlos thinks he is not smart like his brother Diego.

CARLOS'S MOTHER: I don't think that Diego teases him, but Carlos's teachers always tell him how smart Diego is and how much they miss him in their class. We tell Carlos that he is smart, too, and we always put his school papers on the refrigerator next to Diego's papers . . . but sometimes he says that Diego's writing or work is better. We need help with this. We want Carlos to feel that he is smart, too.

MS. MARGRET: Thank you for telling me this. I will try really hard to support Carlos so that he is successful in my class and help him understand that being a successful learner is all about setting goals, working hard to meet these goals, using strategies to make sense of his reading and writing, and learning from mistakes. Let's plan to talk about this when we meet again, or if you want to talk before then, please send me a note or call me with concerns.

Are there other goals that you have for Carlos this year?

CARLOS'S MOTHER: I would like to see him become interested in other kinds of books and reading more than the *Wimpy Kid.* He is interested in the sky but we have had a hard time finding books on that topic that interest him. Also, we wonder why he doesn't do much writing except in his journal.

MS. MARGRET: Thank you for telling me this as it helps me set up goals and activities for addressing these areas. I am hoping that we will meet again in about two months. At that time, I will want you to share what you are observing at home and we can discuss his work this year. I am hoping that we can continue to learn from each other about the best ways to support Carlos.

Analyzing and Using the Data

After the parent conversation, Ms. Margret **analyzes** the information she has collected. First, she reads through her notes, adding missing information and elaborating on notes that were incomplete. She then returns to her outline of questions and statements to guide her thinking about how to categorize all that she has learned.

Next, Ms. Margret identifies the big ideas from the conversation as follows:

- *Who are family members?* There are six people in the home: Carlos's parents, an older brother, Diego, and younger sister, Josie, and Carlos's grandfather.
- *Typical evening at home?* Dinnertime is family time with the goal to share family happenings. After dinner, there is quiet time for reading and homework, and some TV time that the parents try to limit. Ms. Margret makes a note about the reading and TV

watching, identifying questions she will ask Carlos, to learn about his TV and book preferences.

- *Carlos's identity and interests.* Carlos's grandfather and his family immigrated to Kansas from Spain. He and his family were farm workers. He speaks Spanish and has taught the family some words, but English is the primary language in the home (as preferred by the grandfather). Carlos's grandfather is the family storyteller. Carlos is very interested in astronomy—the things in the sky—an interest shared with his grandfather who shares stories about his visits to the Museum of Science and Astronomy on the Canary Islands, when he was in the military and stationed there. Carlos has a "little telescope" at home. He writes about the objects he sees, drawing these for his grandfather, and keeps this in his diary.

  Carlos's family celebrates Thanksgiving and Christmas, but their favorite tradition is listening to their grandfather's stories about Spain and how the grandparents would celebrate holidays. When living in Spain, Carlos's grandfather's family would open gifts from Papa Noel and then go outside on the plaza to talk with neighbors, singing and sharing stories.

- *Carlos's literacy activities.* Carlos likes the *Wimpy Kid* books and keeps a similar diary. He rereads these favorite books and writes and draws pictures in his diary almost every day, following the same format as *Wimpy*. The content is sometimes funny, and sometimes about his family, what happens in school, or what he sees in the sky. Perhaps he will share some pages with me and our class; this will be a choice for Carlos.

- *Expressed concern.* Both parents shared that Carlos feels he is not smart (including not as smart as his brother Diego. Carlos's teachers often tell him how Diego was in their class). They asked for help with this.

Ms. Margret then decides how she will **use these data.** Noting the importance of Carlos's self-esteem, she plans to demonstrate in multiple ways (e.g., positive feedback, celebrating successes, ensuring that he with other students takes leadership roles in her class) that Carlos is successful as a learner and problem solver. She is also planning to have at least one family night with her class and will ask each family to share their favorite traditions or holidays. She searched the Internet and learned that the Canary Island Museum of Science and Astronomy still exists and can be accessed online. She plans to share this Museum with her class when they study the sky and invite Carlos's grandfather to class and with Carlos ask them to talk about objects in the sky and share related exhibits (e.g., Carlos's telescope and drawings).

Ms. Margret decides the **value** of using this assessment strategy is making connections with Carlos's family and **making visible** what they value, how they share family time, their observations of Carlos's interest in school and literacy, and the concern they shared about Carlos's self-esteem. It provided many hooks to her instruction (e.g., writing in diaries, study of objects in the sky)—hooks that she intends to use in class and when continuing the conversations with them. She believes that she has made progress in building a positive relationship with Carlos's parents by **making visible her interests and identities** and hopes to share more about herself and her teaching goals in subsequent meetings.

Power of Conversations with Students as an Assessment Strategy

Asking students about their interests, activities out of school, friends, and how they view themselves as readers can be extremely helpful for teachers to learn about students' identities—their feelings of competence, their interests and goals, their notions of successful readers, and their worries and needs. As students participate in the reading events of a classroom, they develop perceptions of their capabilities and identities as readers (Seban & Tavsanli, 2015). They also develop understandings about how they use reading strategies for making sense of ideas, for learning about their world and the concepts and ideas they encounter in texts, to communicate with others, and to express their feelings and emotions. Reading events may include the range of daily literacy activities in the primary grades (e.g., read-alouds, shared reading, small-group reading, independent reading, and conferences) or in the upper grades (e.g., workshops, individual conferences, digital text development), as well as their involvement in formative and summative literacy assessments. Conversations are useful for exploring students' perceptions of themselves as readers, as we can learn if their perceptions are positive (e.g., I am capable; I am a good reader; I am a problem solver) or negative (e.g., I am not a good reader; reading is too hard for me; McCarthey, 2001; West, 2002).

ASSESSMENT STRATEGY 2.2.

Initial Student Conversation: What Can You Tell Me That Will Help Me Be a Good Teacher for YOU?

Purpose

The first of these conversations should occur early in the school year followed by opportunities for a two-way dialogue that continues throughout the year. The goal is to begin a dialogue that is comfortable and informative, and that encourages a trusting and comforting relationship between teachers and students. Asking students about their interests, activities out of school, friends, and how they view themselves as readers and writers can be extremely helpful for teachers to learn about their funds of identities and to respond to students' differences, expanding teaching practices to include those that are equitable and personable.

Value

Holding conversations between teachers and students is valuable for laying the foundation for building connections with each other, and for teachers to learn about their students. These conversations also provide an opportunity for teachers to describe their interests and activities in and out of school, and their instructional dreams and goals so students can get to know their teachers as people. As students participate in the reading events of a classroom, they develop perceptions of their capabilities and identities as readers. Conversations with students are useful for revealing students' perceptions of themselves and how they use reading strategies for making sense of ideas and for learning how students view their world and the concepts and ideas they encounter in texts.

Procedures

1. **Preparation** for holding student conversations requires clear expectations about the process and how you plan to initiate and sustain the talk. Identify what you hope to learn from the conversation that occurs early in the school year and plan to take notes that will inform your instruction as well as help you plan for subsequent conversations throughout the year.

   Plan for a time that you will meet with each student in your class or classes and a place for holding the 1:1 conversations. For the first conversation of the year, it is useful to assign 10- to 15-minute time allotments for each student (perhaps 3- to 5-minute conversations with early readers and held more frequently) on your instructional calendar. These may be held during recreational reading or partner reading time or other times when students are working independently.

   Typically, these initial conversations can be completed within the first month or 6 weeks of school. Plan also for frequency of follow-up meetings that will occur during the year. Identify how you will follow up after each conversation. Follow-up might include making connections between the curriculum and students' interests and/or questions and/or discussing progress toward meeting goals during conferences.

   - Identify what you will say to open the conversation that will help each student feel comfortable about the meeting while also explaining that this will be one of many conversations during the year.
   - Plan to share some information about yourself, such as your hobbies, family, activities out of school, and your teaching goals for this school year. Think of this sharing as informal and more spontaneous with information interspersed through the conversation, rather than starting with 2–3 minutes that is all about you!
   - Identify a set of questions and/or comments that will engage you and your student in a meaningful conversation. Plan to be conversational. In Figure 2.4, we provide some examples of conversation openers and questions/statements.

2. **Engaging each student in the conversations** during your scheduled time together requires flexibility. Students will often tell you more about themselves when given the opportunity to talk with you, thus eliminating some of the questions that you previewed. Keep plans for the conversation in place but listen carefully and respond directly to the student's comments and observations. You can learn so much about your students as you listen and let them take the lead. And when students don't take the lead, you have a plan for nudging the conversation along.

Collecting, Analyzing, and Using Data

Taking notes is useful for keeping a record of what was said during the conversation.

1. One method for notetaking during the conversation is an open-ended form (see Form 2.2), listing potential questions and statements by topics (e.g., activities out of school, likes and dislikes about school activities, family members, typical night at home). Note main ideas in spaces provided, knowing that you can elaborate on these after the conversation. See filled-in example in Figure 2.5.

2. A second method is developing a checklist that represents topics of interest, also leaving spaces for taking notes, as illustrated in Figure 2.6.
3. We recommend that you avoid tape recording as typically it is not necessary, and for some students, it can restrict what they want to share.
4. Shortly after the conversation, return to your notes to check for clarity and, as needed, elaborate on your initial set of ideas.
5. Analyze the information by identifying categories that represent your main ideas (e.g., reading interests, activities after school) so that you can make connections to future conversations and to your instruction. Identify questions that you might want to ask during subsequent student conversations.

Making Students and Teachers Visible

Holding two-way conversations with your students provides a wonderful opportunity for you to know your students and understand more about their hopes, dreams, interests, and participation in your class. Likewise, students begin to understand your hopes, dreams, and interests. Connections and trust are formed that support your work together and, in many instances, begin a lifelong relationship. Starting the conversation with the name of our strategy, *Initial Student Conversation: What Can You Tell Me That Will Help Me Be a Good Teacher for YOU?*, tells students that you care about them and want to support their learning in your class.

Using open-ended conversation starters
I am so happy that we have an opportunity to talk with each other.
I hope to learn from you how I can be a good teacher for you.
I noticed that you seemed to really enjoy the book I read in class yesterday and want to know more about the kinds of books you like.
I noticed that you seemed to dislike the book I read in class yesterday and want to know more about the kinds of books you hope we will read in class.
What reading activities do you like that we do in class?
Using questions
Here are some of the books we have read in class. What are your favorite ones?
Your parents told me that you read with your grandfather at home. What do you read together?
What else do you do with your grandparents and/or your parents?
Are there favorite activities that you do with your family?
What are your favorite activities that you do with your family at home?
What do you do with your family on weekends? With your brothers and sisters?
Do you like to read and write at home? What do you read or write?
Do you think you are a good reader? Why?
You told me yesterday that you don't like to read in the small group. Let's talk about that to help me understand. Why don't you like that activity?

FIGURE 2.4. Initiating and engaging students during conversations: Examples.

Questions	Teacher notes	Teacher reflections
Do you like to reread some of your books?	I have reread the *Wimpy* Diary books a million times! My mother told me there are 15 books and I found 7 at our community center. I read these when I go to bed or after dinner when it is quiet time.	Look for additional *Wimpy Kid* books. Wonder why he likes these . . . I need to ask this question. Also look for additional diary-type books and *Wimpy* books . . . use these as guides for in-class writing.
Tell me about your reading. I brought some books to the table. Do you like informational books (like these), or books of poems (e.g., *Where the Sidewalk Ends*) or books that tell a story? Or maybe something else?	I like to read about space and things in the sky. I am learning about Ecuador from my grandfather and books we are reading. I want to learn about other places.	Can make multiple connections to our space readings in science and English language arts. And social studies and English language arts connections to places we will visit.
You told me yesterday that you don't like small-group reading. Tell me more about this. Why don't you like that activity?	I don't like to listen to other students read aloud during whisper reading . . . they read too loud and I can't think.	I need to change this practice . . . perhaps move students further apart on the carpet or at the table. Perhaps do more whisper reading during individual conferences.

FIGURE 2.5. Example of open-ended notetaking during student conversations.

Implementation Example

Ms. Margret, the fourth-grade English language arts teacher introduced in our previous example, is planning to hold her first 1:1 conversation with Carlos. Since Ms. Margret teaches three sections of English language arts every day, she knows that her conversations will need to be planned carefully so that she can talk with each student for about 10 minutes across a 4-week period, so that she ends up having conversations with each student three times a year.

From previous records, she believes that Carlos is making good progress with the English language arts curriculum. She knows that Carlos is Hispanic and speaks some Spanish that he has learned from his parents and his grandfather. Both sets of grandparents are from Spain, having emigrated to the United States 40 years ago. Carlos's paternal grandfather joined the military when he was young and was stationed in European countries, including the Canary Islands. Carlos's mother has a 2-year degree in business from a community college and his father completed a bachelor of arts program in business at a 4-year college. English is the primary language spoken in the home.

Ms. Margret observed that Carlos seems very interested in the read-aloud, informational text (*Olinguito, de la A a la Z!/Olinguito, from A to Z!*, by Lulu Delacre) that she is

Topics		
Interest in reading activities	***At-home activities***	***Strategies to address comprehension difficulties***
____ reading at home	____ games with family	____ I think of what I know already
____ whole-class reading	____ sports on weekends	____ I reread
____ small-group reading	____ other	____ I ask my friends
____ reading and writing connections	***Types of reading/writing activities***	____ I skip that part
____ shared reading with peers	____ drawings about texts	____ I stop reading
____ other	____ drawings about life	____ other
Specific types of texts that hold interest	____ writing about texts	***Feelings about reading competence***
____ picture books	____ reading independently	____ I am a good reader
____ poetry	____ other	____ why?
____ informational	***Strategies when facing word recognition difficulties***	____ I worry about reading
____ narrative	____ sound words out	____ why?
____ mixed genre	____ use of pictures	____ other
____ author's series of texts	____ use of meaning	***Worries about reading competence***
____ other	____ try different strategies	____ I don't read correctly
Reading out of school	____ other	____ I don't know all the words
____ quiet time scheduled at home		____ I don't like to read
____ shared reading with siblings		____ why?
____ shared reading with parents or grandparents		____ other
____ other		

FIGURE 2.6. Checklist with topics for notetaking.

sharing with the class. The author invites the reader to travel to the "magical world of a cloud forest" located in the Andes, Ecuador. As readers are introduced by a zoologist to the plants and animals living in the forest, they also learn about a new mammal, the olinguito, that was first identified in 1978. The animals and plants are organized around the sequence of the alphabet with an abundance of colorful and realistic illustrations.

Ms. Margret's **preparation** for her conversation with Carlos begins with thinking about how she will open the conversation and possible questions she will ask. She has learned some information about Carlos's interests from her observations in class and the conversation that she had with Carlos's parents. She **previews** what she will say as she develops a notetaking guide on which she lists open-ended questions and ideas that she will pursue. (See example in Figure 2.5.)

Ms. Margret held her first conversation of the school year with Carlos. We present highlights of this conversation to share what she learned about Carlos and the process that she implemented.

MS. MARGRET: I am so happy that we have a chance to talk with each other as I hope to learn from you how I can be a good teacher for you. As we get to know each other better this year, we will continue to talk about this and I will ask for your help as I learn how to be the teacher that you want and need. I have taught fourth grade for 5 years and I love learning about each of my students.

I have noticed that you are asking questions and talking about the book *Olinguito, from A to Z!* that we are reading in class. I would love to know your thoughts about this book choice and if I should choose similar books for us to read this year.

CARLOS: I really like this book but at first I didn't think I would. The title sounded funny . . . what is an Olinguito anyway! Now I like the title and the other Spanish words. . . . I am telling my grandfather about these words, like bromelias, what a funny word!, and he is telling me in Spanish about the animals and plants in Spain. Some are the same as in the book about Ecuador. I know some Spanish words but I am learning more when I talk with him.

MS. MARGRET: So interesting. I remember telling my grandmother about the books I read in school. When she visited us, we often sat on the porch and she would reread with me my favorite books.

I met with your parents last week at their coffee shop. Tell me about your family members that live in your home.

CARLOS: My mother, father, and grandfather live in my home. Also, I have a brother, Diego, who is older than me, and a younger sister, Josie. I was thinking about Josie when we read the *Fudge* book, because Josie can be mischievous. She plays with my pencils and crayons and moves them to her desk, or she tells really long stories about things that really didn't happen to her. We laugh and then my grandfather will say, "Now, Josie, did that really happen?" And she will say, "No, but it could happen!" She is always sure that her made-up stories could really happen.

MS. MARGRET: Your comments make me wonder about your favorite books. Are there books that are special to you? Do you like to reread some of your books? (*Ms. Margret observes Carlos's nod of agreement.*) Which ones make you want to reread them and why?

CARLOS: I have reread the *Wimpy* diary books a million times! My mother told me there are 15 books, and I found 7 at our community center to read and reread. I read these at night when I go to bed or when we have quiet time after dinner.

MS. MARGRET: Do you like to write? (*After seeing Carlos shake his head yes.*) What do you like about writing? What do you write about?

CARLOS: I think writing helps me think better about the books I read. I told my mother that and she said that this is what happens to her. If she is reading a book with foods to serve at the coffee shop, she writes notes to help her remember the ideas. I write in a diary almost every night. I write about my friends, what I see in the sky, what my grandfather tells me about the sky, and the *Wimpy* books. I write about what I want to remember.

MS. MARGRET: I keep a notebook where I write things that I want to remember. Sometimes I write about the books I read, sometimes I write about things that I have learned and want to share with our class.

What kind of writing do you like to do in school? You can help me plan for the best ways to ask you and the other students to write this year.

CARLOS: In third grade, we learned to write like the author of the books we were reading. I guess that is why I write in a diary because I like the *Wimpy* books. Last night I wrote about the *Olinguito* book in my diary.

MS. MARGRET: That is wonderful. Tell me about your writing last night.

CARLOS: I drew pictures of the animals and plants and then I described them. I wrote like I was a reporter telling my grandfather about what I learned.

MS. MARGRET: Are there things you want to learn that might make you a better writer this year?

CARLOS: My grandfather and mother tell me that I sometimes tell just facts without explaining them. Last night, I drew a picture of the bromelias, I named it, and I said that it grows in the forest. But I didn't explain that it is a plant and it has many characteristics and what makes it live in the forest. My grandfather asked me those questions but I didn't write about those things.

MS. MARGRET: That is a wonderful clue about what we can work on this year. Writing to describe what we are learning is a goal for our writing.

Tell me about your reading. Do you like informational books or books of poems or books that tell a story or maybe something else?

CARLOS: I like to read about space and what appears in the sky. . . . I really like learning about Ecuador and want to read about other places and what happens there. . . . I want to read the next books of Wimp. . . . *Wimpy* books are still my favorite books.

MS. MARGRET: Do you think you are a good reader?

CARLOS: Sometimes I am a good reader. . . . Some other times I am not.

MS. MARGRET: Tell me more. What do you do as a good reader?

CARLOS: I look for clues, like pictures or drawings. Look for special words that the authors use and I try to make sense of them to help me understand what I am reading. Sometimes I reread and reread when I don't understand something.

MS. MARGRET: Good readers often do those same things. Search for clues about the meanings of ideas and words. Reread to make sense of part of the text.

What happens when you feel that you are not a good reader?

CARLOS: Sometimes I don't know what to do when I don't understand what I am reading. I ask my mother or dad or grandfather to help me but I can't help myself. Sometimes I don't know the words and sometimes there are so many things to remember. Sometimes I try to memorize all the things but there are too many things to remember. I don't think I can understand hard books.

MS. MARGRET: Thank you, Carlos, for telling me that and describing what is difficult. Reading hard books can become easier when we learn how to tackle them and try to use strategies we are learning to make sense of words. Let's make it a goal for both of us to work together on that. Many students who read many books have the same dilemma—finding that some books are more difficult than others. Learning how to make sense of them is part of the process of growing as a reader. We can practice some actions that you can take that I think will help you continue to grow as a reader.

We have a plan! I will share some strategies that you can use as you read difficult texts. We will practice these together and with our class. And then when we meet to talk again, we can decide if those strategies are helping your reading.

Analyzing and Using the Data

During Ms. Margret's planning time, she reviewed her notes and filled in missing information from the individual conversations that she held with her students. Next, she read and reread her notes from each conversation and identified clusters of concepts that represented what was discussed before assigning a category title to each cluster. She noticed that some information she was listing was the same as what she heard from Carlos's parents and the repetition is useful for aiding her recall of this information.

For her conversation with Carlos, Ms. Margret organized the information around the following category titles:

- *Family members:* Carlos lives with his parents, his grandfather, and two siblings, Diego, an older brother, and Josie, a younger sister. Carlos's grandfather seems to take an active role in the family conversations and activities.

- *Carlos's literacy identity.* Carlos seems to enjoy reading and writing, and he thinks he is good at both most of the time. He described his interest in the *Wimpy* books, books that he has read and reread "a million times" and the informational book, *Olinguito, from A to Z!*, that we are currently reading. Carlos reads at night when there is family quiet time after dinner or when he goes to bed. Carlos likes to write in his diary, often drawing pictures of what he has read and then writing about the pictures he has drawn. Carlos seems to make connections between books he reads and writes about and with life experiences, such as describing the mischievous acts of his younger sister to similar ones of siblings in the *Fudge* book we read.

- *Carlos's interests:* When reading, Carlos seems to like both humorous stories and informational texts. He expressed his interest in the Spanish words that appear in *Olinguito* and those that he is learning from his grandfather. He talks about books we are reading when he is at home, and he shared that his grandfather, who is from Spain, told him that there are similar plants and animals in Spain. He is interested in space and things in the sky. He wants to read the remainder of the *Wimpy* books, as they are still his favorite, and he likes learning about Ecuador and other countries.

- *Carlos's strategies for reading and writing and expressed needs.* Carlos has developed and is aware of his strategic moves that help his writing and reading, and he described needs for improving reading and writing. Strategies he uses include writing facts and ideas from books that he is reading to help him remember them. When he has difficulty comprehending the texts he is reading, he will reread and looks for clues in the illustrations or when authors use special words.

Carlos indicated that his writing could improve if he told more than just the facts when he writes, adding explanations and descriptions (e.g., descriptions of the plants that grow in Ecuador).

Carlos said that he is "not smart enough to understand hard books." His parents had shared the same concern about Carlos's feeling that he is not "smart."

Next Ms. Margret decides how she will **use these data.** Because she previously had a conversation with Carlos's parents, she starts by comparing her notes and finds that both were useful in helping her understand reading and writing activities in the home, Carlos's book and writing interests, the role of the family in supporting literacy, that Spanish is an interest for Carlos and sometimes this language is spoken at home. During the next conversation, she wants to ask Carlos about his out-of-school activities and interests, especially those that he enjoys with friends. This information can help her learn more about Carlos's funds of identities to which she can make connections in school. More specifically, she learned about two possible problems that they will address in class. Carlos tries to remember everything he reads and finds that it is impossible—"too many things to remember," and that he doesn't "know the words" and their meanings when reading "hard books."

Ms. Margret decides that the **value** of holding this conversation as an assessment strategy is extremely important for **making visible** her interest in Carlos and in making visible Carlos's identities and what he believes are his strengths and needs. She knows that she began to share some information about her identity as his teacher. She hopes to share more about her interests and identities as she continues to learn about those of Carlos in future conversations across the year.

Opportunities for Celebrations of Identities of Students and Families

Several years ago, Vicki visited primary schools in the working-class neighborhoods of Canning Town, Dagenham, and Barking, outside of London, England. Each school identified its goal to achieve equitable learning opportunities for the diverse students and families in their neighborhoods. The schools are hubs for activities in the local communities, offering multiple classes during the day and evening for parents (e.g., learning English, acquiring work-related skills), providing a space for a neighborhood garden in which parents and children planted and harvested produce, and encouraging parents to take part in classroom activities when possible. Multiple languages are heard in the classrooms and hallways, and families' histories and cultural traditions are shared widely, including on school posters developed by the families over the school year. These school visits, coupled with our observations in U. S. schools that celebrate students' cultural identities, influenced our choice of the following two strategies.

ASSESSMENT STRATEGY 2.3.
Celebrating Identities with Students and Their Families

Purpose

The purpose of this strategy is to invite students and their families to share their special traditions and cultural experiences. Assessment of the whole child includes understanding the families and communities from which they come. Teachers can learn about special holidays, celebrations, and everyday family activities that are important to the family. Teachers can engage students and families in this strategy during a school family night or another time that families might come together with their children, such as during a community event held at the neighborhood library. Some schools have established family time during the school day when parents come to work in the school garden or meet with other parents.

Value

This strategy provides a window into the lives and traditions of your students and their families. Teachers can learn what is important to their students' families. And parents have opportunities to learn from each other, often finding that they are more alike than different. During the exchange among families and students, you are making visible multiple funds of identities. Families are communicating with you in ways that may not be typical of your school relationships with families; and families are communicating with each other, often forming bonds of friendship. With this information about students' identities, it is more likely that instruction will be responsive to students' unique capabilities and needs, thus, providing equitable learning opportunities for each student.

Procedures

1. **Preparation** for implementing this strategy begins with building knowledge about your students and their families and planning for meeting with them.

    - Survey your class membership to identify the racial and ethnic groups represented. These might include Native American, Asian, Black, Latinx, Muslim, Native Hawaiian or other Pacific Islander, or White. Each group brings a rich history, rituals, customs, and traditions (e.g., family expressions of values and beliefs, religious gatherings), routines (e.g., expectations for family activities at home), and linguistic and cultural traditions, and sometimes these are held in common across groups.
    - Study the ethnicities of the groups represented in your class by reading about them and talking with coteachers and community leaders. With this information, think about how you will engage the families in this strategy.
    - Decide if the strategy will be implemented at one gathering with the entire class and their families, or if two or three sessions would be optimal for facilitating participation. You will be taking notes during the gathering and want to keep your notetaking manageable as you interact with and observe the students and their families.

2. **Preview** the process you will follow to implement the strategy during the gathering.

- Identify a time most convenient for the families and a place to meet. For example, you might meet in your classroom during a schoolwide family event. If these events don't occur in your school, identify community events, such as book or food festivals, where you might find a convenient and private space for meeting.
- Plan how you will invite families to attend the gathering (e.g., phone calls, notes sent to each home, school liaisons contacting families) and how you will explain its purpose. Explain the purpose for the gathering (i.e., a time for families and students to learn about each other's traditions and customs).
- Determine if school translators or community partners should be invited to support family participation in the event.

Invite each family to bring one artifact with them, emphasizing that each may bring something different (e.g., something they use when they celebrate their favorite holiday, a food that is traditional in their family, a photo or family album, a family quilt). Having an object in hand is often quite helpful for encouraging conversations.

- Plan for an activity that will open the gathering once your students and their families have arrived. For example, if you know that your class is representative of multiple ethnic and racial groups, you might want to read one of the following short texts: *Let's Celebrate: Special Days around the World* by Kate DePalma; *Celebrate! Connections among Cultures* by Jan Reynolds; *If the World Were a Village* by David J. Smith, or *All Are Welcome* by Alexandra Penfold and Suzanne Kaufman. (A brief synopsis of each is provided in Table 2.1). The activity to open this event should reassure parents that you respect and value their backgrounds, cultures, and traditions, and you plan to work closely with them this year.
- Next plan to share your artifact and some information about your own identities (e.g., why you became a teacher, your family background and traditions, your sports or community activities). Typically, your sharing comes before inviting parents to do the same.

TABLE 2.1. Possible Book Selections for Celebrating Family Traditions

Book title	Author	Publisher	Synopsis
Let's Celebrate: Special Days around the World	Kate De Palma	WestMusic	Describes 13 special holidays and customs from cultures around the world with rhyming text and colorful illustrations.
Celebrate! Connections among Cultures	Jan Reynolds	Frozen Land, Vanishing Cultures Series	Photographic exploration of celebrations and customs of seven indigenous world cultures, identifying common rituals.
If the World Were a Village	David J. Smith	Kids Can Press, Citizen Kid	Imagining the world's population—all 6.8 billion—as members of village of just 100 people; diversity represented in this village.
All Are Welcome	Alexandra Penfold	Random House	Discovery of a school where—no matter what—all children have a place, have a space, and are loved and appreciated.

- Ask families to take turns sharing and describing the artifacts that they brought. Students may decide to share for their families. Translators invited for the event may also help families describe their customs and traditions represented with the artifact.
- Preview carefully how you will implement notetaking while parents and students are participating and sharing their information. Consider taking photos, for example, of the artifacts and writing brief notes about each and why they are important to the families.
- Organize a notebook with pages assigned to each family with sufficient space for notetaking. We provide an example in Figure 2.7 (see p. 47) developed by Mr. Blume, the teacher described in our implementation example.
- Last, plan for the closing activity. Return to the opening activity, such as rereading the book that you read initially and close by talking about how you are all different but also alike. Perhaps refer to your notes and provide a brief summary of what you have learned about each family. Or if you need more time to summarize all that you learned, you might explain that your plan is to use what you have learned about each family to make meaningful connections to your teaching.

3. **Engaging parents and students.** Be prepared for multiple reactions from the families who attend your event.
   - Some will be shy, not knowing what to expect. Others will be enthusiastic and eager to share with others.
   - Some families may be most comfortable speaking in their heritage languages, and thus inviting translators, community liaisons, or parents that have collaborated with you previously will support communication across different languages represented.
   - Starting the event by stating your goals clearly and how you hope each will participate (e.g., turn taking, one member shares to start and that one member could be the student) will help to set the tone.
   - Be prepared to listen, to take notes, and to be responsive with lots of praise and excitement.
   - Plan to circle around the room, standing and talking with families as they share.
   - Know when to wrap up and bring closure to the event with a plan for follow-up meetings.

Collecting, Analyzing, and Using Data

Taking notes throughout the assessment strategy will help you collect specific information that is shared by the family.

1. Collecting and organizing information with a notebook may be optimal for collecting data for this assessment strategy. Within the notebook, assign a few pages to each student/family who will attend the event. These pages, with family name identified, may remain blank with notes added as the evening progresses or you may anticipate some organizing headers (e.g., traditions, favorite activities, holidays, ancestor's homes).
2. Plan to analyze the information collected around the categories you established prior

to meeting with the families and those that you might not have anticipated (e.g., common foods that are enjoyed, family celebrations, shared family activities).

3. Develop a list of experiences shared across the families illustrating how families are alike and different. This information will help you make connections to the families and students during future conversations and connections between your instruction and the students.

Making Students and Teachers Visible

At the heart of this activity is a celebration of visible likenesses and differences among the identities of the teacher, students, and families. Teachers develop an awareness of the range of cultural interests and histories of their students, and in turn families learn the same about the teachers and classmates and their families. This activity advances the knowledge of both the teacher and families while also conveying the teacher's respect for students and families and that families' histories are valued in this classroom.

Implementation Example

Mr. Blume is a third-grade teacher who teaches a self-contained class in an elementary school located within an ethnically and racially diverse neighborhood. Mr. Blume knows that he will better understand his students' approaches to literacy if he learns about their families and communities. The school has partnered with community organizations and sponsors multiple activities (e.g., school garden, English classes, parenting classes, and craft activities). Some of the activities are conducted by parent volunteers. Mr. Blume has 22 students within his class, and he has met about 60% of their parents.

Mr. Blume knows that his students represent a range of ethnic backgrounds and that they observe family traditions (e.g., attending religious services, fasting, lighting candles, singing songs) when they celebrate holidays that are special to them throughout the year. For example, he knows that some students' families immigrated from Egypt and celebrate Eid al-Fitr. Others celebrate Passover, and a few attend the Jewish temple that he attends. Some students' families originated from Brazil, and the students talk about the carnivals that are held there each year. Others celebrate Christmas and Kwanzaa. Yet he wants to learn more about these holidays, if and how they are celebrated in the homes, and if there are other traditions that might be more important than holidays to them. He felt that in the past holidays have been glossed over with insufficient information learned by him and his students about actual traditions and customs that families valued.

This focus on customs around holidays will lay the foundation for a continuing study of different cultures and customs. For example, Mr. Blume and his students will study customs and rituals followed by seven indigenous cultures in the world, identifying common and dissimilar customs. This will be followed by thinking of their own classroom as a village representing different cultures and what can be learned from each other. See suggested texts that are listed in Table 2.1 to illustrate the range of readings and content that will be addressed.

Mr. Blume **prepares** for this assessment strategy by reading and rereading several books that focus on customs and family rituals related to how holidays are celebrated within different cultures. He chooses *Let's Celebrate! Special Days around the World* as the text he will read at the beginning of the group meeting. This text describes 13 special holidays from cultures around the world, including the ethnic-related holidays celebrated by most of his students. Mr. Blume knows that holidays across the community are often celebrated in his school, but he hopes to explore more specifically how these holidays engage the family in shared activities that help to define their cultural heritage and traditions. Thus, his goal is to examine these traditions in ways that will provide a frame of reference for himself and for the families that provides a deeper understanding of the different traditions represented in his classroom. With this as a goal, he prepares the following invitation and includes specific questions that he hopes will enable participation and shared learning.

Prior to sending out the invitation, Mr. Blume calls each family and describes the celebration of holiday customs that will be held in his classroom. During the conversation, Mr. Blume reads the invitation that they will receive in the mail and encourages each family to attend and to share something about themselves. For some families with languages other than English, Mr. Blume has engaged a school interpreter to help him communicate with each family on the phone. Through the conversations, he is thrilled to learn that all families will be represented that night. For some families, there may be work or other conflicts but at least one member of the family will accompany each of his students. He then sends home the invitations (see Figure 2.7).

Mr. Blume plans to share how his family celebrated the summer solstice each year while he was growing up. He will describe the games and songs that they sang and how each family member wrote one word in their family journal each year to describe their feelings.

To the parents and students in Mr. Blume's Third-Grade Classroom

YOU are invited to attend an event for

Celebrating Family Traditions with Mr. Blume's Students and Their Families

[Date], 6:30–8:30 P.M., Mr. Blume's classroom

This evening is for you to share with us how your family celebrates special times together. This will help all of us get to know each other and will help me make connections to your children when I teach. I hope this will help me be a better teacher.

Plan to tell us about one special holiday that your family enjoys, by answering these questions:

1. How do you and your family prepare for the holiday?
2. What activities/customs does your family enjoy around the holiday?
3. What are some important words and languages that you and your family use to celebrate this holiday?
4. Why is this time together important to you and your family?

If possible, bring one thing that relates to how you celebrate the holiday—a photo, an object, a food that you make, a family game, a drawing.

FIGURE 2.7. Mr. Blume's invitation.

Mr. Blume learned during his first year of teaching that families had lots to talk about and that he had difficulty taking notes about all that was shared. Since that first year, he has invited two or three guests (e.g., school's bilingual teachers, parents of former students, community representatives) to support his notetaking. He plans to set up white boards and posters in the room so that families can write or draw about activities and other customs that occur on their family holidays. Each family will also display the object that they brought with them. He will take photos of the families and their writings or drawings, and later develop a classroom scrapbook that will be kept in the classroom museum. He will keep these photos as forms of information to analyze as data after the event.

In previous years, Mr. Blume implemented a **variation of this strategy** by inviting smaller numbers of families to attend his family night, holding three family nights in 1 week involving six to seven families each night. This year, though, he is inviting all 22 families represented in his classroom following the procedures he implemented the previous year. He is confident that the strategy will provide rich information and engage families in sharing their customs in ways that will build community.

Engaging Parents and Students

Mr. Blume welcomed the families and their children to this celebratory event. He began with a greeting, introducing the special guests, and explaining how the evening will proceed. He had placed ice and water jugs on a welcoming table along with name tags. He noticed that a few families brought a snack to share with the class and these were quietly placed on the table. He was eager to hear about these foods later in the evening.

After reading *Let's Celebrate! Special Days around the World*, Mr. Blume explained that he would start the celebration with his favorite holiday—celebrating the summer solstice. He referred to a few sketches that he placed on a white board before families entered the room. He acknowledged that this is not a holiday that everyone celebrates, saying that maybe his family should have called it a family tradition. Noting that the summer solstice is recognized as the longest day in the United States, he shared that his family would take a picnic basket to the local park, where they ate their dinner, played games, and hiked through the park. They sang songs before making a bonfire and telling family stories. He sang one of the songs and shared a picnic basket that included foods that his family would have enjoyed during this celebration.

Next and prior to the whole group sharing with each other, Mr. Blume invited each family to take a few minutes to write some ideas or a few drawings related to their chosen holiday on a white board or poster. He explained that he would be taking notes and some photos to help him remember what he learned during the evening. Mr. Blume and his guests circulated and asked questions, took notes, and supported writings or drawings on the posters. Afterward, the parents and their children took time to share their artifacts and describe their holiday activities with the whole group. Mr. Blume noticed that even when a few parents asked their son or daughter to "do the talking," they often added to the conversation.

Olga's family, for example, talked about how Carnivale was celebrated in Brazil and now in their home. It begins five days before Lent. Olga and her parents described Lent as a time to say prayers, eat healthy and less, and prepare for Easter. To celebrate, they usually took a weekend day and joined others in the neighborhood to share food and wear "sparkly" clothes and beaded necklaces. Their neighborhood did not have the parades like in Brazil but they exchanged small gifts and some members of their group told stories about Brazil.

Elif said his family is Muslim. His family described how they observe Ramadan, a religious time for families to pray and fast. They explained that when Ramadan ends, they began the Eid al-Fitr, a celebration. It begins on the first day of a new moon and there is always a special meal served for lunch. Elif's mother said she brought a rice dish that evening for the group to try; this was a dish that she served at home to start the holiday. Elif told the group that the holiday lasted three days, and his grandmother came to stay with them sometimes for it. One of the days the families in the neighborhood would go out on the street and celebrate with each other, eating together and telling stories. Elif's mother said there are traditional folktales that they shared. Sometimes they paraded around the neighborhood greeting their friends and others that lived nearby.

Chandra's parents shared how they celebrate Kwanzaa in their family. Chandra said that her family lit seven candles, one each day. There are three red, three green, and one black. Chandra's mother held up the seven candles and said the red ones represent unity, self-determination, and collective work and responsibility respectively; the black one represents cooperative economics, and the green ones represent purpose, creativity, and faith. Chandra's dad explained that it is not a religious holiday but a celebration of African American culture. He said that they celebrated with family members and neighbors in the community, they enjoyed meals together, and they sang songs and told stories about grandparents and great grandparents.

The evening continued with families and children describing the customs they followed on their holidays that included Christmas, Dia de Muertos (a Mexican holiday), and Passover. Several families brought food to share and all brought an artifact, which included family photos, maps, objects used in the celebrations, and drawings. One student, whose family celebrated Passover, concluded after hearing from the other families that "we all like to eat and sing and tell stories." Mr. Blume picked up on this comment and asked others to share how they were alike (e.g., we celebrate with our families and neighbors) and how they were different (e.g., not all holidays were religious ones, reasons for celebrations were different).

Mr. Blume took photos during the evening and, after 90 minutes, ended the evening by reading the book *All Are Welcome Here,* with the group singing a song Mr. Blume taught them. Families talked with each other and Mr. Blume before leaving, ending the activity after 2 hours.

Analyzing and Using the Data

The next morning, Mr. Blume **analyzed** what he had learned from the data he collected. He found that he was in a writing frenzy (i.e., so much to write and remember) as he tried to capture what he and guests had written as notes and to examine the families' writings and drawings. He decided to set up six columns in his notebook, listing each family name along with the holiday name and preparations in the first column, the activities and customs followed, the artifact and its description, words and languages used, importance, and his own reflections in the five additional columns, respectively. He noted specifically the information contributed by his students during the time when families were sharing. See Figure 2.8 for an excerpt of the notebook page that Mr. Blume developed.

Family holiday	Preparation	Activities	Artifact	Words/languages	Importance	My reflections
Olga's family: Carnivale	Celebration before Lent; during Lent they will say prayers and fast, eating healthy foods	Exchange small gifts with family and friends, neighborhood get-togethers singing and eating. Grandparents tell stories about Brazil	Sparkly clothes and beads	Carnivale means farewell to meat, they will fast and eat less meet during Lent. Portuguese spoken at home and with grandparents	Brings families together to celebrate with elders and to hear their stories, sing songs of families and countries.	Make connections to the importance of our families' stories and celebrations, especially when our community celebrates Carnivale with a neighborhood parade. Social studies connections to Brazil.
Elif's family: Ramadan and Eid al-Fitr	Ramadan is a time of fasting and prayers. Eid al-Fitr follows with 3-day festival with morning prayers (bath before prayers), sweet foods prepared	Ramadan is a time for prayer, fasting, and giving donations to charities Following is Eid al-Fitr, celebrating renewal. Small gifts are given to children; eating outdoors; wear fancy clothes	Green flags and green balloons to decorate homes. Green is a holy color. Brought baklava to share with others.	People greet each other "Eith Eid Mubarak"–which means Blessed Eid–and exchange formal hugs.	Time to pray for forgiveness of sins and to give back to others. Five pillars of Islamic faith: God Prayer Alms Fasting Pilgrimage	Plan to access Metropolitan Museum of Art (NY) that displays Islamic culture and the five pillars. Make connections to readings about pillars of strong communities when we study our community and community of others

FIGURE 2.8. Mr. Blume's notebook pages for families' customs.

Mr. Blume plans to **use these data** in several ways. He will mark on his school calendar when these holidays occur during the school year, making certain that they remind each other about these holidays and how important they are for the families. He plans to continue the conversations with the families and students when he meets with them. And last, he plans to make specific connections to the reflections he made on his data analysis chart. For example, he was very interested in the Kwanzaa candles and thought their meanings had special meaning for the content they would study in literacy and social studies across the school year. He wants to return to these concepts (i.e., purpose, creativity, self-determination, cooperative economics) and develop their meanings as they relate to the texts they will be reading to deepen comprehension of these universal concepts. Mr. Blum believes these concepts will be useful for anchoring text discussions during literacy instruction.

Mr. Blume concluded that the **value** of this assessment exceeded his expectations. He was able to facilitate connections among the families and with himself. And as they made **visible** their customs, their activities, and their feelings about their traditions, Mr. Blume felt better prepared to personalize his literacy instruction in ways that would invite equitable student participation—making connections and responding to his students' interests and backgrounds enables him to recognize the uniqueness of each student in his class. Such information isn't typically captured on traditional achievement or diagnostic texts, but it is extremely valuable for establishing and extending the learning of both the students and Mr. Blume.

ASSESSMENT STRATEGY 2.4.
I Am Who I Am as a Reader

Purpose

This strategy is designed to invite dialogue between teachers and students as both discuss their reading identities. In particular, the conversation should enable students to discuss how they view themselves as readers, what they are learning about the reading process, and information they draw on to guide their thinking about texts.

Value

This strategy provides an opportunity for teachers and students to make visible how they think about themselves as readers. As teachers share their identities, they are making explicit to their students and themselves how and when they read, the strategies they use to guide their thinking, and what they do to fix-up misunderstandings that might occur during the process. Likewise, students can reveal what interests them about reading and the knowledge and strategic behaviors that they might rely on for making sense of texts. For students, especially young children, it may be difficult at first for them to be explicit about what they do as readers and how they feel about reading. Thus, teachers need to model some of these behaviors (e.g., *I love to read mysteries; I reread sentences when I don't understand what I am reading*) and build trusting relationships so that students feel comfortable sharing their worries or problems.

Procedures

1. **Preparation** requires setting explicit goals and identifying questions you will ask. Establish a few goals (e.g., what students choose to read, how students approach a text they are beginning to read) that will help you understand how your student views reading and what they view as strengths and needs. Next identify a conversation starter, such as previous student comments about a book being read during small-group instruction. Plan to hold these conversations at least three times with each student during the school year.

2. **Preview** the process you will follow as you implement this strategy. Decide on the information, such as student interests and their perceptions of themselves as readers (see suggested information identified in parentheses that follow):

   - (*Interests*). Open the conversation by stating the goal (e.g., "I hope to learn about what interests you as a reader. Knowing what is interesting to you as a reader will help me be better teacher for you").
   - To facilitate the conversation, it might be helpful to share what you have noticed about the student's reading (e.g., "I noticed that you were laughing about the cows typing a letter to Farmer Brown, when we read the book *Click, Clack, Moo: Cows That Type* by Doreen Cronin") and then making connections to interests (e.g., "Do you like to read texts that are funny? Ones that tell you about adventures?").
   - (*Students' perceptions of self as a reader*). A follow-up question would address students' perception of their reading actions and questions might include "What makes reading easy for you? What makes reading hard for you? Do you sometimes have problems when you read, such as not knowing all the words or what they mean? What do you do to read better or to help you when you don't understand what you are reading?"
   - (*Students perception of reading as activity*). Additional questions might include "What is the best thing about reading? What are your favorite reading activities in this class or at home?"
   - Throughout the conversation, be prepared to share your interests, what you have noticed about your reading habits, and the strategies you use for problem solving when experiencing difficulty.

3. **Engaging students** in these conversations provides valuable insights about how students think about themselves as readers, their reading preferences, and their reading behaviors. Such engagement can help us understand why students are or are not engaged in reading or the reading activities provided in our classrooms. With this knowledge, we gain clues about how we can support their reading success and involvement and provide instruction that is specific and responsive to who they are as readers.

Collecting, Analyzing, and Using Data

1. Taking notes during the conversation is extremely important for keeping a record of what was discussed and for making comparisons about what you are learning throughout the school year.

   - One method for notetaking is the use of a notebook, with sections assigned to each student. Within the notebook section for each student, identify three columns (see Form 2.3). In the first column, list the questions you might ask, leaving spaces for questions and comments that you add when the conversation takes you in new directions. In the second column, prepare to take (shorthand) notes during the conversation. These notes are ones that you will return to after the conversation, adding comments and interpretations in the third column.

- These notes will continue to develop across the school year, following additional student conversations. We provide an example of a notetaking procedure and data collected during this conversation in Figure 2.9.

2. Take time following the conversation to reflect on what you have learned during your conversations with each student. You will notice and identify specific patterns (e.g., students' interests, feelings of confidence, strategies for problem solving—such as rereading or using other fix up strategies) and make connections to your instruction.
3. Refer to this information when planning your instruction and when planning subsequent conversations with each student.

Questions and comments for book selection: *I Am Enough* by Kelurah A. Bobc	**Student's response**	**Reflections and interpretations**
You seemed to like this book when we were reading it earlier. *Shareeka nods yes!* Why did you like this book so much?	*It is like a song and I can see what the words say.*	*She likes the verse of this book, its lyrical qualities (it seems) but also the book creates pictures in her mind.*
Tell me about your reading. Do you like to read? What do you like to read?	*I am learning to read harder books. Like the books my mother reads.*	*High interest in reading.* *I need to make explicit the growth that she is making as a reader.*
What do you mean when you say you want to read harder books?	*When I read to my sister I read the pictures and didn't need to read the words.* *The books my mother reads are like this (shows how thick they are) and have lots of words. I want to learn how to read those words.*	*Make explicit the words that she is learning and when she is reading "harder" books*
Do you read at home? And what do you read?	*Yes, I read and sometimes I read to my sisters and I read aloud to my mother and father. They always tell me I am a good reader, and I know I am a good reader, but I want to read harder books.*	*Return to this conversation; continue to make explicit the goals we have for her reading and the progress she is making.*

FIGURE 2.9. Example of notetaking during a student conversation about book selection.

Making Students and Teachers Visible

The purpose of this strategy is to make visible your views about reading and your reading habits and strategies while also making visible the same information about your students. The conversations provide a wealth of information, helping you form connections around favorite books or strategies used, building trusting relationships with your students, and identifying students' identities and confidence as readers. More specifically, students will begin to share the strategies they use when reading and if they are trying to apply what they are learning, such as applying new skills to determine word meanings, or to reread sections to interpret inferences made by an author. Learning what students are thinking about themselves as readers, their actions when problem solving, and if and when they are applying what they are learning to their reading is useful for guiding your instructional decisions. Rich diagnostic information is provided by our students, who often have insights that either match our own observations or reveal information that we might have overlooked. We have learned that our students are our best resources when we want to learn more about them! And thus, this strategy can signal to students that we trust their insights and the information they are sharing with us about themselves.

Implementation Example

Mr. Marcus has been a first-grade teacher in this school and neighborhood for over 20 years. The neighborhood is diverse socioeconomically, culturally, and linguistically. Mr. Marcus is African American and celebrates ancestors who came from Nigeria and Botswana on the African continent. And while he does not live in the neighborhood, Mr. Marcus is a frequent visitor to the neighborhood to attend neighborhood meetings, enjoy a cup of coffee after school in the local coffee shops, eat in the many ethnic restaurants, attend religious services of his students' families, and shop in the grocery stores and local markets. Over the years, he has had the opportunity to learn about his students' families, become their friends, and often is called on to stand as a child's godfather during baptisms.

Every school year, Mr. Marcus hosts at least three family nights in his classroom. Attendance has increased significantly since his first year of teaching, and he believes that is because his students and their families have learned to trust him. He often says, "I may not get all the teaching right but I am learning along with my students and their families, and each year I think I am a better teacher."

Mr. Marcus has implemented different strategies during the family nights, including the strategy *Celebrating Identities with Students and Their Families,* described above. One strategy that he always implements is the one we are discussing now—*I Am Who I Am as a Reader.* During that family night, Mr. Marcus often reads from his journal and explains how and why reading is so important to him (e.g., I learn so much, I become a better teacher) and how his reading influences the way he teaches (e.g., I always listen to what my students are telling me about the books that we read). This sharing is typically followed by parents and their children talking about their own reading, and he hears how families participate in a range of at-home reading activities. Throughout the discussion, he makes explicit that reading is certainly more than reading a book. "I'm interested in all of the ways you use reading as you go through your day."

At the most recent family night, Mr. Marcus chose the book *I Am Enough* by Grace Byers to read to the group. He chose this book because he noticed that some families were sharing it with each other in the family community room where parents gathered for daily school activities (e.g., working in the school garden, attending English language classes). He shared the book cover with the families and heard several parents say "I just read that book at home," "I wish I could fix my hair that way," or "that girl looks just like Gracian" (a student who was in Mr. Marcus's class several years ago). Mr. Marcus read aloud, demonstrating the poetic flow of the text—"Like the sun I am here to shine, Like the voice, I am here to sing, Like the bird, I am here to fly and soar high over everything, . . . Like time, I am here to be and be everything I can."

After reading the book, Mr. Marcus led a discussion with high parent engagement, as each told about what they were visualizing as they heard the words or how specific lines made sense to them. From Mr. Marcus's perspective, the book reading seemed to be a "big hit" and the conversations that followed helped him to connect with the families and their children. Mr. Marcus then told the families that he had four copies of the book, ready for checkout and sharing among the families.

The next day in class, Mr. Marcus read the book to his first-grade students. Many had heard the book at the family gathering the night before, but a few students were hearing it for the first time. After discussing the book with each other, some students "acted out" a part that they remembered (e.g., Like the trees, I am here to grow, Like a ladder, I am here to climb, Like the wind, I am here to push).

In **preparation** for implementing the assessment strategy *I Am Who I Am as a Reader*, Mr. Marcus asked his students to write in their journals about this book. He told his students that they could draw a picture about their favorite part of the book, or a picture of a part that they did not like, or they could write about the book.

Mr. Marcus, **setting the goal for the strategy,** explained to his students that he was looking forward to talking about what they put in their journals and that he would share his own journal with them, too.

During the next few days, Mr. Marcus met with each student individually for about 5 minutes to discuss their journals and their views of themselves as readers.

Engaging Shareeka in the Conversation

Today, Mr. Marcus is meeting with Shareeka. He notices that Shareeka drew a picture of herself with hair that is similar to the hair on the girl found on the cover of *I Am Enough*. She also wrote several lines of print, sometvimes using invented spelling—(e.g., Lk the brd, I wnt to fly; Lk the trees, I wnt to clmb and get big.) She titled her journal entry—I am Me!

Mr. Marcus opens the conversation by asking Shareeka to tell him about her journal—what she drew and wrote. Shareeka explains that she wants her hair to look like the girl's hair in the picture and then she reads her lines of print. When Mr. Marcus asks Shareeka about the title, Shareeka says, "The book should be called—I am Me. This is about ME!"

He then shares his journal entries that include: Like the fireman, I put out fires. Like a father, I walk my daughter and son to school. Like a husband, I make dinner sometimes for our family. Like a teacher, I can't wait to see my students every day.

Shareeka listens to what he wrote and they both agree that coming to school is a good thing because they are learning "new things." Shareeka adds that she likes the books that he reads in class and "really liked" *I Am Enough.*

Next, Mr. Marcus and Shareeka engaged in the following conversation:

MR. MARCUS: Why did you like this book so much?

SHAREEKA: Because it is like singing when you read the words. I could see what was happening!

MR. MARCUS: I liked it, too, and it is like a song. Or like a poem. Like the book of poetry that I sometimes read in class.

Tell me about your reading. Do you like to read? What do you like to read?

SHAREEKA: I am learning to read harder books. I used to read to my baby sister and I read those books with lots of pictures and the same words. They were easy to read and I could read the books without even looking at the words. I want to read hard books like the ones my mother reads at nighttime.

MR. MARCUS: What do you mean when you say you want to read hard books?

SHAREEKA: They are big books *(she illustrates with her fingers indicating that they are several inches thick)* and they have lots of words that I don't know how to read.

MR. MARCUS: My goal for you this year is to learn how to read books that you enjoy and that are more difficult than the ones you are reading now. And each year in school, you will be reading and reading, learning how to read the books that you think are difficult now.

I like reading mysteries before I go to bed at night. They are stories where there are detectives and they solve problems for people. Do you read at home? And what do you read?

SHAREEKA: Yes, I read at home, sometimes I read to my sisters and sometimes I sit on the couch and read aloud to my mother or father. They always tell me I am a good reader, and I know I am a good reader but I want to read harder books like them.

MR. MARCUS: How do you think people learn to read?

SHAREEKA: My mother told me that I will learn to read by reading lots of books and that is what I am doing. My older sister, Gracian, won a medal last year in third grade for reading the most books. I plan to win a medal, too.

MR. MARCUS: What is your favorite thing about reading?

SHAREEKA: My favorite thing is laughing when the stories are funny. I don't like sad stories because they make me sad . . . like that book about the animals who were lost from their mother until she found them. I like books about me, too. Really love *I Am Enough* because she is like me.

MR. MARCUS: When you are reading books for our small reading group meeting, what do you do when you find some words are difficult and you don't know how to say them?

SHAREEKA: I try to do what you teached us. I look at letters and say the sounds and sometimes I look at the pictures or think about the story and then say the words. Sometimes I ask you to help me. My mother and father help me, too, with the harder words.

MR. MARCUS: I like how you try to solve the words, and we will continue to practice reading words that are difficult. I have learned to keep new words that I am learning in my journal so that I can remember what those words mean and how to say them. We will start keeping words in your journal, too.

Earlier you said that you are a good reader. Tell me why you think you are a good reader.

SHAREEKA: My sister is a good reader so I try to read lots of books like she does. My mother is a good reader and I want to read the hard books, too. I am a good reader because I read the books you ask us to read in class and I read books at home. But also I am a good reader because I like to read and I understand what I read. You always ask us about the books, and I am able to talk about books and what they mean.

MR. MARCUS: Why is it important for you to be a good reader?

SHAREEKA: So I can learn things and then talk about those things. I want to go to college and be a good reader there, too.

MR. MARCUS: How can I help you become an even better reader? What is it that you want to learn this year to help you as a reader?

SHAREEKA: Oh, that is easy. I want you to help me read the long words. . . . They are tricky for me. Words like "everything" that was in the *I Am Enough* book. And then I want you to work with me to help me understand what I read when I read more difficult books.

MR. MARCUS: Those are wonderful goals, Shareeka. I am writing those in my journal and we will continue to work on both—reading longer words and making sense of what we read.

Thank you so much for meeting with me and helping me understand your goals as a reader.

Analyzing and Using the Data

That evening, Mr. Marcus reflected on the notes he took during his conference with Shareeka. First, he reread his notes and completed some places where he had listed only partial thoughts about the conversation. Next, he analyzed the patterns or big ideas present in their conversation that revealed Shareeka's characteristics about her identity as a reader. These patterns included:

- *Feelings about reading.* Shareeka likes to read and she especially likes silly stories that make her laugh and feels sad with some stories (such as when baby animals are lost from their mothers). She also really liked the book *I Am Enough,* confirming his goal to share books that are multicultural and that represent his students. Shareeka identified with the girl on the cover of her book, and drew a picture of herself with the same hairdo. She said that she liked that book, too, because it was like a song. I need to find some additional lyrical books for her and the class.

- *Purpose for reading.* Shareeka was very specific about the purpose for reading—to learn things so she can talk with others and to know things.

- *How Shareeka views herself as a reader.* Shareeka seems to be highly motivated as a reader and she sees herself as a good reader (agreeing with her parents that she is a good reader). She has several role models at home (older sister, parents) who support her reading.

- *Setting goals for herself as a reader.* Shareeka articulated several goals: reading harder (thicker books with unknown words), learning how to read the "long words," and to make sure she understands what she reads. Shareeka was well prepared to address goal setting and is specific about what she wants to learn next.

After noting the patterns derived from their conversation, Mr. Marcus thought about how he **will use these data.** First, he was pleased that his choice of text, *I am Enough,* was highly appropriate for Shareeka because of the connections she made with it and it served to open a deeper conversation about her reading habits. Now he plans to add books that will appeal to the wide range of diversity in his classroom. He knows how important it is for readers to "see" themselves (both literally and figuratively) in the books that they read. Next, he has very specific goals to guide further instruction: continue to provide positive feedback so that Shareeka continues to know she is a good reader, always check for comprehension of texts they are reading together and ones she brings to their individual conferences, and begin the process of applying the word-solving skills that she knows already and adding new ones to help her read "longer words."

Mr. Marcus reflects on the **value of this assessment strategy.** Mr. Marcus feels that this strategy was very helpful, as it provided a rich set of information about Shareeka. It made visible her feelings about her reading identities and the goals she wants to attain. Also, it provided an opportunity for Mr. Marcus to share some information about himself as a reader and to initiate conversations that will continue throughout the school year.

Conclusion

When we conduct assessments that make students' identities visible, we capture the many ways that students experience life around them and in our classrooms. Similarly, as teachers when we share our identities with our students, we demonstrate that literacy development is more than reading and writing—it is part of a larger context of sharing and honoring the interactions that we have with each other. And with those interactions, our understandings of each other develop and foster instructional exchanges that make known and support our likenesses and differences. And once each individual's experiences and views of the world are made visible, we can think about literacy instruction that is responsive to the uniqueness of each student and our own role in leading this effort.

FORM 2.1

Questions to Guide Open-Ended Notetaking during Parent Conversations

Questions focusing on parents' funds of knowledge/ identities	**Notes taken during conversations**	**Teacher reflections**
What is a typical evening like in your home? A typical weekend? Describe these times together.		
Do you and your children have special interests, things you like to do together?		
Are there other special interests or activities that your child enjoys?		
How many family members live in your home?		

FORM 2.2

Questions and Statements to Guide Open-Ended Notetaking during Student Conversations

Questions	Teacher notes	Teacher reflections
Do you like to reread some of your books?		
Tell me about your reading. I brought some books to the table. Do you like informational books (like these) or books of poems (e.g., *Where the Sidewalk Ends*) or books that tell a story? Or maybe something else?		
You told me yesterday that you don't like small-group reading. Tell me more about this. Why don't you like that activity?		

FORM 2.3

Examples of Notetaking Questions and Comments to Guide Conversations with Students about Book Selection

Questions and comments for book selection: ____________________ ____________________	**Student's response**	**Reflections and interpretations**
You seemed to like this book when we were reading it earlier. Why did you like this book so much?		
Tell me about your reading. Do you like to read? What do you like to read?		
What do you mean when you say you want to read harder books?		
Do you read at home? And what do you read?		

3

Building Trusting Relationships

The Linchpin of Productive and Effective Reading Assessment

> Cultures clearly have powerful influences on how individuals develop. This is seen most easily in the case of children who, as newborns, come into the world with the potential to become a competent and successful member of any human culture but quickly become recognizable as members of a specific culture.
>
> —TUDGE (2008)

"Quickly recognizable as members of a specific culture"—how does this occur? How do we become who we are? How do we become connected emotionally, socially, and behaviorally to a particular family? Community? What makes us thrive as infants? What motivates us to learn the language spoken by those around us? Simply put it's our relationships with others. As humans, we are motivated to be with and to be like the important people in our lives (Sroufe et al., 2005), extending beyond the need to survive to a need to thrive. Who we become; what we value; and in large measure, how we behave stems from wanting to be like those closest to us, the ones who care for us and ensure our survival. Initially, these are family members and central caregivers; as the child's world expands, these include peers, teachers, and friends, so our need to affiliate with others continues throughout our lifetime (Sroufe et al., 2005).

Thus, when children enter school, their relationships with their teachers serve as an important factor in their school performance and behavioral adjustment. We know from research across multiple decades that students at all levels—elementary, middle, and high school—reap academic and social benefits from a positive relationship with their teachers (Gershoff & Aber, 2006). Students who experience a positive relationship with their teachers perceive the learning environment as a safe and secure place in which to learn, and thus are more likely to hold a positive attitude toward school, to stay in school, and to have higher achievement levels than students with less-than-positive relationships with their teachers (Cantor, Osher, Berg, Steyer, & Rose, 2019; Gershoff & Aber, 2006; Hamre & Pianta, 2001). Positive teacher–student relationships appear to be especially beneficial to students in high-poverty urban schools, ameliorating risks associated with poverty such as high rates of high school dropout, low self-confidence and low self-efficacy, resulting in higher academic achievement and more confidence in their future aspirations (Murray & Malmgren, 2005). Unfortunately, when the teacher–student relationship is characterized as negative, teachers' interactions tend to focus on students' behavior rather than their instructional performance. Furthermore, given that these interactions often occur in the presence of other students, they seem to influence students' relationships with their peers (Hughes, Cavell, & Wilson, 2001). Hence, other students are watching, observing, and taking cues from their teachers about how they should engage with their classmates. A student's relationships with their teachers, therefore, serve as an important factor in their success in school, their behavioral adjustment, and their relationships with peers (Cantor et al., 2019)

Darling-Hammond (2021) noted an urgency to meet the needs of students who faced extra challenges during the COVID-19 pandemic. Students from communities of color disproportionately faced negative consequences brought on by the pandemic, for example, higher infection rates, unemployment, and housing and food insecurity. Adding to the trauma were incidents of police shootings of unarmed individuals. Just one of these events would be stressful to children, but the cascading nature of these events—COVID-19, unemployment, food and housing insecurity—resulted in many students experiencing multiple events. We need to move "beyond outdated notions of remediation" (p. 2) to include current understandings from the field of human development. Of primary relevance is the understanding that learning is experienced holistically as an academic, social, and emotional experience, not just an academic or cognitive event. (See Chapter 1, where we draw from human development research to support this phenomenon, as highlighted in our Principle 4: *Reading Assessment Must Account for Reading's Complexity*.) Learning must "lead with social and emotional supports and skills" (p. 2) and more broadly, schools must be reinvented so that relationships become the core of any reinvention.

Even though we acknowledge the powerful contribution of the teacher–student relationship to students' academic well-being, that relationship serves as the core of a more just and humane assessment process. In this chapter, we describe the unique ingredient a positive teacher–student relationship contributes to reading assessment.

Reading Assessment: The Need for a Positive Teacher–Student Relationship

A positive teacher–student relationship is a necessary part of reading assessment when viewed as a humanizing, empowering process that strives to achieve equity. Teachers committed to such an assessment process strive to communicate to their students that each deserves the chance to fulfill their human potential. In response, teachers choose reading assessments that provide them the information they need to design reading instruction aligned with the student's unique needs and strengths. Teachers also view their students as essential partners in the assessment process. Students interpret their teachers' efforts to learn about them as readers as evidence that their teachers care about them as individuals. Assessments that engage students in meaningful ways convey to students that they are vital and knowledgeable partners in the assessment process. The trust engendered by a respectful teacher–student relationship creates the psychological safety students need to share with their teachers their reading interests, strengths, challenges, and to take risks to try new strategies (Johnston, 1997).

Kaufman (2000) wrote about Linda Reif, a middle school language arts teacher who shared that establishing a positive social relationship with her students was a vital prerequisite to establishing an academic one (p. 77). Through her relationship with her students, she built the rapport needed for students to be willing to take risks during writing conferences. That social relationship, she added, created a context in which students believed they could share their perceptions as writers without fear of humiliation (Johnston et al., 2020).

In Chapter 1, we described the research that made clear to us the need for a radically new paradigm from which to create and enact reading assessments. We conducted multiple studies (Bass et al., 2008) to learn about teachers', students', and parents' views about the reading instruction and reading experiences that occurred in their schools. From these studies, we learned that a primary contributor to teachers' and students' negative views was the emphasis placed on improving test scores over supporting meaningful growth as readers. Concerns expressed by the teachers in our studies are echoed by others. Lake (2012), in his book *Letters to Nel Noddings,* shared a letter written by Rachel, a first-year elementary teacher who recounted the frustration she felt when she was to "get motivated" by a "pay for performance" program instituted by her school system. "Basically," Rachel lamented, "our school as well as individual teachers would get more money, not for caring about *students,* but for caring about *test scores.* At every faculty meeting, we were shown graphs of the previous year's achievement test scores, and our administrator admonished us to focus on raising those scores" (Lake, 2012, Kindle Location 1098). This rise in the importance of test scores projects a view of learning as solely a cognitive process, with little consideration of social, emotional, and developmental influences (Koretz, 2017). Such views of learning, we assert, too often lead to a stripped-down version of what it means to be a human engaged in the process of learning and, of relevance to our discussions, the process of building genuine and trusting relationships that support authentic and meaningful assessments.

The View of Relationships That Guides Our Thinking

Like Lake (2012), we look to Nel Noddings to ground our knowledge of the significance of a positive teacher–student relationship in establishing a safe learning environment as well as for guidance on how to enact assessments that reinforce such relationships. As the author of numerous books on caring, Noddings has written extensively about the importance of teachers forming caring relationships with their students and viewed this as an essential aspect of the learning process. We chose one characteristic of caring relationships that we find relevant to the assessments we promote—*Caring relationships prioritize students over academics*—because so many teachers in the studies we described in Chapter 1 spoke of how the persistent and unabating focus on testing impeded their efforts to meet the needs of their students.

For Noddings (2013), whether teaching or assessing students, concerns for their well-being should take priority over the subject being taught or assessed (Noddings, 2013, p. 20). She asserted, "we cannot ignore our children—their purposes, anxieties, and relationships—in the service of making them more competent in academic skills" (Noddings, 2005). As a mathematics teacher, Noddings appreciated the need to develop students' academic capacity, but she asserted that teachers should do so in ways that engender trust.

So, what does it mean when you engage in reading assessments that prioritize students over academics and over test scores? Risko and Walker-Dalhouse (2012) provide guidance for what to consider when situating literacy assessment within the students' perspective. We must, they told us, consider students' cultural, linguistic, and life experiences as valuable resources that can be "leveraged within the assessment process and instruction" (pp. 44–45). We must be open to hearing what students say and when they speak, we must be receptive to what they have to say. "When I care, I really hear, see, or feel what the other tries to convey" (Noddings, 2005, p. 16). Assessment that prioritizes students over academics and test scores changes a teacher's role from a giver of information to one of a learner (Noddings, 2005). As such, teachers believe their students possess valuable and unique information they need to create high-quality reading instruction.

A Positive Teacher–Student Relationship: The Foundational Linchpin for a Just and Humane Approach to Reading Assessment

In our introductory chapter, "The Urgency of Now: Addressing Assessment Inequities," we described four principles that inform our view of reading assessment as a humanizing, empowering process that strives to achieve equity. A positive teacher–student relationship is foundational to each principle, for it provides the necessary emotional and social context within which reading assessment should occur. However, Principle 1 and Principle 2 offer essential features of such a relationship when enacting a just and humane reading assessment process. Principle 1 necessitates that a positive teacher–student relationship must be informed by an equity mindset. Thus, being able to read is necessary for students to fulfill their human potential. Teachers agree and know that to meet the unique needs and strengths of each student they must control what to assess, when to assess, and how to assess their students' reading progress and performance. Principle 2 argues that a positive teacher–student relationship requires that both teachers and students must be visible (i.e., consequential to the assessment process). Teachers are visible when their district and school administrators view them as trusted professionals who can make the decisions necessary so they can meet the individual needs of their students. Students are visible when their needs and strengths, not test scores, become the purpose for conducting assessments.

Peter Johnston, a literacy scholar who has written about assessment for decades, put forth a view of literacy teaching that could be characterized as a human act. In 1997, he wrote, "literacy is not simply an isolated set of skills, but rather a very complex way of interacting with the world, with others, and with oneself. Being literate is as much something one *is* and *does* as skills one *has*" (Johnston, 1997, p. 8; emphasis in the original). Johnston maintained this view in his recent book *Engaging Literate Minds: Developing Children's Social, Emotional, and Intellectual Lives: K–3* (2020). He continued to assert that literacy is a human act as reflected in the quote he chose to begin Chapter 15, "Assessment in Grades Two and Three": "The recognition of assessment as a human project is a necessary starting point. Many decades of fruitless endeavor have demonstrated the folly of attempts to reduce it to an abstract technology" (Patricia Broadfoot, as cited in Johnston et al., 2020, p. 248).

In the next section, we present three assessment strategies that represent Nel Noddings's assertion, "When I care, I really hear, see, or feel what the other tries to convey"

(2005, p. 16). They are designed to assist teachers in their efforts to implement reading assessments as a human project, not a technological exercise. As you consider how you can use these assessment strategies in your practice, these questions may be helpful for guiding your thinking.

- How does the assessment help me understand my role and actions to support a positive and caring relationship with my students?
- How does this assessment help me identify my students' interests and expectations for building and extending strong relationships with me and student peers?
- How does this assessment help me learn about each student's attitudes, goals, and literacy learning? What will become visible about the student as a reader through this assessment?
- How can this assessment make visible my goal for building and sustaining trusting and caring relationships with my students?

ASSESSMENT STRATEGIES: BUILDING TEACHER–STUDENT RELATIONSHIPS

In the remaining part of this chapter, we offer three assessment strategies for making visible teacher–student relationships that support building caring and trusting relationships and enhanced literacy development. These strategies are:

3.1. *Conferencing with Care*
3.2. *Conferencing with Retrospective Miscue Analysis*
3.3. *The Blob Tree*

Conferencing with Care to Build and Nurture Teacher–Student Relationships

Reading conferences are a familiar routine in many literacy classrooms, and they serve many useful purposes. During reading conferences, students can demonstrate their understanding of a recently introduced strategy. Teachers can provide additional support for using a newly taught strategy, and teachers can use them to perform one-on-one assessments, such as an analysis of oral reading. However, we view conferences as more than just opportunities to talk with students about academic matters. Conferences can provide time to build the special and unique relationship between teacher and student (Freire, 1998). This view of teaching as a relationship aligns with our view that assessment is a humanizing, empowering process focused on equity. The assessment strategy *Conferencing with Care* offers a way to demonstrate you care about your students as human beings and are committed to their development as independent, engaged readers.

These brief conferences, typically around 10 minutes, provide a space that illustrates you prioritize your students as human beings and their continuing development as literacy learners. As the year progresses, the teacher seeks to build students' trust so they will be comfortable sharing personal information about themselves as readers—their interests in and out of school, the strengths they think they possess as readers, the challenges they face as readers, and the in-the-head processes they use to comprehend the texts they read.

ASSESSMENT STRATEGY 3.1.
Conferencing with Care

Purpose

Conferencing with Care has two unique purposes. The first is to provide a space for teachers to demonstrate they care about their students as readers and that they view the student as a vital partner in their efforts to advance their reading growth. The second purpose is to build the students' awareness of what they do as readers. This awareness can enhance students' metacognitive skills, a necessary component of becoming an independent, engaged reader. Importantly, the two purposes together provide the psychological safety students require to be comfortable taking the risks needed to share personal thoughts and perceptions about themselves as readers.

Value

The *Conferencing with Care* assessment strategy serves as a value-added component of any reading assessment program. It offers a space where teachers can communicate to students in a one-on-one setting that they care about them as human beings and in their growth as independent, engaged readers. Within these conference settings, teachers become the learner and students become the teacher. As such, teachers seek their students' opinions and input so they can be better literacy teachers for the students. *Conferencing with Care*'s flexible format enables the conference to conform to changes that may occur as the conference proceeds.

Procedures

1. Prepare for the conference, by first identifying the schedule you will follow to conference with each student. Form 3.1 offers a template of a Class Status Chart you can use to record the date of each student conference across the year.
2. Establish a clear goal for each student that specifies what you hope to learn from the student during the conference.
3. Decide how you will initiate the conference and communicate your goal for the time together. Possibilities for opening statements include the following:
    - Beginning with a question that invites the student to talk and share something about themselves as readers. You might ask, "What's the most fun thing you like to do when you are with your friends?"
    - Asking a question that enables the student to identify the focus of the conference. You might ask, "What are you working on as a reader?" Or later when they become more comfortable with the conference and willing to take risks you may ask, "What do we do in class that makes learning to read easy for you? Hard for you?"

- Asking the student to bring an artifact, such as a book they enjoyed reading during independent reading, to the conference. "Why did you choose to bring this book to our conference?"
- Asking the student to elaborate on something you noticed about them as a reader that you want to learn more about: "Today in our reading group, I noticed you . . ."

4. Proceed with the conference as follows. From the start of the conference,

- Position yourself at the student's eye level and look at the student as they talk.
- Review with the student the purpose of these conferences—to learn about them as a reader so you can be a better reading teacher to them.
- Remind the student that you will be taking notes so you can remember what you learn from them.
- Use the question or statement you chose to initiate the conversation.
- Use statements ("Tell me more about the books you like to read"), questions to invite student elaboration ("What makes this book interesting to you?"), and wait time (3–5 seconds).
- Conclude by sharing what you learned from the student and how you will use this information to help you be a better literacy teacher for them.
- Ask the student to tell you what they learned during the conference that will help them be a better reader. At first, students may have little to say about the conference and what they learned about themselves, because they have not been asked this question before. Be patient and continue to offer encouragement. To help your students to answer such questions, it may be helpful, prior to using the Conferencing with Care assessment strategy, to conduct a mini-lesson with the class about how to respond when asked questions like, "What did you learn about yourself as a reader today?" Or "What did you learn today that will help you when you are reading a book?"
- Thank the student for meeting with you and tell them that you look forward to learning more from them that will help you be a better literacy teacher for them.
- Review your notes as soon as possible after the conference and add any information that may be missing or not fully explained.

Collecting, Analyzing, and Using Data

One method for **collecting and recording** information is notetaking. Form 3.2 can be used to collect data on individual students during the conference. Tell the student you will be taking notes and why. We do not recommend audio recording your session because students may be uncomfortable with being recorded.

Be transparent about your notetaking. Share with the student what you are writing and learning: You can do this at the end of the conference to recap the important things you learned from the child.

Analysis of data has three parts. First, **analyze** your procedures and talk during *Conferencing with Care* and your perceptions of the student's responses. Questions such as the following may be useful to analyze your actions.

- Did I seem interested in what the student said? Did I sit at eye level with the student and look at them as they talked?
- Who talked more? If I did, what can I do to make sure the student talks more next time?
- Did I share my notes and/or the photographs I took during the conference?
- Was my focus on quantity, covering several topics, or quality, accomplishing the goal to learn from the students?

Next, questions such as the following may help you analyze your perceptions of the student's response to the conference.

- How would I describe the student's behavior during the conference?
- Did the student ask me questions? If so, what type of questions? Questions about reading: "Are you going to read *Bud Not Buddy* today after lunch?" Questions unrelated to the conference, such as: "When do we go to art?"
- What worked to make the student comfortable? What appeared to make the student uncomfortable?

Additionally, ask yourself questions to analyze what you learned about the student. These questions may include the following.

- What did I learn about the student during this conference?
- What books or topics are interesting to the student?
- What are their out-of-school interests or activities?
- How does the student feel about themself as a reader?
- Did the student express goals for reading? For books to read?
- Did the student share information about reading problems they are experiencing?

The information you gain about the student during the conference can be used to inform your instruction. For example, if you learn that the student likes to read short texts, such as poems, you might choose a poem to use with the student to strengthen reading skills that may be developing or need to be strengthened, such as reading fluency. If you learn that the student's big sister is the one who reads to the student at home, make a note of this so you can find out more from the student, such as what she reads to them. If the sister is a student at the same school, you might make a point to look for the sister to thank her for helping her brother or sister become a better reader.

Use the information to inform how you will conduct your next conference with this student and, if relevant, how to inform conferencing with other students. For example, if you felt pressed for time and ended the conference too abruptly, then review your notes to determine if too many topics were discussed and make a note to focus on the quality of the conference not the quantity of what's covered.

Making Students and Teachers Visible

Conferencing with Care is a one-on-one conversation between you and your students that makes visible the student's interests, their reading strengths and challenges, and the processes they use to construct and deconstruct the meaning of texts. This assessment makes visible to your students that you care about them and that what they say is important and vital to your efforts to help them develop into engaged and independent readers. *Conferencing with Care* provides a method for teachers to create and sustain personal and caring relationships with their students.

Implementation Example

It's 1:00 in the afternoon and Mr. Roberts's second-grade students are scattered throughout the room. As it is early in the year, the students are still becoming familiar with how Mr. Roberts conducts his reading workshop. He dismisses the students from the whole-class activity and tells them that they will now have time for independent reading, as practiced on previous days during the reading workshop period. Some students sit at their desks, others sit on the floor leaning against a wall, while others sit on the rug located in the front of the room. This is the one time during the day when all of Mr. Roberts's students are engaged in independent reading.

Mr. Roberts then prepares to hold individual conferences with his students and plans to implement the *Conferencing with Care* assessment strategy. Prior to the conference, Mr. Roberts checks his conference status chart (Figure 3.1) to identify the students whose turn it is to meet with him and to identify specific goals for the conversations he will hold with each student. He then reminds himself of the two goals for the conference. One, to reinforce to the students that he cares about them as readers. Two, to build the students' awareness of what they do as readers. Mr. Roberts knows it will take time for the students to be comfortable sharing personal aspects about themselves as readers, such as their interests in and out of school, the strengths they think they possess as readers, the challenges they face as readers, and the in-the-head processes they use to comprehend the texts they read. However, he knows that these conferences are valuable for building their awareness of who they are and what they do as readers and that this awareness is foundational to them becoming independent and engaged readers. Therefore, he believes time is well spent conferencing with his students.

For the first 5 minutes of independent reading time, Mr. Roberts sits on the corner of his desk and observes the students as they get settled. Although during this brief period he observes all of the students, he spends more time watching the three students he plans to confer with today. He also waits to begin his conferences, because he knows that during the first few minutes each student must make several key decisions, such as: What will I read? Why did I choose this book, magazine, or other text to read today? Where will I sit? What's my purpose for reading this text today? Thus, Mr. Roberts watches the students and makes notes of what he observes that might inform his conferences with the students.

Mr. Roberts identified three students to confer with today. He decides to begin with Jada (see Figure 3.1). During these first 6 weeks of school, Mr. Roberts has identified Jada as one of the less-confident readers. His goal for this conference is to build Jada's confidence as a reader. To do this, he wants to identify something that interests Jada or something she does that helps her as a reader; Mr. Roberts plans to identify this as an observed strength with the goal *to build on* this. (See Chapter 8 for more information about building on student strengths.) He's eager to conference with Jada to begin to boost her confidence and to build her independence as a reader. He watches Jada for a couple of minutes. He

Student	Date	Date	Date	Date	Date	Date	Date	Date	Date
Alisha	09.10								
Alice	09.10								
Anthony	09.10								
Darius	09.11								
Isaiah	09.11								
Jordan	09.11								
Jada	09.12	10.10							
Juan	09.12								
Keisha	09.12								
Leo	09.13								
Maria	09.13								
Manny	09.13								
Niko	09.17								
Pablo	09.17								
Rosita	09.17								
Van	09.18								
Watkins	09.18								
Wilson	09.18								

FIGURE 3.1. Mr. Roberts's conferencing with care status of class chart.

plans to begin the conference by asking Jada to elaborate on her reasons for selecting the book *Jamaica Tag-Along*, by Juanita Havill, to read independently. He recalls that he read this book to the class the previous week.

Mr. Roberts observed Jada sitting on the rug in the front of the room. The book *Jamaica Tag-Along* is in her lap and she is flipping the pages. She periodically pauses to look at a page. For the conference, Mr. Roberts moves toward Jada and sits in front of her on the rug. He takes notes on his iPad, elaborating as time permits. He will expand his notes further after the conference.

Following is a transcript of the conversation between Mr. Roberts and Jada.

MR. ROBERTS: Hi Jada, this is our second conference where I try to learn something about you that will help me be a better reading teacher for you. I will be taking notes on my iPad so I can remember what I learn.

Today I want to find out how you decide which books to read during independent reading time. I noticed you chose *Jamaica Tag-Along* to read today. Why did you select this book?

JADA: Well, she has a brother like me.

MR. ROBERTS: (*Waits about 3 seconds to give Jada chance to add any other information.*)

JADA: And she's kinda like me.

MR. ROBERTS: She's kinda like you? (*Looks at Jada and waits for her to respond. After 3 seconds with no response from Jada, he continues.*) When I read *Jamaica Tag-Along* last week, what did you notice in the book that's "kinda like you"?

JADA: (*Looks up at the ceiling as though pondering the question.*) Well, she's Black like me, and her brother doesn't want to play with her. Sometimes my brother won't play with me when I want him to.

MR. ROBERTS: So, you like books with characters who are kind of like you?

JADA: (*Smiles.*) I hadn't really thought about that before, but yeah.

MR. ROBERTS: Next time it's hard for you to find a book you want to read during independent reading time, look for a book about girls who are kind of like you. Jamaica is Black like you and has a big brother who sometimes won't play with her like your brother.

JADA: Yeah, and that makes her sad like it makes me sad when my brother won't play with me.

We have a lot of books in our room so when I look at all of those books it's sometimes hard to find the one I want to read. When you read this book to us last week I really liked it, and this morning when I came to school I walked over to the books and found the book and took it to my desk so no one else would get it.

MR. ROBERTS: (*Smiles.*) So this morning when you came to school you planned what you wanted to read during independent reading time? Good plan, huh?

JADA: (*Laughs.*) Yeah.

MR. ROBERTS: Jada, you know what? You just identified a strategy that engaged readers use to choose a book to read. Like you, many readers read books with characters like themselves.

Jada, when we get together on the rug today after reading, will you share with the class how you choose a book to read with characters who are kind of like you? Then, show them a page in the book and tell them how the character is kind of like you. Which page will you show them?

JADA: (*Pauses and flips through the book and stops at the page that shows Jamaica walking behind her brother.*) I can show this page. (*Shows the page to Mr. Roberts.*)

MR. ROBERTS: So, when you show this page, what will you say?

JADA: I'll say that I like books that are about girls who are Black like me.

MR. ROBERTS: How else is Jamaica like you?

JADA: And my brother sometimes doesn't want to play with me. She's sad like me, when her brother won't play with her.

MR. ROBERTS: Here, put a sticky-note on that page so it's easy to find when you share. Let me tell you what I learned from you today that will help me be a better reading teacher for you. (He reads the notes he recorded on his i-Pad.) "Jada likes books with characters who are like her. Knowing this will help me pick books you might like to read."

Can you tell me what you learned about choosing books you like to read?

JADA: That I like books with girls who are kinda like me.

MR. ROBERTS: Thanks Jada for helping me out today. You know, we have just started independent reading, and some of us are having trouble finding books we want to read. So, sharing one of your strategies will help your classmates select books they like to read.

After school, Mr. Roberts analyzes the information he collected during his conference with Jada. He adds that for his next conference with Jada he will discuss how reading books about familiar characters or topics can help us understand what we read. Once he completes his analysis, he looks at the information he wrote during his first conference. He is pleased that in the second conference Jada appeared to be more comfortable. See Figure 3.2 for data and Mr. Roberts's observations from his conference with Jada.

Mr. Roberts uses what he learned from his conference with Jada to guide his selection of books available to the students and to guide his future conferences with her. He also plans to use what he learns from the conferences with all of his students to inform how he conducts these conferences, so they are a place where students feel safe to share personal thoughts about themselves as readers. Mr. Roberts believes he's off to a good start this year in implementing the *Conferencing with Care* assessment and sees it as a **valuable** element in building strong relationships with his students. The conversations during the conferences make **visible** students' self-evaluation as readers, the questions they may have, and skills and strategies they use to support their reading. Mr. Roberts believes that the conversations during *Conferencing with Care* will support his goal to create engaged and independent readers while demonstrating his goal to develop caring relationships with each student.

Conferencing with Retrospective Miscue Analysis

Conferencing with students about their reading and writing demonstrates that the caring, personal relationships being formed between you and your students apply to all that is happening in the classroom. Asking them to reflect on their work, such as strategies they might apply during oral reading, makes explicit that they and their observations are valued. And these conferences provide continuous opportunities for ongoing formative assessments as students share what they know and are learning and misconceptions they might be developing. Conferences about student work can be held with individual students or small groups once every 2–3 weeks, and they are relatively short. Some teachers describe these conferences as embedding short conversations with their students, in the moment of literacy activities, every day all week long.

Conferencing with Retrospective Miscue Analysis emphasizes the students' role in evaluating their oral reading of text and thus, respecting and valuing the reader's self-evaluation is central to this process. Developed by Yetta Goodman in 1996 (Goodman & Marek, 1996), the retrospective miscue analysis (RMA) reflects her "observations that readers' beliefs about themselves as readers often influence their literacy development" (p. 601). The RMA assesses students' analysis of their oral reading as they examine the changes to the text that they made while reading (referred to as oral reading miscues). With teacher

Student/ Date	Conference goal	What I learned from student	What I'll do with what I learned*	What I observed about the student*	How I think I did*
Jada 09.12	Introduce purpose of Conferencing with Care Learn about Jada's interests Make her comfortable	Has 1 dog and 1 cat at home that she helps take care of Has books at home Is read to by her brother	Make a point to tell Jada's brother that by reading to Jada, he's helping her learn to read	Seemed bored Stared at other students as I talked Asked "When do we go outside?"	Jumped in too quickly when Jada didn't respond Sat at eye level Shared my conference notes with Jada Appeared more at ease when she talked about her pets and her brother
10.10	Build her confidence as a reader, so begin conference with a question about the book she chose for IR: "Why did you choose *Jamaica Tag-Along* to read during IR?"	Enjoys reading books with characters that look like her and do what she does Has a big brother like Jamaica who sometimes doesn't want to play with her	Check to make sure we have books Jada would like to read Asked her to share her book selection strategy with the class after IR	Smiled and laughed Added more info when she was given more time Appeared at ease when answering questions	Used wait time Focused on Jada's responses instead of the time

*Use relevant questions on page 69 for help with completing this column.

FIGURE 3.2. Individual student data conferencing with care observations of Jada.

guidance, they are evaluating their miscues and what might have influenced them. Thus, the RMA is designed to capture students' thinking about their reading and knowledge sources (e.g., prior knowledge, language differences, familiarity with text organization, beliefs about reading) that are influencing their reading actions. Additionally, the RMA invites students' problem solving as they identify oral reading miscues that might not make sense and strategies needed for self-corrections. When used routinely, this strategy can become part of your instruction by embedding it in guided self-reflections during oral reading of texts.

ASSESSMENT STRATEGY 3.2.
Conferencing with Retrospective Miscue Analysis

Purpose

Conferencing with Retrospective Miscue Analysis invites students to examine and analyze their oral reading miscues (their changes to the text when reading aloud). With teacher guidance, students are encouraged to make visible their decisions about the text, strategies and skills they applied, their understanding of text meanings, including vocabulary, and their misunderstandings. Routinely, embedded in instruction, this strategy promotes self-reflection and problem solving, as students learn to self-correct and apply new strategies they are learning. Used for assessment purposes, teachers can monitor students' miscues and their application of decoding and comprehension strategies to support self-corrections and making sense of texts.

Value

The value of listening to a student's oral reading and analysis of that reading situates the assessment within an authentic reading opportunity. With continued practice and guidance, students are learning to value their own decision making and are encouraged to be strategic problem solvers. Teachers' records of their observations provide explicit information about students' use of skills and strategies when reading texts aloud, thus determining directions for future instruction that is appropriate for every student.

Procedures

1. **Preparation** begins with sharing the RMA with your students, explaining its purpose, and demonstrating the process.

   - Plan for two to three practice sessions with small groups of students, with the first one focusing on your demonstration.

   - During the **demonstration,** give each student a copy of the text selection you will read aloud, and tape record your oral reading, making miscues as you read. Ask students to make notes on their copies, circling any changes to the text or writing those changes on the text. Tell students that "We will call these changes, miscues." Next, listen to the tape of your oral reading with your students, confirming identification of miscues. You may want to project these on the classroom screen, identifying with simple markings, the miscues that were made, typically by circling the miscues and/or writing changes to the text.

- While you are *not* teaching students the names for types of miscues, you are observing and marking common types of miscues, including substitutions, omissions, insertions, self-corrections, repetitions, and/or attempts at self-correction.
- For the second part of the demonstration, **prepare** a guide that students can use for self-evaluating the miscues that you made. Take students back to the text that you read previously, and if needed, ask them to reread it. Then share a few miscues that you preselected, drawing students' attention to these, recording them on the guide, and asking questions, such as those that are listed in Form 3.3. Ask students to write notes in the second column, describing what they are learning about the miscues (e.g., most of the miscues made sense, used decoding skills to self-correct).
- Plan to discuss students' miscue evaluations and the notes they made on the guide in Form 3.3. During conferencing, enter teacher notes in the third column of the Self-Evaluating Miscues form about the students' self-evaluation and comments. Add questions that you asked, as needed, and a summary of their performance. This form is then kept in each student's portfolio, with additional ones added during the year. We discuss the use of portfolios for assessment in Assessment Strategy 8.2.
- Initially, draw students' attention to the first one or two questions, placing emphasis on meaning or changes to meaning. Gradually add the remaining questions as you continue to guide students' analysis of the miscues.
- Next, implement one to two practice sessions with individuals or small group of students, following the procedure described previously. If meeting with a small group, students can take turns reading aloud on the tape recorder.
- Listen to the tape with the students, circling or writing changes that they made and ask the questions identified in Form 3.3. Continue to model your thinking about the miscues that are identified. You may need to stop the tape at times, providing time for students to mark the miscues.
- Typically, text selections are about 150 to 300 words in length.

2. After completing practice sessions with the students, identify sections of your selected texts to begin the assessment conferences. Texts are typically chosen from those that are part of the current instructional activities. Photocopy the text selections so that you and your students can mark the miscues.

3. **Plan** to hold individual conferences (perhaps over 2 days) with students and **implement** the RMA assessment strategy. If you decide to take 2 days for the conferencing, students will read the text orally on a tape recorder on the first day (for about 5–8 minutes). Analysis and discussion of the miscues would occur on the second day (for about 10 minutes). Students will complete the self-evaluation guide (Form 3.3) prior to your discussion.

4. With **practice,** the time for administering the RMA will become shorter and you may choose to implement a shorthand procedure that involves (a) listening to a student read aloud, (b) marking the miscues on a prepared copy of the text selection,

(c) sharing your marks with the student, and (d) asking students the questions that appear in Form 3.3. *You would not tape record the oral reading for this shorter version of the RMA, but students continue to evaluate their miscues referring to markings that you shared with them.*

5. In preparation for administering the RMA, consider its appropriateness for the age and literacy development of your students. In some schools, the RMA is administered starting in third grade and continued through the upper grades. However, Goodman and Marek (1996) reported that even younger children can be successful with the RMA, as primary teachers notice students' ability to hear "miscues" when their teachers are reading aloud to them, laying the foundation for moving to the RMA.

6. Finally, prepare for collecting and analyzing data about your students' self-evaluation of miscues, as described in the next section.

Collecting, Analyzing, and Using Data

Collecting data involves the following. First, ask students to review their self-evaluation sheet (Form 3.3). Plan to record your observations and notes in the third column while you are discussing the student's self-evaluation. Second, proceed through the markings of the miscues. You may want to draw attention to ones that you preselected as important ones to discuss (e.g., you noticed the use of new strategies, you noticed that there was no attempt to self-correct some miscues).

Next, invite students to discuss the miscues and their self-evaluation, starting with the questions on the guide. During this discussion, add your notes to the third column of the form provided in Form 3.3. In the third column, you might quickly record ideas discussed with each student, comments about how they answered the questions, additional questions that you ask, and an overall summary of their performance, including instructional plans. Your summary and goal setting are shared with the students before the conference ends.

Throughout the conference, remind your students to look again at the miscue marks and refer to their self-evaluation guide as you discuss the questions. Plan to **analyze** the data as you listen to their self-evaluation and the summary statements. Note understandings, use of strategies, and needs.

Making Students and Teachers Visible

Conferencing with Retrospective Miscue Analysis makes visible students' thinking about their miscues and reasons that they may occur. With guided practice, their self-evaluation prompts them to identify strategies and skills they are using successfully or ones for which they need additional instruction and practice. The RMA also makes visible students' use of their own resources, which include their prior knowledge and experiences, their linguistic knowledge, and their interests and goals for reading. Teachers holding the RMA conferences with their students obtain a wealth of information about each student's use of skills and strategies and resources. Teachers also observe the power of students reflecting on their own reading actions as teachers demonstrate their respect and valuing of students' capabilities for self-evaluation.

Implementation Example

Ms. Fareed is a third-grade teacher who teaches English language arts and science to groups of students throughout the day. Her passion for teaching science has been celebrated at her school by both the school leaders and parents of her students. For example, Ms. Fareed is often asked to share her science projects with the community and, in turn, she often requests that parents join her efforts to excite students about science. Together they have held star-watch parties and developed replications of the solar system, both of which became annual school activities. Ms. Fareed has learned that her excitement about science and engaging her students in hands-on activities has helped her build positive relations with her students, their parents, and the school community. She values what she is learning from her students and their families, making projects each year better than the ones completed the previous year.

It is October of the school year and Ms. Fareed and her students are immersed in the study of planets. They are reading about one planet, Pluto, before each student chooses another planet for a small-group research project. Ultimately, each group of students will create a set of Google slides to share with other students what they are learning about the different planets. Two parents are teaming with Ms. Fareed to support the development of the slides (i.e., identifying content learned about each planet, laying out design and content for each slide, finding illustrations, and developing the set of slides).

This week, Ms. Fareed is implementing the *Conferencing with Retrospective Miscue Analysis* assessment strategy to determine her students' performance on the first text of the unit, *Pluto: The Planet That Wasn't*. She wants to know if this text is appropriate for her students and their use of reading skills/strategies that they are learning. This text has free access to educators and is available through Readworks (*www.readworks.org*). She is hoping to learn about students' reading performance on this text so that she can plan instructional supports that might be needed for the students when they read the next texts about planets in the unit.

Today, Ms. Fareed is meeting with her class to **demonstrate the procedure** of the RMA. First, she selects a text, *The Milky Way* (taken from *www.readworks.org*) that students read previously during the development of the unit focusing on space. She shares a copy of the text, which has 161 words, with each student and asks them to listen to her reading, noting any changes she makes to the text while she reads aloud. She asks her students to draw a circle around changes and/or write notes about the changes. She knows that her students will be interested in "finding her changes to the text," as they often look for mistakes on charts and signs in the community (e.g., "fruits" was spelled "fuits" at the market!).

In Figure 3.3, we provide miscues Ms. Fareed made during the demonstration lesson.

Ms. Fareed then asked students what they noticed about her oral reading. Students said that most miscues did not change the meaning. They thought meaning was affected, however, when she omitted the word "dust" and when she didn't say that the planets go "around" the sun in the galaxy. Changing "all" to "are" didn't make sense in the sentence. For instruction, they felt that Ms. Fareed needed to learn to reread for meaning and to learn to self-correct miscues that didn't make sense in the sentences. See Figure 3.4 for the record of student comments. Ms. Fareed agreed with their recommendations.

Line 1: *What is a galaxy?* Ms. Fareed self-corrected her reading of "galaxy" after first pronouncing it as "gateway."
Line 2: *A galaxy is a large group of stars, dust, and gas.* Ms. Fareed omitted the word "dust."
Line 3: *Our sun and all the planets around it are in one galaxy.* Ms. Fareed read "Our sun and all the planets are in one galaxy." She omitted the words "around it."
Line 4: *This galaxy is called the Milky Way galaxy.* Ms. Fareed read this sentence correctly.
Line 5: *All the stars humans can see are the Milky Way.* Ms. Fareed read this sentence correctly.
Line 6: *When it is very dark outside, the stars, dust, and gas all together look like a milky band of light.* Ms. Fareed read the text as "When it is very dark, the stars, dust, and gas are together look like a milky band of light." She omitted "outside" and changed "are" to "all."

FIGURE 3.3. Ms. Freed's reading with miscues during demonstration (actual text provided in italics).

After several practice sessions with individuals and small groups of students, Ms. Fareed set up individual conferences to **implement** the *Conferencing with Retrospective Miscue Analysis* assessment strategy. She plans to ask each student to read the first four paragraphs of *Pluto: The Planet That Wasn't*. The text is presented in Figure 3.5.

Ms. Fareed's first conference is with Tericka, who is always eager to read aloud with Ms. Fareed. Ms. Fareed has observed that Tericka frequently reads quickly and at times does not notice miscues that change the meaning of the texts, and these miscues often affect her overall comprehension of the text. Ms. Fareed plans to examine Tericka's self-evaluation with the RMA to determine if she is beginning to apply the self-correction strategies that the class has been practicing.

After greeting Tericka at the class conference table, Ms. Fareed provides a copy of the text to Tericka and asks her to look over the text and read aloud the first four paragraphs of *Pluto: The Planet That Wasn't*. Before reading, Tericka tells Ms. Fareed that she learned about planets in second grade and that her father took her and her brother to the local planetarium over the summer and that she hopes to learn more about all the planets.

Ms. Fareed did not tape record the oral reading, but instead made simple markings (circles, written notes) for the miscues on her copy of the text. The miscues generated by Tericka are provided on Figure 3.6.

After the oral reading, Ms. Fareed shared her marked copy of the text and together with Tericka they discussed each paragraph and the miscues. During this conversation, Tericka evaluated her reading by responding to the questions on the self-evaluation data sheet (see Figure 3.7).

After completing the *Conferencing with the Retrospective Miscue Analysis* activity, Ms. Fareed studied closely the self-evaluation form and the notes she recorded during the conversation with Tericka to **analyze** the data. She reread Tericka's miscues and the self-evaluation comments. She noted that self-corrections for meaning were strong and that Tericka referred to her prior knowledge to help her pronounce and define "runt." Ms. Fareed was pleased with Tericka's self-evaluation summary and planned to continue practicing with the class strategies to support comprehension and for Tericka, reviewing and

Student: Ms. Fareed **Date:** Demonstration session

Questions I am asking myself Ms. Fareed	**Student notes** Ms. Fareed and students	**Teacher observations/ summary notes**
What are the miscues and do they make sense?	1. Self-corrected "galaxy" for "gateway" 2. Omitted "dust" 3. Omitted "around it" 4. Substituted "all" for "are" 5. Omitted "outside"	1. This made sense 2. Changed meaning 3. Changed meaning 4. Change meaning 5. Did not change meaning
Were the miscues corrected? Should they have been?	Only one miscue was self-corrected	
Do the miscues look like what was on the page?	Omitted words	
Do the miscues sound like what was on the page?	Omitted words	
Why do you think I made these miscues?	Reading too quickly, not attending to meaning and specific words, at times.	
Did the miscues affect my understanding of the text?	Slight changes to text, may not affect over all meaning . . . except for dust is part of the galaxy	
Did I reread to self-correct?	Only one self-correction	
When I self-corrected, did I use the strategy of decoding the word and/or thinking about meaning of the text or another strategy?	Gateway may have made sense but went back and looked at the word letters more carefully to self-correct.	
Did I confirm that my self-corrections made sense? Sounds like language?	Yes.	
Summary: What did I notice about my miscues? What did I learn about my reading? What do I want to learn next?	We learned that Ms. Fareed made sense most of the time, but her omissions/changes of words did change the meaning. Ms. Fareed needs to learn to read for meaning, rereading and self-correcting miscues.	**Summary of student performance and next steps:** Ms. Fareed agreed with the students' recommendations!

FIGURE 3.4. Ms. Fareed's demonstration session notes for self-evaluating miscues.

Pluto: The Planet That Wasn't

Poor Pluto!

It's bad enough to be the runt of the group, but to be told after 75 years that you're not even a member of the club–what an insult!

Pluto was first discovered in 1930. Until 2006, students were taught that it was the ninth and smallest planet in the solar system. Smaller than Earth's moon, it is not even as wide as the United States.

Pluto is made up almost entirely of rock and ice. It is so far away from Earth that the NASA New Horizons spacecraft took almost 10 years to get very close to it. Pluto's full **orbit** around the sun lasts almost 250 Earth years!

But as small as it is, as cold as it is, as far from the sun as it is, for all those years it was **considered** the ninth planet of the solar system . . . until Eris came around.

Eris was discovered in 2005. It is about the same size as Pluto. And like Pluto, it is part of the Kuiper Belt, a ring of objects that circle the outer edge of the solar system.

After Eris was discovered, scientists had to make a decision. Either Eris was the 10th planet in the solar system or it was not a planet at all! And if Eris weren't a planet, could Pluto be **considered** one?

Scientists made new rules for what is counted as a planet, and decided that neither Pluto nor Eris **qualified.**

A new category was created: dwarf planet. The official list of planets in the solar system went from nine to eight, and Pluto and Eris became members of the dwarf planet club. So long for Planet Pluto–but at least it no longer has to be the littlest guy in the club. In fact, Pluto is one of the bigger dwarf planets! Maybe Pluto doesn't have it so bad after all.

FIGURE 3.5. Text of *Pluto: The Planet That Wasn't*. Reprinted by permission from *www.Readworks.org*.

Paragraph 1: *It's bad enough to be the runt of the group, but to be told after 75 years that you're not even a member of the club–what an insult*! Tericka read, "r–unt/SC (self-corrected) and then said "like a small puppy."
Paragraph 2: *Pluto was first discovered in 1930. Until 2006, students were taught that it was the ninth and smallest planet in the solar system. Smaller than Earth's moon, it is not even as wide as the United States.* Tericka reread the words "as wide as" and said "what does wide mean, how can something be as wide as the United States? How would you measure that?"
Paragraph 3: *Pluto is made up almost entirely of rock and ice. It is so far away from Earth that the NASA New Horizons spacecraft took almost 10 years to get very close to it. Pluto's full* ***orbit*** *around the sun lasts almost 250 Earth years!* There were no miscues.
Paragraph 4: *But as small as it is, as cold as it is, as far from the sun as it is, for all those years it was* ***considered*** *the ninth planet of the solar system . . . until Eris came around.* Tericka read "con-sid-red" for "considered." She did not attempt to self-correct this miscue.

FIGURE 3.6. Tericka's reading with miscues (actual text provided in italics).

practicing decoding strategies for multisyllabic words. As the unit develops, Ms. Fareed will revisit the concept "Pluto is not even as wide as the United States," agreeing that additional knowledge is required to understand this sentence. She thinks that the measurement of planets might be one topic to include in the Google slides that the class is developing.

Ms. Fareed believes that this assessment strategy is **valuable** for at least three reasons: one, it made **visible** explicit information about Tericka's miscues and her self-evaluation of these; two, it provided an analysis of Tericka's strategies that she is applying and those needed within future instruction; and three, it was a valuable opportunity to continue building a personal relationship with Tericka and to demonstrate her respect and valuing of Tericka's thinking and engagement.

The Blob Tree Can Help You Build Relationships and Trust with Students

The Blob Tree (Wilson & Long, 2018) assessment strategy assesses how students view reading and can serve as a conversation starter during teacher–student conferences intended to support positive teacher–student relationships. Such relationships can support students' trust in their teacher and beliefs that their teacher cares about them and go a long way in creating the psychological safety students need to take risks to share. Conferencing about students' view of reading also makes visible their strengths, needs, and aspirations as readers. A positive teacher–student relationship undergirds student trust and helps students feel comfortable sharing personal views about themselves as readers. Some students may need more encouragement than others to share those views.

ASSESSMENT STRATEGY 3.3.
The Blob Tree

Purpose

The Blob Tree is a one-question assessment followed by a conversation between teacher and student. Such one-on-one conversations help teachers build a positive relationship with each of their students and demonstrate that each student's beliefs about reading are important to their teacher.

Value

Teachers find value in *The Blob Tree* assessment for several reasons. This assessment is given three times a year and provides a way to examine students' views about reading across the school year. Each blob depicts a different emotion, ranging from positive to negative, with different but subtle depictions. For example, several blobs depict a positive view of reading, such as a smiling blob standing at the top of the tree, a blob smiling and sitting on a limb, and two blobs smiling with their arms around each other. Such subtle depictions offer students a broader, more nuanced, selection of views from which to choose. This expanded selection potentially offers teachers more insights into their students' views about reading.

Student: Tericka **Date:** October 10

Text: *Pluto: The Planet That Wasn't*

Questions I am asking myself	Student notes:	Teacher observations/ summary notes
What are the miscues, and do they make sense? r-unt for *runt* repeated *as wide as* didn't know the word *considered*, mispronounced it Repeated *wide*—that did not make sense to me. How can you measure how wide the U.S. is? I don't know "con-sid-red" but then I read the sentence and it made sense without that word.	Self-corrected *runt* Our neighbors had puppies—well actually their dog had puppies and they had a runt, the smallest puppy in the group I see now sounding it out to pronounce "considred." Still think sentence made sense without that word.	Why did you say "like a puppy"? (asked before T answered, as seen in middle column) That is a great question—when we read more about Pluto let's look for more information about how wide Pluto and the U.S. are and how they are measured! That question tells me that you are using the questioning strategy to make sense of the text. Let's look at the word parts—con-sid-er-ed . . . *considered* Good for you, using the strategy to check for meaning, and I agree that sentence could make sense without that word.
Were the miscues corrected? Should they have been?	Yes, self-corrected the one that didn't make sense, when I said "r—unt" for *runt*	
Do the miscues look like what was on the page?	Yes	
Do the miscues sound like what was on the page?	Yes, when *runt* was self-corrected. No for *considered*	
Why do you think I made these miscues?	I didn't understand *wide* and *considered*	
Did the miscues affect my understanding of the text?	No	

(continued)

FIGURE 3.7. Tericka's self-evaluation of her miscues.

Questions I am asking myself	**Student notes:**	**Teacher observations/ summary notes**
Did I reread to self-correct?	Yes, one time	
When I self-corrected, did I use the strategy of decoding the word and/or thinking about meaning of the text or another strategy?	Thinking about the meaning	Yes, I agree!
Did I confirm that my self-correction made sense? Sounds like language?	Yes	I noticed that you used meaning and what you know about language to help you make sense of the text.
Summary: What did I notice about my miscues? What did I learn about my reading? What do I want to learn next?	I noticed that I was reading for meaning. I want to get better at reading the really big words—like *considered*—and learn what they mean.	**Summary of student performance and next steps:** Agreed with Tericka's summary. She is using the strategy of making sense of the text. I noticed that she also was using prior knowledge, such as what she knew about the word/meaning of *runt*—this is another strategy we are practicing—asking what you know already that can help your comprehension. We have two goals—learn more about "how wide Pluto is" and learn how to read and understand those "big words." Ended the conference by thanking Tericka for reading with me today!

FIGURE 3.7. *(continued)*

Procedures

1. **Prepare** to administer this assessment early in the year to help you get to know each student and their feelings about reading. By having this conversation early in the school year, you can demonstrate that you care for your students and want to build positive, respectful relationships with them, so they feel safe and comfortable sharing their thoughts and feelings.

2. Meet with each individual student—you will only need 3–5 minutes per student. Share the Blob Tree sheet (Figure 3.8) and say, "This is a blob tree. You will notice that each blob has a different look. Some look happy. Some look sad." Point to a blob and ask the student to describe how they think the blob feels. Do this several times until you

are satisfied that the student has a good understanding of the emotions depicted by the blobs.

3. Tell the student, "I've talked with our class about how I want each of you to love reading. I know we enjoy reading more when we read books that interests us. So, in our first reading conference, we talked about what you like to do when you are not in school. Knowing what topics you are interested in helps me choose books you will enjoy in our class library. And I know that you will read more if you like what the book is about. Today I want to find out how you feel about reading. Knowing how you feel about reading will help me when I plan my literacy instruction."

4. Discuss with the student how the different emotions reflect different views of reading. You could say something like the following: "These blobs represent different views

FIGURE 3.8. *The Blob Tree* (Wilson & Long, 2005). Reprinted by permission of the authors.

about reading. I want you to choose the blob that best tells me how you feel about reading. I'm here to support you, so please be honest about how you feel. For example, if you don't like reading, you might circle this blob." (Point to the blob at the top right-hand corner.) "Which other blob could you circle if you don't like reading?" "Which blob might you circle if you like reading?" "Which might you circle if you like reading because it's something you do with others, like reading at home with your sister, or discussing books with other students?" Continue until you think the student understands emotions expressed by each blob.

5. Invite the student to select the blob that best represents their view of reading, by saying something like, "Now it's your time to choose which one of these blobs looks like how you feel about reading. There's not one right answer. Knowing how you really feel about reading will help me be a better teacher for you. I'm the only person who will see which blob you choose. Once you circle your blob, we will have a conversation about your response and feelings about reading."

6. Have a brief conversation with the student about their response and feelings about reading. This is your time to listen and your student's time to talk. This communicates you care about what each student thinks not what you think. You might begin as follows, "I've learned so much from talking with the students about how they feel about reading. Some like reading. Some don't like reading. Some have said that they get nervous when they have to read aloud. We all have different views. Take a moment and look at the blob you selected and tell me why you chose the blob you did." Give the student time to think; resist the urge to talk if the student does not respond immediately. Wait a few seconds. Once the student responds, ask for additional information to help you get a sense of why they feel the way they do about reading.

   Once the student responds, seek their input into what you can do to help them enjoy reading more. You might say, "Each student is different, so I would like to hear what I can do to help you enjoy reading more." You can reference something the student said and ask specifically about the issue and what suggestions they have.

   Keep notes during the conference so that you remember the student's reasoning behind their selection and any other pertinent information, such as the suggestions the student makes or information that helps you better understand the student as a reader Form 3.4 can be used to take notes during a Blob Tree conference.

7. Conclude the conference by letting the student know that you heard them and invite them to add any thoughts. You might say something like, "What you said is important to me, so I want to make sure I heard you correctly. You told me that the reason you selected the blob you did was because . . . You said that it would be helpful to you if . . ." (Name any suggestions the student made.) Ask questions to clarify your thinking: "What else do you want me to know?" End by thanking the student. Remind them you will use this assessment two more times this year to see how their views of reading might change over the school year. After the conference, review your notes and add information that may be missing or not fully explained.

8. Give this assessment three times during the year. Multiple administrations provide a means to track changes across time.

Collecting, Analyzing, and Using Data

You will **collect** data for each student from the blob they selected and from your notes taken during the conference. These data will allow you to look at how the student views reading at the beginning of the year and how their views about reading might change across time.

Analyze the information you collected at the end of your conference conversation with each student. Information gained related to individual students can inform your analysis of the whole class. Consider the following questions to help you interpret the data:

- What other information do you have that might explain the student's response? For example, information gained from an analysis of the student's oral reading could offer insights into why a student might not like to read. (See Assessment Strategy 6.3 for a description of "Oral Reading Analysis.")
- How does the information gained during the conversation explain the student's blob selection?
- Based on your notes and the student's blob selection, what is one action step you can take to help the student move forward in their views about reading?
- Was the student at ease during the conversation? Explain what you observed that led you to your response. If not, what can you do to make the student more at ease when talking with you?
- How would you describe your relationship with the student? If needed, what can you do to strengthen your relationship with the student?

To use the data, reflect on the analysis you performed and, based on what you learned, consider one thing you can do to advance the student's view about reading and one thing you can do to strengthen your relationship with the student.

Making Students and Teachers Visible

Students need to be willing to share their views about themselves as readers. A positive teacher–student relationship is necessary if you want students to be willing to take the risks needed for them to share those views. This assessment makes visible views the student holds about reading. You become visible because you hold the instructional reins and thus control the action steps to take. Further, the assessment provides an opportunity for you to make visible to the students that you care about them and want to help them advance as readers.

Implementation Example

Mr. Taylor, a second-grade teacher, knows that motivating his students to want to read is central to helping them advance in their reading. He has 20 students in his class. He knows that it is his responsibility to make sure the classroom reflects the interests and abilities of his students. Equally as important to Mr. Taylor is to make sure each student knows he cares about them. He believes asking students how they feel about reading provides one way he can communicate to them that he cares and wants to help them enjoy reading and continue to develop as readers.

Mr. Taylor plans to give the first administration of *The Blob Tree* in October. By this time, he believes the students should be developing the trust with him that they need to share their views about reading. The preparation is simple. All he needs to do is make copies of the assessment form and set aside time to meet with each student for 3–5 minutes.

After lunch, Mr. Taylor asks Eloise to join him at a table in the back of the classroom. He introduces the assessment by saying, "This is a Blob Tree. You will notice that each blob has a different look. Some look happy. Some look sad. Some even look angry, and some look frustrated."

Mr. Taylor gives Eloise a copy of *The Blob Tree* and then explains: "You've been in my class for a couple of months, so you know I want to help you love reading. Not all people love to read. If we find reading hard, we may not want to read. If we have not found books we like, we may not want to read. Others may really like reading and read at home. Today I want to find out how you feel about reading. Knowing how you feel about reading will help me be a better teacher for you.

"We just talked about the different emotions expressed by the different blobs. Before we begin, write your name at the top of the sheet. I want you to choose the blob that best tells me how you feel about reading. For example, if you don't like reading, you might circle this blob." (He points to the blob at the top right-hand corner.) "What other blob could you circle if you don't like reading?" (He invites Eloise to respond.) He then says, "If you like reading, you might circle the blob at the top of the tree. If you like reading because it's something you do with others, like your family or with your classmates, you might circle the two blobs smiling and standing with their arms around each other." Mr. Taylor continues until he thinks Eloise has some understanding of the emotions expressed by each blob.

Mr. Taylor says, "Now it's your time to choose which of these blobs looks like how you feel about reading. There's not one right answer. I want to know how you feel, not how you think I want you to feel, so please be honest. I'm the only person who will see which blob you choose." Eloise circles the blob hanging onto the tree.

Once Eloise has circled the blob, Mr. Taylor shifts into the second part of the assessment—holding a conversation with her. He says, "Eloise, take a moment and look at the blob you selected and tell me why you chose the blob you did."

ELOISE: I thought this blob looks like how I feel when I'm in the reading group and I have to read out loud. I don't like reading in front of others because when I read, I don't like the way I sound.

MR. TAYLOR: How do you think you sound?

ELOISE: I'm slow, and others like Holbert don't read as slow as I do.

MR. TAYLOR: You think you read slower than other students in the group. I didn't know you don't like reading in front of others. Eloise, when I listen to you read, I can tell you know most of the words. What would make it easier for you to read in front of others?

ELOISE: Not to read in front of others. (*Laughs.*)

MR. TAYLOR: (*Laughs.*) Well, sometimes I need to listen to you read in the reading group because I learn a lot about your reading. When I hear you or other students read, I might learn which words you know or don't know. When our story has characters who talk to each other, I might learn when you read their conversation that you can make it sound like they are really talking. So, there are times I need you to read in the reading group. Other than not reading aloud in the reading group, what would make it easier for you to read aloud in the reading group?

ELOISE: (*Looks up at the ceiling, then responds.*) Because I read so slow, I'm afraid Holbert or the other kids might laugh at me because I'm so slow.

MR. TAYLOR: Do you remember what I said to your group at the beginning of the year, that we are all learning how to be better readers and that the reading group is one of the places where we learn and practice? Many people, even some adults, do not like to read aloud. In fact, I know there are others in our room who don't like to read aloud. You are not the only one. But I want to see what we can do to make you feel more comfortable.

Let's try this. In our next reading group, I'll have another discussion about respecting each other as readers. This means not to interrupt when someone is reading. It means not rolling your eyes. I will also talk about how we are all learners and we can't expect to be perfect especially when we are learning new things. If we are afraid to make mistakes, it will be harder for us to learn.

ELOISE: (*Smiles.*) Okay.

MR. TAYLOR: (*Takes Eloise's sheet and adds the day's date next to the blob she selected.*) I'll also check in with you in a couple of weeks to see if you are beginning to feel more comfortable reading aloud. Okay? (*Concludes the conference by reviewing the important information shared during the conference.*) What you said is important to me. I learned something that can help me be a better reading teacher for you. You told me that the reason you selected the blob you did was because you don't like reading in front of others, because you think you read too slowly and others may make fun of your reading. I will talk to the group about how important it is for us to respect each other and that we need to know that we can't be perfect when we are learning new things.

Mr. Taylor thanks Eloise and reminds her that she will get a chance to do this assessment two more times later in the year. Once Eloise returns to her seat, he reviews his notes and records his plan to talk to the students about respecting readers and that we must be comfortable as we learn. He notes that he will check in with Eloise in a couple of weeks to see how she is feeling about reading aloud.

To analyze Eloise's data, Mr. Taylor looks at her Blob Tree sheet and uses the questions below to help him expand his understanding of the student's views. Using the questions below, he took notes (see Figure 3.9). He placed these notes in the column for the first administration. (Figure 3.9 also includes notes written by Mr. Taylor about Eloise's blob selections across the school year.)

Student:	**1st Administration** **Date:** October 10	**2nd Administration** **Date:** January 17	**3rd Administration** **Date:** April 5
Eloise	Negative Blob holding onto the tree I don't like reading aloud. I'm worried other students will make fun of me.	Laying on the ground blob I'm getting better at reading, but I can't find a book I like to read during independent reading time	Two blobs w/ arms around each other I really enjoy partner reading.
Actions to build positive relationships	Discuss with her reading group the importance of respecting other.	Share some of my favorite books with Eloise.	Provide regular time for her to engage in partner reading.
Actions to build love of reading	Encourage her to volunteer to read aloud texts she feels comfortable with, so she is more confident reading aloud in her reading group.	Help Eloise find books she loves.	Encourage her to discuss favorite books with her peers.

FIGURE 3.9. Mr. Taylor's *The Blob Tree* conference notes of Eloise across three administrations.

- What other information do I have that might explain the student's response?
- How does the information gained during the reading conference explain the student's blob selection?
- Based on my notes and the student's blob selection, what is one action step I can take to help the student move forward?
- Was the student at ease during the reading conference? What led me to make the response I did? Could this be related to my relationship with the student?
- How would I describe my relationship with the student? If needed, what can I do to strengthen my relationship with the student?

Mr. Taylor reflects on the **value** of this assessment strategy. This assessment makes **visible** the views the students hold about reading. Mr. Taylor chose to give this assessment because he wanted to make these views **visible** to him. He also believes this assessment offers a way to track how his students may change their views about reading over the school year. This assessment offers him the opportunity to make **visible** to his students that he cares about them as readers and as humans.

Conclusion

Positive teacher–student relationships are foundational to everything that occurs in the classroom—actions and reactions, conversations, assessment and instruction, and peer relationships. As teachers convey they care for their students, students view teachers as their learning partners, and in turn, their learning and literacy development are strengthened. Increased are their feelings of confidence, willingness to pursue goals and take risks, and their attitudes toward school. Teachers who care about their students' social, emotional, and academic development find that they are more confident about their assessment and teaching decisions, as they make visible their students' and their own capabilities.

FORM 3.1.

Conferencing with Care Class Status Chart Template

Student	Date	Date	Date	Date	Date	Date	Date	Date	Date

FORM 3.2

Individual Student Data *Conferencing with Care* Template

Student/ Date	Conference goal	What I learned from student	What I'll do with what I learned	What I observed about the student	How I think I did

FORM 3.3

Guide for Self-Evaluating Miscues

Student: ______________________ **Date:** ______________

Questions I am asking myself	**Student notes**	**Teacher observations/ summary notes**
What are the miscues, and do they make sense?		
Were the miscues corrected? Should they have been?		
Do the miscues look like what was on the page?		
Do the miscues sound like what was on the page?		
Why do you think I made these miscues?		

(continued)

Guide for Self-Evaluating Miscues *(page 2 of 2)*

Questions I am asking myself	**Student notes**	**Teacher observations/ summary notes**
Did the miscues affect my understanding of the text?		
Did I reread to self-correct?		
When I self-corrected, did I use the strategy of decoding the word and/or thinking about meaning of the text or another strategy?		
Did I confirm that my self-correction made sense? Sounds like language?		
Summary: What did I notice about my miscues? What did I learn about my reading? What do I want to learn next?		**Summary of student performance and next steps:**

FORM 3.4

The Blob Tree Conference Note Template

Student:	1st Administration Date:	2nd Administration Date:	3rd Administration Date:

4

Using Student Talk to Assess Students' Reading Comprehension

> Have you ever wondered how it is that you can grasp a new meaning, a meaning not your own? Grasping a meaning not our own is necessary to the very act of reading.
>
> —GOWIN AND ALVAREZ (2005, p. ix)

This chapter and the next share a focus on comprehension. In this chapter, we focus on the reader and how to use oral language to assess what students know and understand when reading. In the next chapter, we focus on the text and how to assess readers' ability to grasp the meaning of a text. So, even though many factors play a role in reading comprehension, these two chapters address two primary factors involved—the reader and the text. Specifically in this chapter, we focus on how teachers can support their students' reading comprehension by using student talk to assess the knowledge they bring to the texts they read.

When a reader approaches a novel text, they must grasp a meaning they typically neither originated nor constructed. To grasp the meaning of that text, the reader simultaneously extracts information from the text and constructs meaning by engaging with the text (RAND Study Reading Group, 2002). To construct that meaning, the reader must recruit what they know about (1) the topic, (2) the structure of the written language, (3) the meaning of individual words situated in the context of other words (Clay, 2015), (4) how oral language maps onto the graphic symbols (Perfetti & Dunlap, 2008), and (5) how and when to apply reading strategies. Clay (2005) used the term *working systems* to describe how effective readers orchestrated these multiple information sources when reading. The reader brings this knowledge to assist them in processing every text they read. Important to the focus of this chapter, oral language mediates the development of much of this knowledge (Mercer & Hodgkinson, 2008).

Much more affects students' ability to comprehend text. Fountas and Pinnell (2006) added that "reading, as a thinking process, is part of everything that happens to you as a person and comprehending a text is intimately related to your life" (Fountas & Pinnell, 2006, p. 7). Rosenblatt (2013) described text comprehension as an outcome of the transaction that occurs between a reader and a text. Thus, to be effective stewards of their students' reading development, teachers must learn what students know and bring to the texts they read in class. Reading instruction and by consequence reading assessment becomes a more equitable and humanizing process when teachers contextualize their reading instruction within what students know and understand. To assist in those efforts, we focus in this chapter on how teachers can support their students' reading comprehension by using student talk to assess the knowledge they bring to the texts they read.

The RAND Model: A Heuristic of Reading Comprehension

The RAND Reading Study Group (2002) developed a heuristic for thinking about reading comprehension that supports the need for teachers to learn what their students bring to the texts they read (see Figure 4.1).

Three elements constitute this view of reading comprehension: the reader, who performs the reading, the text, in which the reader engages, and the activity that informs the purpose or purposes for reading the text. In turn, these purposes influence the reader's approaches to the text. For example, reading to locate information in a text might lead a reader to skim the text for relevant key words. A sociocultural frame encircles these three elements. The *socio-* part of sociocultural represents literacy's social origins. Beginning at birth children come to share the meaning of the world held by members of their family and community and instantiated in their shared routines (Razfar & Gutierrez, 2013). For example, *quinceañera* is a Mexican tradition that takes place when a young girl is 15 and celebrates her transition from childhood to adulthood. The *cultural* part of sociocultural represents the knowledge transmitted across generations of how their family and community interpret the world and transmit information (RAND Study Reading Group, 2002). Although each Native American tribe has its distinct practices and traditions, many rely on spoken, as opposed to written language, to transmit cultural knowledge (The Pluralism Project, n.d.).

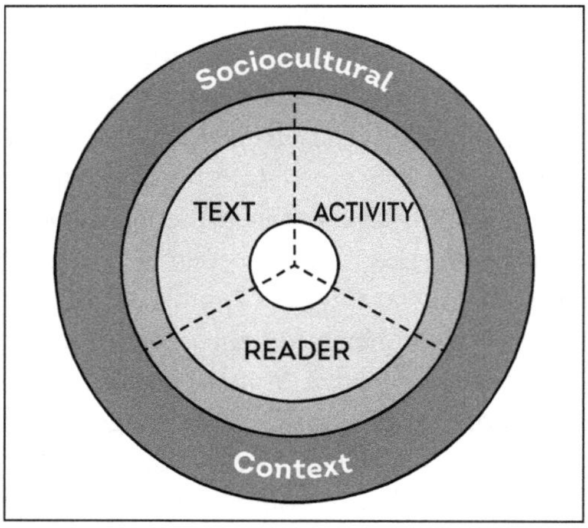

FIGURE 4.1. Heuristic for thinking about reading and comprehension (RAND Study Reading Group, 2002). Reprinted by permission of RAND, permission conveyed through Copyright Clearance Center, Inc.

Encircling the heuristic's elements of the reader, the text, and the activity within a sociocultural context acknowledges the cultural and social influences of reading comprehension. The student's home and community serve as the primary source of these influences. These influences are affected by the outside world from which the students come and the classroom contexts in which the reading occurs. Acknowledging the influential role of the sociocultural context supports our view of a more humane and just approach to assessment; one we describe as a humanizing, empowering process that proceeds through an equity mindset. Accordingly, teachers who seek to promote their students' reading comprehension expand their instruction and by consequence their assessment beyond the students' acquisition of the content that contextualizes the assessments. They know that accuracy in the assessment of their students' reading comprehension requires they consider their students' knowledge, cultural histories, lived experiences, and reading strengths and needs, all which shape their responses to the content (Penul & Watkins, 2019). In this chapter, to assist teachers in those efforts, we examine the use of student talk to assess students' reading comprehension. First, we discuss the unique advantages of using students' oral language to assess reading comprehension. Then, we conclude the chapter with descriptions of three assessment strategies that illustrate the use of student talk to assess students' reading comprehension.

The Unique Advantages of Using Student Talk to Assess Students' Reading Comprehension

Although speaking is only one of six senses humans possess, language stands apart from the others because of how we learn language. Learning language is an intimate process. It occurs in the laps and by the sides of those most important to us (Tomasello, 2003). During the learning process, children grasp the structure or syntax of the language spoken, the intonation of that language, and the phrasing of that language. They also learn the meaning of words, the reasons for using those words, and the time and place to use those words. Miraculously, humans learn all of this without formal instruction but by engaging with others in the daily routines of their lives. The intimacy of this language learning process serves to affiliate us with our family, our community, and the social groups in which we engage (Gee, 2013). This affiliation occurs because language serves as the mode—the delivery system for the spoken words, sentences, and so forth—while simultaneously transmitting the purposes for which language is used as well as the meanings ascribed to those purposes. Essentially, as Halliday (1975, 2004) so succinctly stated, it is through language that we "learn how to mean" (Halliday, 1993, p. 93) like those around us.

Many ways exist to assess the knowledge students bring to the texts they read; we present some in this book. For example, in Chapter 2, which focuses on identity, we show how interviews with students and their parents can be useful in learning about students' life outside of the classroom. In Chapter 3, which focuses on relationships, we show how reading conferences can be used to learn about students' book interests in a way that reinforces a positive teacher–student relationship. In this chapter, we focus on how teachers can use students' oral language to assess what they know and understand when reading. We chose this focus for four reasons, which we examine in turn below:

1. Language use promotes language learning.
2. Oral language mediates thinking.
3. Language makes visible what students know and understand when reading.
4. Language spoken by dual and multiple language learners supports rather than hinders literacy learning.

Language Use Promotes Language Learning

Current usage-based conceptions of language development emphasize that language develops from language use (Tomesello, 2003). That use determines language capacity, such as words known and spoken, syntactic complexity, and the purposes for which we use language. Of most relevance to this chapter is expanding the purposes for which students use language. If we want students to view talk as a means to deepen their knowledge about themselves as readers, then they must be given opportunities to use language for that purpose. When students talk about their reading process, their reading interests, or their reading challenges, they build awareness of themselves as readers (Johnston, 2004). That awareness prepares them to work with their teachers as active partners in their reading growth.

Unfortunately, in most classrooms, teachers control the talk, relegating students to respondents rather than initiators and thereby leaving minimal opportunities for students to talk about themselves as readers. In fact, for decades the most prevalent discourse pattern used to assess students' text comprehension and instruction more broadly is an Initiate, Respond, Evaluate (IRE) pattern (Cazden, 1988; Mehan, 1979). The teacher Initiates the process by asking a question, usually one listed in the instructional materials used to teach reading and one to which the teacher knows the answer. Typically, the student Responds in the form of a one-word or abbreviated answer. The teacher then Evaluates the student's response by acknowledging if the answer is correct or incorrect. The following shows an example of an IRE discourse pattern.

TEACHER *initiates*: Who came to the three bears' house while the bears went for a walk?

STUDENT *responds*: Goldilocks

TEACHER *evaluates*: That's right.

If language use promotes language development, using an IRE discourse pattern to assess students' text comprehension is problematic. Such discourse patterns offer few, if any, chances for students to develop the ability to talk about themselves as readers. Not providing such opportunities consigns students to playing a passive role in their reading development. As a consequence, students look outward, to their teachers' appraisal, instead of inward, to what they know and can do as readers for insights into themselves as readers (Johnston, 2005, p. 685). Teachers fair no better. They look outward for instructional guidance to published materials instead of inward to the knowledge they possess about reading and about the strengths and needs of their students. Essentially, both are rendered inconsequential, invisible, to the instruction and assessment that occurs in their classrooms.

Oral Language Mediates Thinking

By all accounts, reading is a thinking process. We look to Vygotsky's (1978) sociocultural theory to explain the central role language plays in the development of individual thinking and the consequential role one's life experiences play in that development. Sociocultural theory posits that cognitive development results as a consequence of children's social interactions with those closest to them—members of their family and community. Language serves as the primary mediator for these interactions as well as the channel for the transfer of the norms and values held by those important others (Tomasello, Carpenter, Call, Behne, & Moll, 2005). As a result, children interact with their families, and they come to share their families' ways of life and ways of making sense of their world. Thus, individual thinking begins on a social plane, what Vygotsky called an *intermental activity,* and gradually transforms within the child to individual thinking, what he called an *intramental activity* (Vygotsky, 1978).

The process Vygotsky (1978) depicted in his theory illustrates the intimate ways we come to talk and think. Everyday ways of talking and thinking develop through informal interactions with the important others in one's life. The life experiences children accrue are personal and foundational to how they think. Hence, when teachers seek to guide students' comprehension of texts, they should look to the students' life experiences to leverage those efforts.

Language Makes Visible What Students Know and Understand When Reading

Pearson and Cervetti (2017) asserted that since comprehension occurs in the reader's mind, it is a "phenomenon that can only be observed indirectly" (p. 13). When we ask students to retell a story or answer questions related to a text read, those responses are "little more than the residue[s] of the comprehension process" (p. 13). In effect, they serve as proxies for the complex construction and deconstruction that takes place in the reader's mind as they respond to text demands. Moving beyond the residuals of comprehension requires teachers to create opportunities where they can observe their students in the act of reading, writing, and discussing so they can observe how the students go about constructing and deconstructing meaning. Students need to read and write a lot and must be given opportunities to talk and to talk in ways that show what they know about applying reading strategies to deconstruct and construct the meaning of the texts they read (Johnston, 2003). Such opportunities make what students know and understand visible and provide information teachers can use to guide their reading instruction. Once visible, that process becomes something that can be "analyzed, probed, challenged, encouraged, and advanced" (Ritchhart & Church, 2020, p. 24) by both teachers and students.

Language Spoken by Dual and Multiple Language Learners Supports Rather Than Hinders Literacy Learning

Current English-only approaches, English-immersion programs, and programs that offer insufficient time for students to become fluent in a second language produce "vastly inequitable outcomes" (Werblow, Duesbery, & Koulidobrova, 2020, p. 23). These approaches reflect a deficit-based, not an asset-based, perspective of the students for whom they are designed to serve. In fact, Werblow and colleagues asserted that the label *English language learners* implies a deficit view of learners because it attends to what students know about English, while ignoring the knowledge they possess about language derived from years of using their heritage language. In place of using *English language learners,* they suggest referring to these learners as *dual language* or *multiple language users.* These labels embrace the benefits to students of being bilingual or multilingual (p. 23) and encourage students' use of their first language to support their literacy learning.

The idea of *translanguaging* reflects current thinking on the benefits to students of speaking more than one language (Puzio, Keyes, & Jimenez, 2016; Reyes, Iddings, & Feller, 2015). When students use language, they draw from the totality of their linguistic knowledge. For monolinguals, the totality of their knowledge stems from the one language they speak. For dual and multilingual speakers, the totality of their linguistic knowledge includes the knowledge they possess of their first language as well as what they know about English. Orellana characterized translanguaging as a "gift that has been invisible" (Orellana & Garcia, 2014, p. 387). It is a gift because the dual and multilingual students possesses an expanded language tool kit from which to draw, a tool kit comprised of what they know about the multiple languages they speak. It is invisible because too often the richness of bilingual students' linguistic repertoires is not considered, or worse it is discounted. So, to gain an accurate view of multilingual students' linguistic knowledge and experiences, what they know about their home language should be considered along with what they know about English.

Iddings, Risko, and Rampulla (2009) offered an example of how a third-grade teacher, Seth, incorporated ways to engage his dual language learners in conversations that supported the students' use of their heritage language, of English, or of combinations of both. For example, Seth used a "picture walk" to introduce the book *Curious George,* and he asked questions during the reading to check for understanding. Such discussions provided opportunities for students to use their collective language knowledge by allowing them to talk to each other in their first language, in English, or in a combination of both. Given the personal and intimate origins of language development and by using opportunities that invite and make space for his students to use their home language at school, Seth sent the message to his students that their home language is a valuable resource that should be used, not discounted.

To support your efforts to use students' oral language to assess the knowledge they bring to the texts they read and the strategies they use to understand those texts, we present three assessment strategies in the remainder of this chapter. As you read about and consider each of these strategies, the following questions may be helpful to guide your thinking.

- How does this assessment help me identify students' oral language development, vocabulary knowledge, and comprehension?
- How does this assessment help me identify areas of strengths and needs of students in their development of oral language, vocabulary, and comprehension?
- How does this assessment help me understand students' accurate and effective use of oral language, vocabulary, and comprehension skills and strategies?
- How can I apply what I am learning from these assessments to plan effective and appropriate instruction for all students?

ASSESSMENT STRATEGIES: SUPPORTING STUDENTS' ORAL LANGUAGE AND COMPREHENSION

In this section, we share three formative assessment strategies. These strategies are:

4.1. *Vocabulary Knowledge Assessment*

4.2. *Language Detective*

4.3. *T-Chart*

The *Vocabulary Knowledge Assessment* Can Help You Understand What Your Students Know About Vocabulary Words

Vocabulary knowledge plays a critical role in students' comprehension of texts because vocabulary words are labels for concepts and related details that students need to understand and to make sense of the texts they read. The *Vocabulary Knowledge Assessment* is designed to address the complexity of learning words. Vocabulary learning has multiple dimensions and is context dependent, incremental, and develops across the lifespan (Stahl & Bravo, 2010). For these reasons, traditional assessments of vocabulary knowledge such as writing definitions, matching and fill-in-the-blank items, and writing sentences containing target vocabulary words do not provide useful information for teachers regarding students' depth of understanding about a word (Cobb & Blachowicz, 2014; Ganske, 2019). Knowing a word is more than being able to say or identify the definition. Word learning is incremental, so with each additional encounter with a word, students develop a deeper and more complete understanding of the word, its multiple meanings, and its use in different contexts (Paris, 2005).

Used prior to vocabulary instruction, the *Vocabulary Knowledge Assessment* allows students to make visible their depth of word knowledge for words that will be vital for a unit of study or text that will be taught. After instruction, teachers administer this assessment again to determine how students' depth of understanding for the target vocabulary words has developed. The data gathered from the *Vocabulary Knowledge Assessment* can help teachers plan instruction to build and deepen students' vocabulary knowledge.

ASSESSMENT STRATEGY 4.1.

Vocabulary Knowledge Assessment

Purpose

The purpose of the *Vocabulary Knowledge Assessment* (VKA) is to determine students' knowledge of target vocabulary words that are important in units of study, texts, or lessons. VKA is designed to be used as both a pre- and a post-assessment. By using VKA as a pre-assessment, you can gauge students' knowledge of the words, so you can use that data to inform your planning of the lesson, text, or unit. By using VKA as a post-assessment, you can make visible the growth students have made in word knowledge and depth by comparing their pre-assessment and post-assessment data. VKA can be used with an individual student, a small group of students, or the whole class, depending on who will be participating in the lesson, text, or unit associated with the target vocabulary words.

Value

Because what it means to know a word is complex and incremental, this assessment is a useful tool for teachers. It can be used to determine what students know about a word as compared to traditional vocabulary assessments that simply offer a "yes" or "no" determination of whether a student knows a word or not. VKA has the most value when the target vocabulary selection is intentional and strategic.

Procedures

1. Review your plans for the lesson, text, or unit of study, and make a list of words that are likely to be unfamiliar to your students.
2. **Prepare** for VKA by selecting the target vocabulary words. We recommend that you focus mainly on Tier Two vocabulary, which are useful words students are likely to encounter in multiple texts and contexts and which are characteristic of mature language users.
3. By focusing on words that are classified by Beck, McKeown, and Kucan (2013) as Tier Two words (i.e., high-frequency words for mature language users), you can help students develop a vocabulary that will be useful for reading and writing a wide variety of texts. There is also value for including a small number of Tier Three words (i.e., low-frequency words from specific content areas that are needed to understand some lessons, units, and texts). Generally, Tier One words are learned through normal interactions and spoken language, but some students, such as those with special needs or those who are newcomers to English, may benefit from focusing on some Tier One words in VKA. See Table 4.1 for more information about the tiers of

TABLE 4.1. Tiers of Vocabulary Words

Tier	Description	Examples	Considerations for VKA
Tier One	Basic words learned through daily interactions and spoken language	• *book* • *chair* • *green*	These words are generally not included in VKA.
Tier Two	High-frequency, multiple-meaning words that are useful across many texts and contexts	• *between* • *scamper* • *sequence*	These words should be the focus for VKA.
Tier Three	Low-frequency words that are content and context specific	• *photosynthesis* • *Revolutionary War* • *editorial*	A small number of words from this tier can be included in VKA if they are essential to understand for the lesson, unit, or text AND have usefulness in multiple contexts in the future.

vocabulary words that you can consider when selecting target vocabulary words for VKA.

4. Analyze the list of words by asking the following questions:
   - Which words are Tier Two words? (See Table 4.1 for more information.)
   - Of those Tier Two words, which ones are most necessary for comprehension? Most useful now and in various contexts in the future?
   - Are there any other words on the list that are essential for comprehension of the target text or unit of study?
5. Using the analysis you did for step 4, determine which words to include in the VKA. Generally, it is advised to focus on a small number of words for VKA. We recommend four to six words for students in the primary grades and five to eight words for students in the upper elementary grades.
6. For those words that will *not* be included in VKA, determine if they deserve brief attention, such as explaining the meaning of the word directly to the students, or if those words do not require attention at this time.
7. **Prepare** the VKA chart using the template provided in Form 4.1.
8. For the **pre-assessment,** present the VKA to the students and do a demonstration item together. For example, with the word *equivalent,* you might say:

   > Before we begin our next lesson [or text or unit], I want to see how much you know about these words. Be honest because this information will help me plan what to teach and what you already know. Let's do a practice item together. How much do you know about the word *equivalent?*
   >
   > Is it a word you have never heard or seen before? Do you have no clue what it means or how it is used? If so, put an X in the column that says, "No Clue!"
   >
   > If you have seen or heard the word before and have an idea of what it means or how or when it is used, write down what you know in the "I know a little about this word" column. You can write or draw to show what you know about the word.
   >
   > If you are sure you know the word, write or draw everything you know about the word in the column that says "I know a lot about this word." If you need more space, you can use the back of the paper.

9. For younger students, follow the same process for each word on the VKA. For older students, you can simply read each target word aloud and ask students to complete the chart themselves after practicing with the first word.
10. For the **post-assessment** (after you have taught the lesson, text, or unit), give the students the charts they filled out for the pre-assessment and ask them to review each word, determine if their level of knowledge stayed the same or changed, and note any new knowledge they gained about each vocabulary word. You can use the same process outlined above for the pre-assessment. The value of having both the pre- and post-assessments on the same page is to make visible the incremental growth students have made in their knowledge of the target vocabulary words.

Collecting, Analyzing, and Using Data

You will **collect** data on the VKA chart for both the pre-assessment and the post-assessment, so any incremental growth students have made in their knowledge of the target vocabulary words is documented in one place.

For the **pre-assessment,** review each student's chart and identify words that most of the students do not know at all, and target those words for instruction. Next, identify words that most students have some knowledge of and **analyze** what aspects of word knowledge they already have. Consider what else they need to know about the word, its meaning, and its use in the specific context(s) in the lesson, text, or unit. Use that data to plan instruction for those words. Finally, **analyze** the words that students have lots of knowledge of, and determine if that knowledge is accurate, and whether instruction is needed to comprehend key ideas in the lesson, text, or unit of study. Use those data to determine what instruction is needed for those words.

For the **post-assessment, analyze** each student's VKA chart to see what progress they made in developing knowledge for each of the target vocabulary words. If students did not make progress for some words, **use** the data to determine what additional instruction is still needed for specific words.

Making Students and Teachers Visible

VKA is designed for students to make visible all they know about a target vocabulary word. This allows them to demonstrate partial knowledge, knowledge in a specific context, and in-depth knowledge about a word. By comparing VKA data from the pre-assessment to the post-assessment, students' growth in depth of knowledge of a word is made visible. Teachers are made visible in this assessment as they use their expertise to select target vocabulary words that not only are useful within the lesson, text, or unit but also are likely to be encountered and used in the future.

Implementation Example

Mrs. Singh is a first-grade teacher in a suburban school located several miles outside a large city. Her students come from a wide variety of backgrounds, and many of them speak languages other than English at home, including Urdu, Spanish, Assyrian, and Arabic. Because she understands the importance of vocabulary knowledge for comprehension, especially for her students who are learning English, Mrs. Singh uses the *Vocabulary Knowledge Assessment* with her students before beginning a new unit of study. She will soon be teaching a unit on measurement. She has identified five vocabulary words that are essential for her students to understand the unit. All the words are Tier Two words (i.e., *length, width, unit, measure,* and *compare*) that are important in the unit but are also high-frequency words that students will encounter in other contexts.

Mrs. Singh prepares the VKA chart and gives each of her 20 students a copy because they will all be participating in the unit on measurement. She projects a copy of the chart using a document camera and screen in her classroom. She explains to the students, "We are going to do a unit about measurement. In this unit, there are some very important words, and I want to see if you already know any of the words. Please put your name at the top of your paper. The first word is *length*. See me pointing to the word *length?* Can you point to the word too and say it with me? *Length.* If you have never heard or seen the word before, put an X in the column that says, 'No Clue!' If you have seen or heard the word before and know a little about the word, write or draw what you know about the word in this column (she points to it on the document camera) that says, 'I know a little about this word.' Then write or draw what you know about the word here (she points to the Pre/Before section of the chart). If you know a lot about the word *length*, write or draw what you know in the column here (she points to it on the document camera) that says, 'I know a lot about this word.'"

Mrs. Singh and her students continue in the same manner through all five of the words. Because her students are in first grade, they often respond with drawings and single words that may not be fully clear to her. Therefore, she briefly talks with each student after the assessment to make sure she understands what they have written and drawn about each word on the chart.

When she meets with Erik, she puts his chart on the table and says, "Let's talk about what you wrote and drew to make sure I understand what you know about each of these words." Erik nods and says, "Okay." Their conversation is below.

MRS. SINGH: I see that you have not seen or heard the words *width*, *unit*, and *compare* before. For the word *length*, you said you knew a little about the word, and you wrote *neckt*. Can you tell me about what you wrote?

ERIK: I know link is like neckt. Like I can neckt my hands. (*He joins his hands together.*)

MRS. SINGH: I see. You mean that you know the word *link* means to connect or to join together. Is that what you meant?

ERIK: Yeah.

MRS. SINGH: Thanks, Erik. That's great information about the word *link*. This word is *length*. (*She says the word clearly and slowly.*)

ERIK: Oh, that's different.

MRS. SINGH: Do you know anything about the word *length*, Erik?
(*Erik shrugs and shakes his head no.*)

MRS. SINGH: Thanks, Erik. Let's look at *measure*. You marked that you knew a lot about this word, and you wrote, "cokn and bldn with grpa."

ERIK: Yes, I know lots 'cause I cook with my mom and do building things with my grandpa.

MRS. SINGH: What do you measure when you cook and build?

ERIK: I measure 'cause we make soup and cookies and beans. My grandpa measures wood before he saws it, and I help.

MRS. SINGH: Great, Erik. Thanks for helping me understand what you know about these words.

Erik's VKA chart is provided in Figure 4.2.

After Mrs. Singh and her students have finished their unit on measurement, she gives each student their VKA pre-assessment back so they can note whether their knowledge of

Word	No Clue!	I know a little about this word	I know a lot about this word
length	Pre/Before	Pre/Before neckt	Pre/Before
	Post/After	Post/After	Post/After 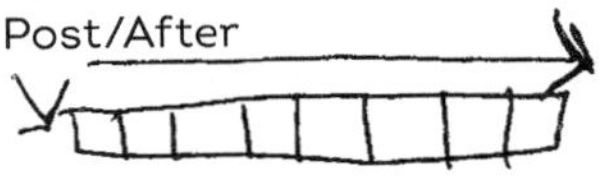
width	Pre/Before X	Pre/Before	Pre/Before
	Post/After	Post/After	Post/After 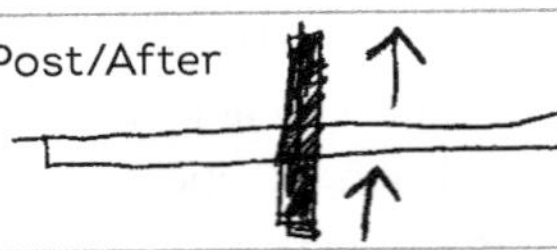
unit	Pre/Before X	Pre/Before	Pre/Before
	Post/After	Post/After 1 2 3 4 5 6 7	Post/After
measure	Pre/Before	Pre/Before	Pre/Before co Rn and bldn wif grpa
	Post/After	Post/After	Post/After
compare	Pre/Before X	Pre/Before	Pre/Before
	Post/After	Post/After mr orls	Post/After

FIGURE 4.2. Erik's *Vocabulary Knowledge Assessment.*

the words increased and if so, what new knowledge they have about the vocabulary words. She explains to the students, "Now that we are done with our measurement unit, let's see what you learned about our vocabulary words." She uses her document camera to display the VKA chart on the screen so all students can see it. She says, "The first word is *length*. See what you put in the Pre/Before section on your chart. I'm pointing to that section on the chart now if you need help finding it."

She takes a moment to make sure each student is looking at the correct section of the chart. She explains, "Now that we are done with our measurement unit, how would you rate your knowledge of the word *length?* If you have never seen or heard of this word, put an X in the 'No Clue!' column here" (she points to the column). Several students laugh, and Mrs. Singh smiles and asks, "What?" Erik raises his hand and says, "We learned it in the unit, Mrs. Singh!" Mrs. Singh smiles and continues, "If you now know a little about the word *length,* write or draw what you know in this column that says, 'I know a little about this word.'" She then says, "If you know a lot about the word *length,* write or draw what you know in this column that says, 'I know a lot about this word.'" She continues, "If you know so much that you run out of space, you can use the back of your paper." Mrs. Singh and her students continue in the same way for the remainder of the words on the VKA chart.

Later that afternoon, Mrs. Singh meets for a minute or two with each student to make sure she understands the knowledge they have now about the target vocabulary. Her discussion with Erik is below.

MRS. SINGH: Hi, Erik. Can you tell me what you drew here to show that you know a lot about the word *length?*

ERIK: Yeah, it's the long part. That's what I drawed. The long part 'cause that's length. I can measure it.

MRS. SINGH: Yes, that makes sense and shows what you know about the word *length.* What about the next one, *width?*

ERIK: I did the same thing. I drawed wide—like width to show what it is.

MRS. SINGH: Yes, I see that. You learned a lot about both of those words from our unit.

ERIK: Yeah, I didn't know 'em before really, but I do now!

MRS. SINGH: Yes, you are learning so much about these words! What about *unit?* Tell me about your drawing in this column. (*Points to the "I know a little about this word" column.*)

ERIK: It's a ruler. It has units to use for measuring things.

MRS. SINGH: Why did you rate yourself as knowing a little about the word?

ERIK: 'Cause other things have units, too, not just rulers.

MRS. SINGH: Thanks, Erik. You are right. The unit of measure for a ruler like this is an inch. We'll learn more about the word *unit* as we apply what we learned to other lessons in the future.

MRS. SINGH: Okay, Erik, the last word is *compare.* Can you tell me about what you wrote for *compare?*

ERIK: More or less 'cause you always say, "Compare, is it more or less?"

MRS. SINGH: Thanks, Erik. I learned a lot about your knowledge of these words. You gained new knowledge about each of these words. You are growing your vocabulary!

At the end of the day, Mrs. Singh notes that several of the students still have limited understanding of the words *unit* and *compare,* and because these are Tier Two words, she considers ways she can use these words in upcoming lessons to help these students (including Erik) increase their exposure to these words to deepen their knowledge of these useful words.

Mrs. Singh believes that the *Vocabulary Knowledge Assessment* is **valuable** because it allows her students to make **visible** what they know about target vocabulary words before and after instruction. VKA also makes **visible** for Mrs. Singh and her students the growth and development of their vocabulary knowledge.

Language Detective Using Student Talk to Support Reading Comprehension

Students need to use language to learn language. If we want students to use language as a means to deepen their knowledge as readers, then they must have opportunities to use language for that purpose. As students engage in conversations with their teachers about texts they read, teachers can use the *Language Detective* assessment to assess the knowledge the students bring to the texts they read and the strategies they use to understand those texts. When they engage in these conversations, the students' words and ideas become part of the learning event. Providing students opportunities to talk about their reading process, their reading interests, and their reading challenges, builds their awareness of themselves as readers. That awareness prepares them to work with their teachers as active partners in their reading growth. Importantly, that awareness also supports their development as independent and engaged readers.

ASSESSMENT STRATEGY 4.2.
Language Detective

Purpose

This strategy serves three purposes: (1) it sharpens students' attention to the content covered during a lesson or a discussion; (2) it makes students' in-the-head strategic processing visible, and once this is visible, teachers can support students' efforts to comprehend texts and, when necessary, clarify misunderstandings; and (3) it enables the teacher to use their students' words to make explicit strategies used to construct and deconstruct the meaning of text.

Value

This assessment addresses two problems teachers face. One, students' persistent problems with comprehending texts. The processes readers use to understand the texts they read reside in the head of the reader, so they are not readily visible to teachers. This assessment makes these processes visible. Two, teachers face the challenge of engaging many of the students in class discussions. Too often the same students participate while others remain silent or talk minimally during class. This strategy offers a way to bring students who may typically be silent into the discussion of the key ideas of the topic presented.

Procedures

1. To **prepare** for the *Language Detective* assessment:

    - Identify a lesson that includes whole-group discussion.
    - Create three language detective signs to place on the language detective students' desks or for students to wear on lanyards around their necks. To create the desk sign, use letter-sized construction paper or another paper type that when folded in half it can stand alone on the desk. Fold the paper in half and using a dark marker write *language detective* on the front. To create the sign to be worn around the neck, use a 4-inch by 6-inch index card or sturdy paper, punch two holes at the top, and string a lanyard or yarn through the holes.
    - Gather six sticky notes for the students to record the ideas they identify during the discussion. Each language detective gets two sticky notes; only one idea is written on each sticky note. Give students a dark nontoxic marker to record their ideas.
    - Get one poster board chart to display the sticky notes generated by the language detectives.
    - Choose three students to be language detectives.

2. Implement the lesson.

    - The language detectives perform the role of observer during the whole-group discussion portion of the lesson. As observers, they become the eyes and ears for the class. Remind them to not worry about spelling when they record their ideas. Instead, they should focus on identifying the ideas from the discussion that they believe are the most important and meaningful.

3. Proceed as follows once the whole-group discussion has ended. The students who participated in the discussion now observe the language detectives as they share their ideas.

    - Invite one of the language detectives to share one of the ideas they wrote on a sticky note.
    - Ask the language detective questions about their idea to make explicit the in-the-head processes the language detectives used to select the idea. Use questions like the following to uncover their reasoning.
        - Why did you choose this as an important idea presented in the discussion?
        - How did you decide this was an important idea?
        - What was said during the discussion that made you think that was an important idea?
        - How did this idea help you understand the content of the discussion?

- Ask if any of the other language detectives selected a similar idea. The other language detectives share similar ideas.
- Invite another language detective to share an idea. Follow the same process as outlined above until all three language detectives have shared their ideas.
- Collect the sticky notes from the language detectives once all ideas have been shared. Place them on the poster board chart at the front of the room.
- Restate the strategies used by the students to identify their ideas.

4. **Engage students as language detectives and as participants.** All students initially will need to have this assessment modeled. With practice, the students will gain expertise in using the assessment.

   - Bilingual and multilingual students may need extra support and encouragement to participate in the discussions and to perform the role of language detective. To provide that encouragement, you can pair bilingual and multilingual students to work together or you can pair a bilingual and a multilingual learner with a native English speaker. When your bilingual/multilingual students share, accept their use of their native language or combinations of their native language and English.

Collecting, Analyzing, and Using Data

Collect data by using the Language Detective Notetaking Template (Form 4.2). The sticky notes also become data. Shortly after the learning event, review your notes; fill in any additional details and information. When needed, rewrite entries with misspellings.

Analyze your data using questions like the following:

- Which strategies did the language detectives use?
- Is there a pattern in the strategies used by the language detectives? Did they use similar strategies?
- When viewed collectively, what strategies were not used that would have been useful?
- Which language detectives share similar needs or similar strengths?

Use the information gained from your analysis to inform future literacy instruction. For example, you could:

- Create an anchor chart to compile a list of strategies used by the language detectives.
- Begin the next literacy lesson by reviewing the strategies listed on the anchor chart.
- Discuss the students' strengths and needs during a future reading conference.
- Form a temporary small group to reinforce the students' understanding and use of the strategies identified during the language detectives' presentation of the ideas.

Making Students and Teachers Visible

This assessment uses student talk to make visible the in-the-head strategies the language detectives used to comprehend content presented in a whole-class discussion. When teachers use the information gained from this assessment to inform their instruction, they make visible that they view their students as valuable partners in their reading growth. The discussions that occurred between the teacher and the language detectives when the students present the ideas they wrote on the sticky notes make visible teachers' commitment to developing their students' ability to construct and deconstruct the meaning of text.

Implementation Example

Ms. Spindle is a fifth-grade teacher who teaches multiple sections of a 60-minute literacy block. She is responsible for teaching all language arts areas: reading, writing, spelling, and vocabulary. The school is located in a rural area where many of the students have family members who live on a farm, work on a farm, or work at the chicken-processing plant located outside of the town. Ms. Spindle has 24 students in this language arts section. Ten of the 24 students are Black, 4 are of Hispanic origins, and 10 are White. Eighty percent of the students in the school qualify for free and reduced-price lunch. Ms. Spindle is African American, and is a long-time resident of this community. As an African American middle-age woman, she grew up listening to her relatives talk about what it was like for African Americans to live in the South prior to and after the passage of the 1964 Voting Rights Act. Ms. Spindle's relatives' remembrances made her realize how the everyday life of people whom she knew was impacted negatively by discrimination. She wants her students to be aware of this part of our country's history, and she chooses to do so through the medium of stories.

To that end, yesterday Ms. Spindle read the book *Freedom Summer* (Wiles, 2001) to her class. *Freedom Summer* tells the story of two friends—Joe, who is White, and John Henry, who is Black. The story takes place in the South in 1964. When she read the book to the students, they discussed the strong friendship that existed between the boys in spite of the differences they experienced growing up in the South in 1964.

Today she will read the book a second time, but this time she will focus on how the author of *Freedom Summer,* Deborah Wiles, uses words to create rich images. The lesson will have two parts. During the first part, the teacher will conduct a whole-class discussion and the language detectives will not participate in the discussion. Instead, they will observe the lesson to identify key ideas presented during the discussion. Each language detective will be responsible for identifying two important ideas expressed during the discussion and recording each on a sticky note.

She has two objectives for the lesson. One, she will use the language detective assessment to understand the in-the-head strategies the language detectives used to identify the key ideas presented during the previous whole-class discussion. Once revealed, Ms. Spindle will use the students' words to make the strategy visible to all students. Her second objective is to explore how the author uses imagery to tell the story and how these images deepen the reader's understanding of the story. She will use three questions to examine how the imagery adds to a reader's understanding of the story. These questions are:

- What do you see?
- What do you hear?
- What do you feel?

In **preparation** for implementing the *Language Detective* assessment, Ms. Spindle chooses three students to serve as language detectives. Ms. Spindle gives each language detective two sticky notes on which they will write their ideas and a lanyard with the words *language detective* to wear around their necks She writes on the white board the three questions (listed previously) that she will use to guide her discussion with the students, and she places in the front of the class the poster board on which she will place the sticky notes after the lesson.

Engaging Students as Language Detectives and as Participants

The students have used the language detective assessment multiple times, and they are becoming more comfortable with talking about how and why they selected the ideas they did. To illustrate the value of their responses, Ms. Spindle uses their words to make explicit the in-the-head strategies they used to identify the important ideas presented during the previous whole-group discussion.

Ms. Spindle offers extra support to her bilingual and multilingual students so they can participate as language detectives or as participants during the whole-group discussion. When they share, they can use their native language or combinations of their native language and English. She uses two ways to support these students. One way is that she allows two or three bilingual and multilingual students to work together. Another strategy that seems to work is pairing a bilingual and multilingual student with a native English speaker.

Ms. Spindle begins the whole-group discussion by explaining that today she will read *Freedom Summer* again. However, today she wants them to pay attention to how the author uses words to paint pictures in their mind. And how these mind pictures deepen their understanding of what happens in the story. She will ask them: What do you see? What do you hear? What do you feel?

The language detectives do not participate in this discussion. As they observe the reading and the discussion, their job is to listen carefully for what they think are key ideas presented during the discussion. When they identify an important idea, they write it on one of their sticky notes. She reminds them not to worry about spelling; rather, they should focus on writing their idea the best they can. Then, Ms. Spindle gives each language detective two sticky notes. She reminds them that they are to choose the ideas they think are important to the discussion.

Ms. Spindle begins the whole-group portion of the lesson by reading the first five pages of *Freedom Summer.* Then she stops to ask the students to listen closely as she rereads the sentence "Henry crawls like a catfish." She asks how these words help them better understand how John Henry swims.

CHANDRA: I know. She says that John Henry crawls like a catfish.

MS. SPINDLE: (*Directs her question to Chandra.*) Do the words help you see, hear, or feel how John Henry swims?

CHANDRA: The words help me see how he swims. He swims like a fish.

MS. SPINDLE: Tell us how you think John Henry swims if he swims like a fish?

CHANDRA: (*moving her hands up and down*) I see that when John Henry swims he moves fast and moves up and down.

MS. SPINDLE: Okay, so it helps you see how John Henry moves in the water.

Anyone else want to tell us how this sentence helps them better understand how John Henry swims?

ISAIAH: Those words help me hear how John Henry swims.

MS. SPINDLE: Interesting. How do those words help you hear how he swims?

ISAIAH: I go fishing a lot and fish make noises when they jump up in the water and they make a splashing sound when they go back in the water.

MS. SPINDLE: So, when you hear those words in your head you hear him making noises when he swims?

ISAIAH: Yeah.

MS. SPINDLE: Hey class, this is interesting. Chandra and Isaiah heard the same words, but the words created different pictures in their minds. So, people can hear the same words, but those words create different images. Chandra and Isaiah have different experiences with fish. Chandra has probably seen fish swim maybe in a lake or in a fishing tank. Isaiah goes fishing a lot. The experiences we have in our lives influence our understanding of what we read. So even though Chandra and Isaiah hear the same words, their different experiences influence how they interpret what they hear.

Ms. Spindle resumes reading *Freedom Summer*, stopping at different places in the book to discuss how the words the author uses help readers to understand the story better. Once she has completed reading the book and discussing the images created by the words, she begins the language detective portion of the lesson.

MS. SPINDLE: Language detectives, now it's your turn. You were our eyes and ears when I read the book and discussed how the author uses words to help us gain a better understanding of the story. Let's see what ideas you identified that you think were important in helping us to understand how authors use words to create pictures in our mind.

Thomas, share what you wrote on one of your sticky notes.

THOMAS: She uses things we know about to help us understand things.

MS. SPINDLE: Give me an example.

THOMAS: She said Joe and John Henry blow water out of their mouths like whales do.

MS. SPINDLE: Do those words help you see, feel, or hear how Joe and John Henry swim?

THOMAS: Helps me see. And I blow water out of my mouth when I swim.

MS. SPINDLE: So, when you hear her words, "They spout like whales," you think spouting like whales is kind of like when you blow water out of your mouth.

THOMAS: Yeah.

MS. SPINDLE: Thomas, you, just like Chandra and Isaiah, put together two pieces of information. You put what you know from your personal experience with what you know about whales to help you understand what it looks like when Joe and John Henry swim on their backs.

That's what we do when we read. And, as we also talked about during the whole-group discussion, we put together what we know from our experiences with what we read to help us understand what we read.

Do any other language detectives have a similar idea to Thomas's?

LOUISA: She said Joe was like a doodlebug.

MS. SPINDLE: Yes, let me read that sentence: "I wiggle in my chair like a doodlebug."

Does that help you see, feel, or hear what's happening when Joe is sitting in the chair?

LOUISA: Helps me see, and I think that means he's excited or something.

MS. SPINDLE: Is he excited or nervous? I'll read that page and let's see if you know why he is wiggling like a doodlebug.

> *Daddy stirs his iced tea and says, "The town pool opens tomorrow to everybody under the sun, no matter what color."*
>
> *"That's the new law," Mama tells me.*
>
> *She heaps my plate with peas and says, "It's the way it's going to be now—Everybody together—lunch counters, rest rooms, drinking fountains, too."*
>
> *I wiggle in my chair like a doodlebug. "I got to be excused!" I shout and run into the kitchen to tell John Henry.*

Louisa, why is he wiggling like a doodlebug?

LOUISA: He's excited.

MS. SPINDLE: Why is he excited?

LOUISA: He wants him and John Henry to swim together. They love to swim, and because John Henry is Black, they can't swim together in the pool.

MS. SPINDLE: Yes, he's wiggling like a doodlebug because he's excited to swim with his best friend.

Louisa, let me tell you what you did that many readers do to help them understand what they read. You put together information on one page, *that everybody will be able to swim in the town pool,* with information the author told us earlier, that *Joe and John Henry were best friends.* You figured out that Joe is wiggling like a doodlebug because he's excited to be able to swim with his best friend.

Shonda, share one of your ideas.

SHONDA: John Henry's brother's face is described like a storm.

MS. SPINDLE: Yes, the author wrote, "His face is like a storm cloud." Shonda, how do these words help you better understand what she is saying about John Henry's brother's face?

SHONDA: Hear and feel.

MS. SPINDLE: Okay, what do you hear?

SHONDA: Storms can be really loud, and Will Rogers was angry about having to put tar on the pool.

MS. SPINDLE: So how does knowing that storm clouds are noisy help you understand that he was angry?

SHONDA: I think he might have made noises because he was angry?

MS. SPINDLE: Interesting. What kind of noises?

SHONDA: Maybe he kicked something on the ground or talked to himself because he's angry about not being able to swim in the pool.

MS. SPINDLE: Yes, and we discussed yesterday that many White people who lived where Joe and John Henry lived did not want African Americans to swim in the town pool. So, they covered the pool with tar so no one could swim. That might have made him very angry.

Shonda, let me tell you what you did that other readers often do to help them understand what they read. You connected what we discussed yesterday about the differences in Joe and John Henry's lives in 1964, with the words the author used to describe John Henry's brother's face. Do any other language detectives have another idea that was similar?

Ms. Spindle continues the discussion until the three language detectives shared all of their ideas. When all language detectives have shared, she collects the sticky notes from the students and places them on the poster board.

MS. SPINDLE: Today we learned that authors create mind pictures with the words they use to help their readers better understand the story. And the language detectives showed us some of the strategies they used to help them identify their big ideas. They showed us how as readers, we:

- Use what we know from our experiences to help us understand what we read.
- Make inferences when we read, when we put our experiences together with the words in the book.
- Put together all of the information in the story not just what's written on one page to understand the story.

She reminds the students to use these strategies the next time they read. She thanks the students just as the bell rings for them to move to their math class.

Using the Language Detective Notetaking Template (Form 4.2), Ms. Spindle reviews the data she collected. First, she reviews her notes, her lesson objectives, and the students' entries on the sticky notes. During this initial review, Ms. Spindle adds missing information and details to the existing information. Next, she looks for patterns across the data. Then she analyzes the ideas shared collectively by the three language detectives and then individually. Her completed form is shown in Figure 4.3. She uses the following questions to identify patterns in the data.

- Which strategies were used by the language detectives?
- Which language detectives exhibited similar needs or similar strengths?
- When viewed collectively, which strategies were not used that would have been useful to their ability to identify key ideas?

Lesson: *Freedom Summer*			
Student	**Idea**	**Strategy used**	**Other information**
Thomas	Joe and John Henry "spout like whales"	That's what we do when we read. To help us understand what we read, we sometimes need to use our experience to help us understand what we read.	Drew from his swimming experiences
Louisa	"Wiggle like a doodlebug"	You put together information not only on one page but with information the author told us earlier in the book. You figured out that Joe was wiggling like a doodlebug because he was excited to be able to swim with his best friend.	Put together information from earlier in the book
Shonda	John Henry's brother's face is described like a storm.	You connected what we discussed yesterday about the differences in Joe and John Henry's lives in 1964, with the words she used.	Used information from the story read the day before
Other notes: These are the strategies identified during the whole-group discussion: • We use what we know from our experiences to help us understand what we read. • We make inferences when we read. We do this by putting together the words on the page with what we know beyond the page. • We use information from earlier in the text to understand information presented later in the text.			

FIGURE 4.3. Example of a *Language Detective* notetaking form for *Freedom Summer.*

Ms. Spindle will use the information as follows:

- Have the students categorize the stickies placed on the poster board to identify similarities in the ideas offered by the language detectives.
- Form a temporary small group composed of students who did not participate in the whole-class discussion to assess their understanding of the strategies covered in the lesson.
- Plan a follow-up lesson to reinforce how to use imagery to help in comprehending the texts they read.

Ms. Spindle believes the *Language Detectives* assessment is valuable because it makes **visible** her students' understanding of the text and their ability to apply strategies to achieve that understanding. Further, being present when the students presented their ideas enabled Ms. Spindle to offer in-the-moment support. When Ms. Spindle used her students' ideas as the basis of her subsequent discussion, it made **visible** to her students that she viewed her students as vital partners in her efforts to advance their reading comprehension. Focusing her lesson on reading comprehension made **visible** to the students that comprehension is important.

The *T-Chart* Assessment Helps Teachers "Look" into Students' Thinking, Understanding, and Knowledge

Teachers can learn a great deal about their students' language, comprehension, vocabularies, and conceptual knowledge by observing what they say and do when engaged in authentic, complex learning tasks with peers. As students solve problems, collaborate, discuss, and apply what they know and are learning to complete tasks across the curriculum, they make visible their thinking, understanding, and application of language and literacy skills and strategies. When teachers observe during authentic tasks, they gain insights about how their students orchestrate their learning by using their background knowledge, language skills including academic vocabulary, literacy skills and strategies, and interpersonal skills. These insights increase teachers' understanding of what their students do and do not understand, what they can and cannot yet do, and how they behave and interact when engaging in authentic learning tasks.

ASSESSMENT STRATEGY 4.3. *T-Chart*

Purpose

The *T-Chart* assessment is designed to document what students say and do while engaged with peers in authentic learning tasks across the curriculum. The data allow teachers to gain insights into the language and literacy skills, strategies, and knowledge that students use as they engage in various collaborative learning tasks.

Value

The *T-Chart* assessment is flexible and can be used to collect and analyze student language and actions while they are engaged with one or more peer(s) in any learning task in any area of the curriculum. Because language and literacy skills and strategies are essential for student learning across the curriculum, this assessment provides a tool for teachers to collect and analyze such data to inform their instructional planning.

Procedures

1. To **prepare** for the *T-Chart* assessment, you will need a blank copy of the *T-Chart* Template (Form 4.3) for each student you will be observing in the group. We recommend that you plan to observe students working as partners or in groups of three to make the assessment implementation more manageable and focused.
2. Determine which students you will observe engaged in which learning task. For example, you may choose to observe a small group of three students in a literature discussion

circle, partners doing a hands-on science activity, or a triad working to solve math problems using manipulatives. A key consideration is that the learning task must be engaging and complex, so you are able to see students use academic language as well as basic vocabulary and apply skills and strategies they have been learning.

3. Plan to observe the partners or small group for about 5–7 minutes by sitting near the students and telling them, "I'm just listening and watching what you do and say so I can learn more about how you are learning. Be sure to talk to each other about what you are doing and thinking as you perform the learning task."
4. Focus on one student at a time by dividing the 5–7 minutes by the number of students in the group. If you have more than three students in the group, you may need to spend more time observing.
5. Using the *T-Chart* Template (Form 4.3), write down what the focal student says, trying to be as accurate and complete as possible. Be sure to record examples of academic vocabulary the student uses as well as examples of the student's use of background knowledge and of language associated with skills and strategies you have been teaching in class. Write what the student does in the form of actions and behaviors, again, trying to be as complete and descriptive as possible.
6. Shift your attention to the next focal student and record what they say and do on a blank copy of the *T-Chart* Template (Form 4.3).

Collecting, Analyzing, and Using Data

You will **collect** data through observing a focal student engaged in partner or small-group learning tasks. You will observe one focal student at a time and record these observations on the *T-Chart* Template (Form 4.3). Your observations will be divided into two broad areas—"What Student Says" and "What Student Does."

For the **"What Student Says"** section, you will record examples of academic vocabulary the student uses; evidence of the student's comprehension, learning skills, and strategies taught in the classroom; examples of background knowledge the student is using; and examples of how the student collaborates with their peer(s).

For the **"What Student Does"** section, you will record data about the specific actions the student takes and the behaviors they demonstrate.

To **analyze** the data you record on the *T-Chart,* first, look at the data in the "What Student Says" column. Look for patterns and information that help you gain insights into what the student is thinking and understanding, and how they are using their literacy and language skills. Record your insights in the "What does it mean?" section of the template. Next, look at the data you recorded in the "What Student Does" column and identify patterns and information that help you understand the student's literacy and learning in the context of this task. Finally, consider what you wrote in the "What does it mean?" section and respond to the question "What should I do next?" Consider how to **use** the insights you gained from this assessment to provide future instruction, support, task selection, grouping, and feedback to enhance the student's literacy learning. Record those ideas in the "What should I do next?" section at the bottom of the template.

Making Students and Teachers Visible

The *T-Chart* assessment makes students' thinking, understandings, and misunderstandings visible. Plus, this strategy reveals students' applications of skills and strategies, including application of background knowledge. Through analysis of the data collected, teachers can make visible their growing knowledge about their students, language, learning, and literacy development.

Implementation Example

Miss Cowlishaw is a second-grade teacher in a small rural school in a county where she grew up. She has only 12 students in her class who come from farms and small towns across the county. In fact, some of her students ride the bus to get to and from school for almost an hour each way! Her students are mostly from lower income backgrounds, and some students' families are migrant farmers who travel to find work planting and harvesting crops. Miss Cowlishaw is a relatively new teacher who has only been teaching for 2 years. Several of her students speak Spanish as their home language, and she has been taking an online course to learn "Spanish for Teachers." The students from migrant families tend to move frequently, so she feels that she always has new students to get to know in her classroom. Miss Cowlishaw reports that she learns a great deal by listening to her students' language and observing them closely because doing so helps her gain insights about their knowledge, comprehension, and vocabulary.

Miss Cowlishaw's students are working with partners to solve subtraction problems using math manipulatives because she wants to see if they are able to use the academic vocabulary associated with subtraction to explain their processes and thinking while solving the problems. She views literacy as a tool that her students need to use across the curriculum, so she is interested if they can read and understand written directions, follow steps in a sequence, and use the academic vocabulary *difference, less than, take away,* and *solve* correctly as they engage in the subtraction tasks. She decides to observe Juan and Hannah. Juan has only been in her classroom for about a week, and Hannah has attended this school since kindergarten. Miss Cowlishaw sits in an empty chair at the table where Juan and Hannah are working with place value manipulatives to complete two-digit subtraction problems. She says, "I'm just going to watch you, so I can see what you are doing as you solve the subtraction problems. Be sure to work together and talk to each about what you are doing as you complete this task. And just pretend I'm not here."

Miss Cowlishaw has two copies of the *T-Chart* Template (Form 4.3) on a clipboard, and she records her notes while observing Juan for about 3 minutes. She then shifts her focus to Hannah. See the notes she took in Figure 4.4.

To **analyze** the data, Miss Cowlishaw reviews the notes she recorded on the *T-Chart*. First, she reviews the data recorded about Juan in the "What Student Says" column and records her insights in the "What does it mean?" section of the template. Next, she reviews the data recorded in the "What Student Does" column and records her insights in the "What does it mean" section. Then, she considers all of the data related to the student and indicates her follow-up actions in the "What should I do next?" section. She uses the same process to analyze Hannah's data.

Focal student: Juan Other student/s: Hannah	Date: March 8 Learning task: Two-digit subtraction
Observations of What Student Says	**Observations of What Student Does**
Academic vocabulary used: minus take away	Actions: Counted out place value cubes, subtracted, identified difference. Wrote the answer on his paper.
Background knowledge student uses: Big one first, then take away Gotta check!	Literacy behaviors: Looked to Hannah and pointed to instructions for her to read aloud.
Skills and strategies taught in class that student uses: Check it. Adds up?	Interactions with peer(s): Waited for Hannah to agree before writing the difference on his paper Pointed and used eye contact to support communication
Teacher Analysis	**Teacher Analysis**
What does it mean? He understands concept of subtraction and has some of the academic vocabulary in place. Knows how to check his answer.	What does it mean? He knew to read directions first, but asked Hannah to do it since he is not confident in his English reading skills. He understood how to use place value manipulatives and how to subtract and check answer.

What should I do next?

- Teach Juan math academic vocabulary: **subtract**, **difference**, **less than**, and **solve** because he has concepts but does not know the vocabulary in English yet.
- Check to see what these words are in Spanish to see if he knows them in Spanish.

(continued)

FIGURE 4.4. T-charts for observing Juan and Hannah in a math subtraction task.

<table>
<tr><td>Focal student: Hannah

Other student/s: Juan</td><td>Date: March 8

Learning task: Two digit subtraction</td></tr>
<tr><td>Observations of What Student Says</td><td>Observations of What Student Does</td></tr>
<tr><td>Academic vocabulary used:
Subtract
Take away</td><td>Actions:
Sets up first problem using blocks. Points to Juan for him to do the next one.</td></tr>
<tr><td>Background knowledge student uses:
Adding makes the answer more than. Subtracting's answer is less than.</td><td>Literacy behaviors:
Appears to read directions silently but reads them aloud when Juan points to them and then to her.</td></tr>
<tr><td>Skills and strategies taught in class that student uses:
Subtract is taking away the number to get the answer.
Add the answer to the take away to see if it checks out okay.</td><td>Interactions with peer(s):
Responds to Juan's request for her to read the directions aloud. Does first problem but then takes turns for rest of problems.</td></tr>
<tr><td>Teacher Analysis</td><td>Teacher Analysis</td></tr>
<tr><td>What does it mean?
Hannah knows some academic vocabulary and process for subtracting and checking answer.</td><td>What does it mean?
She took the lead, but alternated solving problems with Juan. She provided support with reading directions when he requested it.</td></tr>
<tr><td colspan="2">What should I do next?
• See if Hannah can solve problems without place value blocks.
• Teach Hannah academic vocabulary words difference and solve.</td></tr>
</table>

FIGURE 4.4. *(continued)*

Miss Cowlishaw believes the *T-Chart* assessment is **valuable** because she can use it while her students are engaged in a variety of learning tasks throughout the school day. She reports that it does not require any additional time because she would already be observing her students during their partner and small-group work. She uses the *T-Chart* assessment to make **visible** what her students say and do so she can understand more about their learning and identify ways to help them continue growing.

Conclusion

Teachers need opportunities to observe and engage with their students when they are involved in the act of reading, writing, and discussing so they can learn what resources students use as they go about constructing and deconstructing meaning. The assessments in this chapter make visible the resources, such as linguistic and background knowledge, and the strategies used by their students that influence their text comprehension. Furnished with this information, teachers become empowered to develop instruction that is responsive to the strengths and needs of their students.

FORM 4.1

Vocabulary Knowledge Assessment Template

Word	No Clue!	I know a little about this word	I know a lot about this word
	Pre/Before	Pre/Before	Pre/Before
	Post/After	Post/After	Post/After
	Pre/Before	Pre/Before	Pre/Before
	Post/After	Post/After	Post/After
	Pre/Before	Pre/Before	Pre/Before
	Post/After	Post/After	Post/After
	Pre/Before	Pre/Before	Pre/Before
	Post/After	Post/After	Post/After
	Pre/Before	Pre/Before	Pre/Before
	Post/After	Post/After	Post/After

FORM 4.2

Language Detective Notetaking Form

Lesson:			
Student	**Idea**	**Strategy used**	**Other information**
Other notes:			

FORM 4.3

T-Chart Template

Focal student: Other student/s:	Date: Learning task:
Observations of What Student Says	**Observations of What Student Does**
Academic vocabulary used:	Actions:
Background knowledge student uses:	Literacy behaviors:
Skills and strategies taught in class that student uses:	Interactions with peer(s):
Teacher Analysis	**Teacher Analysis**
What does it mean?	What does it mean?
What should I do next?	

5

Assessing Readers' Text Comprehension

> The "noble bubble" . . . the moment when all the notes of each musician slid effortlessly around and among one another so that a piece of music became such a beautiful sound that it captured the spirts of both player and listener and carried them effortlessly upward . . . like a bubble.
>
> —EXCERPT FROM NATIVE AMERICAN LITERATURE (in Krueger, 2020, p. 206)

The coming together of prior knowledge, new ideas, an author's voice, and so much more represents our vision of reading comprehension. Like a "noble bubble" in the quote above, there are multiple influences on reading comprehension and multiple actions required of the reader to be successful. Taken together, they represent if and how well we understand the texts we are reading. Too frequently, however, the goal of achieving the "noble bubble" of comprehension or the bringing together of multiple student and teacher resources is reduced to meaningless and oversimplified text-related activities (e.g., short-answer text questions, multiple-choice questions, required factual recall). For instance, I remember during my first year of teaching, how elated I was when my first-grade students could answer the questions embedded in the curriculum materials and that occurred at the end of each story. And I remember being humbled when my students were unable to answer the final question that I generated: "So what was the story about?" I heard names of people, words, places . . . but no responses indicating that students understood the concepts, the vocabulary, the events, or character motives. My students were simply reciting back what they heard and thought was expected of them, remembering the facts with no thinking required!

In this chapter, paired with the previous chapter, we discuss the importance of reconceptualizing the assessment of reading comprehension within an equity framework. Central to this reconceptualization is implementing strategies that capture the resources that students bring to their learning, including their information sources and their cultural, linguistic, and experiential knowledge. These assessments need to make visible how students approach texts, and the strategies they use to make sense of texts and construct new knowledge. We need multiple and continuous formative assessments if we expect to capture students' identities as literacy learners and the wide range of assets and differences each one brings to texts, especially noting how their knowledge, skills, and strategies may vary with widely different texts in terms of genre, style, language, and information loads. As discussed in the previous chapter, considering the roles of the reader, the (assessment) activity, the text, and the sociocultural context is important to the analyses of reading comprehension.

Decoding and Comprehension in Tandem

Scott Paris (2005) described the developmental trajectories of two categories of reading skills. One is the constrained skills, which consist of learning letters of the alphabet as well as sounds associated with these letters and as they appear in words. These skills are mastered in relatively brief developmental periods. The second is the unconstrained skills, such as vocabulary and comprehension, that are "unconstrained" by time but continue to develop over time (and through adulthood) as knowledge is acquired and readers engage with increasingly complex texts. While decoding skills should be mastered early in a reader's development, text comprehension skills develop alongside the word-learning skills and continue to deepen and enrich the learning of each reader. In Chapter 6, we discuss the importance of constrained skills for decoding words and methods for assessing these skills. Together, constrained and unconstrained skills are two of the elements needed for successful reading development. Both are influenced by students' development of decoding and meaning-based strategies (e.g., identifying and applying sounds and context to support decoding, monitoring comprehension while reading), and methods for assessing these strategies are presented in this chapter and Chapter 6. As addressed in the previous chapter, oral language (listening and speaking) lays the foundation for developing text comprehension and decoding. Thus, across Chapters 4, 5, and 6, we signal the importance of assessing these three areas.

Our approach to assessment across these three chapters is comprehensive and inclusive of the multiple skills, strategies, and knowledges that are developing and supporting each other (e.g., oral and written/text comprehension and decoding) from early reading development throughout life. Thus, our assessments across these three chapters provide data that can be cross- referenced to give a more complete snapshot of a reader's development. We do not advocate the privileging of one area, such as decoding, as more important than the others for early readers. Assuming that these three areas (e.g., oral language, comprehension, and decoding) develop in concert with each other is consistent with decades of research indicating that emphasizing word reading alone results in a knowledge gap that often contributes to later reading difficulties (ILA, 2019a). For example, we learned from the Reading First programs of the early 2000s and the RAND report, *Reading for Understanding* (RAND Reading Study Group, 2002), that instruction focusing largely on decoding words accurately and with fluency had no impact on students' reading comprehension (Almasi & Hurt, 2019), and students with comprehension difficulties often had strong decoding skills. Each area is necessary but not sufficient, and as we explain in this and the previous chapter, reading comprehension is more than the outcome of successful decoding. It is the drawing together of multiple resources to make sense of the texts we read.

Further, we are keenly aware of the overrepresentation of minorities (i.e., African American, Latinx, and Native American students, and English language learners) and students living in poverty within remedial and special education placements, and the underrepresentation of these students within gifted-and-talented special education programs. As discussed in Chapter 1, high-stakes testing practices that drive educational decision making about student placements are narrow in conception and biased in consequences; students' assets that may be different from the mainstream go unrecognized and untapped (e.g., Koretz, 2017). In response to these biases, the assessment strategies we offer across the chapters of this book, and in particular those identified in Chapters 4, 5, and 6, are inclusive of the multiple knowledges, skills, and strategies that each child brings to their reading development. As we illustrate in the assessment strategies that follow in this chapter, multimodal student responses (e.g., oral and written answers, drawings and digital artwork, musical representations) and drawing on home languages can tap the multiple resources that students use to support their text comprehension. And with the rich sets of data that are obtained, instructional decision making and placements are more likely to be representative of students' diverse talents and knowledge.

Reader, Texts, Activity, and Sociocultural Context: *All* Matter When Assessing Comprehension

We elaborate further on the impact of the reader, texts, activity, and sociocultural context on reading comprehension. These are components of reading comprehension as advanced by the RAND Reading Study Group (2002, p. 12). Each element influences the others simultaneously as readers construct knowledge about the texts they are reading (see Figure 4.1).

Reader

As introduced in the previous chapter, the RAND Reading Study Group (2002) made clear that text comprehension is affected by the reader, text, activity, and sociocultural context in which the learning and reading is occurring. Children from birth are comprehending the world around them as they begin to recognize familiar voices and understand the language, emotions (e.g., happiness, apprehension), or intended actions (e.g., good morning, time to wake up) of others. As we discussed in Chapter 4, these understandings increase in leaps and bounds as children acquire their own language and respond to the language of others. With this history of development that all children experience, they come to preschool and kindergarten with a great wealth of information and language that impacts their reading comprehension. This wealth of out-of-school information and language, referred to throughout this text as their sociocultural knowledge, continues to influence their reading comprehension across the grades and throughout life. More specifically, all children bring world and experiential knowledge of the topic, the structure of written language, vocabulary meanings, their interests and expectations for the purpose of the texts they are reading, and their strategies for making connections and constructing new knowledge (see previous chapter for extended discussion of these attributes). Thus, the (assessment) activities that we describe in the following material must make visible the knowledge that students bring to the texts they read (RAND Reading Study Group, 2002). In this chapter, we provide specific guidance for considering students' rich "funds of knowledge" (González, Moll, & Amanti, 2005) when assessing students' text comprehension.

Texts

Just as our knowledge about our students as readers increases our ability to assess their comprehension, we must also understand how text choices impact those assessments. During the last decade, renewed interest in text difficulty has advanced understandings of what makes texts "complex" and, thus, more challenging for the reader. Stylistic elements might include more implicit meanings of words and ideas, frequent uses of flashbacks and flash forwards, complicated graphics, and increased use of figurative language. Additionally, comprehension might be affected by sentence length (with sentences that are excessively long or difficult to comprehend), coherence or lack of coherence of ideas across the text, language clarity and conventionality, and a high conceptual and vocabulary load.

Most important to meet our goal of an equity approach to assessment is the need to examine the texts to determine if the texts represent the students who are reading them. Do they make visible students' attributes, knowledge, and histories? Will students be interested in the texts they read? Do students see themselves, their communities, their languages, and their experiences represented in the texts they are asked to read? Or are the texts written to assume that there is a universal set of understandings that all students have, regardless of cultural and experiential differences? We believe that each of these questions and guidance for their application is unique to our approach to equity-based assessments. The questions we ask, from our viewpoint, must be considered when choosing the texts that might be most appropriate for assessing comprehension, for if these considerations are not addressed, poor comprehension may be the result of a poorly chosen text instead of "failure" on the reader's part.

Activities

The activities or tasks represent the assessment strategies that we recommend. Our goal for these strategies is to capture the readers' thinking and responses to text while making visible in-the-head processes (e.g., making connections to prior experiences or linguistic knowledge) that influence that thinking. The assessment strategies we choose are extremely important for building confidence about our assessment results.

The strategies will assess students' recall of facts, inferences, and critique and application of text information. We seek to understand students' comprehension of major text concepts and supporting details, how they are interpreting what they are reading, how they are perceiving the value and usefulness of the text ideas, and if they are reading for enjoyment and because they are interested in the topic and/or writing style of the author. Each activity makes visible students' thinking and what might be influencing that thinking. Vocabulary assessments are embedded throughout the strategies, evaluating the readers' comprehension of novel and technical vocabulary. Most assessments will require students to read their texts either silently or orally before examining comprehension; some assessments might engage students in listening comprehension.

As cautioned by Valencia, Wixson, and Pearson (2014), choosing texts without a careful analysis of what we ask students to do with those texts (i.e., the activity) can have serious negative consequences. For example, tasks requiring simple literal recall of text information or simple matching exercises may result in false positives, overestimating that students have also developed deep meanings of the text or false negatives, and conversely, judging a lack of literal recall as indicating there is also a lack of deeper understanding. High stakes, standardized tests may provide a profile of students' performance on an array of skill areas, but these items/tasks were developed independent of knowing the readers and/or their instructional history. For example, Valencia et al. (2014) described test items requiring knowledge of figurative and connotative language, which may be inappropriate tasks for the fourth-grade students taking this test.

Sociocultural Context

The sociocultural context refers to how children come to understand their world, learning from their family and community members as they experience language development, shared routines and activities, and meanings associated with multiple actions occurring around them (RAND Reading Study Group, 2002). They represent family and community traditions, expectations for behaviors, and shared home languages and dialects that are part of how families and communities communicate with each other. Students' culture and linguistic histories, including their home languages, are significant to their learning as they influence how students convey their understandings of language and experiences, how they talk about the text ideas, and how they are constructing new understandings. One adaptation that is responsive to students' social and cultural history is considering the implementation of a translanguaging process. To implement, the teacher might observe that students who are actively learning English also rely on their home languages to make sense of the world around them. These students might be hesitant to share their thoughts without the support of their peers. Thus, the assessment activity would move to a group activity, bringing small groups of students together for "group talk" as they take time to talk with each other about the text in their home languages and/or hybrid languages (i.e., a mix of home and school language), debating ideas and constructing meanings, and then sharing back with the teacher how they might convey their understandings in English (Iddings et al., 2009; Jimenez et al., 2015), making visible their understandings as the teacher records information about each students' contribution.

We share an example of how translanguaging can be embedded in an assessment procedure later in this chapter when we discuss the *Think-Alouds* assessment strategy.

Summary

Each of the above elements influences others simultaneously. And thus, reading comprehension is not fixed (Valencia et al., 2014). To achieve a trustworthy understanding of students' comprehension of selected texts requires us to consider how each of the elements influence how they are constructing their own understanding of the text. For example, students with strong prior knowledge of star constellations learned in a previous science unit might couple this information with cultural stories about stars that they heard from community members, and taking these together might elaborate on the text ideas in ways that might not be expected by the teacher. Yet their construction of knowledge is rich with text information, previous learnings, and cultural information brought to the text. Thus, listening to students as they share their understandings and knowing their instructional history and culture will be extremely helpful and necessary to capture how the student is constructing knowledge embedded in the new text they are asked to read.

The ultimate goal for comprehension assessment is to answer the question, "Did the reader understand the text?" To achieve a trustworthy answer, we need to consider how the four elements described above interact and impact text comprehension. There is an urgency for equity-based assessments, particularly in the area of reading comprehension. Moving away from a reductionist approach (e.g., getting the "right" answers) to an approach that is broad based and inclusive of multiple elements when considering students' text comprehension sets up a pathway for informing appropriate and responsive literacy instruction for all students.

In the remainder of this chapter, we present four assessment strategies. Three strategies provide alternative methods (i.e., retellings, think-aloud, questioning) for assessing text comprehension and each focuses on revealing what students are thinking and understanding, with minimal direction and prompting by the teacher. The questioning strategy provides prompting but only after students have shared first their interpretations and understandings of the text. Discussions about the text within all three strategies aim to build two-way conversations that engage students' active participation and personal responses. While the assessment of vocabulary is built into each of the three strategies, a fourth strategy focuses primarily on the assessment of vocabulary. As you read about and consider each of these assessment strategies, the following questions will help guide your thinking.

- How does the assessment help me identify students' comprehension of text ideas, noticing attention to major ideas and supporting details, and meanings of vocabulary?
- How does the assessment help me understand how students are applying comprehension and vocabulary strategies to support their text comprehension?
- How does the assessment help me understand what students are thinking as they construct new knowledge drawing on their own prior knowledge and experiences?
- How can I apply what I am learning from these assessments to plan appropriate instruction that is responsive to students' strengths and needs?

ASSESSMENT STRATEGIES: SUPPORTING STUDENTS' TEXT COMPREHENSION

Assessing reading comprehension can be one of the most challenging tasks that we assume. There is much to consider, including the role of the readers and their in-the-head thinking processes, the texts and their complexities, the trustworthiness of the assessment tasks, and whether the sociocultural context supports the process. To meet the challenges of assessing reading comprehension, we must constantly reflect on our process and ask ourselves, through our assessments, "Did we get it right? Are we confident with our text choices, with our assessment procedures, with our ability to 'connect' with our students?" and so on. As we reflect, we are constantly evaluating our process to ensure that we are capturing and representing well our students' knowledge, their capabilities, their skills, their goals, and their understandings and misunderstandings.

Additionally, we advocate for assessments that capture students' capabilities in ways that go beyond traditional testing procedures. For example, we ask students to sketch and visualize their understandings of texts to aid their oral explanations, we enable students to demonstrate their understandings with multimodal representations of text ideas (sometimes working with peers to display their knowledges), and we invite students to use their home languages (either individually or with small groups) to aid their translation of text ideas and to support their text retellings and think-aloud work. Students' understandings are made visible, and so are teachers' reflections and observations, contributing to a powerful combination for assessing text comprehension.

In this section of the chapter, we offer four assessment strategies with variations for adapting the procedures for the retellings and think-aloud activities:

5.1. *Retellings*
Variation: *Retellings with Multimodal Text Representations*

5.2. *Think-Alouds*
Variation: *Think-Alouds with Translanguaging Applications for English Learners*

5.3. *Questioning of Text Comprehension*

5.4. *Semantic Word Sorts*

Information to Consider When Implementing Comprehension Assessment Activities

Before we describe the assessment strategies for this chapter, we provide questions in Figures 5.1 through 5.4 to guide your preparation and implementation of the four assessment strategies. We believe these questions are unique to our approach to comprehension assessment; our goal is to support your implementation of strong comprehension assessments that consider explicitly the reader, text, assessment activity, and sociocultural context. Please refer to these when preparing to administer each of the following assessments.

Assessing Students' Retellings

One activity that is powerful for assessing students' text comprehension and making visible their understandings is the retelling assessment strategy. Retellings invite students' agency as they explain their text understandings with minimal prompting during *unaided retelling* to the teacher or a peer. Thus, students retell the text in their own words choosing information that is important to them, organize how they want to present their understandings, and generate their literal, interpretive, and evaluative understandings. For the aided retelling that follows the unaided retelling, teachers provide guidance by asking students to explain what they have just shared, tell more about the text information, and/or address information not included in the unaided retelling.

As teachers listen to students' retellings, they are able to assess both understandings and the skills and strategies used to influence those understandings. Listening to students' retellings enables teachers to observe a wide range of strategies, skills, and knowledges

Questions to consider about the reader when preparing for the assessment activity:

- Did I provide sufficient practice of the strategy prior to assessing it?
- Did I model my thinking and how I was constructing text knowledge?
- Did I remind the student of the procedures we will follow and how I will take notes?
- Did I provide sufficient time and a quiet space for inviting each student to participate in the assessment strategy?
- Did I take time to make a connection with the students by remembering shared events or connecting to interests to support the students' engagement?
- Am I prepared to take notes about the reader's performance, reaction, and interest in the text?
- Did I consider the reader's experiences, background knowledge, and instructional history when choosing the text and assessment strategy?
- Did I prompt the student to use background knowledge and experiences to explain understandings of the text?
- Did I start the activity by asking students to tell first what they remember/understand about the reading and end by asking students to share their own perceptions of their performance?

FIGURE 5.1. Questions on the reader.

that students are drawing on to support their retellings. These can include what students choose to say about the text as they recall what is interesting to them, how students organize the information for retellings, the knowledge they draw on to support their retellings, what they are visualizing and inferring about text ideas, and the concepts and vocabulary that they are able to explain. The interpretation abilities of teachers when identifying students' strengths and needs are made visible and usable to guide instruction.

When appropriate, the assessment of student retellings can be embedded within instruction. For example, during small-group instruction, you might ask students to take turns retelling sections of the text while other students continue to read, taking notes for each student. Or you might focus on retellings during individual student conferences.

ASSESSMENT STRATEGY 5.1.
Retellings

Purpose

Asking students to retell a text that they just read or heard with minimal teacher prompting provides a powerful vehicle for evaluating how students are constructing their own meanings about that text; it is a process that makes visible what is happening "within the head of the student"! Too often teacher prompting and questioning that occurs immediately after reading a text intrudes on students' personal reactions and interpretations. Instead, the goal for retellings is to make visible students own interpretations and ownership of text ideas. Also, retellings provide information about students' difficulties and misunderstandings, with students often acknowledging that there were parts of the text that "were really hard."

Questions to consider for text selection:

- Did I choose a text that is appropriate for each student, considering instructional history, cultural and experiential knowledge, interests, and languages?
- Did I consider whether the readers will "see" themselves in the texts, and if not, explain the context for the choice of text (e.g., related to unit of instruction)?
- Did I choose a text appropriate for age and grade level? For example, for adjusting length for young and older readers, for readers experiencing difficulty, as appropriate.
- Did I choose a text that students have not read previously? For example, you could choose the first chapter or part of a first chapter of a text that will be read by the students. Or you could choose a later chapter in a text that students have been reading.
- Did I purposely choose a text that was read previously, assessing comprehension after a rereading of a text or portion of a text?
- Did I choose a text that has a beginning, middle, and ending?
- Did I choose a text that the students have not read previously; or is it important for my goals to assess a rereading of a text?
- Did I choose a text that aligns with my goals for assessment and instruction (e.g., students' ability to determine word meanings by the context; students' use of comprehension strategies; students' use of text structure to guide making sense of the text; and/or students' use of prior texts to make sense of new texts.)
- Did I choose a text that is consistent in style and content with the students' current instruction and their background knowledge? For example, what might I learn by choosing a text that follows an earlier one versus choosing the first text of a conceptual unit?
- Is the text authentic, including illustrations and text characteristics that are embedded naturally in the text?
- At times, will I consider pairing texts with similar content to assess if the former positively impacts comprehension of the second or subsequent texts, as I know this information will help me choose text pairings during instruction?
- Am I choosing texts, across time, that represent multiple genres—narratives, expository, poetry, wordless, digital? (I know that strong comprehension of one genre does not necessarily mean strong comprehension of another genre.)
- Am I choosing high quality texts (e.g., with depth of information, strong organization, concepts that are well developed, rich content to support meanings of unfamiliar vocabulary, plots that are well developed in narratives, main ideas and supporting details are well developed in expository texts, words convey imagery and meaning in poetry)?
- Am I choosing a text that will pose minimal decoding challenges? (If I find that students are making frequent decoding errors, I am prepared to stop and go to another text and/or procedures, such as reading the text to the student to assess listening comprehension).

FIGURE 5.2. Questions on text selection.

Value

Asking students to retell the text that they have just read or has been read to them signals to students that they are knowledgeable. They have the power and agency to organize their understandings and choose what and how they want to share the text information. As students gain confidence in retellings, they learn to identify skills and strategies that are helpful for deepening and extending their text comprehension while also developing a positive mindset about their own capabilities (Morrow, Dougherty, & Tracey, 2019).

Questions to consider when designing the assessment activities/tasks:

- Am I choosing tasks and questions that reveal what my students are thinking and possible reasons for their answers (e.g., background knowledge, strategy use, understanding literal details, generating inferences or predictions, instructional history)?
- Am I prepared to ask questions that reveal my students' understanding of vocabulary?
- Am I prepared to explain the task if it is confusing (e.g., restating the question with examples, provide an example of how I might answer the question)?
- Am I choosing tasks that go beyond short-answer constrained questions or multiple-choice questions?
- When I ask questions or comment, am I supporting a conversation about the text instead of asking too many questions or leading the conversation to an expected answer?
- Am I listening carefully to the students' language and understandings and taking notes and recording my observations?
- Am I prepared to offer supports that might be needed (e.g., moving to a listening comprehension activity if text seems to be interesting but requires more decoding than I anticipated; or moving to another text; or offering a choice of texts)?
- Am I prepared to ask the students to make notes or draw a simple sketch of the text before moving into the assessment strategy? (This technique is optional and depends on the context for the assessment.)
- Am I prepared to ask the students to start the activity by asking what they remember about the text or what they thought about as they read?
- Am I prepared for the procedure I want to follow (e.g., students will have already read the text silently prior to coming to the assessment strategy, students will first read aloud and then discuss the text and I will take notes for both)?
- Am I allocating sufficient time for a careful analysis of students' thinking by considering the actions of the reader, text characteristics, and the context–noting how each of these affect student performances?

FIGURE 5.3. Questions on assessment activity.

Questions to consider about the context for the assessment:

- Have I established a comfortable atmosphere in my classroom and for conducting this assessment strategy (e.g., students are comfortable meeting one-on-one with me; we have practiced this strategy so students know what to expect)?
- Do I have a good understanding of each student's cultural experiences and history and language so that I recognize when students are relying on these resources to explain their text understandings?
- Am I prepared to alter the procedures, such as asking two or three students to jointly retell a text using their home language and English and sharing ideas with each other (i.e., translanguaging)? Am I prepared to take notes that will represent the input of each student's ideas?
- Am I prepared to listen carefully to the language used by each student so that I represent its importance to the students' comprehension of text ideas?

FIGURE 5.4. Questions on sociocultural context.

Retelling is an authentic task representing how we at all ages share our thoughts about the texts around us. Teachers also learn how to interpret and evaluate students' retelling, generating data that guide instructional responses and acknowledgement of students' capabilities and needs.

Procedures

1. The first step for **preparation** is reading the text that you choose and generating notes about main ideas and supporting details.
2. Next is sharing the text with the students (they may read aloud with you, read independently prior to meeting with you, or you may choose to read to them), along with practice sessions for the students to learn what is expected of them when they retell the text information during the unaided and aided retelling.
3. After the students have read the text, provide retelling supports as needed. It may be helpful to provide blank guides to support their retellings. For narratives, the form illustrated later in the chapter with an outline of story elements (Figure 5.7 on pp. 144–145) is useful; for prompting retellings of expository texts, the form presented in Form 5.1 is useful. You may find that students will need to use these blank guides as they retell texts during the actual assessments. Alternately, students may find it helpful to draw a simple sketch of text ideas to support their retellings. Each can support students' recall and organization (without "giving them the answers").

   Plan to gradually withdraw these supports so that students can organize their information without a guide. Keep notes on the quality of retellings that are conducted with and without supports to determine what may be needed for each student.
4. **Plan** for several practice sessions, usually with small groups of students. Start the learning process by modeling how you could organize your retellings, referring to the guides described above and illustrated in our figures. Depending on the length of the text or passage that is read, the teacher may prepare students for retelling the story or the text from beginning to end or instead to retell a preselected section of a (longer) passage.
5. **Preview** the process you will implement during both the unaided and aided retellings.
   - Start by telling students that they will be retelling the text by pretending they are telling the story or talking about the text to someone who has not read it. [It may seem odd to them, at first, when you ask them to retell a text that they have read silently or you have just read to them, and thus provide only a summary. *After all, you have both just read or heard the full story and students may wonder why they are asked to repeat it!*]
   - Plan to implement guidance, as needed, with comments or questions such as, "Can you tell me more about that? What did you mean when you said that?" This guidance, however, is minimal and only required if students seem to get stuck or stop their retelling.
6. Next during the **preparation** is the ***text selection,*** the choice of ***activity/assessment strategy,*** and the ***sociocultural context.*** See Figures 5.2, 5.3, and 5.4 for questions that will guide your preparation in each of these areas.

7. During the **implementation** of the retelling assessment strategy, ask general questions, as needed, that will move the retellings along. The first part of the retelling is the *unaided retelling:*

   - Begin the retelling by asking students to pretend they are telling the text to a friend who has not read the text.
   - Begin the retelling on a positive note (e.g., thanking students for their reading of the text getting us ready for the retelling, showing interest in their retelling!).
   - Occasionally, students have difficulty getting the retelling started. To be supportive, be patient and wait. Also, it might be helpful to have the students close their eyes and think about the text before starting. Some general prompts may be needed, such as, "How would you tell this story to a friend who hasn't read it? Where would you start?"
   - Take notes quietly during the retelling on the prepared notetaking sheet (see the figures and forms presented later in this chapter).
   - As the retelling proceeds, there may be times when the student stops and may need some coaching to continue, such as, "What else would you tell a friend about this text?" (This prompt is especially important for the students who stop after giving a brief summary of the text or if they retell only a part of the text.) Avoid accepting "I don't know" and instead encourage students to think again about the story and share what else they might remember.

   The second part of the retelling is the *aided retelling:*

   - When the student has stopped the retelling, go back over your notes and ask open-ended questions that will extend what has already been shared. Stay close to their retelling ideas when asking them to tell you more about those ideas. For example, "In the beginning of your retelling, you said this, can you tell more about that?"
     - Some examples of open-ended questions are "Tell more about the character" (that the reader mentioned); "Why do you think the character did that?"; "Why do you think that event happened?"; "Which words did the author use to describe the characters?"; "The problem and solution?"
     - Then focus on the text elements—if an informational text—for example, "What do you think was the main idea of the text? What details support that main idea?" Or focus on the story elements—"Where did the story take place? What was the main problem? How was it resolved?"
     - Include questions, as much as possible, that invite deeper thinking, such as, "What questions were you wondering about as you read the text? Do you think the author was trying to teach you something? Does this story remind you of another story that you read?"
     - Additionally, you might decide to tape record the students' retellings so that you can refer back to the taping for your analysis of the retelling. Tape recording the retellings for later listening, however, can be very time consuming and probably is not necessary once you have practiced with a few student retellings.

Collecting, Analyzing, and Using Data

Taking notes during the retelling is important so that you can capture information about the retellings, such as the following:

- what information is shared
- how information is organized
- how important to the text the information is that is shared
- possible strategies used to retell—such as starting at the beginning of text and moving through it sequentially versus starting at the beginning, going to the ending, and then filling in details, or starting at the end and moving back to the beginning and moving forward
- references to prior knowledge and experiences, use of home languages
- stating information that is interesting or "boring"

Analyze each student's retelling to identify patterns of strengths and needs. Learning about students' capabilities to retell texts provides information about their comprehension of main ideas and details, their use of prior knowledge to aid their comprehension, their understanding of vocabulary, their organization of ideas to provide a coherent recall, their interests and use of strategies to make connections across ideas, and their overall understanding of the text. With this information, you are generating implications and directions for your text comprehension instruction.

Collecting and **analyzing data** takes less time with practice. Initially, plan on about 10–15 minutes for students to retell the text, and about 10–15 minutes for analysis (with practice, however, the analysis can be shortened to about 5–10 minutes).

Plan to administer retellings at least four times a year, but many teachers with whom we have collaborated administer weekly retellings, using the scoring sheets we describe below for quick checks of students' comprehension. Some teachers start with the scoring procedure illustrated in Form 5.2 (with 10 questions) for scoring and analyzing weekly or monthly retellings; as teachers become more familiar with retellings the additional procedures are added to the assessment process.

There are at least five ways to collect and analyze retellings, including the use of pausal units, text structural organizers for narratives and expository texts, concept maps, and questions to guide analysis. We illustrate these ways in the following sections.

Collecting and Analyzing Retellings Using Pausal Units

Pausal units can be used when students are retelling relatively short texts or perhaps just a few paragraphs of a longer text, with about 10–25 sentences. For example, if a student is retelling the short poem *Quite an Adventure,* we notice that there are two sentences with multiple phrases. Each sentence is divided into pausal units, defined as the places where you pause when reading the passage. See the slash (/) marks on the passage in Figure 5.5.

Next, write the pausal units in the middle column of a notetaking sheet (see Figure 5.6). Then, examine the pausal units and identify the most important and least important units. Number these units from *1* to *3*, with *1* indicating the most important text information and *3* the least. In the third column, number the order of the student's recall sequence (e.g., what is said first, second, and so on). If you wish you can add spaces between the units, to record what the student says if the text retelling changes the actual wording of the text. A space at the bottom of the form is provided for teacher notes. We provide an example of the process used to collect and analyze retelling data with pausal units in Figure 5.6 (p. 142).

Quite an Adventure

Mrs. Hen, /one sunny day,
Took her chickens /for a walk,
Dick, the youngest, /strayed away
While his mother /stopped to talk.
Then he saw /the strangest sight,
'Twas a monster aeroplane,/
But it gave him /such a fright/
That he scurried /home again!

FIGURE 5.5. Example text, *Quite an Adventure*, parsed with pausal units.

Collecting and Analyzing Students' Retellings with Narrative Guides

The following items represent information that may be included in a narrative retelling; these may vary depending on specific information that is or is not provided in the narrative. Also, these may vary by name or content depending on your instruction and/or expectations. For example, you may identify a problem solution chain as one category instead of a separate heading for resolution (as shown in Figure 5.7, pp. 144–145), or you may include the initiating event as part of the plot episode chain (Morrow, 1986, 2020).

Note. For the purpose of this example of a notetaking form and to adhere to copyright laws, we provide a synopsis of text information in the second column. For your purposes, you may provide either synopses of text information or actual text excerpts taken from your texts of choice.

Collecting and Analyzing Students' Retellings with Informational/Expository Guides

The descriptors presented in Form 5.1 identify information that may be represented in a retelling of an expository/information text. These descriptors may be changed to match the content of your texts of choice. Data are analyzed qualitatively as you identify patterns of strengths and needs. We inserted a column for you to note expected responses for key components (e.g., main idea/concept, supporting details, important inferences, and so on).

Collecting and Analyzing Students' Retellings with Hierarchical Concept Maps

Another way to analyze students' retellings of informational/expository texts is to first draw a teacher-made hierarchical concept map of the text ideas (Asan, 2007; Gowin & Alvarez, 2005), as illustrated in Figure 5.8 (p. 146), and assign points to each element on the map, noting higher-level information that is supported by lower levels of details. This scoring scheme provided in Form 5.2 is especially helpful and explicit about students' identification of major text concepts and higher-level details supporting those concepts versus recalling mostly lower-order details.

Note. It is possible that students have been taught to generate their own concept maps, and if so, ask students to draw a concept map of the text they have read and talk

Directions: Write the student's comments in the spaces next to the pausal units and number the sequence of student's recall of text information in the third column.

Student: Randy **Date:** ____________

Importance (1–3)	Text Pausal Units		Recall sequence
1	**Quite an Adventure**	*It was an adventure*	1
1	1. Mrs. Hen		2
3	2. one sunny day		
1	3. Took her chickens	*and her chickens*	
1	4. for a walk	*were walking*	3
1	5. Dick, the youngest	*Dick*	
1	6. strayed away		
2	7. While his mother		
2	8. stopped to talk		4
2	9. Then he		
1	10. saw the strangest sight	*saw something strange*	5
1	11. Twas a monster aeroplane	*it was a monster airplane*	6
2	12. But it gave him		
1	13. such a fright	*he was scared*	7
2	12. That he scurried		
1	13. home again.	*And he went home*	8
Total number of units – 14 (with title)			
Number of units recalled – 8			
Percentage of units recalled – 57%			
Sequence evaluation – Very Good			
Importance level recalled – 90% (9/10)			
Teacher Notes after Retelling			
I identified Randy's strengths and needs with this analysis. I noted that Randy recalled 57% of the pausal units and included the main idea represented in the title. Randy did not add information to the text. He retold information sequentially, focusing on the most important information. He retold 9 of the 10 most important units, He omitted the information about Dick being the youngest chicken, about mother stopping to talk to others, that Dick strayed away, and that Dick scurried home. He did not make personal connections to the story or an adventure. She concluded that Randy had a strong focus on main ideas and a few supporting details. For my future instruction, I will focus on generating details that support action and that signal the cause of problems.			

FIGURE 5.6. Notetaking with pausal units during student retelling of *Quite an Adventure.* (Student comments are *italicized.*)

about the map for their retelling, starting with "the main idea or concept in this text was" and then continuing with the retelling while referring to the content on the map. Students may generate additional information, but the map provides another source of data for your analysis.

Collecting and Analyzing Students' Retellings with Questions Guiding a Qualitative Analysis

We provide a fifth method for analyzing students' retellings in Form 5.3, a tool that can be applied to retellings of both narratives and expository texts. This is the most streamlined version of analysis for retellings, yet it provides a careful analysis of retellings and is useful for identifying students' strengths and needs for instructional purposes (Irwin & Mitchell, 1988). For this analysis, first generate a written record of the student's retelling (taking notes on top level of data form) and then analyze the retelling by answering the questions that follow.

Making Students and Teachers Visible

Asking students to retell a text that they have read or heard acknowledges to students that how they are thinking about the text and organizing its information is important to you as their teacher. Not being prompted by teacher questions, students take responsibility for what they want to share about the text—the ideas that are important to them, the connections that they make with their own experiences and language, and the organization of ideas that makes sense to them. Made visible then are how students are making sense of the texts they read and the agency they assume when retelling. Additionally, the teachers' role in making sense of the retellings makes visible their observations of the students' strategies and retelling choices. During this process, teachers generate notes about whether students focus on the most important ideas versus less important ideas, if there are personal connections to the text that support comprehension, and if the retelling generates a text that is meaningful—all of this information guides instructional planning. The data and analysis are extremely useful for helping teachers build on what their students know and can do and the areas where further growth might be needed.

Implementation Example

Mx. McCloskey, a fifth-grade language arts teacher, developed and is teaching a unit on the perseverance of inequalities in our society. Mx. McCloskey is nonbinary and uses the pronouns *they*, *their*, and *them*. This language arts unit is part of a larger unit that integrates social studies and a focus on the Great Depression. Mx. McCloskey plans to make connections with inequalities experienced in contemporary society and most specifically inequalities that were revealed during the pandemic of 2020–2021 and beyond. Mx. McCloskey's school is located in a low-income neighborhood. Many of the students and their families experienced difficulties during the pandemic, and recovery continues to be slow. Some students experienced limited access to broadband Internet capabilities, a problem that continued to exist as students began to return to school. Many students experienced food and housing insecurities. Some families moved to family shelters where

Directions. Place a checkmark or assign one (1) point to each element of the story that the student includes in the retelling. One-half (½) point may be assigned if partial information is provided. Follow unaided retelling with teacher questions that are provided.

Student: ______________________ **Date:** ______________

Story elements (organized for unaided retelling)	**Expected response/synopsis of story and teacher notes** Text: *Bud, Not Buddy* by Christopher Paul Curtis	**Student's retelling**
Setting and Characters: Student's retelling includes: • An opening statement • Main characters • Character traits–for all characters, for some characters • Time • Setting/Location *Initiating Event:* Student identifies/describes: • Event(s) that starts the actions of the story or causes the main character to react *Theme:* Student identifies/describes: • Main problem to be resolved and/or goal of main character	Opens at the orphanage Main characters are: Bud Caldwell (10 years old) and Jerry Clark (6 years old) Bud and Jerry are fearful of foster homes Bud holds back his tears–they have stopped coming, but Jerry cries. Bud gives advice to Jerry, trying to help him see that good things can happen–compassionate Bud worries about Jerry because he is only 6 years old and lots happens to a 6-year-old (e.g., losing teeth).	
Plot Episodes: Student's retelling includes: • *Main events/episodes of actions* • *Series of events told in sequential order (all events or partial events)* • *Connections between the events*		

<table>
<tr><td>Resolution:
    Student's retelling includes:
    • Problem/goal solution
    • How character(s) solves problem or meets goal
    • Story ending
Personal Reactions:
    Student may include:
    • A personal reaction or connection to the story theme/events
    • A critique of the story

Highest Score Possible:

Student's Score</td><td></td><td></td></tr>
<tr><td>Questions asked after the retelling is completed (aided retelling):

Ask students to "evaluate" their retellings

Return to retelling and ask questions for clarity or additional information that was not in the retelling

Ask students about vocabulary that may be unfamiliar

Ask questions about vocabulary, if not generated above, such as, "What words did the author use to describe the orphanage? The foster homes? The characters? Jerry's problem? Bud's problem?"

Ask students if they thought text was interesting or important and why?

Ask students how they evaluate their retelling.</td><td></td><td></td></tr>
</table>

FIGURE 5.7. Analyzing narrative retellings with story elements.

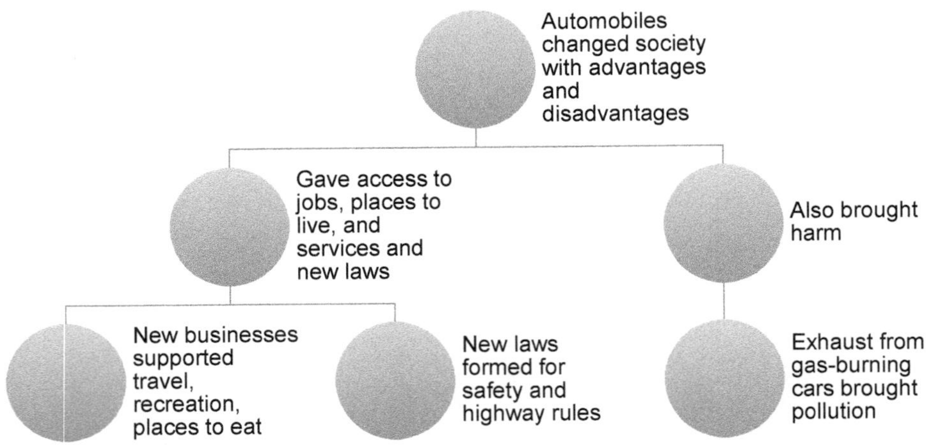

FIGURE 5.8. Example of a concept map to analyze retellings of informational/expository texts background. This teacher-drawn concept map focuses on text that described advantages and disadvantages of the invention of an automobile.

they are remaining for this school year. Some families moved in with other relatives, and others lost one or more parent or another family member to COVID illnesses (during 2020–2021 school year).

Mx. McCloskey plans to ask the students to read *Bud, Not Buddy,* written by Christopher Paul Curtis, as the first text of the unit. This text choice is part of the conceptual unit focusing on the Great Depression and builds on the knowledge that students are acquiring about this historical period. The setting for this text is the Great Depression, in the year 1936, and the story opens with a caseworker assigning two students who live in an orphanage to two foster homes. The students are reading the text independently and/or listening to it with headphones at the listening center. Mx. McCloskey, who read and studied the text prior to meeting with the students, asked them to reread and discuss selected parts of a chapter, or a whole chapter, during small-group instruction.

It is the third month of the school year and the second week of the unit. During the first week of the unit, the students as a whole class viewed and discussed videos and short-text passages about the Great Depression. Students demonstrated their feelings about the hardships with drawings and by writing essays. A few students shared the experiences of their great grandparents, with stories that they heard from their parents. They talked about food shortage and bread lines, and the housing shortage, with many families losing their homes. On Monday of the second week of the unit, the students began to read *Bud, Not Buddy*. Mx. McCloskey decided to ask each student for an individual meeting to talk about selected sections of the text using a retelling assessment activity. Mx. McCloskey wanted to examine the students' comprehension of this text and the concepts associated with the Great Depression. Choosing this activity early in the unit of instruction will enable support for students' comprehension strengths and needs so that each student is building on and extending their knowledge.

Mx. McCloskey **prepared** for the retelling assessment activity by reading and rereading the choice of text and by studying carefully and answering the questions posed in

Figures 5.1 through 5.4. Next, Mx. McCloskey **prepared** the students for the retelling assessment, used for the first time with these students. The students engaged in group retellings about the texts they were reading. Mx. McCloskey modeled thinking and demonstrated explicitly how to organize their thoughts around a story outline (as illustrated in Figure 5.7) that was shared with the students, identifying elements: setting and characters, initiating event, theme, plot episodes, and resolutions. Mx. McCloskey called their attention to possible new vocabulary while modeling thinking about these words. Mx. McCloskey told them when and where the story took place and the problems the characters faced. This preparation occurred each day of the week, with students gradually taking more of an active role in the group retelling. Some days they wrote on the story charts (e.g., as illustrated in Figure 5.7) and other days they used the headers (e.g., setting, time) to guide their retellings.

Prior to administering and **collecting data** with the individual retelling assessments, Mx. McCloskey read and reread the first chapter of the selected text, *Bud, Not Buddy*, and **prepared** a blank story element chart for each student. Mx. McCloskey then completed the chart as a guide to evaluate each student's comprehension (see Figure 5.7). Mx. McCloskey will ask each student to choose a time during the week on a sign-up sheet for an individual meeting to retell the first chapter of *Bud, Not Buddy*. Students were reading the first chapter independently prior to the retelling activity. Mx. McCloskey is eager to learn about the students' comprehension of the text—the connections they may be making, their understanding of central themes, and their possible misunderstandings. Mx. McCloskey will continue to assess their comprehension of this book during the next few weeks and continue the retelling process with additional texts throughout the year.

This morning, Mx. McCloskey is meeting with Jack, who often says that he likes to read, but that he sometimes "skips part of the book I am reading if it is not interesting." Mx. McCloskey is interested in Jack's performance on this first chapter, wondering if he will skip over some of the details about the orphanage and the boys in his "hurry to read the rest of the book."

After greeting Jack, Mx. McCloskey explains that Jack is to retell the first chapter (eight pages) of *Bud, Not Buddy*. Mx. McCloskey explains that, after the retelling, Jack can go back and add information that he remembers but didn't include in the retelling, explaining that there will be some questions following Jack's retelling.

Mx. McCloskey then says, "Now Jack, please retell the first chapter of *Bud, Not Buddy* as if you are telling this information to someone who has not read it. You may use this story guide, if you choose, to help you remember what happened in the first chapter. I will make notes on my chart so that I can remember what you said." Jack's retelling data for both the aided and unaided process are reported in Figure 5.9 (pp. 148-151), and a qualitative analysis of the retelling and a summary of his retelling notes are presented in Figure 5.10 (p. 152)

Mx. McCloskey later that day **analyzed Jack's retelling** performance and concluded that Jack had a strong recall of the story elements, as he correctly identified the characters and setting, the initiating event, the theme, the sequence of events, and the resolution of the problem. He offered details to support his retelling of actions. He made personal connections to the problems in the text (i.e., the boys did not have a home), and he shared his reactions to characters (e.g., I didn't really like the caseworker as she didn't sit down and talk with the boys and help them make the move). He understood that Bud is growing up

Student: *Jack* **Date:** *October 15*

Story elements (organized for unaided retelling)	**Expected response/synopsis of story and teacher notes** Text: *Bud, Not Buddy*, by Christopher Paul Curtis	**Student's retelling** Jack, October 15
Setting and Characters: (5 points) Students' retelling includes:		
• An opening statement	Opens at the orphanage, Bud says "Here we go again"	• *The story happened in 1936, it was the time of the Great Depression*
• Main characters	Main characters are: Bud Caldwell (10 years old) and Jerry Clark (6 years old)	• *The main characters are Bud and Jerry. There is also someone called a caseworker*
• Character traits–for all characters, for some characters	Bud and Jerry are fearful of foster homes Bud holds back his tears–they have stopped coming, but Jerry cries. Bud gives advice to Jerry, trying to help him see that good things can happen–compassionate Bud worries about Jerry because he is only 6 years old and lots happens to a 6-year-old (e.g., losing teeth).	• *I didn't really like the caseworker as she didn't sit down and talk with Bud and Jerry about their new home* • *just gave them orders* • *They must be scared to leave each other but she doesn't help them to not be scared*
• Time • Setting/Location	1936 During the Great Depression, Muncie, Indiana	• *Told time—1936, and Great Depression above*
Total for Jack–4 points (omitted town), told information without T probing		
Initiating Event: (2 points) Student identifies/describes: • Event(s) that starts the actions of the story or causes the main character to react	There are two initiating events 1. Caseworker tells Jerry and Bud they will move to foster homes 2. Bud has a flyer about Herman E. Calloway, a musician. Bud thinks he is his father and plans to find him when he comes to Muncie, Indiana	*The action starts when the caseworker tells Bud and Jerry where they will go when they leave the orphanage.* *I remember that Bud says, "here we go again"* *He tells the caseworker that he is Bud, not Buddy.*
Total for Jack–2 points (only one initiating event)		

<table>
<tr>
<td>Theme: (2 points)
Student identifies/describes:
• Main problem to be resolved and/or goal of main character

Total for Jack–1 point (main goal for story/Bud not identified)</td>
<td>Main problem/goal set up for the story–Bud is looking for his father and a home with him

Goal of first chapter–to find a home that is a good fit</td>
<td>Bud and Jerry are scared about leaving as they didn't like the foster homes where they went before.</td>
</tr>
<tr>
<td>Plot Episodes: (minimum of 4 events for 2 points)
Student's retelling includes:
Main events/episodes of actions
• Series of events told in sequential order (all events or partial events)
• Connections between the events

Jack has 2 points</td>
<td>1. Bud and Jerry are living in an orphanage, which isn't anything like a "home"
2. Caseworker tells Bud and Jerry they will be sent to foster homes–Bud will have an older brother; Jerry will have three sisters
3. Jerry cries, Bud holds back the tears
4. Bud consoles Jerry, trying to convince him that his home will be good with three sisters
5. Boys clean their room and pack their belongings
6. Bud packs his flyer about Herman Calloway</td>
<td>Jerry is to go to a home with three girls and Bud will go to a home with a 12-year-old boy. Bud doesn't cry no more about these homes and leaving the orphanage.

The caseworker takes them out of line. She tells them they won't have time for breakfast but that she has some fruit for them to eat in the car. She tells them to go and pack their bags and to get ready to leave. She tells them they are lucky to have new homes but they don't feel lucky.

Bud tried to help Jerry who was crying—told that the girls will help him in his new home and really like him and hug him all the time, but he—Bud—will probably have to fight the older boy in his family. He could be hit, like Bud was in a foster home when he was younger.</td>
</tr>
<tr>
<td>Resolution: (2 points)
Student's retelling includes:
• Problem/goal solution
• How character(s) solves problem or meets goal
• Story ending

Jack has 1 point–shared how boys prepared for the move, did not explain how the flyer was important to this chapter and the story.</td>
<td>1. Boys prepare to go to their foster homes
2. Bud keeps flyer and his hopes to see his father
3. Says "here we go again"</td>
<td>Then the boys fixed their beds and packed to leave.
Bud has a suitcase—other children just had paper bags. He also has a flyer that he found when his mother died.
Bud says, here we go again.</td>
</tr>
</table>

(continued)

FIGURE 5.9. Example of analyzing narrative retellings with story elements.

<table>
<tr><th>Story elements
(organized for unaided retelling)</th><th>Expected response/synopsis of story and teacher notes
Text: Bud, Not Buddy, by Christopher Paul Curtis</th><th>Student's retelling
Jack, October 15</th></tr>
<tr><td>Personal Reactions: (1 point)
Student may include:
• A personal reaction or connection to the story theme/events
• A critique of the story
Jack has 1 point

Highest Score Possible: 14 points
Student's Score: 11/79% agreement</td><td></td><td>I liked the story okay. I feel sorry for Bud and Jerry. I have two friends who don't have their parents, but they live with their aunts. They didn't have to go to an orphanage or a foster home.</td></tr>
<tr><td>Ask students to "evaluate" their retelling
• Thank you, Jack for sharing your retelling! How would you evaluate your retelling of the first chapter? What was good about your retelling?
• Would you make any changes to your retelling?</td><td></td><td>I thought my retelling was good—maybe not very good, but close to very good. I remembered the characters and their fears about moving to foster homes. I described Bud and Jerry. And I explained how the chapter ended. I would not make changes.</td></tr>
<tr><td>Return to retelling and ask questions for clarity or additional information that was not in the retelling.
• Thank you, Jack. I agree that your retelling was good. You remembered many details and events that occurred in the first chapter! That will help you understand the next chapters.
• Let's think again about the chapter. You said that the boys were living at an orphanage at the beginning of the chapter. Describe what you learned about living at the orphanage.
• We learned about Bud and Jerry–how would you describe their relationship with each other?</td><td></td><td>It was not like home. Everyone had to stand in line for things, such as their food. They had lots of other kids in their bedrooms and they were bad if they misbehaved.
I think they were good friends. And Bud was very caring of Jerry . . . he tried to help him see the good in his new home. He consoled him when he was sad.
I think Bud did console Jerry—tried to make him feel better and to be calm.</td></tr>
</table>

• Interesting that you choose the word *consoled* to describe Bud's actions. We talked about that word last week–how does it fit Bud?		
• Why do you think Bud told the caseworker that his name is Bud, not Buddy?		Buddy is a baby name, and he is older now.
• Why did the author tell us that Bud was able to hold back the tears, that they "didn't come anymore"? Why is this important information?		Bud is older and doesn't want Jerry to see him cry. Also, we are learning that Bud is taking charge of what is happening to him. . . . My mother tells me that I do that—because I am getting older and I want to set an example for my little brother. I think Bud is doing the same.
Ask students about vocabulary that may be unfamiliar • Were there words that didn't make sense to you? What did you try to do to figure out its meaning? Was that helpful? What could you do next time?		There was that one word—flyer—I could pronounce it but I didn't see how it was important. We get flyers from the grocery store that my mother throws away. The flyer in the story was about a singer and Bud thinks it is his father, but it probably isn't.
• Why do you think that the man named in the flyer is probably not Bud's father? • Well, we will learn more about this as we read. You made a reasonable prediction. • How is the word "flyer" relevant to the name Harold Calloway?		I think it is probably not his dad . . . the name is different—Caldwell and Calloway and that would be too unreal.
• What do you think will happen to help Bud solve the mystery of his father?		I think somehow Bud will meet Harold Calloway and learn the truth.
• Bud says "here we go again" two times in this chapter. Why did the author tell us that?		I think the author tells us that because Bud has been sent to different foster homes before. That is sad.
Additional possible questions • Did you like this chapter? Did you learn something new? Did you try new strategies to help you understand the story or the words? Do you think you will enjoy reading the rest of the book? Why or why not?		I just read all the words and thought about what they meant and I didn't need to try any of our new strategies. I like action stories better, but I will learn more about Bud and this Harold Calloway and this is somewhat interesting to me.

FIGURE 5.9. *(continued)*

Student: *Jack* **Date:** *October 15*

Questions	**Teacher observations/analysis**
1. Did the student include information that is directly stated in the text?	Yes
2. Did the student generate plausible inferences about information that is stated directly or indirectly in the text?	Yes
3. Did student include the main ideas or most important ideas of the text?	Some of these
4. Was student's retelling accurate?	Yes—sequential, across episodes
5. Did student explicitly apply comprehension strategies, such as connecting prior knowledge to text to support sense making, generate summary statements, generate generalizations or conclusions that relate to the real world, revise retelling during the process seeking accuracy, and/or make explicit connections across ideas?	Connecting to prior knowledge Made explicit connections across ideas Generated summary statements
6. Did the reader identify and define possible new vocabulary, including disciplinary vocabulary, that was embedded in the text?	Contained few disciplinary vocabulary, made personal connections to the word *flyer* to understand it but didn't understand its significance to the story. Understood words such as *foster home* and *orphanage*.
7. Did the student ask to look back at the text or illustrations/photos to support retelling?	No
8. Did the reader provide personal, creative, or affective responses to the text?	Yes—especially affective responses to boys and their life in an orphanage and foster homes
9. Was the retelling organized logically while representing accurate content?	Yes
10. Did the retelling demonstrate appropriate language conventions (e.g., sense of audience, sentence structure, use of text vocabulary)?	Yes
Other	

FIGURE 5.10. Qualitative analyzing of text retellings. The following list of questions is provided to guide observations and notetaking when analyzing students' retellings. This information would be included in the teachers' note section and applies to scoring with pausal units, story elements, or informational text units (Irwin & Mitchell, 1988).

and wants to be called Bud (not Buddy). Jack literally defined *flyer* but didn't understand the importance of the flyer as an initiating event for future actions. He predicted that Herman Calloway would not be Bud's dad. While preferring action stories to this one, he expressed interest in continuing with it to learn what happens, and he thought his retelling performance was good using descriptors that corresponded to their study of narratives (e.g., characters and events, the problem). For future instruction, Mx. McCloskey plans to meet with small groups of students once the retellings are completed and review the first chapter. During that review, Mx. McCloskey will ask students to talk about the "flyer" and to identify reasons for the author including that information. This will lead into a discussion of the importance of initiating events and clues that authors provide to forewarn students about upcoming happenings.

Mx. McCloskey is pleased with the retelling assessment strategy. For Mx. McCloskey the **value** of listening to each student's retelling far outweighs the use of the end-of-chapter questions that are provided in the teachers' guide. Mx. McCloskey was able to **make visible Jack's comprehension,** his personal connections, his organization of ideas, his evaluation of the text, and his elaborations on each of the story elements. In the past, the use of questions in the teacher's manual typically resulted in one-word answers or less information about how the student was making connections about the parts of the story. Mx. McCloskey felt that the retelling **made visible the power to guide Jack's retelling** during the aided portion, and to **analyze useful information** that will inform instruction.

VARIATION OF ASSESSMENT STRATEGY 5.1.
Retellings with Students' Multimodal Representations

We have collaborated with teachers who are helping their students develop multimodal representations of the texts they are reading. Multimodal projects can vary widely, with students developing comics or graphic novels (with or without written text), newspapers, posters, story boards, and digital texts. Each text that is created typically has more than the written text, but would include drawings, sketches of people or events, layers of paper adhered to each other to enhance drawings, development and/or selection of photos and digital artwork, and so on. If creating digital texts, drawings and selected music can accompany the texts that are written and/or students may dictate the text for each of the drawings they provide on the computer screen. As students make decisions about the modes they want to convey meanings of texts represented in their retelling, they are deepening their comprehension and their ability to communicate that meaning with others.

1. ***So how can these multimodal representations enable a retelling assessment?*** Following are procedures to engage students in multimodal text retellings:

- What comes first? Engage students in multimodal text development by first examining models of projects—for example, graphic novels developed by students, a digital story on the computer developed by the teacher and/or students.
- With teacher guidance, they discuss the composition and the audience. The teacher

would provide modeling with examples and support to each student or groups of students.

- Next, students in pairs, small groups, or independently identify their audience (e.g., parents, students in another class, peers in the classroom).
- With teacher guidance, they *set a goal* (e.g., tell the events of the first chapter of *Bud, Not Buddy* during the depression era and living in an orphanage without a home). Next, they would learn to *create a story board* that might include these steps—identify idea to be developed, learn about the information with resources, *collect photos or illustrations* (e.g., orphanages in history, photos of the Great Depression), and last, *put it all together* to create the text.
- Next, they find resources (pens, different colors of paper, digital editing materials) and learn how to incorporate these into a draft of their final project.

2. ***How can I collect assessment data with multimodal text retellings?*** Retelling data are collected on the selected retelling analysis forms identified above once the "text is created" by asking students to tell the text that was created. Additionally, talking with students during the process provides additional data about the students' thinking—their choice of topics, resources, and their interpretations and conclusions.

3. ***Are there examples that would help me develop this procedure?*** Frequently teachers in your school are developing multimodal projects in their classrooms, and they may provide examples and advice for developing these texts. Talk with your colleagues and seek their advice. Additionally, Bridget Dalton and her colleagues provided examples and procedures for developing digital texts and retelling procedures (Dalton et al., 2015). Vivian Vasquez (2010) demonstrated how to implement and develop multimedia/digital texts within text sets to enhance comprehension.

The Think-Aloud for Tapping Students' Comprehension

Asking students to "think aloud" about what they just read is valuable for informing teachers and students about how they are thinking about and processing text information. This assessment activity occurring during the reading of text makes visible students' thinking *during* reading instead of *after* the reading of a full text or text selection. With a think-aloud as an assessment strategy, students reveal their comprehension of the text *and* multiple skills and strategies, such as their use of prior knowledge, how they may be using the context of what has been read so far to clarify meanings of vocabulary, and/or if students are questioning as they read while trying to make sense of the text. Like the retelling strategy that was introduced previously, students will require instruction with teacher modeling and practice using the think-aloud before it is used as an assessment strategy. Further, like retellings, thinking aloud about segments of a text is a strategy that students can adopt and use independently for self-monitoring and enhancing their comprehension. Also, think-aloud as an assessment strategy can be embedded within instruction by asking students to take turns during a small-group activity while you take notes and other students continue to read. The think-aloud can also be a focus on individual conferences that you hold with students about their reading.

ASSESSMENT STRATEGY 5.2.
Think-Alouds

Purpose

Asking students to think aloud about parts of a text that they have just read makes visible how they are constructing meaning and if they are monitoring their own abilities to make sense of the text. A few pages of text are parsed into meaningful units, such as a sentence or every few sentences, a paragraph or maybe two paragraphs, and students are asked to explain what they are thinking as they are reading. Students need to be taught how to "think aloud" while reading through explicit instruction, and such demonstrations can help them understand how readers "monitor" their own comprehension.

Value

As students learn how to think aloud about texts they are reading, they are learning to be strategic to support their comprehension. With continued practice, the think-aloud activity makes visible, to both teachers and students, how they are monitoring their comprehension. Making visible the skills, strategies, and self-monitoring capabilities provides a rich source of information to inform instruction and teachers' evaluations. The *Think-Alouds* assessment procedure is highly engaging as an instructional tool. Additionally, teachers' observations and analysis of students' think-aloud comments make visible their ability, quite explicitly, to capture their students' comprehension strengths and needs—the "thinking in the head" of students becomes visible and when captured provides teachers with information that will guide instruction and supports for each student.

Procedures

1. **Preparation** begins with explaining the *Think-Alouds* procedure to your students and engaging them in two to three practice sessions prior to using it for assessment purposes. These sessions can occur during whole-class instruction with additional practice during small-group meetings.

2. **Prepare** a list of think-aloud strategies that you will want to model for your students during the practice sessions and encourage them to use these as they practice their own think-aloud strategies. See Figure 5.11 for a listing of possible strategies that students use to support their text comprehension.

3. **Plan** for your practice sessions by including the following components:

    - First, name the *Think-Alouds* assessment strategy and explain its purpose. For example: "Today you will be reading short segments of a story/text and then asked to tell what you are thinking as you read." Additionally, you might say, "When we read, we think about the words on the page and their meanings, we try to make sense of the photos or illustrations. These are all the things you do as a reader."
    - Second, model the think-aloud strategies you are using by reading a small

section of the selected text (i.e., one sentence at a time or one paragraph at a time) stopping to share what you are thinking at each pause.

- When modeling, you might tell your students "I will demonstrate what I would say during a think-aloud if I am reading the first lines of a nursery rhyme (or another text of your choice). I am reading *Humpty Dumpty*." Continue to model thinking after each text section, as follows. (See full example in Figure 5.12, illustrating what teacher says and comments).

Helpful Strategies
Restatement–student presents literal paraphrase of idea
Rereading–student will read phrase or part of text to understand (may explain this)
Use of text elements–student refers explicitly to illustrations or text markings provided by the author and/or illustrator
Personal identification–student uses background knowledge, experiences, or feelings to relate to passage
Stated failure to understand word or idea–student actually states that they don't understand word or ideas
Stated success to understand word or idea–student states that they understand a word or idea
Use of context to define a word–student explains that they decided meaning of a word by using context, may continue to read and then confirm the meaning
Elaborate and infer–student adds information to story, makes inferences, and elaborates on text in plausible ways
Synonym substitution–student uses another word for word in text
Metaphors–student says that one thing or idea is "like" another
Hypothesis generation–student makes predictions, or questions what they are reading
Use of information about the story–student relates information of theme or "big idea" of text to understand ideas that follow or refers to previous parts of text to assist comprehension of text or to represent a "running story"
Visualization or imagery–student describes mental images or what "they see"
Self-questioning–student questions idea to decide meanings of words or ideas
Nonhelpful Strategies or Reasons Student May Not Be Strategic with Meanings
Decoding–student has problems with the word(s), can't pronounce, and makes no attempt to fix-up for attaining meaning
Limited knowledge about text concepts or background knowledge–student doesn't have information to support getting meaning from text
Strategy not relevant–student uses illogical strategy, or uses tangential or unrelated information
Use of nuclear referents–student describes ideas with vague "he" or "she," not identifying referent of these pronouns in a meaningful way

FIGURE 5.11. Strategies that students may display during think-aloud.

- After reading the line "Humpty Dumpty sat on a wall," you might say the following: "I see that Humpty Dumpty looks like an egg in the photo. I wonder why he is sitting on a wall and how did he get there? Notice how I used the photo to help me identify Humpty Dumpty. Also, I asked questions because I didn't understand why an egg would be sitting on a wall."
- After reading the next line, "Humpty Dumpty had a great fall," you might say, "I was thinking 'Oh no! If the egg falls, he will break. I dropped an egg off our kitchen counter just this morning and it made a mess on the floor. I think Humpty Dumpty will make a mess on the ground.' Notice that here I made a connection to my own experiences and I made a prediction about what will happen to Humpty Dumpty."
- After reading the last line, "All the King's horses and all the King's men couldn't put Humpty together again," you might say, "I was right, Humpty Dumpty broke into pieces and made a mess. I wonder though why the King's horses would be brought in to put the egg back together. That really doesn't make sense." Here the teacher is demonstrating a confirmation strategy, questioning the content, and concluding that part of the text did not make sense.
- Engage students in the guided think-aloud, during which you practice together, guiding their use of strategies; additional practice can follow with peer groups practicing the think-aloud strategies.

4. **Decide** if students should read and think aloud after each sentence or after each paragraph. Typically, younger readers might think aloud after reading each sentence within 10–12 consecutive sentences; older students might think aloud after reading each paragraph within a 5–8 paragraph segment. The goal is to provide a sufficient amount of text for the students to read so that you can identify patterns of strategies that they may be using to make sense of the text. Typically, students would start reading at the beginning of the text, or at the beginning of a new chapter. However, this procedure might vary depending on your goals. For example, it could be that you will want to assess how well students make sense of a middle part of a text or a chapter when the information becomes more challenging or technical.
5. As you **prepare,** review the strategies you expect your students might use. You will code the strategies displayed by students' during their think-aloud (Olshavsky, 1977; Wilhelm, 2001). We offer a suggested list of strategies your students may use in Figure 5.11.
6. Finally, **prepare** your data collection process, as described in the next section.

Collecting, Analyzing, and Using Data

There are two considerations for data collection. First, you might want to tape record and, if possible, transcribe what each student said during the *Think-Alouds* assessment. This, of course, is the most thorough method for data collection but not the most practical. With practice, notetaking is sufficient for record keeping and data analysis without tape recording the process. Second, identify a notetaking method that is useful for you for **collecting and analyzing data.** Here are suggestions.

- Photocopy the sections of the text that the students will read (with a photocopy for each student) and then beside each printed text segment on your copy, write the student's think-aloud statements. If you find there is insufficient space for your comments, the next procedure may be useful.
- Set up a data sheet as illustrated in Form 5.4. We provide an example of student data and teacher comments in Figure 5.12, as illustrated with the *Humpty Dumpty* text and example above. The tool for collecting each students' think-aloud statements lists each text segment that the student will read followed by a second column for recording what the students says, and a third column for teacher notes and analysis. Strategies students are using are identified in the third column.

Making Students and Teachers Visible

There are multiple advantages to asking students to think aloud about their reading. It helps students make visible and monitor their own thinking and how they are organizing and interpreting the text. It also makes visible to students the strategies they might be using, or need, such as rereading sentences, looking back at earlier text parts to make connections, defining vocabulary words within the context of this new text, and so on. These strategies also become visible for the teacher and provide the opportunity to observe the students' thinking and to make connections to past and future instruction. Decisions for instructional direction, that are teacher-directed rather than following a script in a manual, are made visible with the analysis of the think-aloud comments; actual data are provided to support teachers' independent planning.

Text segment	Student's think-aloud statements	Analysis of think-aloud statements
Humpty Dumpty sat on a wall.	*I see that Humpty Dumpty looks like an egg in the photo.*	Referred to the photo in the text. Uses prior knowledge (egg lookalike).
	I wonder why it is sitting on a wall? How did it get there?	Self-questioning
	Notice how I used the photo to help me identify Humpty Dumpty.	Stated success to understand an idea.
	Also, I asked the question—why would an egg be on a wall?	Stated success to understand an idea.
Humpty Dumpty had a great fall.	*I knew that would happen.*	Confirms his prediction; states success to understand.
All the king's horses and all the king's men couldn't put Humpty together again.	*He couldn't be fixed. A cracked egg can't be put back together.*	Literal restatement. Use of prior knowledge.

FIGURE 5.12. Example of what might be said during a practice think-aloud session: Humpty Dumpty example with analysis.

Implementation Example

Ms. Johnson is a second-grade teacher who began her teaching at the Wickley Elementary School 7 years ago. Wickley is located in a city center and children from the neighborhood attend this school. About 33% of the students come from low-income families. Twenty-three languages are represented in the school, with the majority of students speaking either English (67%) or Spanish (24%) at home. Ms. Johnson lives in the community and often takes part in a community theater for Black artists.

While the students in Ms. Johnson's class are referred to as "strong readers" by the school principal (they score average or above-average on oral reading and decoding tests), Ms. Johnson is worried about their comprehension beyond the literal level. She observes that her students often read words correctly when reading aloud, and they answer correctly most literal questions that appear on the school tests, but they don't seem to bring their own imagination, interpretations, and world experiences to what they are reading. This year, she has extended her emphasis on telling stories through songs and with the dramatic arts, often writing short plays for her students that invite them to express themselves by "making believe you are the character in the play. Become that person!" Ms. Johnson has also placed more emphasis on the use of comprehension strategies to support comprehension, as illustrated above in Figure 5.11.

To address her concern about text comprehension, Ms. Johnson decided to develop a literacy unit around a set of wordless picture books. In small groups, she and her students have "read" the books *Tuesday* (about an unpredictable Tuesday) by David Wiesner, *Sidewalk Flowers* (about the experiences of a father and daughter as they find wildflowers on their walk and small acts of kindness) by JonArno Lawson, and *Pool* (about two shy children who meet and become friends at a pool, and their imagination takes them on an underwater journey) by Jihyeon Lee.

Early in the unit, Ms. Johnson modeled her own thinking by demonstrating how to read the clues from the illustrations to interpret and make sense of the illustrations. She carefully modeled the think-aloud strategies that are presented in Figure 5.11 at each stopping point where she demonstrated her own think-aloud. Gradually, she shared the think-aloud strategy with her students, asking them to read as a group short sections of text and guiding their think-aloud activity for each of the sections as they read the text. Ms. Johnson has kept notes about her student observations, and she is learning that her students are participating and using their strategies and language and their imagination to explain the text segments. They seem to be comprehending the books and frequently they identify that they are strategic (i.e., "I understood that illustration or that word"; "I am picturing that as I read"). Yet students' sharing of their understandings and think-aloud statements is more representative of "group talk." Some students seem to wait for others to lead, offering few of their own interpretations or strategies. The question now for Ms. Johnson is about individuals and if this unit is impacting the use of strategies to support the comprehension for every student. For that reason, Ms. Johnson is meeting individually with students and asking them to think aloud while "reading" the illustrations on each page of the wordless book *Journey*, by Aaron Becker.

To prepare for administering the *Think-Aloud* assessment strategy, Ms. Johnson first examined and addressed the questions identified in Figures 5.1 through 5.4. She is confident that the days of practicing the strategies has helped prepare her students and they understand what is expected of them when she asks them to "think aloud."

Ms. Johnson provided two implementation examples for the *Think-Alouds* assessment strategy. The first was to engage students in a think-aloud with a wordless book. The *Think-Aloud* was implemented after the second-grade students had practice "reading" wordless books and participating in a group think-aloud. The second was to examine students' think-aloud while reading a text that was part of a text set that was organized around major concepts. Ms. Johnson was interested in knowing if understanding an earlier text would support comprehension of a related text and if students would draw on their prior knowledge, as a comprehension strategy.

Today Ms. Johnson is meeting with Christina. Christina is bilingual (fluent in both Spanish and English) and one of the students in her class described as a "strong reader" because her reading accuracy on short passages is typically 98–100%. Her retelling scores typically are at or above 80%, but most often she has more difficulty with higher-level questions (inferential, critical thinking).

To begin the session, Ms. Johnson and Christina look at the book jacket of *Journey* (illustrating a girl in a boat traveling into a huge castle, or maybe it is fort). Next, they flip through each page, with Christina commenting on what she sees in each illustration. Occasionally, Ms. Johnson asks only four guiding questions to support the development of the text using only the pictures: "What else do you see?", "What do you think that means?", "What do you think will happen next?", and "How did you know or how did you figure it out?" This last question focuses specifically on strategies that students might be able to name and recognize they are using. Ms. Johnson explained to her colleagues that when she first started to use the think-aloud strategy, she asked many, many questions but gradually found that just a few prompts were needed as students learned to think aloud as they practiced this activity with different texts. Fewer questions enabled the students to share what they were thinking, and it enabled her to hear the voices of her students as they demonstrated strategies they used to make texts "come alive for them."

Ms. Johnson was eager to analyze Christina's think-aloud performance that is presented in Figure 5.13. Ms. Johnson concluded that Christina applied multiple strategies to her reading. She made connections within the text to support comprehension of the title and events, she asked herself questions to guide her thinking and stated her success in understanding, she drew on her prior knowledge to interpret events and differences between modern-day methods of transportation and former ones, she provided multiple details of the illustrations, she generated multiple inferences about the girl and being lonely and a metaphor ("this is just like me"), and she generated hypotheses about future events. Each of these strategies supported her comprehension as she made sense of text ideas and vocabulary.

A few weeks later, Ms. Johnson met with each student and asked them to "think aloud" about the book the class was reading, *How the Stars Fell into the Sky: A Navajo Legend*, by Jerrie Oughton. This text is part of a text set that has engaged the students for 3 weeks to learn about Native American's folktales. They are talking about the contribution of these folktales to the history of the United States. Last week they read *The Story of the Milky Way: A Cherokee Tale*, a tale about when the world was new and there weren't many stars in the world and the problems created by a giant spirit dog who was forced to go into the sky and became a great band of stars, the Milky Way.

The analysis of Christina's second think-aloud statements, presented on Figure 5.14 (p. 163), provides a rich source of information about Christina's text comprehension.

Text: *Journey* by Aaron Becker **Date:** November 5	**Student's think-aloud** Christina	**Teacher coding of strategies applied by student**
Opening: Ms. Johnson opens the reading by saying "Today we are going to read a book called *Journey* by Aaron Becker. There are no words in this book. You will be the author and tell the story from the illustrations.	I know what "journey" means—it means going on a trip, like in that book—A Ticket Around the World—that you read to us.	Stated success in understanding the title–drawing on her prior knowledge of the book that was read to her in class.
Book jacket with title, author *A little girl, holding a red marker is in a red boat moving in water toward a big castle/walled town.*	This little girl has a red pencil or marker and she is sitting in a red boat—going on a journey—and it looks like she is going toward a big castle. The doors are open for her to enter. I wonder if she is afraid all alone in the boat.	Stating what is shown on the cover/illustration. Self-questioning–Will girl be afraid?
Endpapers at beginning and end of book *Numerous methods of transportation are shown–sailboats, train, air balloon, car, airplane.*	These pages show different ways we can go away . . . Oh I get it, different ways to go on a journey—there are many sailboats—that one looks like a pirate ship. There is an air balloon and an airplane—it looks different from the Delta plane I saw at the airport. So we can take a journey on a boat, an air balloon, a boat—not a pirate ship—or a car.	Inference–makes connection between objects and title. Draws on prior knowledge to name objects, differences from modern day methods of transportation. Elaborates on illustrations and uses information about the illustrations to connect to journey/ways to travel.
Title page Title and author, *Little girl on a red scooter. Brick wall, Chinese lantern hanging on a tree. Street sign with bus stop times.*	Here we meet the girl at the beginning of the story. She is riding a red scooter. There is a street sign and a funny lamp on the tree.	Stating what she observes in the illustration. "funny lamp"–does not know its name but knows infers that it is a lamp.
Pages 1 and 2 *Three children playing, boy stands alone with purple marker in his hand; girl has her scooter on the pavement as she sits on stoop of a house, looking sad.* *In the house, Dad is working at his computer in a home office, Mother is cooking and on the phone in the kitchen, sister is reading and on her phone on the couch in the living room.*	And now we meet a boy with a purple marker. The girl is not talking with him but she is sitting on a step outside of a house. It must be her home because we see inside. Her dad is working in his office, her sister is reading a book, and her mother is talking on a phone. No one is talking with the little girl.	States details of the illustration. Inferences–about her home, parents and sisters, and no one is talking with her.

(continued)

FIGURE 5.13. Example of a data sheet for collecting and analyzing think-aloud statements.

Text: *Journey* by Aaron Becker **Date:** November 5	**Student's think-aloud** Christina	**Teacher coding of strategies applied by student**
Page 3 *Girl takes her red scooter in the house and tries to talk with mother, who is on phone, then takes a red kite to Dad but he is busy on the computer, then she goes to her sister with a red ball but her sister is busy.*	The girl takes her red scooter to her mother, she takes a red kite to her Dad's office, and she takes a red ball to her sister. This is just like me—sometimes I don't have anyone to play with me and my family ignores me.	States details of each illustration. Metaphor and personal identification–"this is just like me."
Page 4 *Girl goes to her room and sits on her bed . . . looking sad. Cat is sleeping, air balloon hangs over her bed and a map of the world is on the wall.*	She looks sad and alone . . . she is not even playing with the cat that is sleeping. Look there is an air balloon in her room—that journey again!	Inferences–about girl's feelings. Uses information about theme/title to make connection to later part of text–about the air balloon in the room–journey again.
Page 5 *Girl looks at the floor . . . sees papers on the floor and a red marker. Cat is walking out of the room.*	I wonder what she will do with that red marker. She had it in the boat on the cover.	Uses information about theme/title to make connection to later part of text. Self-questioning–red marker in the boat on the cover.
Page 6 *Girl begins to draw . . . a round top, it is a red door and she opens it and walks through it.*	This is make believe, it isn't real—she draws a door with her red marker and walks through the door.	Hypothesis generation to draw conclusion–this is make believe.
Pages 7 and 8 *As she comes out of red door, with the red marker in her hand she walks into a forest . . . with a stream. The forest is lighted with many Chinese lanterns. It looks misty.*	That is beautiful . . . a beautiful forest and those lights . . . [looks back to title page] the same lights that we saw there [pointing to title page] are everywhere. This looks like a fantasy land.	States what she sees. Makes connection of information on the title page–the same lights are everywhere. Elaborates with inference–this is like a fantasy land.
Pages 9 and 10 *Girl walks over to little bridge and sees her reflection and the reflection of the red marker. She leans over and draws a boat on the water and then gets into the boat.*	Oh no! Now she is drawing her red boat and will sail away in it . . . to the castle that we saw before.	States what she sees. Inferences–she is going to the castle.
Page 11 *The row boat is moving with the girl in it down the stream. Now we see that she will enter a town with bridges and domed buildings. It is more than the castle that was shown on the book jacket.*	It is a very big castle—this is a fantasy land—maybe it is more than a castle but a fantasy land. Now I wonder if the boy with the purple marker will be there???	States what she sees. Confirms inference–this is a fantasy land. Self-questioning–will we see the boy with the purple marker, brings story information forward.

FIGURE 5.13. *(continued)*

Text: *How the Stars Fell into the Sky: A Navajo Legend* by Jerrie Oughton **Date:**	**Student think-aloud** Christina	**Teacher's records/notes**
Title page	*This story goes with the one we read last week about the Cherokee Tale. How we got a Milky Way of stars.*	Draws on background knowledge related to prior instruction, and brings forward previous story read in class.
Page 1: The day ends and becomes night. The First Woman tells the First Man–our people need to see our laws.	*They want to write the laws for everyone.*	Literal restatement– does not mention the characters.
Page 2. Illustration of Navajo woman and man standing in a desert–cactus plants in illustration.	*All those plants that are in a desert—like our terrarium. They must live in the desert. We read that some Native Americans lived in Arizona, that has a desert.*	Personal identification–draws on background knowledge about plants, desert, and Navajos in Arizona.
Page 3. Illustration of dark brown waves. The man suggests writing laws in the sand; but the woman says they will blow away.	*I didn't think that was sand in the picture—but I see that it is. And sand does blow away—like at the beach.*	Use of text elements–explains failure to understand illustration of sand. Draws on background knowledge–sand will blow away, like at the beach.
Page 4. Illustration of dark blue waves of water. The man quickly says to write the laws on the water. But the woman says they can't do that because they will disappear right away.	*That is the waves of the water . . . but you can't write on water.* *You can write with water, like those pens that have water and colors appear on the page.*	Uses text element and prior knowledge–waves of the water in abstract illustration. Prior knowledge–you can't write on water. You can write with water.
Page 5. The man looks at the woman and sees stars–her jewels–all around her . . . "like a blanket." Then write them in the sky! Use your jewels to write them.	*Jewels to become stars. . . . Does that mean her necklace or are those jewels that look like stars on the blanket?* *The Milky Way folktale also had few stars in the sky—is that why these folktales talk about stars all the time.* *Were there no stars in the sky already?*	Lots of questioning here–seems to be unsure of what is meant by stars and jewels–and writing with these. Asks question–self-questioning. Makes connection for former Milky Way folktale. Sets up questions that we will need to address with additional resources.
The woman begins to place stars in the sky, writing the laws.	*I wonder what she is writing, what are the laws.*	Self-questioning continues.
A coyote appeared and offered to help her.	*Oh no . . . the coyote will cause trouble. Just like the dog did in the Milky Way story.*	Personal knowledge, making connection to previous text again. Generates hypothesis–coyote will cause trouble.

FIGURE 5.14. Example of a data sheet for collecting and analyzing think-aloud statements. A summary is provided for each page, rather than the original text.

Christina's performance revealed a strong use of her prior knowledge (e.g., you can't write on water) and drawing on prior readings to help her understand this new text. She asked questions that were important and will require us to read some additional sources. She shared excellent questions and monitoring of her own understanding. For future instruction, Ms. Johnson will return to the notion of "writing with jewels" to put stars in the sky—a tricky concept that was not understood, and one that is central to understanding this text.

Overall, Ms. Johnson shares with her colleagues the **value** of the *Think-Alouds* assessment strategy. She tells them that it provides a "window" into her students' thinking and consequently provides data that help her understand the strategies her students are using, the ones that they need to develop, and if and when they are monitoring their own comprehension. Plus, she realizes that with the use of the think-aloud strategy she is better informed—"oh so much better," as she would declare! She is **making visible** her knowledge about her students and her application to guide her instruction in ways that are specifically responsive to each student's needs and strengths.

VARIATION OF ASSESSMENT STRATEGY 5.2.

Think-Alouds with Translanguaging Applications for English Learners

Ms. Johnson is teaching in a school where multiple languages are represented. In her second-grade classroom, she provides opportunities for her students to meet in small groups to discuss the texts they are reading—some are texts that the teacher reads to them, some are texts read during small-group instruction, and some are texts that students are reading independently. The texts include wordless books, as described above.

Ms. Johnson has learned that the translanguaging strategy has at least three benefits. One, it honors students' languages and demonstrates the value of having multiple languages to support text comprehension (e.g., as students connect words across languages or events across countries and customs). Two, comprehension is supported through the opportunity to discuss with peers and elaborate on text meanings. Thus, leveraging students' strengths supports their learning and comprehension. Three, students seem to be more engaged with the text and realize they can be successful when provided a chance to talk with peers. Additionally, parent support is very popular in Ms. Johnson's classroom.

1. ***How can a translanguaging activity enable students' think-aloud performance?*** Following are procedures to engage students in translanguaging to support the *Think-Alouds* assessment strategy:

    - The translanguaging activity begins with the teacher modeling the process. For example, Ms. Johnson invites students who have similar home or first languages to meet with her in small groups. Ms. Johnson is a fluent Spanish speaker but often she invites parents or a bilingual teacher representing other home languages to meet with her and her groups of students. Teachers who speak English only can follow the same procedure, asking students to tell the text in their own languages to demonstrate the process and/or invite parents or the school's bilingual teacher to support the modeling process.

- During the practice sessions, model a think-aloud strategy following a procedure very much like the one illustrated above. For example, Ms. Johnson selects text segments within the English text and models her thinking in Spanish or asks the parent or colleague to do the same in the chosen language. She might read part of a text in English or ask the parent/colleague to read parts of the text. They, too, would model their strategies in the home language of the students in the group.
- While practicing, students then are asked to talk with a partner in their home language about texts they are reading, sometimes sentence by sentence or after a few sentences. Then students come back to the group and share what they were discussing.
- After several practice sessions, implement the think-aloud procedure by (a) identifying text parts students are to read and discuss with peers who speak a similar home or hybrid language, (b) telling students to push back their chairs from the table or group so they can talk with each other, (c) asking students to then come back to the group and explain what they discussed, and (d) taking notes on the data forms for each student, recording what students share with the group, their disagreements and agreements, and their use of strategies to resolve text meanings.

2. ***How can I collect think-aloud assessment data with translanguaging?*** Think-aloud data are collected on the notetaking forms we provide above and the procedure follows the steps above with the added ones for translanguaging. Data are collected for each student in the group as they share their thinking in English, and after their discussions with peers using their home languages. Thus, native English teachers take notes when students are sharing their thoughts in English. If you speak the home languages of your students, you may decide to take notes in the home languages and in English. For example, Ms. Johnson, who is fluent in Spanish, takes careful notes both during the peer-group discussions and within full-group discussions. At times, she invites a parent or the school bilingual teacher to observe her students who speak a language other than Spanish. She observes think-aloud strategies but also rich discussions among the students—often disagreeing with each other and learning strategies to come to a conclusion about the text meaning.

3. ***Are there examples that would help me develop this procedure?*** Iddings, Risko, and Rampulla (2009) provided an example of a third-grade teacher, who was a native-speaker of English, during the implementation of a translanguaging activity. Demonstrated are the interactions between the students and the teacher and the supports to aid comprehension and students' think-aloud actions. Daniel, Jiménez, Pray, and Pacheco (2017), bilingual teachers, provided examples of the use of scaffolds to support translanguaging and students' comprehension, aiding think-aloud performance.

Questioning to Assess Text Comprehension

The strategy that we recommend for *Questioning of Text Comprehension* is one that engages students in a discussion of their interpretations of the text ideas. Too frequently, text questions are shallow and ineffectual during assessments and instruction (RAND Reading Study Group, 2002). They can focus primarily (or solely) on literal recall of details, giving the students the impression that they are to memorize the facts as they read so that they can tell these back during the discussion. Instead, we recommend generating questions that invite both literal and higher-level comprehension of text, questions that attempt to have students connect the ideas as they develop a coherent understand of text meanings, and questions that make visible students' thinking and use of strategies.

The greatest limitation to *Questioning of Text Comprehension* as an assessment strategy is its design; questions represent the understandings and ideas of the person asking the questions. Thus, they frequently impose interpretations and understandings *on the reader* and direct how and what students are thinking about the text (Lipson & Wixson, 2013) and the answers they provide. Often these are heavily text dependent, signaling to students that they are to memorize information that can be lower-order details and not connected to main ideas. We strongly recommend that questions be asked after first capturing students' thinking that is independent of prompts. For that reason, we recommend starting with retellings and/or think-aloud assessments followed by questions. Both retellings and think-aloud assessments make visible how students are constructing their knowledge and text understandings. As we take notes about their thinking, we find windows of opportunity to ask questions such as "Can you tell me more about that?" or "You described the character as *bizarre*—what did you mean by that? What does that word mean?" Revisiting what the student has said usually leads to questions that follow naturally and can include "tell more," "explain further," or "can you summarize all that you said about the pelican and its habitat?" Additionally, you may find that entire sections of a text were omitted, and thus questions might take the student back to the text to assess comprehension (e.g., "I noticed that you didn't talk about the text section focusing on predatory birds. What did you think about that information?").

For the most part, our comprehension questioning strategy emphasizes open-ended and more general questions, such as "tell me more," while also focusing on the range of comprehension skills students are learning (as presented in Figure 5.15). The questioning procedures we recommend are flexible in style and can be applied to all texts regardless of structure or purpose. Our strategy design avoids taking students through the text in a linear progression (e.g., what happened first, what happened next, what is next?) unless sequencing is your specific goal for that selected text. The progression of questions we recommend would also avoid following a strict adherence to the text structure unless that is your instructional goal. For example, a narrative is written to include elements such as the setting, characters, problem, events, and problem solution—and while we would embed questions about these elements within the questioning procedure, we would not take students through each of these step by step (e.g., first, what is the setting; second, who are the characters) as though we are following a story grammar formula to develop the questioning.

We avoid the above two questioning procedures and associated explicit examples because too often they signal to students that they are to remember the facts or details as the most important aspect of comprehension. Also, progressing through the lineup of questions illustrated in the above examples can reduce attention or avoid altogether the central concepts and the depth of meaning that the authors convey. The end result may be a factual recall of details that may be "accurate" but are not conceptually coherent (Risko & Walker-Dalhouse, 2012). For example, students reading an informational text about pelicans might recall the details about their physical characteristics, their eating habits, and their habitat, and miss entirely the author's discussion of why their webbed feet are important for swimming or their cooperative behaviors when they fish and fly together, or the important ecological role they play in the food chain.

Across instructional plans, commercial programs, and testing programs, questioning remains the most used strategy for assessing comprehension. Some questioning procedures are not helpful for either assessment or instruction. For example, as we discussed in Chapter 4, an IRE pattern, a teacher-led question-and-answer procedure, focuses primarily on literal thinking and moves quickly, without much time for student thinking. Instead, we recommend attention to open-ended questions, ones that probe more deeply in response to students' answers, and ones that create dialogue to assess how students are constructing knowledge from their texts. Additionally, even though there are numerous ways to classify questions (e.g., literal, inferential, evaluative, critical), there are numerous debates about these classification systems, and in the end, we find that definitions for each of these can vary greatly and there is limited evidence that parsing questions into a wide variety of "levels of questions" adequately or accurately represents different "levels of thinking" (Lipson & Wixson, 2013).

Given the above concerns, we have two recommendations:

1. First, worry less about how you are labeling the questions. We present labels for our questions in Figure 5.15 because those are ones that are useful for us. You may be more

Question types	**Focus of questions**
*Prior knowledge/funds of knowledge	Asking students what they knew about the topic or experienced. Could include questions students had before reading the text
Literal	Recognizing/recalling factual content
Inferential	Reasoning about content based on evidence
Application	Using and applying information (may include predictions)
Analysis/Evaluation	Judging worth and value, contribution
*Vocabulary	Asking students meanings of words in passage, including discipline-specific vocabulary. What did that word mean? Did the author's use of that word help you understand that part of the text? How?
*A summary question	What was this text all about?
Student question(s)	Student generates questions, spontaneously or with prompting, asking the author or seeking other sources
*A personal reaction question	Do you think this text was worth reading? Why?
*A personal reflection/self-evaluation question	How do you evaluate your comprehension of this text? Explain.

FIGURE 5.15. Types of comprehension questions. We recommend that you add the questions with an asterisk (*) to any questioning scheme you implement.

familiar with another classification system and you may have learned a system that lines up with your school curriculum and your teaching goals. We recommend that you keep labeling the question types that you have practiced and that match up well with your expectations of what are considered plausible answers for the questions you ask; thus, you will meet the criterion for choosing (and labeling the) tasks that are appropriate for your context and your students. To us, how questioning is implemented and the associated results are far more important than what the questions are called.

2. Second, start the process of questioning about a text by first asking students for a least a brief recall of the text—what do you remember about the story or text you just read? The information provided sets the scene for further elaboration and critique, and your questions then are tailored to start with the students' own thinking before going deeper into the text information, as appropriate and relevant to your goals.

The questioning procedure we illustrate in the following assessment activity extends beyond the two recommendations we make above. It seeks to assess students' understanding of central text concepts and their supporting details, to assess whether students are comprehending the text as a coherent whole rather than its bits and pieces. This strategy is one we recommend both for comprehension assessment and for instruction, as it signals to students that organizing what may at first appear to them as disparate facts actually are supportive of each other when developing our understanding of texts. For example, once students understand the concept that pelicans have an important ecological role in the food chain, the details of a pelican's physical (e.g., webbed feet), behavioral characteristics (e.g., moving and flying in groups), and eating habits (e.g., eating some small vertebrates and bringing home the food of the day) are more easily remembered and understood. Students are not recalling a set of isolated facts that might not add up to a more complete understanding of pelicans and their significance in the environment.

Since questioning strategies are frequently embedded in text discussions, we suggest that, when appropriate, you collect data on individual students during text discussions. Setting up data sheets for each student, especially during small-group or individual conferences, can support data collection that is embedded within your instructional routines.

In the following example of our assessment strategy, we develop further our notion of text questions that aim to measure students' understanding of coherence and the melding of the important concepts and ideas with their supporting details.

ASSESSMENT STRATEGY 5.3.

Questioning of Text Comprehension

Purpose

Questioning for text comprehension is designed to make visible students' comprehension of text concepts and supporting details. The questions require students to recall, interpret, integrate, analyze, and evaluate text information. Additionally, the questions ask students to derive main ideas and major text concepts and to use and apply information to solve problems, make predictions, and/or identify future questions to be answered. As students are answering the questions, teachers can observe and document what students are remembering, the connections they are making across text parts, their use of prior knowledge, and the strategies they draw on to support their thinking.

Value

Understanding how students are comprehending texts lies at the heart of literacy instruction, for our goal as literacy teachers is to support students' text comprehension, their strategic use of meaning-getting strategies, and their developing knowledge. Additionally, questions include open-ended directives, such as, "What were you thinking when you answered that question?" and once asked, these can encourage students to self-evaluate their own thinking.

Procedures

1. The first step to **prepare** is to refer to Figures 5.1 through 5.4 to guide your consideration of the reader who will be assessed, your choice of text, the design of the assessment activity, and elements of the sociocultural context. You will be identifying what you know about the **reader**'s instructional, sociocultural, and linguistic histories and how you might draw on that information as you use questions to assess text comprehension. For the **text choice**, you will decide if it will be a narrative or an informational, digital, poetic, or wordless text. How you design your activity will establish your procedures.
2. When you think of the information in Figure 5.3, specific to your questioning procedure and consistent with the style of those questions are these additional ones:
   - Should I provide aids to support comprehension, such as an outline of a story grammar or an informational text map? Perhaps younger students' comprehension would benefit with the use of puppets or props (and these were used previously during the practice sessions). Perhaps students are keen to dramatize parts of the story.
   - Decide if you will allow text look-backs to aid students' recall, and if so, under what circumstances and how often.
   - Should I read the text to the student for a listening comprehension activity, or if the student is reading, should they read orally or silently?
   - Did I prepare my students to understand what is required of them when I ask questions seeking specific types of information (e.g., literal, inferred, evaluative)?
3. Next is **preparing** a set of questions to initiate and sustain the conversation around the text. Expect that additional questions will be accessed naturally during your conversation and when needed for clarification of ideas.

   - Start with the types of questions (using labels that are familiar to you). The question types may vary by name but should include the ones that assesses the range of skills represented in Figure 5.15. Note that questions on the figure include those that identify students' funds of knowledge or prior knowledge. We always ask students what questions they might have for the author or that would take them to additional resources.

- Refer back to Figure 5.7 (on story elements) or Form 5.1 (on informational text elements) to further guide question development, as appropriate for instructional goals and text choice. For example, you may ask students where and when the story took place (setting questions) or what started all the action or problems in the story (initiating event question).
- If seeking an organization for your questions, you might consider organizing them as in Figure 5.15—around those questions that seek literal (in the text) information, inferential information (going beyond the text or putting ideas together across text parts), critiques of information, and personal reactions and evaluations (how this makes sense to me and the world). Added to this are questions that focus on concepts (what the text is all about). *Not in this order, though, as questions should be embedded naturally and as appropriate within a conversation rather than presented as a drilling procedure!*

4. During **implementation** of the questioning strategy:
   - Plan to start by asking the reader to tell what they remember about the text.
   - Following this brief retelling, implement questions to help the reader elaborate on what they have just said, and to access the forms of information that you are seeking (e.g., narrative information).

Collecting, Analyzing, and Using Data

The most important procedure for implementing the questioning assessment strategy is to plan to engage in a conversation with your student, listening carefully to what each student says, and build off what they have shared with the next questions that you have planned. Be prepared to follow a different order to the questions, taking the lead from the student's comments and add or delete questions, once again as appropriate to continuing the text conversation. This is not an opportunity for a fast-paced questioning and answering session, but instead the opportunity to query the student's thinking by acknowledging and building on what they are sharing.

When preparing to collect data using the questioning strategy, prepare a notetaking record sheet, such as the one presented in Form 5.5, listing the questions you plan to ask, a column to record the student's responses, and a column for your interpretations and notes. You might want to add extra rows allowing you to add questions based on what your student is telling you about the text. Also, consider if you should tape record your conversation.

Making Students and Teachers Visible

Asking students questions about their reading with open-ended and probing questions that are embedded within text conversations makes visible how students are coming to understand the texts they are reading, including their understanding of both literal and higher-level information and the strategies they apply to merge text information with their prior knowledge, their experiences, and their expectations for the text. Teachers also make visible their own thinking about texts as they generate questions and initiate deeper conversations about texts, thus, providing a wealth of information about students' text comprehension and their expectations and use of information they are gathering.

Implementation Example

Mr. Rabin has been teaching fourth grade for 20 years, and for the last 5 years he has taught science and the English language arts at an inner-city school, the Phoenix school, that stresses teaching across the curriculum, with science, math, and history integrated with the English language arts curriculum. Problem-based learning units organized around major concepts engage students in identifying and solving real-world problems. A mid-income community with most parents working in local factories, restaurants, or grocery stores, students' parents and families are often engaged in the units of instruction (e.g., planting and tending to organic food gardens while studying plant growth and problems associated with pesticides). Thirty-three languages are represented in this school, with the primary languages of English (67%) and Spanish (29%), and a small number of Haitian (2%) and Somali (2%) languages. Most children in Mr. Rabin's class have attended the Phoenix public school since kindergarten and will go on to a middle school when they enter fifth grade.

Mr. Rabin and his students are engaged in a 6-week unit focusing on the climate, with two major threads: (1) impact of climate change on weather conditions, and (2) harsh weather conditions that don't seem to be related to climate change. For both, Mr. Rabin's students are learning about the effects of these two conditions and identifying what they can do in response.

Mr. Rabin's students are identifying problems associated with weather conditions and setting goals for themselves and their families that will help them know how to respond. Students are reading multiple texts, writing summaries of what they read, and meeting in small groups or individually with Mr. Rabin to discuss their readings and what they are learning. Today, Mr. Rabin is meeting with Karin to discuss *Tornado: The Story Behind These Twisting, Turning, Spinning, and Spiraling Storms,* by J. B. Fradin and D. B. Fradin (a National Geographic Book for Kids). The class has learned about climate changes due to human actions and the climate getting warmer, but this warmer climate is not making U.S. tornadoes any more frequent. Scientists are studying the relationship between tornadoes and climate change, and they are hypothesizing that climate change may have something to do with shifts in the location and the timing of tornado threats.

Listed in Figure 5.16 are the questions posed by Mr. Rabin when he met with Karin, and her answers. Before he began to ask questions, he encouraged Karin to look back through the chapter, rereading chapters—and to quickly make some notes or sketch some simple drawings to remind her of information about the tornadoes. He explained that he would ask some questions about what she read but was eager to hear her thoughts about tornadoes and possible questions she might have after reading the latest chapter. His goal was to hold a conversation about the text rather than drilling her with lots of questions, one right after the other. He often asked her to "tell more," encouraging her to elaborate on her answers. Mr. Rabin took notes as he and Karin discussed the *Tornado* text, as illustrated in Figure 5.16.

Mr. Rabin identified several strengths that Karin demonstrated during their text conversation. She brought her prior knowledge and experiences (*The Wiz* video) associated

Text: *Tornado* by Fradin and Fradin Student: Karin T. Date:

Type of question	**Student responses**	**Teacher's notes/ observations**
When we started to study tornadoes, what did you think about?	I remember when I was little watching movie The Wiz—and there was this awful sound and then a tornado took Dorothy to Kansas. I was always scared but then I couldn't wait to see it again.	K. was familiar with the sound of tornadoes. Use of prior knowledge.
Did you have questions that you hoped to answer about tornadoes?	I wonder if we could learn how to stop tornadoes.	Interesting questions–seemed to know that they are problematic–draws on prior knowledge to advance her thinking.
What stands out as the most memorable thing that you learned in this chapter, called "Twister Predictions"?	The scariest parts was the first sentence —it said that tornadoes are one of the most difficult weather types to forecast accurately!	Literal recall.
Why did that scare you? Tell more about your feelings and reactions . . .	Well., tornadoes are so dangerous and if weather forecasters can't warn us, we are all in trouble. But when people can be warned, no one may be injured—that is what happened when a second tornado hit Tinker Air Force Base in 1949.	Elaboration of literal information.
What happened when the first one hit?	The warnings didn't happen and eight people were killed, and airplanes and buildings were damaged.	Literal recall.
Why did the author write about these two tornadoes?	Because this is when they learned that weather forecasters could predict tornadoes and save lives and property. Before they thought they couldn't do this. They called this the Birth of Modern Tornado Forecasting—I love that title for a story I could write! I could apply it to Wiz!	Literal recall.
Gee that is interesting . . . How would you apply it to Wiz?	I would make drawings—one with tornado taking Dorothy to Kansas; and second one with a warning—and Dorothy has packed what she wants to take with her to Kansas! That would be cool.	Applying what she is learning about forecasting to the Wiz!
There were photos of a tornado. What do these photos tell us?	Oh, yes . . . they showed the tornado coming toward the camera than the funnel cloud, and then passing over the camera, and then going off in the distance—it was a sequence of things.	Literal recall of the photos.
That makes me wonder how tornadoes are formed . . . what did we learn?	For tornadoes to occur, they need warm, moist air, unstable weather conditions, and really, really strong wind moving in different directions—they call this wind shear. I think that is what causes those loud, loud noises of a hurricane.	Literal recall, inferences about conditions producing the sounds of a tornado.

(continued)

FIGURE 5.16. Example of questions and notetaking for responses to questions.

Type of question	Student responses	Teacher's notes/ observations
What do scientists need to know if they are going to forecast a tornado?	*They need to know how to read the radar images—they are called Doppler radar images—they have these big radar systems that detect wind speed. Wind speed is recorded . . . and then on a map there are these large, large red blobs—indicating that a tornado is in the area.*	Literal recall, vocabulary and tornado conditions described.
Did you have questions about how this works?	*Well I understand that they can detect a tornado by measuring the wind speed, but I made a note about this—it says that the radar reveals a picture that looks like a fishhook on the screen. . . . That comes from a rotating motion, the book says. But I think the author could have been more clear about this or show a picture of this . . . that is not very clear to me. I need to look that up somewhere else.*	A concept that was not understood . . . and Karin is seeking additional information–evaluates the text, having copied the sentence from the text and concluded that the author did not explain this very well. Analytical and evaluation work, seeking additional information.
That is an excellent suggestion–where will you look and will you share with me what you learn?	*I am going to go to YouTube and hope to find a picture or an illustration to help me understand this.*	Going beyond the text to seek additional information.
What words will you use to search for this on YouTube?	*Let's see—I can ask for tornado photos and Doppler—or even better—what is a hook echo for a tornado/Doppler radar.*	Good plan for seeking additional information; clear understanding of missing information that is needed.
Are there other questions you would ask the author? Other words that aren't clear?	*I would ask the author to define radar for readers who don't know what it means. I know that radar is like a detective—it detects or tells us about things, like the weather because I watch the weather forecasts with my Dad every morning.*	Strong analysis of *detects*–makes association with detective.
That reminds me, when the author uses the words "wind shear"–what does that mean?	*That means wind is crazy—going in different directions and fast, some faster than others.*	Good understanding of *wind shear.*
How do you evaluate this book–Would you recommend it to others? Is it valuable and worth reading?	*Yes, I like it—the photos and illustrations are very helpful and I learned about what causes tornadoes. I wish scientists knew more about climate change and tornadoes. We need to know more, but the author says it is difficult to draw conclusions about this. That's important to know, too.*	Connections to our climate change discussions . . . and reasoning for value of this text.
How do you evaluate your reading and understanding of this book?	*I had a very good understanding of tornadoes in this chapter, although I need to know more about that hook echo—I didn't understand that. I could define most words and I now know what cases tornadoes.*	Self-evaluation–identified strengths, misunderstanding. Corresponded to my observations.

FIGURE 5.16. *(continued)*

with tornadoes to the text to support her comprehension. Her literal recall was strong, and she often elaborated on the details and made plausible inferences. She accurately represented the text photos and graphs and accurately applied vocabulary to explain actions of scientists and tornado conditions, such as wind shear. She referred to the word *detective* to analyze the meaning of *detect.* She noted that she did not understand what was meant by a *fishhook* on the radar screen, indicating that more information is needed to understand the radar process, how tornadoes are detected, and how to interpret the radar symbols. Her self-evaluation represented what Mr. Rabin observed, and together they decided that reading additional resources was needed to support comprehension of the detection systems for tornadoes.

Mr. Rabin used his data analysis to guide his instructional decisions for the next texts he would read with Karin and other students in the class. The **value** of the questioning strategy, especially held as a conversation, helped him to probe Karin's comprehension and learn about her own interpretations and needs. Plus, this process **made visible** the information that Karin brought to the text, her prior knowledge that aided her comprehension. Mr. Rabin also **made visible** his own hunches about Karin's comprehension, confirming for him how to proceed next with his instruction.

Semantic Word Sorts to Assess Comprehension of Text Vocabulary

Students' understandings of word meanings within texts is foundational to their reading comprehension. Readers experience comprehension difficulties when they do not understand most of the words in a text or words represent important, higher-level information. To develop vocabulary knowledge, students need repeated exposure to words, opportunities to use their words when talking with others, especially during text discussions, and when writing. During instruction, students need both implicit and explicit instruction to help them gain word meanings, use them meaningfully, and understand how words "work together" to create meaningful networks (e.g., are climate words; Neuman & Wright, 2013). Numerous literacy educators provide guidance for developing students' reading and writing vocabulary, strongly recommending teaching vocabulary in rich contexts (e.g., during text discussions, mapping relationships among words) and moving away from rote learning of words and their definitions (e.g., Cobb & Blachowicz, 2014; Ganske, 2018, 2019).

As an instructional tool, semantic word sorts build students' vocabulary knowledge and knowledge of semantic relationships across words. Students, with teacher modeling, learn to apply definitions to sets of words and then place them in categories with other words that are related (e.g., climate words, weather words). As students develop their comprehension of words and their meanings, including multiple meanings and meanings that are content specific, students are building and extending their knowledge. As they learn to increase associations among words and categories of words, they are more likely to remember and use these words when talking with others, when writing, and when supporting their text comprehension.

Sorting words is also a dynamic tool for assessing students' vocabulary knowledge. Asking students to sort words by their meanings has the advantage of observing how students' think about the meanings of words and how they apply what they are learning to form relationships among words. We learn if students are building semantic and conceptual networks as they build knowledge of new vocabulary words. Semantic word sorts require students to determine the meanings, even multiple meanings of words, through categorization. When students sort words into categories, they are confirming their understandings of words, comparing and contrasting meanings of words, and determining how to classify words within semantic categories.

Semantic word sorts are frequently embedded within instruction to build vocabulary knowledge, and thus, collecting assessment data for individual students using data collection sheets for each student can occur during group instruction and/or when holding individual reading conferences.

ASSESSMENT STRATEGY 5.4.
Semantic Word Sorts

Purpose

Semantic Word Sorts as an assessment strategy provides valuable information about students' vocabulary knowledge and ability to form semantic relationships across words.

Value

To comprehend texts, students need to understand most of the words in a text. Assessing vocabulary knowledge with word sorts provides information about the knowledge students are building as they identify relationships among words. Students who are able to define vocabulary and form semantic networks among the words are more likely to remember and use these words when reading texts, in their oral language, and when writing.

Procedures

1. If your students are unfamiliar with word sorts, **plan** for several practice sessions before administering them as an assessment activity. The practice sessions, and the assessment meetings, can be implemented within small-group instruction. The practice session would include the following steps:
   - After reading sections of a text with your students, explain that "we will be reading and defining some words, taken from the text we just read. After defining the words, we will look for words that seem to be related to each other."
   - Next, show your students a set of word cards (in larger card forms so that all students can see the cards; could be projected on the classroom screen).
   - Explain what you are thinking as you read and define each card.
   - Next, model how you are forming (or placing words in) categories—I notice that *greenhouse gas, fossil fuels,* and *carbon dioxide* are words associated with climate change; and I notice that *temperature, humidity, precipitation,* and *air pressure* are weather words; so I will move these cards together and form a new grouping of the words.
   - Ask the students to take a turn defining and sorting the practice words.

- Provide each student with a bag full of words (the number will depend on your goals and age of students).
- As students read each card, ask them to define and sort the words, telling you the definitions and their reasons for placing words in categories that are teacher provided or student generated. If this is a small-group activity, take time to talk with each student about their definitions and categories.

2. Once students have had sufficient practice with word sorts, **plan** for the sorting assessment activity by first revisiting your instructional goals for word learning, and identifying and listing specific words that you expect students are learning and can apply meaningfully to categories that you choose or that they generate.
3. Next, organize the words into semantic categories and decide if you will provide the label for the semantic categories or if students will be asked to generate their own categories.
4. Choose an array of words that can be represented in at least two categories and as many as four or five, as appropriate for your students and your goals.
5. Write the words on notecards and present them to the students in a random order.
6. During **implementation,** ask students to read and define each word to themselves and then group words that seem to be related to each other, or ask students to place the word cards in the categories that you provide. Once students generate their word choices for each category, ask them to share their thinking about the words, define each word, and explain their reasoning for grouping words together.
7. It is possible that you will observe students creating and re-creating their groupings of words. When they seem to arrive at their final categories, ask students about the changes they made and why. You are learning additional information about how students are making choices about the related meanings of the words, with strategies of self-correcting or explaining that some words have multiple meanings and can be placed in two or more categories.

Collecting, Analyzing, and Using Data

Collecting student data occurs after students have made decisions about placement of words into categories. Plan to engage students in conversations about the words—how they are defining each and why they choose words for each category. Student data are collected when students explain the meanings of words and their reasoning for placing words in categories either that they generate or that are provided.

Prepare a notetaking sheet to record each student's performance when asked to define words on the word sort activity (see Form 5.6). Four columns are provided, with the first column to list the words, a second column for indicating if the word is defined correctly with a + or –, a third column for notes about what the student said, and a fourth column for teacher interpretations and notes about the student's performance.

Analyze the data to determine understandings or misunderstandings about the word meanings, identifying next steps for vocabulary instruction.

Next, prepare a notetaking sheet to record each student's performance when sorting words into semantic categories (see Form 5.7). In the example provided, words will be grouped within four categories/groups. The number of columns will vary depending on the number of categories you anticipate are possible for your choice of words. A last column is provided for teacher notes and a row at the bottom of the form is provided to record student comments. Additional columns can be added if students generate plausible categories beyond what you anticipated.

Making Students and Teachers Visible

Semantic Word Sorts is a powerful tool for making visible students' developing vocabulary knowledge and their abilities to derive semantic relationships among words; with such development the power of text comprehension and application of vocabulary that are greatly enhanced. As teachers observe this development, they are observing language acquisition as it is happening and gathering explicit data of instructional supports that may be needed to continually enhance their instruction and their students' learning.

Implementation Example

We are returning to Mx. McCloskey's classroom to observe how *Semantic Word Sorts* are administered to assess students' vocabulary development. Recall Mx. McCloskey is a fifth-grade language arts teacher who is teaching a unit that integrates social studies and the English language arts to focus on the Great Depression. Currently they are reading *Bud, Not Buddy*, by Christopher Paul Curtis, as the first narrative in the unit.

Today, Mx. McCloskey is administering the *Semantic Word Sorts* assessment activity with small groups of students who will gather at the communication table within the classroom. Mx. McCloskey's first group of students is composed of five students, including Jack. We met Jack earlier in this chapter, when Mx. McCloskey analyzed his retelling.

First, Mx. McCloskey distributed a set of 12 word cards, prepared prior to the group meeting, for each student in the group. The following words were taken from the first five chapters of *Bud, Not Buddy*:

> *temporary, cheerful, tiptoed*
> *crouch, frightened, frown*
> *limited, nudge, helpful*
> *glum, foster care, grateful*

Mx. McCloskey set out the array of 12 cards and explained that each student was to do the same, and then read the words, think about how to define them, and then organize them in groups that seemed to fit together. Students were to generate their own categories. Mx. McCloskey asked the students to work independently and silently for this activity. After providing sufficient time for students to work independently, Mx. McCloskey conferenced with each student as they shared their definitions of words and the semantic clusters they formed, explaining why words were chosen for each set of words.

Jack's performance on word definitions is reported in Figure 5.17. Mx. McCloskey noted strong understandings of the selected words, with the exception of the word *glum*. Jack explained that he didn't use that word and was unsure of its definition. Ms. McCloskey plans to revisit this word and other words that students confused in future instruction.

Next, Mx. McCloskey analyzed Jack's performance when forming semantic categories. His performance is reported in Figure 5.18. Once again, Mx. McCloskey observed Jack's strong understanding of the targeted words, with the exception of *glum*. Jack was able to explain his reasoning for his choice of categories and seemed to have a strong understanding of the semantic relationships among the words.

Mx. McCloskey plans to implement the semantic word sort assessment strategy on the next day, with categories that will be teacher generated. First, Mx. McCloskey will

Student: Jack **Date:** ________

Words	Definition met expectations	Student comments and/or definitions	Teacher comments/ interpretations
temporary	+		
crouch	+		
limited	+	Like limited supplies of pens	Good association
glum	?/ +	Not sure, I think it means sad. I don't use that word.	Will return to this word in next chapters
cheerful	+		
frightened	+		
nudge	+		
foster care	+		
tiptoed	+		
frown	+		
helpful	+		
grateful	+		

FIGURE 5.17. Student performance on semantic word sort.

Student: *Jack* **Date:** ______

Words to be sorted	Group 1	Group 2	Group 3	Group 4	Teacher notes
	temporary	*nudge*	*glum*	*cheerful*	
	foster care	*crouch*	*frown*	*helpful*	
	limited	*tiptoed*	*frightened*	*grateful*	
Student explanation of semantic grouping:	"short amount of time"	"actions of Bud" when trying to leave the Amos home	"Sad/worried feelings of Bud"–so *glum* had to go here as it didn't fit the cheerful words that are opposite. It just sounds sad.	"Feelings that are opposite to what Bud felt"	Strong performance for generating semantic categories–we will revisit *glum*

FIGURE 5.18. Student performance when sorting words into semantic categories—*Bud, Not Buddy*, Chapters 1–5.

ask students to define the following second set of words and phrases from Chapters 1–5 of *Bud, Not Buddy:*

gave assurance, hard-headed
insistent, moved like a tornado
on-the-lam, never standing still
flower-to-be, kept secrets
absent

Next, Mx. McCloskey will ask them to sort words into semantic categories, by choosing words that describe three characters: Bud, Mother, and Grandfather. Mx. McCloskey will assess whether students can assign these words meaningfully, as presented in Figure 5.19, and thus extending assessment of their vocabulary knowledge.

Mx. McCloskey is pleased with the information that is gathering with the *Semantic Word Sorts* assessment strategy, as the sorts provide precise information about whether students can define the selected vocabulary words. *Semantic Word Sorts* make **visible** students' definitions of vocabulary words and the strategies they are applying to generate semantic relationships. In addition to collecting information about students' performance on the two tasks (defining and forming relationships), Mx. McCloskey values the explicit attention to forming the semantic categories and thus helping students see the relationships among words and ideas represented in the texts they are reading.

Word sort for characters/ characteristics– *Bud, Not Buddy,* Chapters 1–5 Student: Date:			
	Bud	**Mother**	**Grandfather**
	gave assurance	*kept secrets*	*hard-headed*
	flower-to-be	*moved like a tornado*	*insistent*
	on-the-lam	*never standing still*	*absent*

FIGURE 5.19. Student performance when sorting words into semantic categories for character descriptions—*Bud, Not Buddy,* Chapters 1–5.

Conclusion

We began this chapter by advocating for achieving the "noble bubble" of text comprehension assessment. The assessments described within this chapter demonstrate methods for capturing students' comprehension of texts while also making visible the multiple resources they bring to a text. Central to the "noble bubble" is a focus on equity, assuring that students' cultural, linguistic, and experiential knowledge is seen as a resource to be tapped and acknowledged explicitly during assessments and instruction. Also, the assessment strategies provide power to the teacher who can apply what is learned about the students to instruction that is responsive to each student. Each assessment supports and make visible rationales for instructional decision making.

FORM 5.1

Qualitative Analysis for Informational/Expository Text Retellings

Directions: Listed below are qualities of retellings to guide your analysis of a students' informational/expository text retelling. A section for notes following each statement can be used for you to record your observations. You may want to add and/or delete statements to correspond to your teaching goals and the student's history of instruction.

Student: ______________________________ **Date:** ____________________

The reader . . .	**Expected responses by the reader**	***Yes, no, or partially,* and student comments**	**Notes**
1. Identifies most important main ideas–concept/theme/problem			
2. Explains supporting details for all important main ideas			
3. Generates inferences around main ideas			
4. Generates inferences around supporting details			
5. Summarizes parts or the whole text			
6. Draws on prior knowledge to support retelling			
7. Offers plausible opinions, interpretations, and/or critiques			

(continued)

Qualitative Analysis for Informational/Expository Text Retellings *(page 2 of 2)*

The reader . . .	Expected responses by the reader	*Yes, no,* or *partially,* and student comments	Notes
8. Generates questions			
9. Derives plausible conclusions not stated by the author			
10. Suggests applications of main ideas to real-world happenings, beyond the text			
11. Provides sequence, coherence, and completeness of ideas			
12. Provides incomplete retelling			
Summary:			

FORM 5.2

Scoring Protocol for Analyzing Concept Maps

Directions: Analyze the student's retelling by identifying students recall of the central concepts, major supporting ideas, and lower-level details (Gowin & Alvarez, 2005). The middle column is provided to record student statements and the third column is provided for teacher's notes and comments. Points are assigned according to the level of information generated in the retelling.

Student name: ______________________________ **Date:** ____________________

Points assigned for level of recalled information *(noting correspondence to information generated on teacher map):*	**Student comments:**	**Teacher notes:**
Level One—Central concept(s) of text—5 points (for each central concept identified)		
Level Two—Major supporting details—4 points (for each)		
Level Three—Descriptive information/lower-level details—3 points (for each)		
Level Four—Descriptive information/lower-level details—2 points (for each)		
Level Five and beyond—Descriptive information/lower-level details—1 point (for each)		
Links drawn to indicate relationships across supporting details—10 points (for each cross link)		
Teacher summary of observations:		
Total score possible:		
Student's total score:		
Percentage of ideas represented in retelling: ____________		

FORM 5.3

Qualitative Analysis of Text Retellings

Directions: Generate a written record (can be in summary form) of student's retelling in Part A of data form. Analyze quality of retelling by answering the questions in Part B and identifying strengths and needs and directions for instruction.

Part A. Student's retelling

Student: ______________________________	Date: ____________________

Part B.

Questions	**Teacher observations/analysis**
1. Did student include information that is directly stated in the text?	
2. Did student generate plausible inferences about information that is stated directly or indirectly in the text?	
3. Did student include the main ideas or most important ideas of the text?	
4. Was student's retelling accurate?	

(continued)

Qualitative Analysis of Text Retellings *(page 2 of 2)*

Questions	**Teacher observations/analysis**
5. Did student explicitly apply comprehension strategies, such as connecting prior knowledge to text to support sense making, generate summary statements, generate generalizations or conclusions that relate to the real world, revise retelling during the process seeking accuracy, and/or make explicit connections across ideas?	
6. Did student identify and discuss/define appropriately possible new vocabulary, including disciplinary vocabulary, that was embedded in the text?	
7. Did student ask to look back at the text or illustrations/photos to support retelling?	
8. Did student provide personal, creative, or affective responses to the text?	
9. Was the retelling organized logically while representing accurate content?	
10. Did the retelling demonstrate appropriate language conventions (e.g., sense of audience, sentence structure, use of text vocabulary)?	
Teacher Summary: Patterns of strengths/ needs	
Suggestions for instruction:	

FORM 5.4

Data Sheet for Collecting and Analyzing Think-Aloud Statements

Student: ______________________________ **Date:** ____________________

Text segment	Student's think-aloud statements	Analysis of think-aloud statements

FORM 5.5

Questions and Notetaking for Responses to Questions

Student: ______________________________ **Date:** ____________________

Text: ____

Questions/type	Student's responses	Teacher's notes/ observations

FORM 5.6

Student Performance on Word Definitions in Word Sort

Student: ______________________________ **Date:** ______________________

Words	Definition met expectations	Student comments and/or definitions	Teacher comments/ interpretations

FORM 5.7

Student Performance When Sorting Words into Semantic Categories

Student: ______________________________ **Date:** ____________________

Words to be sorted	Group 1	Group 2	Group 3	Group 4	Teacher notes
Student explanation of semantic grouping:					

6

Assessing Constrained Skills within the Big Picture of Reading

> Literacy is a big thing we do in life, not a little thing we do on worksheets in school.
>
> —MR. RIVERA, THIRD-GRADE TEACHER

Literacy assessments that provide *big picture* information are those that make visible the strategies and skills that we use when decoding words, reading fluently, and making sense of texts. As we discussed in Chapters 4 and 5, the assessment of students' unconstrained skills will identify if students are generating understandings of text that make sense, relate and extend prior knowledge, build vocabulary and information for problem solving and argumentation, and provide pleasure and memorable experiences to support their text comprehension. Alongside and in concert with the unconstrained skills we use when reading, are the constrained skills of phonemic awareness, phonics, and fluency that work in tandem to support students' text comprehension.

When students develop constrained skills, they have the ability to learn sounds associated with letters and letter combinations and to blend these sounds to pronounce meaningful words. When taught constrained skills in combination with unconstrained skills, readers are learning to draw on multiple sources of information, such as prior knowledge, vocabulary, and text comprehension, to support their word learning within authentic reading contexts. And while we want readers to learn how to use constrained skills to pronounce words accurately, we also want them to identify if the words they pronounce sound right and make sense (Duke, 2020). As words are pronounced and read within meaningful texts, readers use their knowledge and text comprehension strategies to monitor their word pronunciation (e.g., does that word sound right? does that word make sense in this context?). The goal for instruction is to develop students' strategic use of both constrained and unconstrained skills and knowledge to cross-check (across multiple sources of information) their word pronunciations (Scanlon & Anderson, 2020).

Unconstrained skills continue to develop over time, while constrained skills are generally learned and mastered during early literacy development. Because these skills support each other, our assessments must account for this relationship and ultimately help us answer the following big picture questions: Are my students applying their skills of phonemic awareness, phonics, and fluency to make sense of texts that they are reading and writing? Are they strategic as they monitor meanings of words they pronounce? The answers to these questions guide our teaching as we prompt children to monitor their word reading and comprehension and apply strategies to fix-up what they have read if it does not make sense or sound right (Duke, 2020).

Too often, however, assessments identify constrained skills, typically assessed in isolation, that may be mastered and those that are needed, but stop short of making students' application of these skills visible within authentic reading contexts. In this chapter, we identify concerns associated with assessments of constrained skills and provide guidance and specific examples of assessments that address these concerns—placing the measurement of constrained skills within authentic reading and writing contexts *and* using the data collected on these measures to inform instruction. Our approach aligns to Milner's view of equitable assessments that "gauge student learning, development, and improvement over time" and are "used by teachers to adjust their practices (how they teach, what they teach, when they teach, and so forth) to respond to and meet the needs of students" (2018, p. 89).

An overarching problem we feel we must address is that constrained skills (and unconstrained skills, too) are often assessed through standardized tests that rank, label, and sort students based on the results of a single assessment. For several decades, standardized tests have been criticized for being biased against students from diverse backgrounds, specifically students of color, and more recently, researchers, advocates, and educators have argued that such tests are racist and have been so by design from the beginning (Gates, 2019; Knoester & Au, 2017; Soares, 2020). For example, the Scholastic Aptitude Test (SAT), which is often used to determine college admission, was originally designed by Carl Brigham who was a proponent of eugenics (Gates, 2019). The eugenics movement supported improving the genetic quality of the human race by excluding groups deemed to be inferior and promoting those who were deemed to be superior. In his book *A Study of American Intelligence* (1923), Brigham argued that standardized testing was a means for upholding racial purity and ensuring the superiority of White Americans. The focus of our book does not allow us to discuss the racist history of standardized tests fully, but we did want to acknowledge that this history of racism in standardized testing informed our commitment to developing the humanistic, student-centered, equitable approach to assessment that we advocate in this book.

Now, getting back to the assessment of constrained skills, one specific concern relates to measures of constrained skills within isolated tasks that make assessment of these skills look easy, such as accuracy checks that assess knowledge of letters and their sounds presented one at a time and out of authentic contexts, or timed oral reading fluency exercises that identify the number of words read accurately. Such measures are the most troublesome because they are the least helpful in guiding instruction. The lure and danger of 1-minute fluency probes, for example, illustrate how something easy to assess and teach can be overused to make decisions about instruction (e.g., increasing rate of reading) without concomitant attention to whether students are drawing on multiple unconstrained skills (e.g., prior knowledge, text meaning, syntax, word meanings) simultaneously to understand the texts they are reading while increasing their accuracy and all aspects of fluency (i.e., accuracy, rate, and prosody). This narrow view of assessment advocated by the No Child Left Behind Act and the Reading First program lead to a narrow view of instruction that prevents students from developing into strong readers. Unfortunately, this narrow view tends to be common in underresourced schools that primarily serve students from low-income and diverse backgrounds. Teale, Paciga, and Hoffman (2007) explained that this situation creates a curriculum gap, which they defined as the "absence of or insufficient attention to curriculum elements critical for success in reading and writing" (p. 345).

A second concern relates to the messaging given to students, teachers, and parents when we assess constrained skills outside of authentic reading and writing contexts. Students and parents are misled to believe that students will be successful readers once they can "sound out" all the words presented on lists (and sometimes nonsense words), read fast, match definitions to words on worksheets, and so on. These assessment routines signal to teachers that what and how we assess should be given high priority for what and how we teach. In short, what we assess is what we teach (Johnston & Costello, 2005). The more we undersample the range of skills and abilities that children can use or are developing within our assessments, the more our instruction will fall short of meeting the goal of developing strong readers. By viewing reading as a simple set of skills, we limit our ability to develop critical readers who comprehend complex texts. The end result is preventing equitable access to high-quality reading instruction to help all students develop into critical readers.

Unfortunately, too often instructional programs are deemed successful if skills are taught well with little attention to their application to authentic tasks of making meaning during reading and writing. Associated with testing isolated skills is the false assumption that once skills are mastered, they will be applied automatically to aid comprehension. The goal for assessment, in our view, is to signal to students the importance of these skills as part of a larger process. Teachers need to be intentional about selecting assessments, such as the ones we illustrate in this chapter, that address what is important in literacy and to communicate this to students.

As readers and writers, our students need to understand and use constrained skills, but that knowledge is not sufficient for proficient literacy development. Reading is more than reading fast or being able to read words correctly. It is about using those constrained skills in combination with unconstrained skills to unlock meaning, to communicate, to learn new things, and so on, and that is the big picture—the goal for our instruction. Assessments, then, must provide a comprehensive view of students' skill and strategy development within the context of the real acts of reading and writing.

A third concern is about the privileging of performance assessments over process ones.

To be more specific, assessments need to measure *processes*—capturing the strategies and skills students use while they read or spell words, determine meanings of vocabulary, comprehend texts, and read fluently, and *performance*—what students produce after reading and/or writing (Afflerbach, Cho, Crassas, & Kim, 2019). A performance assessment, for example, could be an oral reading sample that provides information about mastery, such as whether each student is reading the words correctly when reading aloud. Conversely, process assessments might involve listening to students producing sounds for letters in a word. As we listen to each student, we learn how they approached the task and what knowledge they used. For example, when reading the word *block*, one student may say *-bl* and *-ock* and then produce the word while another student may produce a sound for each individual letter, as *-b, -l, -o, -ck*, before pronouncing the word, and a third student may produce the sounds but have difficulty reading the whole word. Listening to each student and keeping records of students' attempts at reading words with phonics clues provides information about patterns that characterize a students' use of phonics skills. Collecting this information across multiple samples and identifying patterns of a students' conception of using phonics for sounding out words provide invaluable information for informing instruction.

As we see in the above examples, both performance and process assessments provide information about student progress in meeting goals for literacy development. Performance assessment provides periodic checks to identify the skills students are able to apply to a reading or writing product. This information is useful to note learning and progress with learning goals over time. Conversely, process assessments are valuable as they make visible how the product was achieved, how students process text and use skills and strategies to obtain meaningful responses in "real time" (Afflerbach et al., 2019, p. 315).

To clarify our thinking about reading as a big thing we do in life, not what's done on worksheets in school, we draw on the work of Andrea A. diSessa (2018), an education researcher. diSessa has advocated for thinking about assessment (and instruction) within a conceptual framework relevant to the kinds of assessments demonstrated in this chapter. To explain his framework, diSessa has discussed the issue of students learning in "bits and pieces" and invites us to think about how we might use this knowledge in meaningful ways. He has argued that those "bits and pieces" of knowledge acquired over time and through different experiences lay the foundation for acquiring new information (e.g., sounds and letters of a word) and in the long term integrating the parts into wholes (reading words and understanding their meanings).

Additionally, the process of knowing bits and pieces and the integration of these into deeper understandings also signals to students what it means to become a learner or a reader. Thus, for assessments to be optimal, we must assess the breadth of student knowledge, including the partial knowledge and the knowledge that is in development. If we are to provide instruction that is responsive to students' development of "bits and pieces," we must listen carefully and capture the skills and strategies in development. A relevant example is how linguistically diverse learners may draw on "bits and pieces" of their languages while becoming literate in more than two or more languages.

The goal to understand students' partial understandings of information or the "bits and pieces" has a strong evidence base. Years of systematic investigations on how people learn (Bransford, Brown, & Cocking, 2000) and how young children develop as literacy learners (Clay, 1982, 2001) provide rich descriptions of children's emerging understandings of the world. They begin at a very young age and it is their partial understandings of information that help them acquire new knowledge. For example, Clay (1982) identified multiple early literacy behaviors (e.g., directionality of print in a text, awareness of words and letter clusters, expectations for generating meaning from pictures) that very young children acquire through their experiences with books and writing. It is this information that children integrate when beginning to read and that becomes a powerful foundation for acquiring new knowledge of print and texts. She concluded that as children gain more control over their use of early literacy behaviors, such as grasping the directionality of print or the sounds of letters, they become able to apply that understanding in progressively complex ways, such as pointing to individual words as they read. Similarly, Bransford and his colleagues (2000) concluded that initial understandings of students should be identified and engaged because they can serve as a foundation when asking students to grasp new concepts and information.

Our long-term goal for assessment, then, is to move along a continuum. We want to make visible the bits and pieces of knowledge that students are acquiring (e.g., letter names, letter sounds, word pronunciations, word meanings, and so on). And we want to know if and how students are understanding how this knowledge is being used and applied to make sense of text information, the big picture of reading and writing. We want our assessments to help us understand not only what students are learning about the bits and pieces, and how they are applying these to reading and writing, but as diSessa (2018) suggested, we want to know if students are learning what is expected of them as readers and writers.

In the remainder of this chapter, we present five strategies you can use to assess your students' constrained skills in meaningful contexts. Each of the assessment strategies addresses our key principles of ensuring the visibility of both students and teachers, addressing the complexity of reading, being embedded in the daily activities of teaching and learning, and operating from an equity mindset. As you read about and consider each of these assessment strategies, the following questions will help guide your thinking.

- How does the assessment help me identify students' partially learned constrained skills that are still in development? Those that have not been learned?
- How does the assessment help me understand the constrained skills that students have acquired and are applying as they read?
- How does the assessment help me understand how students apply constrained skills over time? In different contexts?
- Through use of the assessment, what can become visible about the student as a reader that I can use to plan and provide appropriate instruction that is responsive to students' differences?

ASSESSMENT STRATEGIES: SUPPORTING STUDENTS' CONSTRAINED SKILLS

In this part of the chapter, we offer five strategies for making visible students' knowledge and use of constrained skills. These strategies are:

6.1. *What Can You Show Us?*

6.2. *Running Records*

6.3. *Oral Reading Analysis*

6.4. *Elkonin Sound Boxes*

6.5. *Developmental Spelling Assessment*

The What Can You Show Us? Assessment Strategy Puts a Spotlight on Students' Knowledge of Constrained Skills in Text

Unlike traditional skills assessment, the *What Can You Show Us?* strategy (adapted from Richgels, Poremba, & McGee, 1996) is implemented with groups of students and thus is embedded within your instruction during large- or small-group meetings with students. It is open-ended, student-centered, and asset-focused. When you ask a group of students, "what can you show us?," they can go in any direction they wish without the limits of questions that are often used in assessments. Because this assessment strategy is open-ended, students are likely to share things they notice and know that are beyond what you might expect. This process can extend your understanding of students' knowledge and use of constrained skills rather than limiting you to simply check whether they are using a specific skill. Thus, you are likely to learn students' skill processes *and* performance. Because this assessment is student-centered, it allows you to gain an understanding about what each student knows and can do, so you can adjust instruction to meet their needs and advance their development and progress. Finally, this assessment is asset-focused because what students share—whether it is an accurate and complete understanding, bits and pieces of a skill, or a misunderstanding—is valuable for planning and implementing instruction to support each student's literacy learning.

ASSESSMENT STRATEGY 6.1.
What Can You Show Us?

Purpose

This formative assessment strategy makes visible students' knowledge and use of constrained skills within the context of shared reading of authentic texts. If used regularly, this strategy can become an assessment routine that is embedded in your teaching of shared reading, guided reading, and close reading. This assessment strategy uses an equity lens because it makes visible and values what each student brings to reading the text.

Value

The value of embedding this assessment in teaching routines is that it allows the teacher to evaluate regularly how well students apply constrained skills within meaningful contexts to make sense of words and ideas.

Procedures

1. In the **preparation** stage of this assessment strategy, the teacher selects a text that is related to the curriculum and the constrained skills students are learning. These texts can be children's literature, informational texts, or teacher-written materials such as a chart story. The text can be a new text or it can be one that has been shared previously.
2. In the **previewing** stage, the teacher displays the text or an excerpt. The teacher invites students to look at the text and to talk to each other about what they see and understand in the text.

3. The **student demonstration** phase is the heart of this assessment strategy. Before the teacher and students share in reading the text, the teacher invites volunteers to individually show something they know about the text. This assessment strategy allows children to engage with the text using their current understandings and abilities related to constrained skills. It also allows the other students to learn about the text from their classmates and the constrained skills that others notice. During the student demonstrations, the teacher is an observer and helper, but the students take on the role of teacher as they show what they know about the text. The teacher takes anecdotal notes using a chart similar to the one provided in Figure 6.1.

4. During the **applications stage,** the teacher uses the insights gained from the student demonstrations to guide the shared reading process by offering opportunities to apply and extend the constrained skills students demonstrated. In future lessons, the teacher will introduce instruction on new skills that were identified as areas of need through the student demonstrations.

Collecting, Analyzing, and Using Data

We recommend that you take anecdotal notes using a format like the one provided in Form 6.1. You can do this using a paper form on a clipboard, or you may want to create the form on an iPad or tablet so you can record the data digitally. The key is to review the anecdotal notes carefully to identify patterns that can guide your planning for group lessons as well as determining areas of instruction for individual students.

Making Students and Teachers Visible

Because this strategy invites students to show what they notice, know, and wonder about in a text, it allows them to make their understanding of and use of constrained skills visible. Students are also able to show how they use their constrained skills to make meaning and understand the text. By using this strategy regularly so it becomes an assessment routine during shared reading, guided reading, and close reading; students will have time and structure to share their observations, understandings, misunderstandings, and questions about constrained skills in the context of authentic and meaningful texts. Teachers can make their observations and insights about students' literacy learning visible by recording, analyzing, and using the anecdotal notes they take to develop and guide future instruction to meet the needs and build on the strengths of all students.

Implementation Example

Miss Watson teaches kindergarten and uses the *What Can You Show Us?* strategy almost daily to assess her students' knowledge and application of multiple skills with a particular focus on constrained skills. As part of her shared reading routine, she always begins by asking students, "What can you show us?"

In the **preparation** stage, Miss Watson develops a chart story that provides a short text with several high-frequency words her students should be able to identify on sight—*is, the, I, do, you.* The text also illustrates the use of capital letters to start sentences and use of end of sentence punctuation.

During the **previewing** stage, she provides about 5 minutes for students to look at, read, and discuss the text with their peers. During this time, she observes carefully and takes brief anecdotal notes (see Form 6.1 for a template) about what students are discussing as well as which students are not participating so she can follow up with those students individually at a later time.

In the **student demonstration** stage, Miss Watson invites several students to come up—one at a time—to point out what they know about the text. Since some of her students tend to be shy or hesitant to share, she also invites these students to share when she observes that they are sharing something with their peers during the previewing stage.

One day, she displays this text about spring.

Spring
Spring is here.
Birds chirp.
Flowers bloom.
The sun shines.
I like spring.
Do you?

Jaime volunteers, "Spring is in there three times," and then points to the word each time it appears in the text. Sasha explains, "Sun starts with *s* just like my name." Darius excitedly shares, "I see birds in the picture." Oskar points out, "I see periods at the end of the lines." Wei points to the question mark and says, "This is a question!" Manuel says, "I think *is* is like *es en español*."

As several other children share, Miss Watson continues to take very brief notes (see Form 6.1 for a blank template) so she can use those data for future instructional planning.

Miss Watson then shifts into the **applications stage** where she addresses what the students showed they knew, and she provides opportunities for students to apply this knowledge. For example, Jaime showed the word *spring* and Miss Watson invites the children to focus on the word *spring* as she points to the word each time it appears in the chart story. She then invites several students who did not participate in the student demonstration stage to come up and highlight the word *spring* as they read it aloud. Miss Watson reminds the students that Sasha noticed that the word *sun* begins with the letter *s* just like her first name. She explains that Darius noticed the birds in the picture and asks a volunteer to point out the word *birds* in the text. She discusses what letter *birds* begins with, and invites several students to come up to the chart story to point at the *b* and then read the word *birds*. She then asks the students to talk about the kinds of things they might see birds doing in the spring. Several students offer ideas such as flying, chirping, eating worms, and laying eggs. Miss Watson also draws the students' attention to the periods that Oskar pointed out. She asks several students to highlight the period at the end of the sentences. She then refers to what Wei shared about the question at the end of the story. She asks a student to highlight the question mark on the chart story. She comments that Manual shared that *is* in English looks similar to *es* in Spanish, and Manuel smiles and nods. She explains that using a language that is spoken at home is a good tool to help you learn English.

Miss Watson also focuses on **collecting, analyzing, and using data** throughout the assessment strategy. To see her notes, see Figure 6.1. She documents her observations during the student demonstration and application stages of the strategy. She also notes which students are not participating or sharing to guide her data collection, analysis, and follow-up instruction.

Later in the day, Miss Watson begins **analyzing the data** in her anecdotal notes in three ways. First, she looks to see what the kindergarten curriculum expects of students in terms of constrained skills and how her students performed against these expectations. Second, she analyzes each student's performance to identify known skills. Third, she identifies which constrained skills students do not yet have control over and those with partial control, such as the beginning sound of *spring*. She considers her findings from these analyses as well as patterns students have demonstrated over time in instructional strategies and other assessments. For students who demonstrate control over specific constrained skills, she makes plans to observe them closely to see if they apply these skills

Text: Spring chart story

Constrained skills to look for from curriculum: beginning consonant sounds, capital letters, and periods

Date: January 28, 2021

Student name	Observations related to constrained skills	Next steps for assessment and teaching points
Jaime	Identified *spring* in text all 3 times	Can he identify the word in another context?
Sasha	Noticed that *sun* starts with *s* like *Sasha*	When reading with Sasha, ask her to find other words that start with *s* and help her read them.
Darius	Found birds in the picture	Work with him to use picture cues to help him read words and simple texts.
Oskar	Pointed out periods at the end of each sentence	When reading with Oskar, observe if he knows to pause when he sees a period at the end of a sentence.
Wei	Pointed out the question mark and knew its meaning	When reading and writing with Wei, observe whether he knows to raise his voice when reading a question.
Manuel	Noticed that *is* in English is like *es* in Spanish	Help Manuel look for other cognates so he can link his knowledge of Spanish and English.

Ideas for next group lesson: Look for capital letters and talk about how every sentence begins with a capital letter. Look for words that start with the same letter as their names. Do a think-aloud about how to use picture clues to help figure out words.

Students to follow up with and why: Maurice, Shelby, Raven, and Max didn't participate. Do this assessment with each of them individually to get more information about what they notice.

FIGURE 6.1. Example of an anecdotal record form for *What Can You Show Us?* strategy.

when writing in their journals or reading other texts. For students who did not participate or those whose responses demonstrated they need assistance with specific constrained skills, she makes plans for small-group instruction and individual conversations.

Miss Watson believes the **value** of this assessment strategy is that she can gain insight into the range of things that students know (and do not know) about applying constrained skills to a text. Because the focus of this assessment is open-ended, she has an authentic look into her students' understanding of a text and knowledge of constrained skills, which often go beyond what she would normally teach to her kindergarten students. This assessment strategy invites all of her students to make **visible** what they notice, know, and have misunderstandings about when applying constrained skills to reading the text. She learned that this assessment strategy encourages her linguistically diverse learners to make connections from their heritage language to English and her students who speak other dialects to make meaningful connections to the text. By making these connections visible, she is able to identify ways to leverage those linguistic assets to help her students develop as readers. She considers this to be a generative assessment because students generate responses that show how they apply and combine their knowledge and skills. She then uses this information to be strategic, intentional, and student-centered in her instructional planning.

Assessing Students' Oral Reading: Key Considerations for Strategies 6.2 and 6.3

One of the most common approaches to assessing a student's oral reading is to listen to the student read a text. Doing so can provide you with rich data to help you understand the many dimensions of a student's reading. When appropriate oral reading can be embedded within your instructional routines, such as asking students to read aloud to you during small-group instruction while other students are reading silently or during individual conferences with your students. Keeping notes of the oral reading performance by each student occurs during these readings.

We provide two specific assessment strategies—*Running Records* (6.2) and *Oral Reading Analysis* (6.3)—that offer you two frameworks for how you can assess oral reading. A running record is a fairly structured process that includes error analysis and self-correction rates so you can gain insights into the strategies that students use and do not use when reading. In the *Running Records* assessment strategy, we use the term *error analysis,* which is consistent with Marie Clay's approach (2019). You may be familiar with the term *miscue analysis,* which engages a similar process, but its formal approach has specific differences from error analysis. For more information about miscue analysis, we recommend that you consult Goodman, Watson, and Burke (2005).

Sometimes oral reading assessments focus only on accuracy and reading rate, and we think that is a problem. While determining accuracy is helpful, it is the error analysis process that provides you with information about the student's use of both constrained skills and unconstrained skills, reading strategies, ability to self-correct, and use of self-monitoring to ensure that reading makes sense. Also, error analysis helps you identify the skills and strategies that have not been learned and the "bits and pieces" that are still in development. Therefore, we urge you to always look closely at a student's oral reading errors to identify patterns and "idiosyncratic processing" or skills and knowledge that are in development (Clay, 2019, p. 51) to inform your instruction for that specific student. When we use the word *miscue* in the *Oral Reading Analysis* assessment strategy, we are referring to students' reading of text when they say something that deviates from what is in the text. Such miscues provide valuable information about the skills and strategies the students did use to make sense of words that were not known to them. For example, if a student reads "poodle" for *puddle* and "blend" for *bland,* we know they recognize the beginning and ending sound but need instruction on the vowels or vowel combinations that follow the initial sound(s). Additionally, they need to be coached to determine if their word choice makes sense in the context of the sentence or text. This approach to miscues relates to the bits and pieces that are known as the foundation for subsequent instruction.

The oral reading assessments that follow align with Milner's (2018, p. 89) approach to assessment for equity because they can be used to gauge student learning, development, and improvement over time; help you adjust your teaching practices to be responsive to your students; and are a natural part of classroom activities and therefore are not intimidating to students.

Determining reading rate can also be helpful to ensure that a student reads at a rate that will support comprehension and allow them to read text commensurate with classroom expectations. For example, Laurie worked with a fifth-grade student who read 27 words per minute while his classmates read at an average of 100 words per minute. The student was frustrated that he was never finished reading texts in school when his peers were done, and at home, he spent countless hours just trying to get through his reading assignments. We understand that rate matters, but it is not the only or even the most important thing you can learn from assessing a student's oral reading. If you want to add the assessment of a student's reading rate to either the *Running Records* or *Oral Reading Analysis* assessment strategy, please do so, but we caution you against only assessing reading rate and not looking at error or miscue analysis, reading behaviors, affect toward reading, comprehension, or other key indicators of how a student reads a text. Furthermore, some assessments of reading rate focus on having a student read aloud for 1 minute and then stop. Such a practice sends students the message that rate is the most important aspect of reading, and this approach also does not encourage students to read continuous text, which can reinforce the fallacy that reading is about speed and not about understanding the text.

ASSESSMENT STRATEGY 6.2.
Running Records

Purpose

In our view, this diagnostic assessment strategy provides you with some of the most useful information for understanding how to design instruction to meet the unique needs of your students. It does so by allowing you to collect data about a student's constrained and unconstrained skills through their oral reading of an authentic text. Running records can also help you plan instruction and gain insights into how students go "about understanding what they are reading" (Johnston, 2000, p. 39), sometimes referred to as in-the-head processes. Running records allow you to determine accuracy and analyze errors to see if students are using meaning cues, structure cues, and visual cues (i.e., looking at letters to map on the corresponding sounds) as well as their ability to self-correct their errors. Running records can also document change in a student's reading over time (Clay, 2019).

Value

The *Running Records* assessment strategy has value for several key reasons. Running records can be done at any time, with any text, and the teacher only needs a sheet of paper, a pencil, a student, and a text to implement this assessment strategy. Because running records are so easy to implement, teachers can use them frequently to learn about and understand their students' oral reading. Running records allow the teacher to analyze a student's oral reading strategies to determine if students are using phonics, knowledge of language structure, text meaning, and background knowledge, and if they are able to make self-corrections.

Procedures

1. To **prepare** for this assessment strategy, you will need to consider your text choice and review previously collected data about the student's reading. On a sheet of paper, write the student's name, date, book title and pages read, and any other relevant information, such as whether the book is new to the student, has been read by the student before, or has been read aloud to the student. See Form 6.2 for the recommended format for a running record. You can also simply use a blank sheet of paper that contains the same information as Form 6.2. If you are just starting to use running records, you may wish to create a small table tent or index card with any notations that you find difficult to remember so you can use it as a quick reference to help you get more familiar and confident with implementing running records. Once you have used this strategy a few times, you will be more comfortable just taking notes in the moment.
2. Ask the student to read the text aloud. Tell the student that you will be taking a running record so you can understand their reading better. Let the student know that they can look at the record after they read and you will explain it to them if they wish.
3. As the student reads, write a check mark (✓) for each word read correctly. Arrange the check marks the same way the words are organized on the page so you can tell which check mark represents each word. Here's an example of the text, what the student read, and the running record.

   Text: It was a cold and rainy day.
   Sally was sad.
   She wished she could play outside.

   Reader: It was a cold and rainy day.
   Sally was sad.
   She wished she could play outside.

   Running record: ✓ ✓ ✓ ✓ ✓ ✓ ✓
   ✓ ✓ ✓
   ✓ ✓ ✓ ✓ ✓ ✓

4. Record the student's errors as they read. Oral reading errors include omissions, substitutions, insertions, self-corrections, repetitions, attempts, and those requiring teacher support. The definition of each of these errors and a method for recording these on a running record are provided in Table 6.1.

TABLE 6.1. Oral Reading Errors and Scoring Procedures for a Running Record

Error	Definition	How to record
Omission	The reader omits or skips over a word and does not read it.	Use a dash to show that a word was omitted. Text: It's my birthday! Reader: It's—-—birthday!
Substitution	The reader substitutes a different word for the one in the text.	Write the word the reader says and later add a line below it and write the word that is in the text. boy ——— day
Insertion	The reader adds a word that is not in the text.	Write the inserted word, add a line underneath the added word to show that there was no matching word in the text. Text: It's my birthday! Reader: It's always my birthday!
Self-correction	Reader makes a self-correction while reading, indicating reader may be self-monitoring and cross-checking by applying visual, meaning, and/or structure cues.	Write "SC" on the running record. was |SC ——— saw
Repetitions	Reader rereads a word, phrase, or sentence.	Record the repetition with the letter R and a line above the word(s) to show what segment of text was repeated. Text: It's my birthday! It's time for a party. Reader: It's my birthday! It's time it's time for a party. Running: ✓ ✓ ✓ Record ——— ✓ ✓ R ✓ ✓ ✓
Attempts	If the reader does not recognize the word right away, they may try to figure it out. Attempts to problem-solve provide you with information about strategies the reader uses to figure out words.	Record each attempt. Text: My dog is big and brown, and his name is Buster. My dog is big and b / b / br/ brown, and his name is B / Bus/ Buster ✓ ✓ ✓ ✓ ✓ b/b/br/ ✓ ✓ ✓ ✓ B/Bus/✓ ——— ——— brown Buster

(continued)

TABLE 6.1. *(continued)*

Error	Definition	How to record
Teacher support	Generally, the teacher does not intervene with a student's reading during a running record. However, if a student is stuck or has made multiple errors that have caused them to stop or appear frustrated or confused, it may be helpful to say, "Why don't you try that again?" and direct them back to the beginning of the sentence or section where they got stuck.	Record this intervention by writing TA (try again) in the running record. Text: The owl screeched in the distance while the full moon shone. Reader: The owl screeched in the dis / dis / distand / distand? when the? ✓ ✓ ✓ ✓ ✓ dis / dis / distand / distand? when the ?] TA (under the line:) distance while
Teacher support (2)	Occasionally a student will simply stop reading when they encounter a word, and you may wish to provide the word for them. This should be done as infrequently as possible.	If you provide a word, write the letter T in the bottom right corner of the running record line. Text: The wind cut like a knife through the night. Reader: The wind cut like a [Teacher tells *knife*] Running Record: ✓ ✓ ✓ ✓ ✓ knife | T

Collecting, Analyzing, and Using Data

A teacher can **collect** a great deal of information while taking a running record. The teacher can use the data collected about words read accurately, determine error rate, error analysis, self-correction rate, omissions, substitutions, and insertions as well as repetitions, monitoring for meaning, and problem solving of words. In addition, if the teacher had to prompt the student to "try that again" or had to supply a word for the student, those data will also be included in the running record.

Analyzing data from a running record can be done in several steps. Therefore, we have numbered the following processes to help demonstrate a step-by-step process the teacher can use to analyze running record data.

1. Calculate the error rate by counting each omission, insertion, substitution, and teacher intervention (i.e., "try that again" or teacher supplies a word). Do not count self-corrections because the student eventually reads the word accurately. Divide the number of errors by the number of words in the text read by the student, and multiply that number by 100 to get the error rate as a percentage: Error rate = (number of errors/number of words) × 100. For example, if a student had 6 errors on a passage with 149 words, the error rate would be (6/149) × 100 = 4%.

2. Determine the accuracy rate by taking the error rate and subtracting it from 100%. Take that number and divide it by the number of words in the text read by the student, and multiple it by 100 to get the accuracy rate as a percentage. Accuracy rate provides a useful rule of thumb or estimate for teachers about whether a book is easy

for the student, appropriate for instruction, or too difficult. Accuracy rate = (number of words – number of errors)/number of words × 100. For example, if a student read 149 words and made 6 errors, the accuracy rate would be (149 – 6)/149 = (143/149) × 100 = 96%. According to Marie Clay (2019), if a student's accuracy rate is 95% or higher, the text can be considered easy and appropriate for independent reading. If a student's accuracy rate is 90–94%, the text is appropriate for instruction. If a student's accuracy rate is 89% or lower, that text can be considered hard for the student, and they may require a good deal of support to read the text.

3. By calculating self-correction rate, the teacher can gauge if students are monitoring their reading and applying strategies to fix their errors. Students who do a fair amount of self-correcting are more likely to be able to make progress as readers with relatively little help. A self-correction rate of 1:3 or lower is a good sign that a student is able to apply self-correction independently. To calculate the self-correction rate, add the number of errors and the number of self-corrections and divide by the number of self-corrections. Self-correction rate = (errors + self-corrections) /self-corrections. For example, if that same student had 4 self-corrections and 6 errors, the self-correction rate would be (6 + 4) / 4 = 2.5. The self-correction rate is written as a ratio of 1:2.5, which means that the student corrects one out of every 2.5 errors. A self-correction rate of 1:3 or lower shows that a reader is monitoring their reading and applying strategies appropriately to fix their errors.

Analyzing errors is an important part of using running records. Look at each error to determine what type(s) of information the reader used. We use the approach that Clay (2019, p. 72) offered for identifying the types of information students used when making oral reading errors: M (meaning), S (structure), or V (visual). Consistent with her procedures, consider the sentence only up to the error to analyze M, S, and V information. Some teachers find it helpful to ask these questions as they do error analysis (Clay, 2019, p. 72).

Meaning (M)—Did the meaning of the messages of the text influence the error? Perhaps the reader brought a different meaning to the author's text.

Structure (S)—Did the structure (syntax) of the sentence up to the error influence the response? If the error occurs on the first word of the sentence, it is marked as positive for structure if the new sentence could have started that way.

Visual information (V)—Did visual information from the print influence any part of the error: letter, cluster, or word?

For each error, note if the student used M, S, and/or V information, and mark this on the running record in the right column (see Form 6.2). Some errors will reveal use of more than one type of information, so circle any that are appropriate for each error.

Look at how many Ms, Ss, and Vs are circled to identify patterns of which types of information the student used and which cueing system/s the student might need additional instruction and practice with to use in their reading.

Look at all instances of problem solving to determine what strategies the student used to try and figure out words. Finally, review any instances of the student "getting stuck" and needing the teacher to prompt them to "try that again" or waiting for the teacher to supply the word. See Figure 6.2 for a complete listing of scoring conventions for running records based on the work of Clay (2000).

There is a great deal of data a teacher can be **using** from running records for instructional purposes. First, a running record is a snapshot of a student's reading; therefore, teachers are encouraged to look at a student's reading over time to see progress or lack thereof. Teachers can use running records as a gauge of what level of text is appropriate for a student to read independently, for instruction, or with significant support. In addition, teachers can gain insight on a student's use of information sources, self-correction, and problem solving. These data points can be used to inform the teacher's instructional planning.

Making Students and Teachers Visible

Running records make a student's reading processes visible to the teacher. These include students' assets in the form of knowledge, use of skills and strategies, and reading behaviors. Running records rely heavily on a teacher's expertise, professional knowledge, and ability to draw insights about a student's reading. Therefore, teachers are very visible throughout all phases of implementing, analyzing, and using results of running records.

1. *Omission.* Count as one error each word in text that is omitted. If a line or sentence is omitted, each word is counted as an error. If pages are omitted, words on those pages are not counted as errors.
2. *Substitution.* Count as one error each substitution of a word or part of a word that is in the text. Substitution of a proper noun is counted only once.
3. *Insertion.* Insertions can have more errors than there are words in the text. Count each word that is inserted as an error.
4. *Self-correction.* If a child succeeds in correcting a previous error, this is recorded as a self-correction, and not an error.
5. *Repetition of single words.* Repeated errors, such as repeating *ran* for *run,* counts as an error every time. Repetition of the same error for proper nouns, e.g., *Mary* for *Maru,* counts as an error only the first time.
6. *Repetition of word, phrase, or sentence.* Repetitions are not counted as errors, when words are read correctly. If some words in the phrase or sentence are not corrected, count as an error each misread word.
7. *Attempts.* If a child tries several times to read a word or parts of a word, record all trials. There is no penalty (does not count as an error) if the child succeeds in saying the correct word after these attempts. If the correct word is not attained, all the attempts on the same word is counted as one error.
8. *Language representation.* When children's reading represents their language patterns, such as *pitcher* for *picture* or *gonna* for *going to,* each is counted as correct, and not a reading error. Also, saying a word as two words (e.g., a/way) is considered a pronunciation error, and not a reading error.

FIGURE 6.2. Scoring conventions for running records.

Implementation Example

Miss Carter is a second-grade teacher who implements guided-reading instruction in her classroom, and she uses running records regularly with her students. This is her second year teaching, and she has found that running records have become so much easier for her to use because of the practice she has had. She also finds that running records offer her some of the most valuable information about each student's reading.

Miss Carter is working with a small guided-reading group, and when it's time for the students to read to a partner, she asks Javy if he will read with her so she can take a running record. Javy is a linguistically diverse learner who receives support from a bilingual teacher in a small-group format every afternoon for 30 minutes. Miss Carter tells him, "Javy, I'd like to take a running record so I can understand your reading better. You can look at the record after I'm done, and I'll explain it to you if you wish." Javy smiles and nods his understanding.

Miss Carter points to page 27 to show Javy where to begin reading. "Javy, please start reading here." Javy begins to read and Miss Carter takes the running record, being careful to record a check mark for each word read correctly and organize the check marks in the same way the text is organized. She records the errors Javy makes, and she also notes a self-correction he makes when reading the title. The running record is provided in Figure 6.3. The text he read from the book *Horrible Harry in Room 2B,* by Suzy Kline, is provided below.

> *Harry's Triple Revenge*
>
> Sidney brought a book of bird stickers to Room 2B. He said he had a page of blue jays, a page of robins, and a page of something else.
>
> "What's the something else?" Ida asked.
>
> "It's a secret," Sidney said, looking at Harry.
>
> Harry lowered his eyebrows. "I know what the other stickers are. Don't you, Doug?"

Afterward, Miss Carter asks Javy if he'd like to look at the running record, and he enthusiastically responds, "Yes!" She shows him the running record and explains what each check mark means as well as the errors and self-correction she noted. She tells him, "You are making good progress in your reading. What did you notice about your reading?" Javy responds, "I noticed that I could read some of the words, even the hard words." "Yes, you were able to read most of the words accurately, and you used self-correction, which shows me you are monitoring your reading to make sure it makes sense. I notice that you used problem solving to keep trying to figure out the word *eyebrows.* Can you tell me about what you did to figure out *eyebrows?*" Javy responds, "I knew *eye.* I figured out *br* and then thought what made sense." Miss Carter smiled, nodded, and said, "um-hum" in response to Javy's explanation. "And how did you figure out *revenge?* First you said *raven*—what made you say *raven?*" Javy said, "I saw the *r* at the beginning of the word and yesterday we saw that film about ravens and how they eat small things that live in the sand along the ocean." Why did you change to say the word *revenge?*" Javy explained, "I looked more at the word and there was no *a* for the second letter, and how can you have triple ravens? That didn't make sense."

Miss Carter then goes on to say, "I noticed that you said *página* for *page* each time you read the word." Javy smiles and says, "Oh, I think I said it like Spanish, not in English!" Miss Carter nods, and says, "Yes, the words *page* and *página* are cognates. That means the

Name: Javy Date: 11-3-21	E	SC	E	SC
Book: Horrible Harry in Room 2B			MSV	MSV
✓✓ raven | SC / revenge		1	m s (v)	(m) s (v)
✓✓✓✓✓✓✓				
✓✓✓✓✓✓✓✓ página / page ✓				
✓✓✓ página / page ✓✓✓✓ página / page				
✓ somethin' / something ✓				
✓✓ somethin' / something ✓✓				
✓				
✓✓✓✓✓✓				
✓✓				
✓ blowed / lowered ✓ eye/br/eyebrows / eyebrows ✓✓✓	1		m (s)(v)	(m) s (v)
✓✓✓✓✓✓✓				
✓				

Words (W) = 60

Self-Corrections (SC) = 1

Errors (E) = 4

Error Rate (ER) = (E/W) × 100 = 4/60×100 = 6.7%

Accuracy = (W – E)/W × 100 = 60-4/60×100 = 93.3%

Self-Correction Rate = (E + SC)/SC = 1+1/1 = 1:2

NOTES: Javy did not read the two questionmarks in the dialog. He used self-correction and applied problem solving to figure out the word "eyebrows." He used the cognates página/page.

FIGURE 6.3. Javy's running record for *Horrible Harry in Room 2B.*

words have the same meaning and are almost the same in English and Spanish, but they are spelled and pronounced a little differently. Using cognates can help your reading and writing in both English and Spanish." Miss Carter points to the word *page* in the text, and Javy nods and says, "It's *page*. That's in the story." Miss Carter nods and then says, "Is that English or Spanish?" Javy responds, "English. *Page* is English." Miss Carter nods and continues, "I noticed that you didn't read the question marks when reading the character dialog—when they were talking to each other. I know that reading dialog is new, but it's important to help you understand what you are reading. We can work on reading dialog with questions tomorrow so you can get more practice." Miss Carter thanks Javy for reading with her, and she takes a moment to wrap up the guided-reading group and for students to return to their tables. Running records can be implemented very quickly. In fact, by the time Javy returns to his seat, only about 5 minutes have passed.

Miss Carter quickly analyzes the data from the running record by calculating error rate, accuracy rate, and self-correction rate. She analyzes errors by determining if Javy used meaning, structure, or visual information or a combination to try to figure out unknown words.

Finally, Miss Carter looks at the running record and compares it to the one she took of Javy's reading about 2 weeks prior. She notes an improvement in his accuracy rate and self-correction rate. She also sees that he is not overrelying on visual cues like he was previously, and sometimes he draws on structure information and his prior knowledge and experiences to help him figure out a word (e.g., *raven*). She knows that prior knowledge about words and their meanings can help students try to make sense of words that they are trying to identify. She noted that his pronunciation of *something* is consistent with his oral language, at times dropping the last sounds of words. This is a pronunciation error and not a reading error. Javy read the word *page* as *página,* using the Spanish word instead of the English. Because he is a linguistically diverse learner, she is teaching him to recognize that some words are cognates—those words that are in similar in more than one language. Miss Carter knows that using cognates is a strength that benefits his reading in both languages; therefore, she views this as a representation of his language and not an error. She noted that he omitted the question marks when reading the dialog in the text so she plans to address this in guided-reading instruction tomorrow as well as in her upcoming reading conference with Javy at the end of the week. She notes that the text was similar to the one he is reading with his small reading group. During their next conference, she plans to ask Javy to read a slightly more difficult text to determine how he is applying his skills and strategies with a text that is slightly more challenging. Miss Carter places the running record in Javy's folder on the counter behind the guided-reading table so she can use it for planning and also to document his reading development over time.

ASSESSMENT STRATEGY 6.3.
Oral Reading Analysis

Purpose

Oral Reading Analysis is a diagnostic assessment that allows you to determine a student's current knowledge and ability to use constrained and unconstrained skills to read a specific text. By observing carefully, recording data, and analyzing it for patterns, you can gain insights into a student's knowledge and use of phonics, knowledge of high-frequency words, and oral reading fluency (i.e., rate, accuracy, and prosody) to read a text. In addition, you can observe and gather data about a student's specific reading behaviors such as chunking word parts, decoding by analogy, applying letter–sound correspondences, using syntactic and semantic cues to confirm word choice, monitoring for understanding, and self-correcting. You can also assess the student's affect while reading the text.

Value

The value of listening to a student's oral reading is that it provides you with an authentic opportunity to observe a student's reading of a connected text to see how the student applies constrained and unconstrained skills that support decoding, reading, and understanding the text, as well as to observe their specific reading behaviors and affect while reading. Because this assessment strategy is flexible, the student can read a longer piece of text to allow you to gain additional insights into how the student engages with and navigates the text. Furthermore, because you are observing a student engaged in real reading in real time, you can see in all its complexity exactly what they do and what they bring to the reading task.

Procedures

1. In **preparation** for this assessment strategy, select a text for an individual student to read. You will have many choices of what text to select depending on your instructional goals and your knowledge of the texts your students have read previously. So, you may choose a more complex text, one that corresponds to texts the student has read with instructional support, one that is about a topic that interests the student, or a text that has language or structures that may be new to the student. Choice of text requires your thoughtful consideration to ensure the text is appropriate for the student in terms of complexity and length and will provide you with useful data about the student's reading. You will need to review how you will record your observations and the notations you will make when observing oral reading errors.
2. Invite the student to read a section of the text aloud. Tell the student, "Please read this aloud for me. I'll be taking some notes while you are reading so I can understand your reading better."
3. Observe carefully for the student's affect, use of constrained skills, and reading behaviors.
4. Record your observations using a chart such as the one provided in Form 6.3.
5. Ask the student to share something they noticed about their own reading. Follow up by asking the student what they would like to work on next as a reader. Record that information in the corresponding section of Form 6.3. Thank the student for reading with you.

Variations in Procedures

You can apply this assessment strategy in a small-group setting such as guided reading using an instructional-level text. In this context, while students read with a partner, you can observe and record data representing each student's oral reading.

Beyond asking the student to reflect on their reading overall, as is done in step 5 of the procedures, you may find it helpful to identify a specific miscue that you are not sure how to analyze and interpret and ask the student, "Can you tell me what you did to try and figure out this word?" This type of discussion can lead you to gaining greater insights on how the student approaches unknown words and the types of strategies and prior knowledge they are using (and not using) when reading. We examine students' miscues to determine how students' prior knowledge and experiences may influence their word reading and whether this knowledge aided their reading and understandings or whether a difference in meaning and word choice occurred. This analysis of students use of (or inattention to) prior knowledge and experiences informs our instruction. Students' cultural histories and experiences can aid word identification and word learning. We want to acknowledge to students the importance of bringing prior knowledge to a text to aid word learning and comprehension while also helping students listen to their own reading and determine whether they are making sense with their choices.

You can also listen to a student's oral reading in a more structured format by doing a running record so you can analyze the student's reading errors to learn more about the types of information, such as text language and grammatical information and text meaning information, the student uses when reading. See Assessment Strategy 6.2. *Running Records* for more information on implementing this variation.

Collecting, Analyzing, and Using Data

You can collect data about the student's reading using Form 6.3. You will want to have a copy of the text the student is reading so you can follow along. While the student is reading, fill out the sections of Form 6.3 that address affect, constrained skills, and reading behaviors. There is also blank space on the form for you to add specific things you want to observe in alignment with your curriculum, state standards, or developmental expectations.

After the student has completed the oral reading, review your notes, identify patterns, and fill in the "What could it mean" section for each column. Finally, consider the data and your analysis, as well as your previous observations of the student's reading over time to note any next steps for future instruction or goals for student reading performance.

Making Students and Teachers Visible

When you use *Oral Reading Analysis* as an assessment strategy, you must rely on your own knowledge about reading development and curricular expectations, as well as what you know about the student from your observations of the student's reading over time. This assessment strategy makes the teacher's knowledge and expertise visible and places decision making about instructional planning directly into the hands of the teacher.

This assessment makes the student's knowledge, use of skills, reading behaviors, affect toward reading, background knowledge, and linguistic resources visible while they read an authentic text. Furthermore, because you ask the student to reflect on their own oral reading, they are able to see and understand themselves as readers.

Implementation Example

Mr. Rivera is a third-grade teacher who finds that *listening to a student's oral reading* is one of the most effective ways to gather diagnostic assessment data about his students' reading and to observe how students' reading behaviors, ability, and strategy use change over time. During independent reading time, he generally asks a student to join him at the back table so he can listen to them read. One Tuesday afternoon, he decides to select an informational text about birds to use with one of his guided-reading groups later in the week. He asks Sophia, one of the students in the group, to join him to read a few pages of the text. He wants to see how she will read the text because it is at a slightly higher level than most books they have read previously, and it includes a number of multisyllabic words that contain familiar prefixes such as *re-*, *pre-*, and *un-*, as well as suffixes such as *-er*, *-est*, *-ful*, and *-less*.

Mr. Rivera has set up a routine in his classroom where he asks each child to join him periodically to read to him. As soon as Mr. Rivera calls Sophia, she quickly heads to the back table and eagerly responds to Mr. Rivera's request to read a few pages aloud. As she reads, he begins to observe closely, and notes that she seems relaxed and when he asks her to share something she notices about her reading, she smiles broadly before responding. He records his notes as she reads aloud (see Figure 6.4), and he notes that she is able to read high-frequency words easily and without hesitation. He also notes that she slowly and methodically chunks multisyllabic words such as *re/lax/ing*, *use/less*, and *help/less/ly* accurately, and then she reads the whole word. He notes that her accuracy is good, her rate is a bit slow, and her prosody is poor in terms of expression and phrasing. He also notes that she went back and self-corrected the word *wing*, which she had read as *win*. When he asks her afterward why she went back and self-corrected that word, Sophia responds, "It didn't make sense so I went back and read it again."

To **follow up**, Mr. Rivera asks Sophia to share something about her reading, and she responds, "I did good with the long words, but I didn't read with expression." He also shares that he noticed she paused before reading the word *weightless*, and he asks her, "How did you figure out that word?" She responds, "I looked at parts I knew. I saw *less*. I knew it, but the first part was hard." He probes further by asking, "So what did you do to figure it out?" After a moment Sophia responds, "I looked at the letters and tried to think what made sense. So I read *weightless*." Mr. Rivera thanks her for her input and asks her what she thinks she should work on next as a reader. She thinks for a moment and says, "I need to read long words without having to chunk all of them." He nods and responds, "That's a good goal, and I'm sure we can work on that in our guided-reading lessons this week." He then comments, "Do you agree that you didn't read this text with expression?" Sophia nods, and explains, "I was so worried about the big words. I forgot to read with expression." Mr. Rivera smiles and says, "There's a lot to think about when you are reading. That's why practice is so important! We can work on your fluency—specifically your expression—during guided reading, too." He then thanks Sophia, and she returns to her desk to resume her independent reading.

While implementing this assessment strategy and afterward, Mr. Rivera is focused on **collecting, analyzing, and using data** to understand Sophia's reading better. When Sophia is reading, he jots down his notes in the rows that address "What does the student do?" and "What does the student say?" (see Figure 6.4). He also records what Sophia shares about her own reading.

Afterward, as he reviews his notes (see Figure 6.4), he also reflects on what he knows about Sophia as a reader over time. More specifically, he considers his observations and her performance in guided reading, her participation during shared reading, and her engagement during independent reading times. By analyzing the data from the

Name: Sophia **Date:** 10-2-2020

Text: Wild Birds

Text characteristics (circle those that apply):		**Ind. level**	**Instr. level** (circled)
Unusual language	**Familiar topic**	**Unfamiliar topic**	**Other (specify)** Multisyllable words w/prefixes & suffixes (circled)

Record data about the three areas of affect, constrained skills, and strategies. Include specific examples as much as possible.

Specific things to observe for: decoding multisyllable words using prefixes and suffixes

Affect when reading • Emotions • Attitude • Physical responses	**Constrained skills** • Phonics (specify phonic elements) • High-frequency words • Oral reading fluency o Accuracy, rate, prosody	**Reading behaviors** • Figuring out unknown words • Use of information sources to figure out unknown words • Monitoring • Self-correcting
What does the student do? Eager to read Relaxed Smiled	What does the student do? Chunked multisyllable words using prefixes and suffixes Read high-frequency words accurately	What does the student do? She used self-correction (win to wing) and was able to explain what she did (used visual and meaning cues)
What does the student say?	What does the student say? "I looked at parts I knew." "I looked at letters and tried to think what made sense.">"	What does the student say? "It didn't make sense so I went back and read it again." "I looked at the parts I knew."
What could it mean? She is positive about reading and understands that she has strengths and areas where she can improve.	What could it mean? Sophia is able to apply skills of decoding in a methodical way. She applies her knowledge of high-frequency words by reading them automatically.	What could it mean? She monitored and used visual clues and meaning to figure out unknown words. She self-corrected an error by using visual information & meaning.

What does the student say about their own reading?

"I did good with the long words, but I didn't read with expression." "I need to read long words without having to chunk all of them."

Next steps and/or goals

Practice reading multisyllabic words to develop automaticity. Reread texts to focus on prosody—specifically expression and phrasing to support her comprehension development. Help her build on her strength of using meaning cues. Observe her reading of multisyllabic words and reading prosody in other settings.

FIGURE 6.4. Example of a record form for listening to a student's oral reading.

Oral Reading Analysis assessment in tandem with data and observations of Sophia's reading engagement, affect, and performance over time, Mr. Rivera is able to develop a clearer understanding of Sophia as a reader, including that she is using meaning cues such as "What makes sense?" He records those insights in the "What could it mean?" section. In the "Next steps and/or goals" section of Figure 6.4, he writes, "practice reading multisyllabic words to develop automaticity" and "re-read texts to focus on prosody—specifically expression and phrasing to support her comprehension development." He also notes that her use of meaning cues is a strength that she can build on to support her reading. He adds these goals to his guided-reading instructional plans, and because reading fluency is an important aspect of reading development in third grade, he makes a note to himself to observe Sophia's reading of multisyllabic words and her reading prosody in other situations throughout the coming days to gain greater insights into how she performs related to these goals while she is reading various texts in different contexts. Once he gathers this additional data, he will determine what types of fluency instruction and practice to implement with Sophia.

Mr. Rivera believes that the **value** of this assessment strategy is the opportunity to closely observe a student reading an authentic text in a 1:1 setting. By observing carefully, he can gain insights into what the student does, what they struggle with, the ways they use constrained skills, the reading behaviors they demonstrate, and their affect when reading. This assessment allows Mr. Rivera's students to make **visible** what they do as readers when reading an authentic text that the teacher has selected to gain insights into their ability to apply specific constrained skills. Furthermore, because this assessment includes the student's reflection on their reading, it also makes visible a student's self-perceptions. Mr. Rivera describes this assessment as seeing a "movie" of the student's reading as compared to traditional assessments that are more like a photo. This assessment also makes visible Mr. Rivera's knowledge and expertise related to reading development, and he uses both to inform his future instruction.

Using *Elkonin Sound Boxes* to Observe (and Understand) Student's Thinking about Phoneme Segmentation and Blending

Sound segmentation and blending are considered among the more difficult phonemic awareness skills for young children to learn, but they are foundational to developing phonics and decoding skills. Most phonemic awareness assessments determine that yes, a student can do this specific task, or no, they cannot. While that type of data has some value, it does not provide information on what students are thinking and how they approach tasks and try to solve problems. *Elkonin Sound Boxes* and other assessment strategies that require students to physically do something—such as segment words into sounds or form words with given sounds—and then to explain what they have done, provide multiple opportunities for you to see students' thought processes and problem solving as well as their knowledge and use of constrained skills. This assessment strategy can be administered during individual conferences with students, and/or during small-group instruction with data collected for each student.

ASSESSMENT STRATEGY 6.4.
Elkonin Sound Boxes

Purpose

Elkonin Sound Boxes can be used as an assessment to understand how young children segment sounds in a spoken word and then blend them to say the word. Elkonin (1971) created this strategy to help children develop the important phonemic awareness skills of sound segmentation wherein they segment words into individual sounds or phonemes by moving a token into a box for each sound they hear in the word and then blending the individual sounds together to say the word.

Value

Elkonin sound boxes allow you to gain insights into a child's development of phoneme segmentation and blending, which are key foundations for understanding the alphabetic principle in decoding and spelling. You can actually see the child's thinking while they segment words as they push tokens into boxes and then move their fingers under the tokens to blend the sounds into the word. The movement of the tokens provides young children a physical reinforcement of processes performed "in the head." By making their thinking visible, you can determine where they are in their phonemic awareness development rather than just whether they get the answer correct or not. Using data you collect through this assessment, you can determine how children segment and blend words with two sounds, three sounds, and more, as well as words with digraphs (two letters that make one sound), blends (two or more letters that blend together but have separate sounds), and end with a silent *e*. Using these data, you can determine what instruction and practice individual students need to develop these important phonemic awareness skills.

Procedures

1. In **preparation** for the strategy, you will need a template like the one in Figure 6.5. You will also need to gather three to five tokens, such as counters, pennies, or cubes,

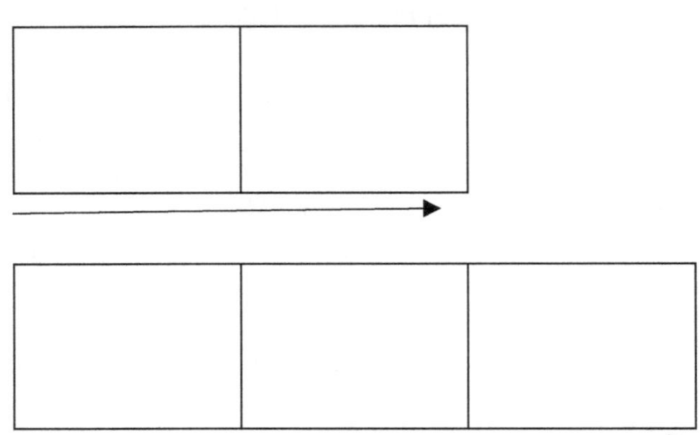

FIGURE 6.5. *Elkonin* sound boxes template.

for each student. Prepare a list of words that are organized by increasing difficulty. See Table 6.2 for a recommended progression from easy to more difficult. You can also progress to words with four and five phonemes for students who are further along in the development of their phonemic awareness skills.

2. Remind the student that words are made up of sounds and explain that they will practice hearing the sounds in a word. Be sure to emphasize that they should focus on the sounds they hear, not the letters.
3. If this is a new strategy for the student, model the process with two or three words to ensure that the student understands the task. Point to the set of boxes that has two squares. Explain that the student will move one counter into one square for each sound they hear. Model how to do this with the word *it*. Place two counters above the squares. Say the word *it*. Ask the student to say the word after you. Then, pull down one counter into the first square as you say /i/ and the second counter as you say /t/. Then run your finger along the arrow underneath the box to blend the sounds back together to say *it*. Repeat with one or two examples to ensure the student understands the process.
4. Ask the student to segment and blend several words of increasing complexity using the chart provided above for guidance. Record the student's performance on Form 6.4.
5. Ask the student to explain what they did for the last word they segmented and blended to gain insight into their understanding of these phonemic awareness skills.

Collecting, Analyzing, and Using Data

As the student segments and blends each word, record those data on Form 6.4. You will also want to record the student's response to step 5 in the procedure to get additional data on their understanding of segmenting and blending processes. Review the student's performance, considering their ability to segment simple and more complex words with two phonemes, three phonemes, and so on.

TABLE 6.2. Word Lists for Two and Three Phonemes in Progression of Difficulty

Word lists for two and three phonemes	Examples
Two-phoneme words (short vowels; no vowel or consonant combinations)	*at, in, on, up*
Three-phoneme words (CVC words; short vowels)	*mat, red, sit, lot, run*
Three-phoneme words (CCVC or CVCC with blends or doubled consonants)	*glad, mess, skin, drop*
Three-phoneme words (CCVC or CVCC with digraphs)	*hang, them, chip, sock, hush*
Three-phoneme words (CVCe—with silent *e*)	*same, fine, home, cube*
Two- and three-phoneme words with vowel combinations and diphthongs	*day, team, light, coat, loop, boy, cow, lawn*

Based on the student's performance as well as observations of the student's ability to segment and blend phonemes during shared reading, guided reading, and other settings, you can get a complete picture of this aspect of each student's phonemic awareness. Using these data, you can determine if you need to provide instruction and practice with simple one-, two-, or three-phoneme words or with words with additional phonemes and more complex features such as blends, doubled consonants, digraphs, silent *e*, vowel combinations, and diphthongs.

Phonemic awareness is a necessary foundation for reading development, but as a set of constrained skills, it is insufficient by itself. Therefore, once the student is able to segment and blend words with four or five phonemes, you can move on to the most challenging aspect of phonemic awareness—phoneme deletion and manipulation. With phoneme deletion, the child is asked to say the word with the beginning or ending sound removed. For example, "What word do we have if you say *cat* without the /k/?" (*at*). With phoneme manipulation, the child is asked to "play with" sounds in the word to make a new word. For example, "Take the word *pot* and change the /p/ to /h/. What's the word?" (*hot*). While instruction of phonemic awareness skills is important, it should be a small portion of your instructional time. Once students have gained control over phonemic awareness skills, you can stop teaching and assessing phonemic awareness skills. You can then focus on other constrained skills such as phonics and fluency, while emphasizing vocabulary and comprehension instruction, because being able to understand what one reads is the real purpose of reading.

Making Students and Teachers Visible

Some phonemic awareness assessments focus only on whether a student is able or unable to complete a task. While that type of information may be somewhat helpful, it is more valuable to understand how a student approaches, understands, and completes the task. With Elkonin sound boxes, students are able to demonstrate their phonemic awareness skills by physically moving counters as they segment the word and sliding their finger along the arrow below the boxes as they blend the word so you can see what they understand as well as where their understanding breaks down. In addition, by asking students to explain how they segment and blend one or more of the words, you can gain greater insight into their understanding of these phonemic awareness skills.

Your knowledge as a teacher is front-and-center during this assessment strategy, as you must understand the progression of words from simple to more complex and have a good understanding of phonemic awareness to develop your word lists. In addition, your knowledge of your students and their phonemic awareness skills is essential during this assessment as you determine if you should continue assessing the student or if you have reached a point where they require more instruction and practice. Knowing that your students' pronunciation of sounds and words may be consistent with their regional dialect or their home language while learning English, it is important to consider this information, accepting these representations, when evaluating their performance on these tasks. Such recognition acknowledges students' use of their language information and accepts these differences as part of their language development.

Implementation Example

Mrs. Anderson teaches first grade. She has been teaching segmenting and blending during shared reading and guided reading, and she wants to assess several of her students' skills using Elkonin sound boxes. She prepares a list of words that have two and three phonemes and include complex features such as CVC*e* words as well as those with vowel combinations and diphthongs. She also prints out a page with two, three, and four Elkonin sound boxes and gathers round plastic counters that are each about the size of a penny. Finally, she prints out a copy of Form 6.4 and fills in the two left columns with the words she plans to use for assessment (see Figure 6.6).

Mrs. Anderson sits at a kidney-shaped table with Katelyn, one of her first-grade students. She explains to Katelyn how to use Elkonin sound boxes following the procedures described above. She demonstrates the process with the words *up* and *mat.* She then asks Katelyn to segment and blend the word *cup,* and when Katelyn does this correctly, Mrs. Anderson moves to the list she has prepared with the following words: *chip, sock, hush, same, home, day, team, loop.* As Katelyn segments and blends each word using the Elkonin sound boxes, Mrs. Anderson records her responses (see Figure 6.6). She then asks Katelyn, "Can you tell me how you segmented and blended the word *loop*?" Katelyn responds, "I stretch out the word and put a counter in the box. Then I say the whole word." Mrs. Anderson smiles, and asks, "When you push a counter in the box, what does that mean?" Katelyn pauses for a moment, furrowing her brow, and then says, "It's because it's for each sound." Mrs. Anderson follows up by saying, "Each sound that . . . ?" Katelyn smiles and finishes the sentence by saying, "that is in the word."

Mrs. Anderson thanks Katelyn and tells her that she is making good progress with her segmenting and blending skills. She then asks Katelyn to return to her seat. Mrs. Anderson makes a few notes on the record sheet and jots down her plans to practice segmenting and blending words with vowel diphthongs and combinations as well as introducing words with four phonemes. She then asks Raul to join her at the table to assess his segmenting and blending skills.

Developmental Spelling Assessment Views Spelling from an Equity-Minded Lens

Traditional spelling tests are a cornerstone of language arts assessment in many schools, but by only marking words as correct or incorrect, they have very limited value. On the other hand, by taking a developmental spelling view and looking to see what spelling features students are using and noting patterns in how they spell words, you can make visible what students understand about constrained skills, those they apply, and those they still need to learn. You can then use these data to plan and deliver spelling and instruction that is appropriate for your students. This assessment strategy can be embedded within your whole-class and small-group instruction routines.

ASSESSMENT STRATEGY 6.5.
Developmental Spelling Assessment

Purpose

Understanding your students' developmental spelling will provide you windows into their thinking and use of constrained skills, such as letter–sound relationships. By asking emergent spellers to spell challenging words, they must apply their current understanding of

Name: Katelyn **Date:** November 6, 2020

Target word	**Number of phonemes and complexity**	**Segmenting** ✓ = correct Record errors	**Blending** ✓ = correct Record errors
chip	3 ch digraph	✓	✓
sock	3 ck digraph	✓	✓
hush	3 sh digraph	✓	✓
same	3 CVCe	✓	✓
home	3 CVCe	✓	✓
day	2 ay diphthong	Segmented ay	✓
team	3 ea vowel combo.	✓	✓
loop	3 oo vowel combo.	Segmented oo	✓

Select at least one target word. Ask student to tell you what they are doing. Record what the student says to document their understanding of segmenting and blending.

"I stretch out the word and I put a counter in the box. Then I say the whole word. It's because it's for each sound . . . that is in the word."

Katelyn segmented and blended *loop* correctly this time.

Analysis:

Inconsistent performance with 2 and 3 phoneme words with vowel diphthongs and combinations. Able to blend all words correctly.

Next steps:

Observe Katelyn segmenting and blending words in shared reading and guided reading.

More practice with segmenting words with vowel diphthongs and combinations. Also introduce words with four phonemes.

FIGURE 6.6. Example of a record sheet for *Elkonin* sound boxes.

letter–sound relationships. The spellings are not counted as correct or incorrect; rather, you will analyze them using a developmental scale to understand each student's spelling development so you can plan appropriate instruction.

Value

Spelling and phonics can be thought of as different sides of the same coin. A *Developmental Spelling Assessment* is quick and easy to administer to a group of students. Because you can analyze each word to see what spelling features a student is using or not using, you can gain important insights into their understanding of sound symbol relationships that can inform your instruction. You can create your own word lists to provide you with the information you need to plan phonics and spelling instruction so that students have strong skills in these areas that they can apply to their reading and writing.

Procedures

1. **Prepare** the list of words you want students to spell that align with the types of spelling features your students need to be learning according to your curriculum and your knowledge of spelling development. Or use this list from Johns, Lenski, and Elish-Piper (2002), if it is appropriate for your students.

   drop, faster, liked, back, monster, mess, packet, make, earn, greet

2. Tell the students, "Today we are going to spell some words. Some of the words will be hard, but don't worry. Just spell them the best you can by making good guesses about the sounds you hear and the letters that spell those sounds. This is not for a grade, but it will help me understand how I can best teach you about phonics and spelling."
3. Ask each student to number a sheet of paper from 1 to 10 and to write their name on the top of the page.
4. Dictate the list of 10 words. After saying each word, use it in a simple sentence. For example, if the first word on the list is *drop*, say, "*Drop* . . . Do not drop the dish when you dry it." Continue through the list of words. Repeat words and sentences as necessary.

Collecting, Analyzing, and Using Data

Review each student's spellings by using the developmental spelling features listed in Table 6.3. Do not focus on whether the child spelled correctly or incorrectly, but look at the types of spelling features they did use. You will likely find that some of the students' spellings do not map neatly onto the examples provided for each stage so you will need to use your best professional judgment to determine which stage most accurately represents the students' spellings. It will also be helpful to consider what you have observed about students' spellings in other settings such as in their daily work, journals, and shared writing. Using all of this data, determine which spelling stage most accurately describes most of the words the student has spelled. You may find it useful to look at the results for a group of students or your whole class to form short-term instructional groups to teach and practice specific spelling patterns.

TABLE 6.3. Developmental Spelling Features

Precommunicative	Semiphonetic	Phonetic	Transitional	Conventional
Random letters or symbols	*dp*	*dop*	*dropp*	*drop*
Random letters or symbols	*ft*	*fasr*	*fastr*	*faster*
Random letters or symbols	*lt*	*likt*	*licked*	*liked*
Random letters or symbols	*bk*	*bak*	*backe*	*back*
Random letters or symbols	*mtr*	*mostr*	*monster*	*monster*
Random letters or symbols	*ms*	*mss*	*mes*	*mess*
Random letters or symbols	*pt*	*pkt*	*paked*	*packed*
Random letters or symbols	*mk*	*mak*	*macke*	*make*
Random letters or symbols	*en*	*ern*	*earn*	*earn*
Random letters or symbols	*gt*	*gret*	*grete*	*greet*

Making Students and Teachers Visible

Rather than showing only which words they can spell correctly and which they cannot, this assessment provides a window into each student's understanding of sound–symbol relationships. By analyzing students spelling patterns, you can identify those spelling features they have control over and which ones they are not yet using conventionally. The *Developmental Spelling Assessment* makes your knowledge about sound–symbol relationships and spelling development very visible as you analyze and interpret the students' spellings. Gentry (1981) identified the following developmental spelling features (children's examples are shown in Table 6.3):

- *Precommunicative:* Children use letters and letter-like symbols when writing words, but they do not correspond to sounds. This is the earliest stage of spelling development.
- *Semiphonetic:* Children know that letters represent sounds. Spellings are telegraphic and usually focus on beginning and sometimes ending sounds.
- *Phonetic:* Children spell words like they sound, and all phonemes are usually represented.
- *Transitional:* Children focus on how words appear visually. Spellings demonstrate an understanding of common spelling patterns, but they may be applied incorrectly.
- *Conventional:* Children spell words correctly.

Implementation Example

Mr. Hu teaches second grade, and he just administered the *Developmental Spelling Assessment* to several of his students. He looks at Omar's assessment and identifies developmental spelling features in Table 6.3. He records Omar's spelling as shown in Figure 6.7. He also

Target word	Omar's spelling	Spelling stage
drop	*drop*	Conventional
daster	*fastr*	Transitional
liked	*likt*	Phonetic
back	*bak*	Phonetic
monster	*monster*	Transitional
mess	*mes*	Transitional
packed	*pakt*	Phonetic
make	*mak*	Phonetic
warn	*ern*	Phonetic
greet	*gret*	Phonetic

FIGURE 6.7. Omar's spelling identified by developmental spelling stages.

considers his observations of Omar's spelling over the past few days. Omar is a linguistically diverse learner whose home language is Arabic. Omar receives English as a second language (ESL) support daily, and Mr. Hu and Mrs. Ramirez, the ESL teacher, have both noted that he is making good progress on his reading, writing, and speaking in English. Mr. Hu remembers the following spellings that Omar used in his journal yesterday (*take/tak*; *smile/smil*; *happy/hapy*). He combines those data with Omar's spelling on the assessment. He concludes that Omar is at the phonetic stage of spelling and specifically that he needs to provide Omar with instruction about spelling words with the silent *e* (VC*e*) pattern. Mr. Hu uses this basic approach to assessing students spelling development, but he knows that other teachers may use more complex models such as those advocated by Ganske (1999) and in *Words Their Way* (Bear, Invernizzi, Templeton, & Johnston, 2008).

Conclusion

Constrained skills in reading are like building blocks—they are necessary, but they are not sufficient on their own. In each of the five assessment strategies we shared in this chapter, the constrained skills are nested within authentic contexts of reading or writing so you can obtain a sense of how your students are applying those skills. While it may seem easier to assess constrained skills in isolation, the real value of these assessment strategies is that they allow you to make visible your students' thought processes, use of strategies, understandings and misconceptions, and assets such as background knowledge and linguistic resources.

FORM 6.1

Anecdotal Record Form for *What Can You Show Us?* Strategy

Text: ____

Constrained skills to look for from curriculum: ____

____

Date: ______________________

Student name	Observations related to constrained skills	Next steps for assessment and teaching points

Ideas for next group lesson: ____

____

Students to follow up with and why: ____

FORM 6.2

Running Record

Name:	**Date:**	**E**	**SC**	**E**	**SC**
Book:				**MSV**	**MSV**

Words (W) =

Self-Corrections (SC) =

Errors (E) =

Error Rate (ER) = (E/W) × 100 =

Accuracy = (W – E)/W × 100 =

Self-Correction Rate = (E + SC)/SC =

NOTES:

FORM 6.3

Record Form for Listening to a Student's Oral Reading

Name: ______________________________ **Date:** ______________________

Text: ____

Text characteristics (circle those that apply):		**Ind. level**	**Instr. level**
Unusual language	**Familiar topic**	**Unfamiliar topic**	**Other (specify)**

Record data about the three areas of affect, constrained skills, and strategies. Include specific examples as much as possible.

Specific things to observe for: ______________________________________

Affect when reading • Emotions • Attitude • Physical responses	**Constrained skills** • Phonics (specify phonic elements) • High-frequency words • Oral reading fluency o Accuracy, rate, prosody	**Reading behaviors** • Figuring out unknown words • Use of cueing systems • Monitoring • Self-correcting • ______________ • ______________
What does the student do?	What does the student do?	What does the student do?
What does the student say?	What does the student say?	What does the student say?

(continued)

Record Form for Listening to a Student's Oral Reading *(page 2 of 2)*

Affect when reading	**Constrained skills**	**Reading behaviors**
What could it mean?	What could it mean?	What could it mean?
What does the student say about their own reading?		
Next steps and/or goals		

FORM 6.4

Record Sheet for Elkonin Sound Boxes

Name ______________________________ **Date** ____________________

Target word	Number of phonemes and complexity	Segmenting ✓ = correct Record errors	Blending ✓ = correct Record errors

Select at least one target word. Ask student to tell you what they are doing. Record what the student says to document their understanding of segmenting and blending.

Analysis:

Next steps:

7

Using Assessment to Support Students' Development of Agency

> If teaching is to be effective with young children, it must assist them to advance on the way to independence.
>
> —MARIA MONTESSORI

The goal of an equitable education is to help all students become independent learners (Hammond, 2015, p. 14). An equitable education, however, requires more than just access and opportunity. If we truly want to leverage education as a tool for empowerment and for promoting social and racial justice, we must choose instructional and assessment practices that honor the dignity that is inherent in each student by virtue of their humanity (Cobb & Krownapple, 2019). When we use formative assessments, we make students visible and help them find and amplify their own voices so they can become self-directed, independent learners who have decision-making power in their education and lives. In short, agentive learners have voice, choice, and ownership of their learning (Gilchrist, 2018).

Formative literacy assessment offers the promise of empowering all students to be agents who have control over and the power to act on their education and lives rather than just being passive participants who lack control, autonomy, and power (Freire, 2005). Bandura (2008) defines being an agent or having agency as being an active participant in one's life events, not just being a product of those events. Perhaps an easy way to think about the concept of agency is to imagine students as drivers for their learning rather than passengers who are simply along for the ride. For example, when students set goals for their learning, self-assess their performance and progress, understand and articulate their strengths and areas of need, and tell their teachers the types of feedback and support they need, they are demonstrating their agency as learners.

A practical definition of student agency is a "student's ability to have ideas, to have intentions, and to exert influence and take actions in the learning context" (Vaughn, Premo, Sotirovska, Erickson, 2019, p. 428). According to research from the American Institutes for Research conducted by Zeiser, Scholz, and Cirks (2018), agentive students have high achievement and engagement in school because they manage their learning and take an active role in pursuing and internalizing new learning through collaborating, communicating, and engaging in the classroom and world. Zeiser et al. also examined what teachers did to support students becoming agentive learners, and found five things that effective teachers do:

1. Develop personal relationships with students.
2. Guide students in the process of asking for feedback.
3. Use student goal setting as a foundation for learning in the classroom.
4. Expect students to provide input on key decisions in the classroom that affect them and their learning.
5. Use formative assessments, like the ones presented throughout this book, to promote and measure student agency.

Gerzon and Jones (2020) argued that "formative assessment has the power to advance achievement only when students come to see themselves as responsible for, and agents of, their own learning" (p. 2). Therefore, as a starting place, assessment practices must "focus on providing ways to make students' current knowledge and understanding visible (e.g., through what they say, do, make, or write)" (pp. 2–3).

Now, let us look at agency more specifically in the context of literacy education. Agentive students are strategic, goal directed, and willing to take risks to solve problems and address challenges. Johnston (2004) asserted that teachers can do simple things to foster students' agency as readers, such as providing opportunities to stop and talk about their thinking (while reading), so students can gain more control over their own reading and comprehension processes. When students have agency, they "can influence and make decisions about the reading process when they are able to evaluate their progress to determine whether their reading is successful or unsuccessful and then to make adjustments as needed so that they can reach their goal" (Almasi & Hurt, 2019, p. 238). When students are willing to take risks and try new ways of thinking and processing text, they begin to understand when a text does not make sense that they have the agency to take action to try to make sense of the text. In this process, "Students determine *whether* they need to be strategic, *when* they need to be strategic, *where* they need to be strategic, and *how* to be strategic. Such agentive behavior is necessary to help students transform themselves from passive to active participants in the reading process" (Almasi & Hurt, 2019, p. 240). For an example of how think-aloud procedures can be used to illuminate student thinking while reading, see Chapter 5, Assessment Strategy 5.2.

So, what specific steps can teachers take to move toward formative assessment that informs and supports the development of their students' agency? As advised in Chapter 3, it is important to build positive, respectful relationships so you can establish a trusting, caring partnership with each student. By doing so, you can foster an inclusive, equitable classroom community that promotes respect, risk taking, safety, and agency. Such classroom climates are important for all students, but especially for students from diverse backgrounds, including immigrants, refugees, emergent bilinguals, and others from traditionally marginalized groups, who may feel they are too different to be part of the classroom community (McNeill, 2020). We like to refer to such classrooms as safe <u>and</u> brave spaces. The term "safe space" has been used widely to focus on creating classrooms where students and teachers "share air time, actively listen, show empathy, respect confidentiality, participate fully, assume good will, [and are] sensitive to feelings and others" (Anti-Defamation League, 2019, p. 1). However, such safe spaces are not sufficient for creating truly equitable, inclusive classrooms that foster and support student agency. By focusing on creating safe *and* brave spaces, we can build contexts where students and teachers understand that they may feel uncomfortable at times, but that is part of growing and taking ownership for one's own learning while also addressing difficult issues such as bias, social justice, and racial justice. When confronting such uncomfortableness, "a brave space is one in which we take risks, doing so with care and compassion" (Anti-Defamation League, 2019, p. 1), so each member can act upon the world, be fully visible, share their voice, chart their path, grow, thrive, and succeed (Arao & Clemens, 2013).

When you create a safe *and* brave space, students (and teachers) are comfortable taking risks, challenging assumptions, asserting what they need to grow, and teachers are routinely seeking and using input from students not only to guide their individual learning but to determine classroom processes and practices. In addition, in such classrooms, teachers must commit not just to student-centered instructional practices, but take it a bit further—to student-directed instruction and assessment. Teachers can do this by creating regular opportunities and channels for students to ask for feedback and assistance that meet their needs as learners. This overlaps with the importance of student-initiated goal setting that focuses on goals that are meaningful and relevant to the student, promoting ownership and engagement in learning. In addition, teachers must seek student input in meaningful and honest ways so they can understand the impact of their instruction, classroom activities, classroom procedures, the curriculum, and other aspects of literacy learning. Such input is essential for teachers to reflect on, revise, and refine their instruction so it is as effective and relevant as possible. More importantly, this process shows students that through their agency, they are truly partners with their teachers, and they play the most important role in their own educational experiences. For these reasons, we argue that formative assessment is an essential tool for supporting students' literacy development through agency.

In the remainder of this chapter, we present four assessment strategies that will help you learn about your students' agency as they develop as self-directed, independent learners and readers who have voice, choice, and ownership of their learning. The assessments we present in this chapter frame agency as a developmental process and help teachers to document and analyze their students' progression from passive students to agentive learners. By using these assessments, we can ensure we are not only providing opportunities for students to develop agency, but we have data to guide the support, feedback, and modeling students need to take ownership of their learning. As you read about and reflect on each of these assessment strategies, these questions will help guide your thinking.

- How does the assessment reveal student voice and choice?
- How does the assessment identify students' strengths and areas for growth related to voice, choice, and ownership of learning?
- How does the assessment help me understand the opportunities and support that I do (and do not) provide to support student ownership of learning?
- How can I use what I learn from these assessments to foster student voice, choice, and ownership of learning?

ASSESSMENT STRATEGIES: UNDERSTANDING STUDENTS' AGENCY AS LEARNERS

In this part of the chapter, we offer four assessment strategies that will help you (and your students) understand their agency as learners who are developing into self-directed and independent individuals and who take the lead in their own learning. These assessment strategies are important facilitators for equitable education because they put students in the center of their learning and support their development of voice, choice, and ownership. These assessments align closely with Zeiser et al.'s (2018) findings, as noted above, of five things teachers can do to support students' development of agency: (1) develop personal relationships with students, (2) guide students to ask for feedback needed to support their learning, (3) use student goal setting to frame learning, (4) expect student input on key decisions, and (5) use formative assessments such as those that follow.

The assessment strategies in this chapter are:

7.1. *Teacher Self-Evaluation of Opportunities for Student Agency*

7.2. *Student Agency Questionnaire*

7.3. *Student Self-Assessment*

7.4. *Goal Setting*

Teacher Self-Evaluation of Opportunities for Student Agency Can Help You Support Students' Development as Agentive Learners

Typically, the focus of literacy assessment is on the student, and that is right where it should be. However, this assessment is different in that it focuses on your classroom and the opportunities you provide for students to develop voice, choice, and ownership of their learning.

For students to develop as independent and agentive learners, they must first be able to make choices, which fuels their voice, and leads to the development of independence and ownership over their learning. Zeiser et al. (2018) asserted that teachers are central to supporting student independence and agency through the opportunities they provide and the instructional approaches they use. If numerous meaningful and authentic opportunities are not available for students to develop their agency, and instructional approaches are mostly teacher-centered, those things will be barriers to student progress. Therefore, before you consider assessing students' agency, you will want to first assess your classroom through an equity lens to evaluate the opportunities you do (or do not) provide and the degree to which you implement instructional approaches that encourage all students to make choices, express their voices, and develop ownership for their learning. If you do this self-evaluation early in the school year, it will provide you with useful information to ensure you are creating a classroom context that will help all students develop and use their agency. If you determine that you need to add opportunities or adjust instructional approaches, you can implement them for a period of time and then complete the self-evaluation again later in the year to gauge progress or the need for further changes.

ASSESSMENT STRATEGY 7.1.

Teacher Self-Evaluation of Opportunities for Student Agency

Purpose

This self-evaluation is designed for teachers to understand the instructional practices and classroom opportunities they provide to nurture student voice, choice, and ownership of learning. It also helps teachers identify areas where they can enhance their teaching and creation of meaningful classroom opportunities for students to develop as agentive and independent learners.

Value

For education to truly be equitable, all students must have the opportunity to develop confidence in their voices, to make their own choices, and to take ownership for their learning so they can become lifelong learners who are equipped to meet the needs and opportunities in their lives. An education that trains students to comply, to follow directions, and to re-create only what has been previously created, is not the type of education needed to advance our democratic society and promote social and racial justice for all. Therefore, the *Teacher Self-Evaluation of Opportunities for Student Agency* is a first step for teachers to use self-evaluation to analyze and revise their teaching approaches and student-learning opportunities that provide a safe and brave space where all of their students can develop into independent, agentive learners.

Procedures

1. To **prepare** to complete the *Teacher Self-Evaluation of Opportunities for Student Agency* (Form 7.1), first consider and reflect carefully on the instructional approaches and classroom opportunities you provide to your students. It may be helpful to look through your lesson plans, classroom schedule, curriculum, and classroom procedures to help you determine how to fill out the self-evaluation.
2. As you prepare to complete the self-evaluation, be sure to be honest, because the purpose of this self-evaluation is to improve your practices and classroom opportunities associated with giving your students voice, choice, and ownership of their learning.
3. For each question, record brief notes and apply a rating of *daily, sometimes,* or *never* to reflect whether students have the opportunity in your classroom every day, on some occasions, or not at all.

Collecting, Analyzing, and Using Data

You will **collect** data through completing the self-evaluation. To begin **analyzing the data,** tally the number of prompts you rated in each category—*daily, sometimes,* and *never*—and record that information near the bottom of Form 7.1. Look at the items you rated as *daily* and consider what you do to provide these opportunities daily and to offer instruction, support, and feedback to help students develop in each area. Reflect on the things you and your students do to make these practices part of your classroom daily. For questions you rated as *sometimes,* consider steps you can take to move toward *daily.* Finally, look at the items you rated as *never* and consider how you can address this facilitator of agency so that you do it at least *sometimes* in your classroom.

Look at the prompts that focus on the three components of agency: *choice* (prompts 1–5), *voice* (prompts 6–7), and *ownership* (prompts 8–14). See if there are patterns within or across the components. For example, check to see if you rated one component higher than others. If so, consider why that might be. Or did all of your *daily* or *never* answers end up in one component? Consider what that might mean.

To **use the data,** select a few prompts you want to address so you can move your ratings to the next higher level, with *daily* being your ultimate goal. If you have lots of prompts where you want to enhance your practice and your students' opportunities for growth related to agency, we recommend that you select two or three of them to focus your efforts, so you are more likely to be able to successfully move them closer to the rating of *daily.* Write those items at the bottom of Form 7.1 and jot down action steps you can take to address them. Each semester, you can retake the self-evaluation and identify additional prompts to address through specific action steps.

Making Students and Teachers Visible

The *Teacher Self-Evaluation of Opportunities for Student Agency* puts the focus on teachers themselves through the self-evaluation they do to look critically at their instructional approaches and the classroom opportunities they provide for students to develop voice, choice, and ownership of their learning. As teachers reflect on what they are doing as well as areas they can enhance, they are making their teaching philosophy, practices, and priorities visible not only to themselves but to their students, who will experience learning in the classroom that the teacher designs and facilitates. The realities of being a student in the classroom can be illuminated as teachers complete the self-evaluation, reflect, and take action to ensure their teaching methods and classroom opportunities support student independence and agency.

Implementation Example

Mr. Lee is an experienced fifth-grade teacher. His former students often come back to visit him once they graduate and begin middle school because they remember how enthusiastic, fun-loving, and kind Mr. Lee was to them during their final year in elementary school. They often describe how much they enjoyed book clubs, student-directed projects, group work, hands-on learning activities, and service-learning trips into the local community. Several of his students from last year, Colin, Lucia, Faith, and Rehan, described him in an end-of-the-year assembly as "awesome," "the best teacher ever," "a cool guy," and "my favorite teacher." This year, his Asian students, Ying, Ji-ah, and Kyung, often comment how much they like having a teacher "who looks like them," and this means a great deal to Mr. Lee because he is the only male teacher of color in his entire elementary school.

While it may appear to his students, colleagues, and others that Mr. Lee is an exemplary teacher, he is always reflecting on his teaching and considering ways he can improve his teaching and his students' learning.

Mr. Lee's students live in a large suburb about 30 minutes outside of a major city. The community is highly diverse, and the enrollment at his school has large percentages of Black, Latinx, Asian, and multiracial students, with about 20% of the students identifying as White. Mr. Lee came to the United States from South Korea when he was a child, and he remembers how challenging it was to learn English, adjust to a new country, and make friends. He has worked hard over the years to create a classroom that is a safe and brave space for all his students, and recently he has become concerned about how well he is preparing his students for middle school and beyond. He has been trying to shift his teaching toward more student-centered and student-directed approaches, but he worries that some of his students who are linguistically, culturally, and racially diverse, as well as his students who have special needs, may not be developing into independent learners. Therefore, as he prepared to start a new school year—his 14th year of teaching—he decided to complete the *Teacher Self-Evaluation of Opportunities for Student Agency* to consider and reflect on how well he is doing with putting student independence and agency at the center of his teaching and classroom.

Mr. Lee filled out the self-evaluation a couple of weeks into the new school year once he had gotten to know his students, establish relationships with them, and introduce and establish classroom procedures with his students. His completed self-evaluation is provided in Figure 7.1.

After completing the self-evaluation, Mr. Lee realized that his students did not have as many opportunities to make meaningful choices or share their voices as he wanted. He also realized that his students did not have as much ownership for their learning as he had assumed they did. Because his class generally runs smoothly, his students are engaged, and they report enjoying being in his class, he thought that he was doing enough to develop their agency. The *Teacher Self-Evaluation of Opportunities for Student Agency* reminded him of the importance of reviewing and reflecting on his teaching and his student experiences to ensure that he is doing all he can to help his students develop into independent learners. Mr. Lee realized that simply providing opportunities for students to develop agency was not enough. He understands now that he needs to actively teach, model, and provide feedback so students can develop as agentive learners. Mr. Lee is committed to the action plan he developed to address the one item he rated as *never* and three items he rated as *sometimes* that he thinks are vital for moving his classroom and his teaching toward more opportunities and support for students to develop independence. He plans to complete the self-evaluation again in about a month to see what progress he and his students have made as well as new action steps he needs to develop to enhance his teaching practices and the opportunities he provides to his students that support their development as independent learners. Mr. Lee believes this assessment has great **value** because it allows him to reflect deeply on how he encourages and supports student agency in his classroom. Through completing the self-evaluation, he can make his practices **visible,** so he can analyze and understand them through the lens of student agency.

Prompt (C) choice, (V) voice, (O) ownership	**Notes**	**Daily, sometimes, or never**
1. Students make choices about what they learn in the classroom. (C)	For inquiry projects students chose their own topics. Otherwise, the curriculum is predetermined by the district and to a lesser degree by me.	Sometimes
2. Students make choices about how they learn in the classroom. (C)	I give students choices like to work alone or with a partner, sit at your desk or on the rug, work at the computer to read the digital text or read the book, and so on, but the choices are kind of limited.	Sometimes
3. Students make choices about what activities they do in the classroom. (C)	I give structured choices like play a review game or do a computer activity. Choices are limited and provided by me. I wonder what students would choose if I left it more open-ended.	Sometimes
4. Students make choices about how they demonstrate their learning. (C)	For projects I give the students a list of choices, and I include one that says "you design it" so students can come up with their own ways to demonstrate what they have learned. They don't pick that option often, however.	Sometimes
5. Students make choices about the books and other texts they read in the classroom. (C)	This is an important part of the classroom. Students always pick what to read for free-choice reading and for inquiry projects. They also have some choices for group activities.	Daily
6. Student voices are an important part of decisions about important things in the classroom. (V)	We have weekly classroom meetings where we talk about what we are doing, what's coming next, what's going well, and what we can do better.	Sometimes
7. Students share their ideas, opinions, and suggestions freely with me and their classmates. (V)	At our weekly classroom meetings and conferences, I really encourage students to share their voices, but sometimes I think some students might be hesitant to do so.	Sometimes
8. Students set goals for their own learning. (O)	We do goal setting during reading and writing conferences. We also do goal setting as part of portfolio assessment.	Sometimes

(continued)

FIGURE 7.1. Example of a *Teacher Self-Evaluation of Opportunities for Student Agency.*

Prompt (C) choice, (V) voice, (O) ownership	**Notes**	**Daily, sometimes, or never**
9. Students understand learning is a process and try to solve their own learning challenges first before asking for help. (O)	*The students are used to doing this. Their teachers last year emphasized this idea, so the students understand that learning a process that is ongoing. They are great at trying to solve problems themselves, using resources, and then finally coming to me.*	*Daily*
10. Students ask questions, seek input, and use feedback to revise their assignments and projects. (O)	*Students do ask questions and for input sometimes, but it usually general. They only use specific feedback to revise their work in writing workshop. I never really thought about how to use revision in other parts of the curriculum.*	*Sometimes*
11. Students self-assess their own learning and progress. (O)	*We do self-assessment with portfolios, but I need to look for ways to do this across the curriculum.*	*Sometimes*
12. Students are responsible for their own learning. (O)	*We do goal setting and self-evaluation sometimes, but that's all.*	*Sometimes*
13. Students take learning risks. (O)	*I encourage students to do this, and I am starting to hear them encourage one another and to do so. I need to link risk taking to the idea that failing is an important part of learning.*	*Sometimes*
14. Students understand getting stuck, being confused, and failing are part of the learning process. (O)	*I encourage taking risks, but that is as far as we've gone. I have never really talked about the struggles of getting stuck, being confused, and failing on early attempts as important parts of being independent, self-directed learners. We have lots of work to do here.*	*Never*

Scoring and Analysis

How many prompts did you rate in each category?

Daily: *2 questions (#5 and 9)*

Sometimes: *11 questions (#1, 2, 3, 4, 6, 7, 8, 10, 11, 12, and 13)*

Never: *1 question (#14)*

What patterns do you see within or across the three components of Choice, Voice, Ownership?

- Choice (#1, 2, 3, 4, 5)
- Voice (#6, 7)
- Ownership (#8, 9, 10, 11, 12, 13, 14)

Not really. The responses were varied for choice and ownership, and for the two items about voice, I rated them both as "sometimes."

(continued)

FIGURE 7.1. *(continued)*

Action steps I plan to take to move toward the rating of *Daily*	
Prompts to Address	**Action Steps**
1	Students love and do a great job with inquiry projects, so I want to expand student choices for what to learn. I will look at how I can provide more choices for science and social studies topics. I can bring the idea of student input to our next weekly classroom meeting to get students' ideas for giving them more choices in the curriculum.
3	This prompt is similar to #1. I want to bring this to our next weekly classroom meeting to see what types of learning activities the students think will support their learning. After I hear their ideas, I can think of how to incorporate their ideas into our classroom.
10	Students do ask questions and seek input sometimes, but it is often general, such as, "What should I do here?" or "What do you think of what I did here?" I think I need to model for students how to ask questions and make requests for input to get more specific and actionable feedback. I will consider how I can do this in guided reading, in writing workshop, and in individual conferences with students. In writing workshop students use feedback to revise their drafts and final products, but I just realized I don't encourage revision in other areas of the curriculum. The goal of learning is to gain control over or master the content, skill, or process, so I need to encourage revision elsewhere in the curriculum. I am not sure what this could look like. I plan to talk to my teammates and to post this question on Twitter to see if other teachers have ideas to share with me.
14	I need to introduce the ideas that getting stuck, being confused, and failing are important parts of learning. I will share examples from inventors, athletes, and other famous people. I will share an example of my own, like when I was trying to learn to write an article critique for a graduate class. I completely misunderstood the assignment, spent a lot of time stuck and not knowing what to do, and in the end, I got an F on the first one. I was so embarrassed, but I talked with the professor, who explained the purpose of the assignment, the expectations, answered my questions, and offered to read a draft of my next critique before I turned it in. I will invite the students to share examples of when they have been stuck, confused, and/or failed in early attempts to do something and how that supported their learning. We have lots of work to do here so I hope I can rate it as "Sometimes" in the future.

FIGURE 7.1. *(continued)*

The *Student Agency Questionnaire* Can Help You Understand Student Experiences Related to Voice, Choice, and Ownership of Learning

Using the *Teacher Self-Evaluation of Opportunities for Student Agency* (Assessment Strategy 7.1) can provide teachers with useful data and reflective insights. However, until teachers get direct and honest input from students, teacher perceptions of student opportunities to develop voice, choice, and ownership of learning will only represent part of the picture. For example, teachers may believe they are offering lots of choices, but students may feel like they are expected to make certain decisions. Teachers may think they are seeking student input on important decisions, but students may feel hesitant to share input they feel may offend or upset their teachers. Therefore, the *Student Agency Questionnaire* allows teachers to assess students' encounters in the classroom to understand how students see, value, and experience opportunities for choice, voice, and ownership of learning. This assessment is easy to administer to the whole class or to groups of students at the same time, and the data will help teachers understand how their students are developing as independent learners who are confident using their voices, making reasoned choices, and taking ownership for their learning. Patterned to align with the *Teacher Self-Evaluation of Opportunities for Student Agency* assessment and drawing inspiration from the work of Leap Innovations (n.d.), we developed the *Student Agency Questionnaire*. The results of the student questionnaire can be compared to the findings from the teacher self-evaluation, and they can also be used to learn more about how students feel in general about their opportunities for choice, voice, and ownership of their learning. These insights can help teachers ensure that the experiences and opportunities they provide to their students are truly nurturing students development as independent learners.

ASSESSMENT STRATEGY 7.2.
Student Agency Questionnaire

Purpose

The *Student Agency Questionnaire* is designed so teachers can learn about their students' experiences and beliefs about the classroom opportunities they have to make meaningful choices related to their learning; to develop and voice their ideas, suggestions, needs, and concerns; and to take ownership for their learning. This assessment can be used on its own, or it can be used in tandem with the *Teacher Self-Evaluation of Opportunities for Student Agency* to compare teacher insights and reflections with those of their students to ensure that all students have meaningful opportunities to develop into independent learners.

Value

The *Student Agency Questionnaire* provides teachers with information about how students feel about and take advantage of the opportunities provided for them to make choices, share their voices, and take ownership for their learning. Just because a teacher adopts teaching approaches and provides opportunities aimed at developing student agency and independence does not mean that students experience them in that way. Furthermore, students may be early in their development of independence, and this assessment will help teachers identify where students may need support and encourage them to develop and exercise their agency. By asking students directly about their experiences and perceptions, teachers can determine the efficacy of their efforts to develop and support student agency. In addition, the data teachers gather can provide insights on what they can do to help students develop confidence to take steps toward independence.

Procedures

1. To **prepare** to administer the *Student Agency Questionnaire* (Form 7.2), determine if you will give it to the whole class or a small group of students. Some students may be uncomfortable sharing their honest responses with their teacher, so consider whether to have students put their names on the survey or not. The benefit of including names is so you can tailor supports and opportunities to specific students, but the challenge of including names is that some students may provide the responses they believe their teachers want rather than their honest responses.
2. Distribute a copy of the questionnaire to each student. Read these instructions aloud:

   "An important goal in our classroom is for each student to develop into an independent learner. An independent learner makes choices, shares their ideas and input with their teacher and classmates to support their learning, and takes ownership for their learning. As a teacher, it is my job to create a classroom that helps you become an independent learner. This questionnaire will help me do a better job at creating a classroom that supports your development as an independent learner. It will also help me understand areas where you feel you need more support or that are uncomfortable to you and how we can work together to support your independence as a learner. For each prompt I read to you, consider if the statement describes you daily or almost every day, if it describes you sometimes, or if it never describes you. If you want help in this area, mark 'yes' in the column at the right, and jot down any notes that you think might help me support your development as an independent learner. There are no right or wrong answers, so please respond in the way that best describes your experiences in our classroom."
3. Read each prompt aloud using this format:

   "Number 1. I make choices about what I learn in the classroom. Does this prompt describe your experiences daily, sometimes, or never? Circle the response that best describes your experiences in our classroom. If you need help to do this, please write *yes* in the column. If you selected *never*, please jot down information to explain why not."
4. Continue in this way until you have read all prompts on the questionnaire.
5. Thank the students for their honest responses. Collect their questionnaires.
6. You may also wish to complete brief individual conferences after students complete the survey to understand more fully the students' perceptions and comfort with exercising their developing independence as learners. In addition, these individual conferences

can help teachers learn from students about the specific strategies they use and where they need additional support.

Collecting, Analyzing, and Using Data

You will **collect** data from the completed *Student Agency Questionnaire.* To **analyze** the data, tally the results for each survey using the bottom section of the assessment template provided in Form 7.2. Next, combine the results from each student's questionnaire to show the results for the whole class or group using the template in Form 7.3. Look for patterns by asking yourself the following questions:

- What items did most students respond to with *daily?*
- What items did most students respond to with *sometimes?*
- What items did most students respond to with *never?*
- Is there a pattern for items in each of the following sections?
  - Choice (#1, 2, 3, 4, 5)
  - Voice (#6, 7)
  - Ownership (#8, 9, 10, 11, 12, 13, 14)
- Is there a pattern *across* the three sections (Choice, Voice, Ownership)?
- Note your insights for each item in the column at the right.
- Look at the column for "Do you need help in this area?" Are there any patterns? Record those items where students report they need help at the bottom of the column.
- Look at the column for "If you marked *never,* explain why not." Review student responses to get a sense of where students are in their development of agency as well as any barriers to student independence for each prompt. Look for patterns and record your insights at the bottom of the column.
- If you conducted individual student interviews, add those data to Form 7.3 and use them to cross-check the other data you collected.

> If you also completed the *Teacher Self-Evaluation of Opportunities for Student Agency* (Assessment Strategy 7.1), follow these steps to analyze and use the data. If you did not complete Assessment Strategy 7.1, skip this section and go down to the paragraph labeled "Using the Data."

- Add your results from the *Teacher Self-Evaluation of Opportunities for Student Agency* assessment (Form 7.2) near the bottom of Form 7.3 and then compare whether the results are consistent or inconsistent.
  - If the results are consistent across the *Teacher Self-Evaluation of Opportunities for Student Agency* and the *Student Agency Questionnaire,* you can feel confident that the data are accurate and can provide useful information to guide your reflection and action planning related to developing and supporting student agency.
  - If the results are inconsistent, use the questions below to consider why that might be.
    - Are you confident that your self-evaluation was accurate and complete?
    - Do you think that students were comfortable sharing their honest responses?

    - Do you think the language in some items may have confused students?
    - Can you think of other reasons that the results might be inconsistent?
  - Look for patterns across the three types of prompts (Choice, Voice, Ownership) from the *Teacher Self-Evaluation of Opportunities for Student Agency* and the *Student Agency Questionnaire*.
    - If the results are consistent, you can feel confident that they are accurate and can provide useful information for your reflection and action planning.
    - If the results are inconsistent, consider why that might be by using these questions.
      - Are you confident that your self-evaluation was accurate and complete?
      - Do you think students were comfortable sharing their honest responses?
      - Do you think the language in some items may have confused students?
      - Are there other reasons the results might be inconsistent?

Using the Data

Reflect on the analysis you completed and identify a few prompts you want to address with the goal being to move future responses closer to *daily*. We recommend that you focus on no more than three or four prompts so you can develop a manageable number of action steps to implement in your classroom. Record that information in the Action Planning section at the bottom of Form 7.3.

Making Students and Teachers Visible

The *Student Agency Questionnaire* gathers information about student experiences and perceptions of the opportunities they have in the classroom to make meaningful choices, share their voices, and take ownership of their learning. This assessment puts the focus on students' experiences and perceptions to help teachers learn about the ways students understand and "live in" the classroom regarding agency. The assessment also sends a message to students that their experiences and perceptions are valuable and important in the classroom, which can support their level of comfort and confidence with developing as agentive learners. Teachers demonstrate their interest in their students' genuine input and insights about experiences and opportunities related to agency in the classroom. By doing this, teachers help their students understand that they are focused on planning instruction and classroom opportunities that will help all students become independent learners.

Implementation Example

A few weeks after he completed the *Teacher Self-Evaluation of Opportunities for Student Agency* (Assessment Strategy 7.1), Mr. Lee, a fifth-grade teacher in a very diverse elementary school, administered the *Student Agency Questionnaire* to all 26 of his students at the same time. One afternoon, he told the students he needed their help to make sure he was doing all he could to help them develop into independent learners. He explained that he had a questionnaire he wanted them to respond to with their honest answers, so he could learn about what he is doing successfully and areas where he can improve. He handed out paper copies, so each student had one, and then Mr. Lee gave the students the choice of whether to put their names on their questionnaires or not.

Mr. Lee read the instructions for the questionnaire aloud, saying:

> "An important goal in our classroom is for each student to develop into an independent learner. An independent learner makes choices, shares their ideas and input with their teacher and classmates to support their learning, and takes ownership for their learning. As a teacher, it is my job to create a classroom that helps you become an independent learner. This questionnaire will help me do a better job at creating a classroom that supports your development as an independent learner. It will also help me understand areas where you feel you need more support or that are uncomfortable to you and how we can work together to support your independence as a learner. For each prompt I read to you, consider if the statement describes you daily or almost every day, if it describes you sometimes, or if it never describes you. If you want help in this area, mark 'yes' in the column at the right, and jot down any notes that you think might help me support your development as an independent learner. There are no right or wrong answers, so please respond in the way that best describes your experiences in our classroom."

Mr. Lee read each prompt aloud using the following format:

> "Number 1. I make choices about what I learn in the classroom. Does this prompt describe your experiences daily, sometimes, or never? Circle the response that best describes your experiences in our classroom. If you need help to do this, please mark 'yes' in that column. If you selected *never*, please jot down information to explain why not."

He continued in this way until he reached the final item on the questionnaire.

The administration took about 10 minutes from start to finish. Mr. Lee thanked his students for sharing their ideas and experiences with him, and then he invited the students to begin work on their group projects in social studies.

At the end of the school day, Mr. Lee reviewed each student's questionnaire, and he noted that 22 of his 26 students had put their names on their papers. He smiled and inferred that many students probably felt comfortable with him knowing what their responses were. He then tallied each individual student's responses using the space at the bottom of the questionnaire.

Next, Mr. Lee compiled the results for the whole class using the template provided in Form 7.3. He looked for patterns for each item, for the three categories of questions—Choice, Voice, Ownership. Because he had previously completed the *Teacher Self-Evaluation of Opportunities for Student Agency* assessment (Form 7.1; see Figure 7.1 for Mr. Lee's completed evaluation), he used the questions provided in the section "Comparing Results from *Student Agency Questionnaire* and *Teacher Self-Evaluation of Opportunities for Student Agency*" of the template to consider and record his insights. Finally, he reflected on the prompts provided in the **Action Planning** section of the template to record his ideas for specific steps he plans to take to enhance student experiences and opportunities for developing as independent learners.

After reviewing the student questionnaires, Mr. Lee wanted to make sure the data accurately reflected the students' experiences and perceptions of their own agency development. He decided to conduct brief individual conferences with students to cross-check the data from the questionnaires and see if there were additional useful insights he could gain. He decided to ask four open-ended questions for the individual conferences:

1. Is there anything else you want me to know about your making choices?
2. Is there anything else you want me to know about you using your voice?
3. Is there anything else you want me to know about you taking ownership for your learning?
4. Is there anything else I can do to help or support you in these areas?

Mr. Lee sat at the conferencing table near the back of the room, and invited the students, one-by-one, to speak with him over the next 2 days. He jotted notes on a sheet of paper and then added the relevant information to Form 7.3. Most of the individual conferences lasted only 1–2 minutes, so the time needed was minimal. Many of the students responded that they didn't have more to share, but some did offer useful insights. For example, here is the conference Mr. Lee had with one of his students, Ava.

MR. LEE: Hi, Ava. I want to ask several quick follow-up questions related to the *Student Agency Questionnaire* we did yesterday.

AVA: Okay.

MR. LEE: Is there anything else you want me to know about your making choices?

AVA: (*After a pause.*) Hmmmm. I guess I make the same choices, like for books. I probably need help, you know, with choosing different kinds of books.

MR. LEE: (*Nods.*) Is there anything else you want me to know about you using your voice?

AVA: Ummm. Sure. I'm usually okay talking and asking questions, you know. Sometimes I have ideas, but I'm not sure if I should share them.

MR. LEE: Can you tell me more?

AVA: (*Nods.*) Like when we do something as a whole class, I don't use my voice as much. Or, like, if I don't get it, sometimes just wait to see if I can figure it out.

MR. LEE: Is there anything else you want me to know about you taking ownership for your learning?

AVA: I think it's like growing up, kinda. I'm more responsible 'cause it's fifth grade, you know.

MR. LEE: (*Smiles.*) Is there anything else I can do to help or support you in these areas?

AVA: (*Looks thoughtful.*) To use my voice, sometimes I need more time. You know, to figure out what I want to say. Maybe you could wait longer?

MR. LEE: That's a great suggestion. Is there anything else I can do?

AVA: (*Pauses for a few seconds to think.*) You could help me make different choices, you know, for books. And maybe for who I work with. You know, so I don't always make the same choices.

MR. LEE: (*Smiles.*) Thanks, Ava. I appreciate you sharing your ideas.

AVA: (*Smiles back as she gets up and walks back to her seat.*) Sure, Mr. Lee.

Mr. Lee believes that the *Student Agency Questionnaire* has **value** because it provides him with data that make his students' perspectives **visible** so he can make sure he is providing opportunities and support for his students to develop as agentive literacy learners. To see the notes Mr. Lee recorded as well as his analysis and plans for use, see Figure 7.2.

Student Self-Assessment Can Help You Understand Your Students as Agentive Learners

When students engage in self-assessment, they develop a learning orientation rather than a grading orientation. In other words, self-assessment makes the learner's progress, struggles, and goals visible rather than simply earning a grade or number of points (Walsh, 2016) that may, or more likely may not, reflect their actual learning. Furthermore, the *Student Self-Assessment* strategy promotes the students' ownership of learning as they develop an understanding of their own strengths and areas of need and make decisions about where to focus their efforts on future learning. *Student Self-Assessment* can be embedded into daily literacy activities that teachers are already implementing, such as conferencing and independent reading. The real value of *Student Self-Assessment* is its emphasis on students being in charge of and responsible for their learning—important steps toward becoming independent learners. Another use and benefit of *Student Self-Assessment* is it provides useful data for you to reflect on your classroom climate, instructional methods, and learning opportunities to see if they are effective at promoting student voice, choice, and ownership of learning.

ASSESSMENT STRATEGY 7.3.
Student Self-Assessment

Purpose

Student Self-Assessment is a powerful and flexible assessment strategy that provides useful data as well as advances student learning and agency. It can be implemented in conjunction with almost any learning activity, assignment, or assessment that you are already implementing. You just need to use a few prompts to guide students to think about and reflect on their strengths, areas of need, and next steps for their learning. By design, *Student Self-Assessment* is a venue for student voice, which is an important step for students to take leadership for their learning. In addition, choice is a key feature of *Student Self-Assessment,* wherein students determine how to use the results of their self-assessment to advance their progress—helping them develop ownership for their learning.

Prompt (C) choice, (V) voice, (O) ownership	**Tally of student responses**	**Notes and insights**
1. I make choices about what I learn in the classroom. (C)	2 Daily 22 Sometimes 2 Never	Sometimes is the most common answer for this item and for the other prompts about choice.
2. I make choices about how I learn in the classroom. (C)	7 Daily 19 Sometimes 0 Never	I am not surprised about the Sometimes answer being the most common here. I don't provide that many choices about how students can learn.
3. I make choices about what activities I do in the classroom. (C)	2 Daily 23 Sometimes 1 Never	Sometimes is the most common answer, and that matches what I expected.
4. I make choices about how I demonstrate or show my learning. (C)	0 Daily 25 Sometimes 1 Never	This is what I expected the most common response would be.
5. I make choices about the books and other texts I read in the classroom. (C)	22 Daily 4 Sometimes 0 Never	This is the only Choice prompt that has mostly Daily responses. It appears that having students make choices about books and texts is seen as a choice they can make daily. Since choice is the first step toward independence, I need to look for ways to increase student choice-taking related to items 1–4.
6. I am involved in decisions about important things in the classroom. (V)	6 Daily 20 Sometimes 0 Never	Since we only have classroom meetings once a week, I am not surprised to see Sometimes as the most common response.
7. I share my ideas, opinions, and suggestions freely with my teacher and classmates. (V)	21 Daily 5 Sometimes 0 Never	This made me smile! I have worked hard to create a safe and brave classroom with the students, so I am glad that most students responded Daily, and the rest responded Sometimes.

(continued)

FIGURE 7.2. Example of data summary, analysis, and plans for use of a *Student Agency Questionnaire*.

Prompt (C) choice, (V) voice, (O) ownership	**Tally of student responses**	**Notes and insights**
8. I set goals for my own learning. (O)	8 Daily 17 Sometimes 1 Never	Since we only do "official" goal setting for self-selected reading and for writing workshop, I am not surprised that most responded with Sometimes. I wonder if those who responded with Daily are thinking about how they are working toward those goals they set on a daily basis. Are there other ways I can incorporate goal setting, so students are focused on their goals daily?
9. I understand learning is a process and try to solve my own learning challenges before asking for help. (O)	23 Daily 3 Sometimes 0 Never	This is great but not a surprise. Since students learned this in fourth grade and I see it consistently in the classroom, this response confirmed what I expected.
10. I ask questions, seek input, and use feedback to revise my assignments and projects. (O)	0 Daily 23 Sometimes 3 Never	This item made me think that I need to do more of having students revise their work once they've received feedback. We only do it for writing and sometimes for projects, but I need to reconsider that and see if there are other ways we can add in revision.
11. I assess my own learning and progress. (O)	4 Daily 22 Sometimes 0 Never	I am not surprised that most of the students responded with Sometimes. That's what I expected they would say.
12. I am responsible for my own learning. (O)	23 Daily 3 Sometimes 0 Never	This is AWESOME! I wasn't sure they would respond this way because many of the students still look to me for grades or praise to keep working.
13. I take learning risks. (O)	23 Daily 3 Sometimes 0 Never	I know this was a big focus in fourth grade so it's great to see so many responses of Daily now that the students are in fifth grade.
14. I understand that getting stuck, being confused, and failing are part of the learning process. (O)	1 Daily 2 Sometimes 23 Never	I knew this would be an item that students would not connect to in their own experiences. I have been stressing risk taking, but I have not broached the ideas that getting stuck, being confused, and failure can be valuable parts of the learning process. This is something I need to start addressing with the students.

(continued)

FIGURE 7.2. *(continued)*

Analysis of *Student Agency Questionnaire*	
What items did most students respond to with *daily, sometimes,* and *never*?	Daily: 5, 7, 9, 12, 13 Sometimes: 1, 2, 3, 4, 6, 8, 10, 11 Never: 14
Is there a pattern for Choice (1–5), Voice (6–7) and Ownership (8–14)?	Choice items were mostly *sometimes* with one *daily* One Voice item was *daily* and the other was *sometimes* Ownership items were all over the board with three *daily*, three *sometimes*, and one *never*
Is there a pattern across the three sections (Choice, Voice, Ownership)?	Mixed results across all three areas, but Choice and Voice didn't have any *never* responses. Ownership seems to have the most variation.
Is there a pattern for the areas where students report they need help? If so, describe.	Mixed responses for areas where they need help, but two areas mentioned by multiple students were more time to formulate responses and help expanding reading interests and choices.
Is there a pattern for the reasons that students reported *never* for some prompts? If so, describe.	No, the responses are varied.
Comparing results from *Student Agency Questionnaire* and *Teacher Self-Evaluation of Opportunities for Student Agency*	
How do the *Student Agency Questionnaire* results compare to the *Teacher Self-Evaluation of Opportunities for Student Agency* results? What is consistent? What is inconsistent? What insights can you draw from comparing these data?	The results are quite consistent. This is good because it seems that the students and I are on the same page about the opportunities they have in the classroom for choice, voice, and ownership. We both rated item #14 about failure as *never* so that is an area where I need to do some work with the students.
When comparing the results from the *Student Agency Questionnaire* and the *Teacher Self-Evaluation of Opportunities for Student Agency*, what confirms your perceptions? What surprised you? Why?	I anticipated that the students would choose *sometimes* for most of the items, and they did. I predicted they would say *daily* for #5, and they did. I hoped they would choose *daily* for #9, and I was pleased that they did. I was surprised that they responded *daily* for #7, 12, 13. I rated those as sometimes. Wonder if they are internalizing ideas from #7, 12, and 13, and I'm not observing carefully enough to see them in action.

(continued)

FIGURE 7.2. *(continued)*

Individual Student Conferences *(if conducted)*	
Did the conferences confirm or refute findings from the questionnaires? Describe.	*The conferences mainly confirmed but added more depth to the data from the questionnaires. I got useful "why" information from the students as well as specific ideas of what I can do to support their agency development.*
Important insights gained from the conferences.	*As I reflect on the individual student conferences, I gained the following important insights:* • *Give students more time to share their voices. Some students are stuck making the same choices.* • *Some students see ownership of their learning as developing responsibility as fifth-grade students, but is that enough? Do they think it's just doing what's expected or are they taking the lead and advocating for what they need to be successful learners?* • *Most students talked about choices of what they read and who they work with, but what other choices should they be able to make about their learning? I need to reflect on this more.* • *When we do large-group activities and discussions, am I providing enough opportunities, support, and encouragement for students to share their voices?*
Action Planning	
Based on the available data, what specific prompts do you want to address in your classroom?	*As I planned from the* Teacher Self-Evaluation of Opportunities for Student Agency, *I need to work with the students to understand that getting stuck, being confused, and failing are important and valuable parts of the learning process.* *I know that choice is the first step toward independence, so I want to work on giving the students more choices about what they learn, how they learn, what activities they do, and how they demonstrate their learning.*
What specific action steps can you take to advance student agency in our classroom?	*I already started introducing the idea of failure as part of the learning process when I set that as an action step from my* Teacher Self-Evaluation of Opportunities for Student Agency. *I plan to link the idea of taking risk with the likelihood of failure and how we can analyze that failure to guide and improve our learning.* *At our next weekly classroom meeting, I will talk with the students about the importance of choices for developing independent learners. I will ask them to help me identity additional ways they can make choices about what they learn, how they learn, the activities they do, and how they demonstrate their learning. I will make a chart with their ideas, and I will encourage the students to make more choices for a week. We will reflect on what worked and what we need to change so that students can have more control over the choices they make. This process will also reinforce the importance of the students' voices as they help to create our classroom opportunities and expectations for student choices. I also need to remember to give students time and multiple invitations to share their voices, especially in larger group settings.*

FIGURE 7.2. *(continued)*

Value

The value of the *Student Self-Assessment* strategy for students is multifaceted. First, it provides a vehicle for students to develop and share their voice, provides choice for next steps in their learning, and supports their progress toward ownership of their learning. Furthermore, student self-assessment has important value for teachers. Because students identify and reflect on their strengths and areas for growth, teachers can plan instruction that supports each student's progress and engagement. Teachers can also use insights from *Student Self-Assessment* to reflect on and engage in their own self-assessment of their classroom climate, learning opportunities, and instructional approaches. In addition, as students become more comfortable with sharing their voice, exercising choice, and taking ownership of their learning through their self-assessment, they develop into fully engaged and independent learners—the ultimate goal of equitable education.

Procedures

1. To **prepare** for *Student Self-Assessment,* select an assignment, work product, or particular point in time when you want students to reflect on and evaluate their own performance and progress in learning. For example, you might choose to apply *Student Self-Assessment* with a writing project that students are completing, after reading a book or as they are learning a challenging skill or strategy such as making inferences. You may also want to use *Student Self-Assessment* in conjunction with another assessment such as *Retellings* (Assessment Strategy 5.1) or *Questioning of Text Comprehension* (Assessment Strategy 5.3).
2. **Prepare** several questions to guide the *Student Self-Assessment* process. Using a consistent set of questions (with some modifications as described below in #3), students can get familiar with the format and internalize the questions to guide self-assessment of their work and learning. Three general questions that can be used with and adapted to a variety of settings and situations are:
   - What am I doing well that I should continue doing?
   - What do I need to work on?
   - What specific things can I do to improve?
3. If you have been teaching specific skills, strategies, or content that you want to be the focus of *Student Self-Assessment,* you can revise the questions to be more focused by adding information such as the italicized text below. For example, if you have been working on strategies to monitor comprehension, the questions might be modified as follows:
   - What am I doing well *with monitoring my comprehension that I should continue doing?*
   - What do I need to work on *with monitoring my comprehension?*
   - What specific things can I do to improve *my comprehension monitoring?*

   If you have been working on a specific skill such as identifying setting and its purpose in a narrative text, the *Student Self-Assessment* questions could be revised in this way:

- What am I doing well *with identifying setting and the purpose it plays in narrative text?*
- What do I need to work on *with identifying setting and the purpose it plays in narrative text?*
- What specific things can I do to improve *my ability to identify setting and the purpose it plays in narrative text?*

4. Invite students to consider, reflect on, and record their responses to the self-assessment questions in writing. Afterward, meet with each student individually to discuss their self-assessment. Or, if you prefer, students can complete their self-assessment verbally with you in an individual conference format. While it may be tempting to take the lead and tell the student what you have observed or think they should work on, the power of *Student Self-Assessment* is for students to develop as agentive, independent learners who can reflect on and take ownership of their own learning by identifying their strengths, areas of need, and ways they can continue to grow and develop as learners.
5. Finally, discuss and have students record their plan of specific things they will do to keep growing as learners.
6. Check in with each student frequently about their progress. Because developing agency will be new to many students, be sure to provide encouragement and prompts to scaffold students' efforts to engage in meaningful self-assessment.

Collecting, Analyzing, and Using Data

There are two types of data to collect, analyze, and use with *Student Self-Assessment*. First, you will want to **collect data** on the specific strengths, areas of need, and next steps that students identify so you can provide appropriate instructional support and follow up with them afterward on how they are doing with their specific plan to improve or enhance their learning. When you meet with each student to review their *Student Self-Assessment*, you can take notes using a chart like the one in Form 7.4.

By reviewing your notes over time, you will be able to **analyze** your students' progress on the skills, strategies, and content they are learning and gaining control over as well as their development of agency for their own learning. To do this, it will be important to date your notes and to not only review the current *Student Self-Assessment* data but look back at previous notes as well. By focusing on the student's responses to the question, "What specific things can I do to improve?" you can **use** that information to record your "Teacher insights and notes" and determine ways you can support the student's efforts and growth as a learner.

The second type of data focuses on the student's development of agency. At the bottom of Form 7.4, there is a place to record insights and notes about the student's agency related to their learning.

More specifically, you will **collect** data on your observations of whether they demonstrated their voice during the process by sharing their ideas and insights freely about what they are doing well and what they need to work on; whether they were able to make choices independently about what specific things they can do to improve; and whether they showed ownership of the self-assessment process by taking the lead and demonstrating confidence, or if they needed substantial support, prompting, and encouragement from the teacher to complete the process.

To **analyze** these data, you will need to date your notes and look for patterns across the areas of voice, choice, and ownership as well as comparing notes from previous self-assessments to see if the student is making progress in developing agency. You will need to **use** this information to plan additional scaffolding, modeling, encouragement, and feedback to assist the student in developing agency for their learning.

Making Students and Teachers Visible

Student Self-Assessment is intentionally designed to reveal students' voices and choices. Because students identify and reflect on their strengths, areas of need, and actionable steps they want to take to enhance their learning, they are able to make themselves visible as learners. These are important steps for students to move themselves forward toward becoming independent learners. With the *Student Self-Assessment* strategy, teachers step out of the spotlight and encourage students to take center stage as experts on their own learning. This does not, however, remove teachers as a key part of the *Student Self-Assessment* strategy. Teachers may appear to be in the background, but their role is essential through offering questions to guide students' self-assessment process, facilitating discussions to help students analyze and reflect on their own learning, and using data from the process to guide instruction and support for student agency development.

Implementation Example

Mrs. Njuguna teaches first grade, and she uses *Student Self-Assessment* regularly with her students to foster her students' engagement and ownership of their learning. Nico is a 6-year-old student in her class. Mrs. Njuguna has been teaching her students to use self-assessment since early in the school year. During whole-group lessons, small-group reading instruction, and in individual conferences, she has been laying the foundation for self-assessment by modeling, thinking aloud, and facilitating discussions to help her students understand how to engage in this assessment process.

One day in October she is meeting with a guided-reading group with five students—Aja, Jaxon, Emma, Danny, and Nico. They have been learning common sight words: *he, was, that, she, on, they, but, at, with, all.* They have practiced reading, writing, and playing matching games with the words for several days. They have read the words with partners on flash cards and as a group in sentences in chart stories, and they have copied and written the sight words in sand trays and on individual whiteboards. Mrs. Njuguna asks the children to practice their sight words with a partner, and she focuses her attention on Nico.

Mrs. Njuguna tells him, "Nico, let's do a quick self-assessment so you can share how you are doing with your sight word learning with me." Nico smiles and says "Okay." Mrs. Njuguna is prepared with a copy of Form 7.4 on her laptop computer so she can take notes while meeting with Nico and add her insights afterward. Her completed form is provided below in Figure 7.3.

MRS. NJUGUNA: Nico, what are you doing well that you should continue doing to learn your sight words? (*She points to her temple to demonstrate that she is thinking and gives Nico a moment to think about his response. Nico shrugs his shoulders and looks confused.*) What are you doing good at with your sight words?

NICO: I can match 'em fast.

MRS. NJUGUNA: (*Smiles.*) That's important! Good for you! Is there anything else with your sight words that you are doing good with?

NICO: (*Pauses for a moment.*) I can read 'em if I match 'em.

MRS. NJUGUNA: (*Nods.*) So, you can read them when you are playing matching games. Is that right?

NICO: Um-hum.

Student: Nico	Date: Sept. 21
Question	**Student response**
What am I doing well that I should continue doing?	Match sight words and read them while matching.
What do I need to work on?	Reading sight words in chart stories. Writing and spelling sight words.
What specific things can I do to improve?	Practice at home. Participate more in reading group when reading and writing sight words.

Teacher insights and notes on student learning: With minimal prompts, Nico was able to identify his strengths and areas of need. His insights match my observations. His ideas for next steps are appropriate since he has not seemed to do much practicing with sight words outside of his guided-reading group. I will follow up with him tomorrow to ask him how his plans for improvement are going.

Teacher insights and notes on student agency: Nico was engaged during the Self-Assessment process, and he shared good insights and awareness about his own learning.

- **Voice:** Nico was very open to sharing his ideas and plans. He seemed comfortable with minimal prompts and a little thinking/wait time.
- **Choice:** Nico was able to choose two specific things he can do to improve with sight words. He did not need prompting to do so.
- **Ownership:** Nico seemed comfortable taking the lead while engaging in Self-Assessment and taking on some ownership for the process and for his next steps. I will follow up to see if he is able to follow through with his plans or if he needs additional support.

FIGURE 7.3. Example of a *Student Self-Assessment* template.

MRS. NJUGUNA: Is that something you want to keep doing to help you with sight words?

NICO: Yeah!

MRS. NJUGUNA: What do you need to work on with sight words?

NICO: (*Furrows his brow for a moment, then responds.*) I need to read 'em on the chart . . . and write 'em—spell 'em.

MRS. NJUGUNA (*Smiles*): Those are great ideas, Nico. I agree that those things will help you learn your sight words. What specific things can you do to improve with sight words?

NICO: (*Smiles sheepishly.*) I can practice more at home. I can pay more 'tention when we're 'posed to practice reading and writing 'em.

MRS. NJUGUNA: Nico, those are great ideas for how you can take ownership for your learning of sight words. Let me know what I can do to help you with these plans.

Thanks, Nico, we are now going to read the sight words in a new chart story so you can try your plan to practice and participate during this activity. I'll check in with you soon to see how your plan is going and how you are doing with reading and writing your sight words.

Mrs. Njuguna believes that *Student Self-Assessment* has **value** as an assessment strategy because it makes her students' learning and agency **visible** so she can use those data to plan instruction and support her students' development and progress.

The *Goal Setting* Assessment Can Help You Learn About and Promote Student Agency

Goal setting can increase student motivation, performance, and attention and effort toward goal-relevant tasks (Schunk, 2001). Furthermore, goal setting contributes to the development of self-regulation, which is a critical component of independent learning (Schunk, 2003). Three specific goal attributes contribute to student learning, motivation, and self-regulation—specificity, proximity, and difficulty (Cabral-Márquez, 2015). Goals that are specific provide details about the actions and effort needed for success. Such goals boost students' self-efficacy because their specificity makes it easy for students to assess progress and self-regulate their efforts toward attainment. Proximity refers to how far the goal goes into the future. Goals that can be met in a short time frame such as a day or a few days result in high motivation and self-evaluation of progress, especially for younger children. While older students can set long-range goals and stay focused on them for a period of time, it can be helpful to break longer-term goals into several subgoals that can be attained in a shorter time period such as a few weeks. Finally, difficulty is the third attribute of goals that we need to consider. Moderately difficult goals have the greatest influence on motivation and performance (Schunk, 2003).

To use *Goal Setting* as an assessment, teachers can add it to literacy instructional activities and routines they are already implementing in their classrooms, such as conferencing, portfolio assessment, and student-directed work time in literacy centers or stations. Through *Goal Setting*, teachers can address students' abilities to set goals that are specific, proximal (attainable in a fairly short time), and moderately difficult and to use self-regulation and self-evaluation to monitor their progress toward meeting their goals. The *Goal Setting* assessment process contributes in several meaningful ways to students' development as independent and agentive learners. First, it provides a frame work for them to make choices about what goals to set, to share their voice in meaningful ways as they direct their learning through goal setting, and to develop ownership of their learning as they work to meet their goals. Teachers provide structure and support by conferencing with students when they set their goals and checking in with them regularly to monitor their progress and provide feedback to guide their process toward attaining their goals.

ASSESSMENT STRATEGY 7.4.
Goal Setting

Purpose

Goal Setting is both an instructional process and an assessment. Most students need to initially be taught how to set goals that are specific, proximal, and moderately difficult as well as how to monitor their progress toward attainment. Once students learn that process, the focus of *Goal Setting* can shift to assessment of students' ability to set goals, to self-regulate their motivation and efforts, to self-evaluate their progress, and to attain their goals. All these things contribute to students' development as independent learners. You can add *Goal Setting* to conferences, portfolio assessment, student-directed work time in literacy centers or stations, independent reading time, or other already-established instructional activities or routines in your classroom.

Value

Goal Setting is valuable because it is a lifelong skill that supports students' development as independent learners in school, and it also has applications outside of school and in adult life.

Procedures for the First Time You Introduce *Goal Setting*

1. **Prepare** to introduce goal setting by asking students if they have any personal goals they would like to achieve. If students have difficulty thinking of goals to share, you can share some of your own goals, such as organizing a closet, painting your apartment, and earning a master's degree.
2. Ask students to think of a goal they have set or would like to set in the future. Encourage students to share their goals with the group or a partner.
3. Explain that goals have three important attributes or characteristics. They are **specific, proximal,** and **moderately difficult.**
4. Tell students that goals can be general or **specific.** For example, a general goal would be to eat a healthy diet, while a specific goal would be to eat at least five servings of vegetables and fruits each day. Tell the students that specific goals are the best because they help you know exactly what to do to reach the goal.

5. Ask students if the goal they thought of is general or specific.
6. Explain that goals should be **proximal** which means that they can be attained, or met, in a relatively short time frame such as a few days or a few weeks.
7. Ask student to think back to the goal they discussed a few minutes ago. Ask them to think about what the time frame for the goal is. Is it a few days, a week, or a couple of weeks? If so, it is proximal, meaning that it can be met in a relatively short time frame. If it is for a longer period of time, it may be harder to reach.
8. Tell students that some goals are hard, some are easy, and some are in-between. Explain that goals that are not too easy and not too hard are the best goals because they provide some challenge but are still attainable. These goals are called **moderately difficult.**
9. Ask students to think about the goals they were just sharing and consider the level of difficulty of their goal.
10. Tell students that they will be setting goals for their self-selected reading because doing so will help them to develop into independent learners who have ownership over their own reading.
11. Ask students to think of a personal reading goal that is **specific, proximal,** and **moderately difficult** but attainable within a few weeks. Remind them that a specific goal tells exactly what they aim to do, a proximal goal can be met in a relatively short time, and a moderately difficult goal is challenging enough to be motivating but not so challenging that it feels impossible to reach.
12. Ask students to share their goal ideas with a partner to solicit feedback on whether the goal is specific, proximal, and moderately difficult but attainable in 3 weeks.
13. Listen in on the partners and offer feedback to help students understand how to set goals that are specific, proximal, and moderately difficult yet attainable.

Procedures for *Goal Setting* Assessment

1. To **implement** *Goal Setting,* confer with each individual student as they set two or three goals. We recommend beginning with goal setting focused on self-selected reading, since students already have a great deal of choice and autonomy in this area and are likely to be more confident and comfortable with goal setting in this area. As students get more familiar with goal setting, the focus of the goals can broaden to other areas of the curriculum or their work habits.
2. For the first *Goal Setting* cycle, we recommend choosing a short time frame, such as 2–3 weeks. In this procedure, we will show how the process can be implemented over a 3-week period.
3. Prior to meeting with each student, ask them to come prepared with ideas written down for the goals they would like to set. Remind students to think about goals that are specific, proximal, and moderately difficult.

4. Review what the student has prepared for their goals. Discuss each goal to ensure it is specific, proximal, and moderately difficult. Pose questions to help students revise their goals to address the three goal attributes.
5. If students are stuck coming up with goals, suggest that they consider a genre or author they would like to read, the amount of time or number of days per week they want to read, ways they want to share the texts they are reading, the number of pages or books they want to read, and so on. Sample goals you can use as models for self-selected/recreational reading include:
   - Read three nonfiction books on the same topic in a 3-week period.
   - Read a fantasy chapter book in 1 week.
   - Read an online magazine article on current events every day for 1 week.
   - Read for 30 minutes, 6 days per week for 1 month.
   - Read a biography in 1 week and tell a classmate three interesting things about the person.
   - Read three chapter books in 3 weeks. One will be a mystery, one will be a graphic novel, and one will be science fiction.
6. Once the student is satisfied with their goals, make sure they have them written down in a notebook or folder that is designed for goal setting. You may wish to set a time frame of 2–3 weeks for the first cycle of goal setting. Eventually, you will want students to set their own time frames for their goals.
7. After 1 week, hold a brief conference with each student to discuss their progress toward their goals. Things to discuss include identifying goals that have been met early, asking if the student needs help locating reading materials or resources related to their goal, or discussing if the student wants to abandon, modify, or add reading goals.
8. After 1 more week, hold another brief progress conference with each student.
9. At the end of the 3-week cycle, meet briefly with each student to co-evaluate their goal attainment. Be sure to discuss what went well, any problems they encountered, and what they can do in the future as they set and work to attain their goals.
10. Repeat the *Goal Setting* assessment but shift more responsibility to the students for setting and monitoring their goals, extend the time frame for goal attainment, and consider expanding the focus to another area of the curriculum, such as writing.

Collecting, Analyzing, and Using Data

In addition to each student's written record for their self-selected reading goals, you will want to **collect data** about the process, progress conferences, and attainment of each goal. In addition, you will want to **collect data** about the degree of independence students demonstrate while *Goal Setting*. We recommend using a template such as the one provided in Form 7.5 to **collect data** for each student's progress with *Goal Setting*. You can then **analyze data** from Form 7.5 for each student and **use** the data to guide your approach to working with students in the next goal-setting cycle.

Making Students and Teachers Visible

Goal Setting is a student-centered process that invites students to choose and voice their goals and to engage in self-regulation and self-evaluation in the goal-attainment process. By creating and working toward self-developed goals, students identify and share their priorities, motivations, and efforts. They also learn about themselves in terms of motivation and commitment to attaining goals and share these insights with their teachers and families. Teachers serve as facilitators and coaches through the *Goal Setting* assessment process. Their knowledge of the curriculum, their students, and psychological processes such as motivation, self-efficacy, and self-regulation are visible as they provide and eventually withdraw appropriate scaffolding for their students.

Implementation Example

Miss Lopez teaches third grade, and she uses *Goal Setting* with her students on a regular basis. She often embeds it into the reading conferences she does with her students or she adds it as a literacy center or station where she works with individual students to practice specific skills and strategies. In the beginning of the year, Miss Lopez focuses the goal-setting process on student self-selected reading. As the year progresses, she works with students to set goals for writing and for their learning in science, social studies, and math. Her goal is for all 23 of her students to get so comfortable with setting goals, monitoring their progress, and attaining their goals that they internalize the process and become goal-directed—a key aspect of being independent learners.

Miss Lopez introduces the concept of goal setting with her third-grade students one afternoon. The students are seated on the carpet with their personal whiteboards on their laps, and Miss Lopez is seated on a stool near a large whiteboard. She asks the students, "Have you ever set a goal?" Several students raise their hands to share.

CHARLIE: I did. For catching fly balls. I practiced with my stepdad almost every night.

MARISOL: I set a goal to do a round-off back flip in gymnastics.

FAISEL: I want to learn Arabic, so I study it in Saturday school.

MISS LOPEZ: Those are great examples of goals. Some examples of goals I have set are to organize our classroom library, to write a classroom newsletter every week for the whole year, and to save money for a vacation.

Some goals take a short time, like organizing the classroom library. I could do that in a day or two. Other goals take longer, like writing a classroom newsletter each week for the entire school year, and some take even longer, like saving money for a big vacation.

Miss Lopez asks each student to write a goal they have set or would like to set on their personal whiteboard. She asks each student to turn to an "elbow partner" to share their goals and discuss whether each goal is specific, proximal, and moderately difficult. She tiptoes around the carpet to observe what students have written and to check in when they seem stuck. She pauses next to Abir, a new student who is just learning English, and her partner, Will. Miss Lopez smiles and says, "I'm so glad to see you helping each other! Abir, can you tell me about your goal?" Abir lowers her eyes and shrugs her shoulders. Will chimes in, "Abir, your goal is great! Want me to help share it?" Abir nods and smiles slightly. Will begins, "I will learn . . ." Abir quietly continues "English," and Will concludes, "by the end of third grade." Miss Lopez smiles and says, "Abir, that is a great goal! Can you share it with the class?" She nods yes and looks at Will, and he adds, "I can help if you want." Abir nods.

Miss Lopez asks for several students to share their goals. First, she calls on two volunteers—Mia and Zeke.

MIA: To paint my bedroom with my mom by the end of this month.

ZEKE: To do a 360 on my skateboard before winter starts.

MISS LOPEZ: Those are both good goals. Let's hear from a couple more of you. Hmm . . . Abir, will you share your goal, please?

ABIR: (*quietly*) I learn English . . . (*She points to Will.*)

WILL: . . . by the end of third grade. (*Abir and Will turn toward each other and smile.*)

MISS LOPEZ: Will, can you share your goal?

WILL: I will learn my 3 multiplication tables by the end of next week.

MISS LOPEZ: Those are all great goals. We are going to work on setting goals for our self-selected reading. You may want to set a goal that focuses on the genre or author you want to read. Maybe you want to set a goal to read about a certain topic. You might want to set a goal about how you will share what you are reading. Or you might want to set a goal to write about what you read. Maybe you want to set a goal for the number of books, pages, days, or minutes you read. Please think about two or three goals you would like to set for the next 2 weeks. I will meet with each of you individually at the conferencing table over the next few days to discuss your goals.

The students return to their seats, and Miss Lopez writes a schedule on the whiteboard for goal conferences. She asks students to have their draft goals written down in their reading notebook when they come to their conference.

Wednesday	**Thursday**	**Friday**
Addison	Harper	Max
Zeke	Marisol	Jayla
Sarah	Hector	Will
Charlie	Riley	Tiana
Joo-Hee	Abir	Christopher
Jamal	Chaitanya	Faisel
Mia	Mickey	Gracie
Bella	Cameron	

On Friday, Miss Lopez calls Jayla to the conferencing table. She begins, "Jayla, can you share the goals you are considering for your self-selected reading?" Jayla opens her notebook and says, "I have three." Miss Lopez replies, "That's a great number. Let's look at them to make sure each is specific, proximal, and moderately difficult. Together they look at Jayla's notebook, where she has written:

1. To read lots of genres in 2 weeks.
2. To tell my friends about all of the books I read in 2 weeks.
3. To read for lots of time every day for 2 weeks.

Miss Lopez continues, "For the first goal, is it specific?" Jayla scrunches up her face and murmurs, "I dunno." Miss Lopez smiles. "What genre or genres do you want to read in the next two weeks?"

JAYLA: Historical fiction—can I just put that?

MISS LOPEZ: Yes, that makes your goal more specific. Do you want to say what type of book or the number to make the goal more specific?

JAYLA: (*Pauses for a moment.*) Yes, one chapter book that's historical fiction.

MISS LOPEZ: Good plan, Jayla. That's very specific. Let's continue with goal one. You have a 2-week timeframe, and that's proximal. Is the goal appropriately difficult?

JAYLA: (*Shakes her head no.*) It should be two—one book for each week.

MISS LOPEZ: (*Nods.*) So, I think this is your revised goal—"To read 2 historical fiction chapter books in 2 weeks." Is that accurate?

JAYLA: (*Smiles.*) Yep. That's my goal.

They continue their conference with discussing the two remaining goals. In the end, Jayla settles on these revised goals and writes them in her reading notebook:

1. To read two historical fiction chapter books in 2 weeks.
2. To tell at least one friend about each of the two historical fiction chapter books I read in 2 weeks.
3. To read every day for at least 30 minutes for 2 weeks.

Miss Lopez then shifts the discussion to Jayla's preparedness to work on her three goals. She asks, "Jayla, do you have ideas for the historical fiction chapter books you want to read, or do you need help finding some?"

JAYLA: I wanna read books Addison and Tiana told me 'bout.

MISS LOPEZ: I love to read books that my friends recommend to me, too. You set three excellent goals, Jayla. Each goal is specific, proximal, and moderately difficult. I'll check in with you next week to see how you are doing with your goals. If you need my support sooner, let me know by signing your name on the conference request sheet taped on the corner of the conferencing table.

JAYLA: (*Picks up her notebook and stands up.*) Okay. Thanks, Miss Lopez.

The conference took a total of 5 minutes, and Miss Lopez scheduled all the conferences during self-selected reading time to ensure that she had sufficient time to meet with each student. Some of the conferences were a bit longer or a bit shorter, but on average they were 5 minutes. With the 23 students in her class, it took about 115 minutes—just under 2 hours—to conduct all of the *Goal Setting* conferences.

One week later, Miss Lopez meets for a brief goal-progress conference with each student, using the same schedule as the previous week, but these conferences are shorter—1–2 minutes on average. Miss Lopez calls Jayla to the conference table to discuss her progress toward her goals. She says, "Jayla, let's talk about how you are doing with each of your goals. Let's start with number one and go through all three of your goals."

JAYLA: (*Opens her notebook to the page with her goals.*) I'm doing good with goal 1. I already read one book. I started the second one. I really like historical fiction.

MISS LOPEZ: Thanks for that update. How about goal 2?

JAYLA: I talked to Gracie about the book I finished. I think she wants to read it. I can't finish this goal 'til I'm done with my second book.

MISS LOPEZ: It looks like you are making good progress on goal 2. What about goal 3?

JAYLA: I'm reading way more than my goal. Like an hour some days!

MISS LOPEZ: (*Smiles.*) Jayla, that's great that you are exceeding your goal. That means you are going beyond what you set.

Miss Lopez thanks Jayla for the progress update and encourages her to stay focused on her reading goals for the upcoming week. Jayla nods and returns to her seat. At the end of the 3 weeks, Miss Lopez checks in with each student for about a minute to see how they did with attaining their goals. During this brief check-in, she jots notes on the *Goal Setting* Progress Template (see Figure 7.4). While meeting with Jayla, Miss Lopez asks, "Jayla, how did you end up doing with your three goals?"

JAYLA: (*Smiles widely.*) I met 'em all!

MISS LOPEZ: That's great that you met all of your goals, Jayla. How does that make you feel?

JAYLA: Great! I love this goal stuff!

MISS LOPEZ: Did the goals help you want to read?

JAYLA: Yes, I wanted to read more and more 'cuz of my goals and 'cuz I love historical fiction!

MISS LOPEZ: Thanks, Jayla. We will be doing goal setting again next week, but this time we'll make the goals for a longer period of time.

Miss Lopez believes the *Goal Setting* assessment is **valuable** because it situates her students as leaders for their own learning and helps them identify actionable goals to work toward to grow as readers. With this assessment, she also gains useful insights because it makes **visible** her students' perceptions of themselves as readers that helps her provide appropriate support and opportunities.

Miss Lopez is pleased that most of her students attained all of their goals. She knows that she will be shifting the focus for *Goal Setting* in the future to extend the time frame for the goals, and after another round focused on self-selected reading, she plans to have students set goals for their writing. She also reflects on the ways her students demonstrated their independence and agency during the *Goal Setting*. Most students were able to choose

Student Name: Jayla

Date	Goals	Attainment • Full • Partial • Not attained	Notes
9/18	1. To read two historical fiction chapter books in 2 weeks. 2. To tell at least one friend about each of the two historical fiction chapter books I read in 2 weeks. 3. To read every day for at least 30 minutes for 2 weeks.	Full Full Full (she exceeded by reading up to an hour each day)	Jayla's initial goals were general, but with a little prompting, she was able to develop appropriate goals. She didn't need help finding books because she wanted to read books recommended by her friends. At her progress conference, Jayla was on track and didn't need any support or resources to meet her goal. At the end of the 2 weeks, she not only met all of her goals. She reported that she "loves" goal setting and it made her want to read more. For the next round of goal setting, I will let Jayla take the lead to demonstrate her independence and only support her if asked to do so.

FIGURE 7.4. Example of a *Goal Setting* progress template.

goals that were meaningful to them and met the criteria for good goals—specificity, proximity, and moderate difficulty. Most students were able to voice their ideas freely and to advocate for the goals they wanted to set. Finally, most of the students were able to take the lead with their goals and to demonstrate a degree of ownership over the process. A few students needed more encouragement, coaching, and support, but Miss Lopez is prepared to begin removing some of that scaffolding as they begin round two of *Goal Setting.* Miss Lopez also intends to reduce the amount of conferencing for students who needed little to no support from her so they can be more independent with their goal setting.

Conclusion

The goal of equity-focused education is for all students to become independent learners who make choices, share their voices, and take ownership of their learning. To reach this goal, teachers must provide opportunities, support, and space for students to take on increasingly more responsibility for their own learning. By using the formative assessments described in this chapter, you can intentionally focus on nurturing your students' agency through collecting useful and actionable data that can guide your instructional approaches and the experiences students have in the classroom.

FORM 7.1

Teacher Self-Evaluation of Opportunities for Student Agency

Prompt (C) choice, (V) voice, (O) ownership	**Notes**	**Daily, sometimes, or never**
1. Students make choices about what they learn in the classroom. (C)		
2. Students make choices about how they learn in the classroom. (C)		
3. Students make choices about what activities they do in the classroom. (C)		
4. Students make choices about how they demonstrate their learning. (C)		
5. Students make choices about the books and other texts they read in the classroom. (C)		
6. Student voices are an important part of decisions about important things in the classroom. (V)		
7. Students share their ideas, opinions, and suggestions freely with me and their classmates. (V)		
8. Students set goals for their own learning. (O)		

(continued)

Teacher Self-Evaluation of Opportunities for Student Agency *(page 2 of 3)*

Prompt (C) choice, (V) voice, (O) ownership	**Notes**	**Daily, sometimes, or never**
9. Students understand learning is a process and try to solve their own learning challenges first before asking for help. (O)		
10. Students ask questions, seek input, and use feedback to revise their assignments and projects. (O)		
11. Students self-assess their own learning and progress. (O)		
12. Students are responsible for their own learning. (O)		
13. Students take learning risks. (O)		
14. Students understand getting stuck, being confused, and failing are part of the learning process. (O)		

Scoring and Analysis

How many prompts did you rate in each category?

Daily: ____________________

Sometimes: ____________________

Never: ____________________

What patterns do you see within or across the three components of Choice, Voice, Ownership?

- Choice (#1, 2, 3, 4, 5)
- Voice (#6, 7)
- Ownership (#8, 9, 10, 11, 12, 13, 14)

(continued)

Teacher Self-Evaluation of Opportunities for Student Agency *(page 3 of 3)*

Action steps I plan to take to move toward the rating of *Daily*	
Prompts to Address	**Action Steps**

FORM 7.2

Student Agency Questionnaire

Prompt	Circle the best response	Do you need help in this area?	If you marked *never*, explain why not.
1. I make choices about what I learn in the classroom.	Daily Sometimes Never		
2. I make choices about how I learn in the classroom.	Daily Sometimes Never		
3. I make choices about what activities I do in the classroom.	Daily Sometimes Never		
4. I make choices about how I demonstrate or show my learning.	Daily Sometimes Never		
5. I make choices about the books and other texts I read in the classroom.	Daily Sometimes Never		
6. I am involved in decisions about important things in the classroom.	Daily Sometimes Never		
7. I share my ideas, opinions, and suggestions freely with my teacher and classmates.	Daily Sometimes Never		
8. I set goals for my own learning.	Daily Sometimes Never		

(continued)

Student Agency Questionnaire *(page 2 of 2)*

Prom	Circle the best response			Do you need help in this area?	If you marked *never*, explain why not.
9. I understand that learning is a process and try to solve my own learning challenges before asking for help.	Daily	Sometimes	Never		
10. I ask questions, seek input, and use feedback to revise my assignments and projects.	Daily	Sometimes	Never		
11. I assess my own learning and progress.	Daily	Sometimes	Never		
12. I am responsible for my own learning.	Daily	Sometimes	Never		
13. I take risks when learning.	Daily	Sometimes	Never		
14. I understand that getting stuck, being confused, and failing is part of the learning process.	Daily	Sometimes	Never		
Tally of student responses for each rating	Daily	Sometimes	Never	Notes	Notes

FORM 7.3

Student Agency Questionnaire—
Data Summary, Analysis, and Plans for Use

Prompt (C) choice, (V) voice, (O) ownership	**Tally of student responses**	**Notes and insights**
1. I make choices about what I learn in the classroom. (C)	____ Daily ____ Sometimes ____ Never	
2. I make choices about how I learn in the classroom. (C)	____ Daily ____ Sometimes ____ Never	
3. I make choices about what activities I do in the classroom. (C)	____ Daily ____ Sometimes ____ Never	
4. I make choices about how I demonstrate or show my learning. (C)	____ Daily ____ Sometimes ____ Never	
5. I make choices about the books and other texts I read in the classroom. (C)	____ Daily ____ Sometimes ____ Never	
6. I am involved in decisions about important things in the classroom. (V)	____ Daily ____ Sometimes ____ Never	
7. I share my ideas, opinions, and suggestions freely with my teacher and classmates. (V)	____ Daily ____ Sometimes ____ Never	

(continued)

Data Summary, Analysis, and Plans for Use *(page 2 of 4)*

Prompt (C) choice, (V) voice, (O) ownership	**Tally of student responses**	**Notes and insights**
8. I set goals for my own learning. (O)	____ Daily ____ Sometimes ____ Never	
9. I understand learning is a process and try to solve my own learning challenges before asking for help. (O)	____ Daily ____ Sometimes ____ Never	
10. I ask questions, seek input, and use feedback to revise my assignments and projects. (O)	____ Daily ____ Sometimes ____ Never	
11. I assess my own learning and progress. (O)	____ Daily ____ Sometimes ____ Never	
12. I am responsible for my own learning. (O)	____ Daily ____ Sometimes ____ Never	
13. I take learning risks. (O)	____ Daily ____ Sometimes ____ Never	
14. I understand that getting stuck, being confused, and failing are part of the learning process. (O)	____ Daily ____ Sometimes ____ Never	

(continued)

Analysis of *Student Agency Questionnaire*	
What items did most students respond to with *daily, sometimes,* and *never?*	
Is there a pattern for Choice (1–5), Voice (6–7) and Ownership (8–14)?	
Is there a pattern across the three sections (Choice, Voice, Ownership)?	
Is there a pattern for the areas where students report they need help? If so, describe.	
Is there a pattern for the reasons that students reported *never* for some prompts? If so, describe.	
Comparing results from *Student Agency Questionnaire* and *Teacher Self-Evaluation of Opportunities for Student Agency*	
How do the *Student Agency Questionnaire* results compare to the *Teacher Self-Evaluation of Opportunities for Student Agency* results? What is consistent? What is inconsistent? What insights can you draw from comparing these data?	
When comparing the results from the *Student Agency Questionnaire* and the *Teacher Self-Evaluation of Opportunities for Student Agency,* what confirms your perceptions? What surprised you? Why?	

(continued)

Data Summary, Analysis, and Plans for Use *(page 4 of 4)*

Individual Student Conferences *(if conducted)*	
Did the conferences confirm or refute findings from the questionnaires? Describe.	
Important insights gained from the conferences.	
Action Planning	
Based on the available data, what specific prompts do you want to address in your classroom?	
What specific action steps can you take to advance student agency in your classroom?	

FORM 7.4

Student Self-Assessment Template

Student:	Date:
Question	**Student response**
What am I doing well that I should continue doing?	
What do I need to work on?	
What specific things can I do to improve?	

Teacher insights and notes on student learning:

Teacher insights and notes on student agency:

- **Voice:**
- **Choice:**
- **Ownership:**

FORM 7.5

Goal Setting Progress Template

Student: ____

Date	**Goals**	**Attainment** • Full • Partial • Not attained	**Notes**

8

Starting with Student Strengths

> The real voyage of discovery consists not in seeking new landscapes, but in seeing with new eyes.
>
> —MARCEL PROUST

Today's students often come from backgrounds that are very different than their teachers', and while students bring different experiences, knowledge, and resources to their learning, it is important to understand that these differences are not deficits. Teachers who teach with an equity mindset see the inherent dignity of each student. They view each student as a unique and competent individual who brings valuable resources to their learning, including academic skills, lived experiences, linguistic resources, funds of knowledge, and interests. If we view our students with a strengths-based lens, we can see their "differences as assets rather than deficits" and use their strengths "as building blocks for instruction" (Griffith & Lacina, 2018, p. 513). Taking a strengths-based view, we can see all learners, including those who are linguistically diverse, as having rich linguistic knowledge, valuable lived experiences, and relevant prior knowledge that they can bring to learning English, literacy, and other areas of the curriculum (Martinez, 2018). Martinez explained that by identifying and building on all students' strengths, we can make visible and leverage "their brilliance, their competence, and their tremendous potential" (p. 521). Furthermore, by identifying and then teaching to students' strengths, including academic and literacy strengths, we can improve student engagement (Sternberg, 2000; Sternberg & Grigorenko, 2000) and learning outcomes (Hammond, 2015; Sternberg, 1988).

A Strengths-Based Approach to Assessment

In order to focus our instruction on student strengths, we must also approach assessment using a strengths-based lens that identifies students' academic strengths as well as their personal, social, linguistic, and cultural strengths. The Victoria Department of Education and Early Childhood Development (2012) asserted that assessment should be designed to discover what children know and understand as well as who they are as individuals, based on what they create, write, draw, say, do, and demonstrate in other ways. When we focus on identifying students' strengths through the assessment process, we can make visible the knowledge, skills, and resources that students already possess so we can use those as building blocks to support and enhance student learning.

Why are strengths so important to teaching and learning? If we look at self-efficacy theory, we can begin to see the "why" behind focusing on students' strengths in assessment and instruction. The belief a person has about their ability to succeed is called self-efficacy, and it contributes to how they persevere in the face of difficulty, set goals for themselves, and attribute their success or failure (Bandura, 2001). A person's self-efficacy varies across domains such as math, soccer, baking, or reading and situations such as taking a test, practicing a skill, playing before a crowd, completing an assignment, or reading for enjoyment. Self-efficacy affects the activities an individual chooses to do as well as their effort and perseverance (Bandura, 1977).

Let's look at Sam, a third grader who has high self-efficacy for reading mystery books, so he is likely to read more mystery books and to put forth effort and persevere until he identifies clues to solve the mysteries. On the other hand, Sam has low self-efficacy for decoding multisyllabic words, and he tends to skip those words, guess without working through the whole word, put forth limited effort, and give up after a brief period of time. Applying this knowledge about Sam, his teacher, Miss Hsu, uses a strength where he has strong self-efficacy—reading mystery books and solving mysteries—as a building block for instruction. Miss Hsu decides to use an excerpt from a mystery book to begin instruction on decoding multisyllabic words by looking for prefixes, suffixes, and root words. Sam is very willing and interested to engage in decoding instruction and practice within the mystery text. After several decoding lessons in mystery texts, he begins to apply his newly developed decoding skills in other texts because he feels more confident in his ability to read multisyllabic words. In short, people tend to get better at what they are good at already because they engage in that activity, put forth effort, and stick with it until they complete the task and reach their goal. On the other hand, when someone struggles with a specific task or skill, they tend to avoid it, put forth little effort, and quit quickly. This situation is sometimes referred to as the Matthew Effect (Stanovich, 1986) wherein "the rich get richer and the poor get poorer." In other words, if a person is able to build on their strengths, they can continue to grow and improve. If a person is forced to work only on areas where they struggle and have low self-efficacy, they are likely to make limited progress or growth.

Bandura (2012) argued that a person's self-efficacy is also affected by their sense of belonging and the social context. Teaching is a relationship between teacher and student within the classroom setting. It's important to note that these contributors to self-efficacy are primarily within the control of teachers as they design their classrooms, build relationships with students, promote an inclusive classroom community, establish a positive climate, develop routines, and create spaces and opportunities for students to grow and succeed. Additionally, "Self efficacy and sense of belonging can be influenced by a variety of circumstances such as racism and poverty" that the individual cannot control (van der Putten, 2017, p. 3). Therefore, teachers must understand their students' lived experiences and funds of knowledge (González et al., 2005) to create productive learning opportunities and experiences for all students.

Traditional approaches to assessment focus on comparing a student's performance against a set of criteria or standards to determine what the student can and cannot do and what the student knows and does not know. Within this paradigm of assessment, the teacher identifies areas of weakness for the student and then provides scaffolding to boost the student to higher levels of performance or completion of more complex tasks. What can happen, however, is that the student may believe that the scaffolding and teacher support are provided because they are not capable of completing the task on their own. Because they don't believe they are able to do the task successfully, they may demonstrate less effort, which can lead to even lower performance. Let's look back to the example with Sam. He is able to decode single-syllable words easily and without support. His teacher, Miss Hsu, points this out to him and explains, "Sam, you are very strong at reading one-syllable words. You can use that strength to read words with two or three syllables. Let me show you." She helps him break the words *something, however,* and *without* into syllables, to decode each syllable, and then to blend them into the word. Because he knows that he can decode one-syllable words, he is confident that he can decode each syllable—even when the word has two or three syllables. This is an example of what Dyson (1990) described as a weaving metaphor for assessment and instruction that incorporates both scaffolding and the resources, interests, and intentions of the individual child. Dyson emphasized the importance of starting with the child by explaining that children "must build upon the behaviors they already control, the resources they have. To put it simply, nothing comes from nothing" (p. 211).

If we seek to "see with new eyes" and embrace Dyson's (1990) weaving metaphor, assessment can become an ongoing process or orientation toward careful observation, listening, and conversation rather than an end in and of itself. Researchers from WestEd (Kusimo et al., 2000) argued that in order for assessment to be truly useful for promoting student learning, we need to make its "process equitable and beneficial for students and teachers alike" (p. 9). More specifically, Afflerbach et al. (2019) argued that because our understanding of reading is broad, "we must strive to develop assessments that describe the complexity of student reading growth" (p. 312) and provide us with clear information about how students engage with text, apply strategies, and make meaning as they are reading. Davis (1998) explained that many traditional reading assessments are "thin," meaning that they only provide part of the picture of the student as a reader, learner, and individual and tend to "be silent about students' motivations, or self-efficacy, factors that clearly influence students' reading, strategy use, higher-order thinking, and reading achievement" (Afflerbach et al., 2019, p. 312). To overcome the limitations of "thin" assessments, we can use classroom-based assessments of reading processes, such as *Running Records* (Assessment Strategy 6.2), *Oral Reading Analysis* (Assessment Strategy 6.3), *Retellings* (Assessment Strategy 5.1), and *Think-Alouds* (Assessment Strategy 5.2), and focused observation like *Kidwatching* (Assessment Strategy 8.1). These types of assessments allow us to observe students as they engage in the act of reading so we can learn about their decoding, use of prior knowledge, fluency, comprehension, and self-monitoring by observing their reading behaviors directly.

To embrace this approach to classroom-based assessment, we can adopt Calkins's (2003) view of assessment, which she described as "the thinking teacher's mind work" (p. 85). In this approach, the teacher takes a stance of curiosity in order to figure out what strengths the student brings to the learning situation. By developing this insider view, teachers can reveal students' strengths and use those as building blocks for instruction. Because students are able to build on their strengths, they are more likely to have strong self-efficacy and attribute their performance to effort and perseverance, which will encourage them to stay engaged in their own learning. As veteran ESL educator Laura Lenz (2016) explained, "When you point out kids' strengths, they grow in confidence. They know you see them. You see the whole individual, not just an empty vessel that needs to be filled with your knowledge" (section 6, para 2).

In the remainder of this chapter, we present five strategies that will help you to reveal your students' strengths so you can use them as the foundation for student-centered instruction. As you read about and consider each of these assessment strategies, the following questions will help guide your thinking.

- How does the assessment help me identify students' academic, personal, social, linguistic, and cultural strengths?
- How does the assessment help me understand how students use their strengths when reading?
- Through use of the assessment strategy, what can become visible about the student as a reader that I can use to plan and provide appropriate instruction?

ASSESSMENT STRATEGIES: IDENTIFYING AND STARTING WITH STUDENTS' STRENGTHS

In this part of the chapter, we offer five assessment strategies that will help you (and your students) identify their strengths so you can use these as a springboard for instruction. These assessment strategies are:

8.1. *Kidwatching* (with anecdotal records)
8.2. *Portfolios*
8.3. *Can You Help Me Understand?*
8.4. *Literacy Provision Inventory*
8.5. *Photo Elicitation Interview*

How *Kidwatching* Can Help You Identify and Understand Your Students' Strengths

Kidwatching is an approach to assessment that allows you to learn about your students so you can determine how to best support them as learners. Owocki and Goodman (2002) described kidwatching as "a state of mind . . . for gathering and reflecting on data. It is about getting to know students through observing them intelligently" (p. 2). Kidwatching assumes that every student has strengths, so the focus is for teachers to take note of what students know and can do in order to understand the ways that they construct, express, and apply knowledge. Morrell and Morrell (2018) described kidwatching as a way to identify each student's **genius** and **passion.** Kidwatching helps teachers adopt an asset-based lens that enables them to implement culturally responsive instruction because they know who their students are, understand and value their students' genius and passion, and engage in self-evaluation and reflection to enhance their teaching. Using this information, teachers can then shape the curriculum and instruction to provide teaching that is responsive to each individual student. In other words, kidwatching is not the end—it is the beginning of helping teachers understand student learning in rich, deep, meaningful ways so they can plan and provide effective instruction (Kuby, 2010).

You may be wondering what makes kidwatching different than just observing students as they read, write, and interact in the classroom. Kidwatching is a comprehensive approach to observing, reflecting, and applying your insights to teaching. Kidwatching comprises the following processes: "building an insider view of the community, understanding how language and literacy develop, organizing a rich environment for learning, interacting with children, observing and documenting children's knowledge, analyzing data, fostering children's self-evaluation, engaging in self-evaluation of teaching, and using evaluation to inform instruction and build curriculum" (p. 3). If that sounds like a lot, it *is*—a lot of powerful information to guide your instruction and improve your practice. Kidwatching is a new way of observing your students closely and intentionally, but it can be incorporated into your typical literacy instructional activities and routines, making it simple to use in your classroom.

ASSESSMENT STRATEGY 8.1.
Kidwatching

Purpose

The *Kidwatching* assessment strategy is a systematic yet personalized approach to observing students "intelligently" so you can understand their language and literacy in authentic contexts (Kuby, 2010; Owocki & Goodman, 2002). Kidwatching assumes an equity stance on the part of the teacher because the heart of this assessment strategy is to identify and understand what students know and can do—in other words, to understand the strengths they bring to their literacy learning. Kidwatching assumes that ALL learners have strengths and assets they bring to their literacy learning, and through kidwatching, teachers can observe, document, and use those strengths and assets to create a rich learning environment, inform instruction, build curriculum, and reflect on their teaching.

Value

The value of kidwatching is multifaceted. Its most obvious value is that it provides a structured process that teachers can use to observe, document, analyze, and apply insights about students' literacy learning to plan and implement instruction that is personally meaningful and relevant. If we dig more deeply, kidwatching has the potential to transform how teachers approach assessment and instruction to ensure they view their students through an equity-focused lens that allows them to see every student as a competent learner who has many strengths that can support and enhance their learning. In addition, kidwatching provides opportunities for students to self-evaluate their own literacy learning, which can support their engagement and make them self-directed learners, and it helps teachers reflect on and improve their teaching as well.

Procedures

1. There are multiple steps to consider as you **prepare** to implement the *Kidwatching* assessment strategy. First, the teacher must strive to have an insider view of the classroom community and commit to understanding the language and literacy development of each student. By adopting this approach to assessment, the teacher can implement kidwatching as an intelligent and reflective observer.
2. Another consideration you will need to address as you **prepare** to implement kidwatching is to select a literacy-rich context in which to observe students. By observing in literacy-rich environments, we increase opportunities for students to show us their strengths. Examples of literacy-rich contexts include partner reading, literacy center or station time, inquiry project work time, shared reading, independent reading time, and reading or writing workshop.
3. You will also need to **prepare** a plan for which students you will observe and when. Usually focusing on two or three students a day works well and can be manageable. While there is not a perfect schedule for kidwatching, many teachers find that observing two to three students per day allows them to focus on each student about every 2 weeks.
4. Finally, you will want to **prepare** a few guiding questions to focus your observations, especially if kidwatching is new to you. For example, you might use questions such as, "What print concepts does the student demonstrate?" if you are a kindergarten teacher who has been teaching this foundational knowledge or "How does the student interact with text when reading with a partner?" if partner reading is an important portion of your literacy block. Your questions should align with your understanding of language and literacy development, your curriculum, your previous observations of the specific students, and the compelling questions you have about your students as literacy learners.
5. While you are implementing the kidwatching assessment, your primary focus needs to be observing and interacting with students using interpretive probes, such as "Tell me why you chose to do it that way," "What did you wonder about?" or "Explain what you just did and why."

Collecting, Analyzing, and Using Data

You will need to **collect data** by recording your observations as anecdotal notes, but you will want the method to be easy to implement so it does not distract you from observing and interacting. One easy way to collect data is to have a notebook or three-ring binder with a section for each student. Using sticky-notes, you can write the child's name, date, and information about the observation on each note. At the end of the day (or when you have a break during the day), you can take about 10 minutes to organize the notes into the notebook and add any relevant details or information about the literacy context and your observations. Some teachers find that they prefer to collect data digitally on an iPad or computer using Google forms saved on Google Drive or using other easy-to-use digital tools.

Next, you will be able to **analyze the data.** Because observation dates are recorded on the anecdotal notes, you can view the notes sequentially to check for progress and changes over time. In addition, because the literacy context is also recorded on each anecdotal note, you can determine how the student engages with literacy in different settings and situations and for different purposes.

Another important level of analysis is to consider what strengths each student demonstrates and what passions (interests and motivators) they exhibit. As you record this information in your notebook, you can consider implications for your teaching, such as how to build on strengths, grouping, strategy instruction, individualized support, text selection, classroom literacy climate, ways to include interests, and opportunities for applying what students are learning.

Since **students' self-evaluation** is an important way to promote engagement in their own learning, you will want to meet periodically with each student to discuss your observations from kidwatching and invite them to share additional information and insights about their own literacy learning and development. For example, you can ask questions such as:

- What are some things you are learning?
- How is your learning going?
- How are you using reading and writing in school? Outside of school?
- What are you doing well?
- What is hard for you? What can I do to help?
- What excites you about your learning?
- What is a goal you have for your reading?
- What can I do to help you achieve your goal?

An important part of kidwatching is for you to reflect on and **self-evaluate your teaching.** By carefully observing your students' progress, you can consider questions such as these that can also help you address equity in your teaching.

- When I look at a list of my students' names, can I identify strengths and passions for each student? If not, what can I do to gain these insights?
- How am I honoring and building on each student's strengths? If I am not, why not? What can I do to change that?
- Do I have a good understanding of each of my students as a literacy learner? If not, what questions do I need to pursue through additional kidwatching?
- Which students are usually engaged? Which students are usually not engaged?
- What might be blocking some students' engagement?
- How can I modify the learning environment to engage more students?
- Am I honoring and building on all students' strengths? If not, why not? What can I do to change that?
- What instructional strategies or activities might better support my students' engagement and literacy learning?

As you are implementing *Kidwatching*, you can use what you are observing and learning to plan and adjust your instruction to build on each student's strengths, leverage their passions, and address areas where further growth is needed.

Making Students and Teachers Visible

Just as the name of the assessment strategy says, kidwatching is all about closely watching students' literacy behaviors, language, interactions, and personal characteristics. By observing across time and in different literacy-rich contexts, teachers can develop a clear understanding of each student's strengths, thus making each individual student visible as a literacy learner. Teachers are also very visible in the *Kidwatching* assessment strategy because they must use their knowledge of literacy development and of their students to strategically and intentionally observe, document, analyze, and apply what they are learning about each of their students.

Implementation Example

Miss Garcia is a kindergarten teacher who has been teaching for 3 years. This year is the first year she is teaching all-day kindergarten, and she is excited to be able to spend all day with her 20 students. Most of her students are native English speakers, but she has four who are bilingual learners. She started using *Kidwatching* during her student teaching when her mentor teacher showed her how she used it. Miss Garcia grew up nearby, lives about a mile from the school, and she has many friends and family members who live and work in the community. In addition, this is her third year at this school and she spent the first few weeks of the year getting to know each of her students and meeting with their families. Therefore, she already has an insider's view of her classroom community, and she is confident in her understanding of early literacy development and the kindergarten curriculum. She devotes 2 hours of each day to literacy, and her students participate in a variety of reading and writing instruction and practice. She is also intentional about incorporating reading and writing instruction into science, health, social studies, and even math so she can help her students see and use literacy as a tool across the curriculum. She has a classroom library, lots of environmental print around the classroom, and reading and writing tools and supplies including technology and digital texts as well as centers where they can compose their own digital texts.

Because she uses kidwatching almost every day, she no longer needs to spend much time on the **preparation** steps such as planning a schedule for kidwatching, developing guiding questions, and determining how to record notes—these have become routines in her teaching. She has developed a schedule that allows her to focus on two students each day, and by the end of 2 weeks, she is ready to start over again. If she has questions about a student or feels like she needs more information about their current strengths and passions, she will add a third student on some days. Miss Garcia uses her previous anecdotal notes and interpretations to develop questions to focus her kidwatching. For example, today she will be observing Noemi and Frank. Noemi is a bilingual learner who was born in Mexico and came to the United States about a year ago. Frank is also a bilingual learner, but he was born in the United States and attended a preschool program that was taught in English. Miss Garcia consults her latest notes for these two students and develops the specific questions she will be seeking to answer through her kidwatching. She determines that she wants to observe both Noemi's book-handling skills and her ability to stay engaged with a book during independent reading, and to see if Noemi understands that we read words (not pictures). When consulting her notes for Frank, she determines that she will observe him during shared reading to see if he can read along with repeated phrases and if he can demonstrate understanding of 1:1 correspondence. She also plans to see what she can learn related to the students' interests and passions related to literacy.

Miss Garcia uses kidwatching to observe Noemi and Frank, and she jots a few words on a sticky-note for each student, and when they are outside for recess, she fills in more details about her observations (as shown in the column "Anecdotal notes" in Figure 8.1). After school that day, she looks at her notes and the previous ones for each student, and she fills in the "Analysis and insights" column by reviewing previous notes for each student and considering what she knows about kindergarten student's literacy development. As she **reviews and analyzes the data,** she tries to focus on what she observed and what it means in terms of the student's literacy development and engagement. She then marks each strength with an asterisk (*). Finally, she makes notes in the "Follow-up" column about what she will do next, such as plans for instruction, ways to build on strengths, and questions she wants to consider when she next observes each student. Figure 8.1 shows the pages from her notebook that capture her anecdotal notes, analysis and insights, and plans for following up.

The next day Miss Garcia speaks with Noemi and Frank briefly to engage them in some **self-evaluation.** She asks Noemi, "What do you think you are doing well as a reader?" Noemi responds, "Lots of books." Miss Garcia smiles, and says, "Yes, that's great. You seem to really like the books I read aloud to the class." Noemi nods enthusiastically. Miss Garcia goes on to say, "The best way to become a good reader is to read and read!" She then asks, "What do you want to work on as a reader?" Noemi takes a moment and then shrugs her shoulders and says, "Words." Miss Garcia smiles and says, "That's a great goal, Noemi! It's important to be able to read the words. We can work on reading sight words today in center time and during shared reading and guided reading." Noemi responds with a smile. When Miss Garcia speaks with Frank, she asks him, "What are you proud of as a reader?" Frank looks serious and then responds, "I like it!" Miss Garcia smiles and responds, "Yes, you do!" She then asks, "What is something you would like to work on as a reader?" Frank smiles and says, "Read big, big books!" Miss Garcia comments, "That's a good goal, Frank."

Later that week, Miss Garcia looks back at her *Kidwatching* notes from the previous 2 weeks. She **reflects on her teaching** by considering whether all students are engaged in literacy lessons and experiences, and she carefully reviews her notes for her bilingual students who are new to English. She confirms that her bilingual students have many strengths, and they enthusiastically participate in reading experiences throughout the day, but several of them, including Noemi, are not learning English sight words as easily as some of their classmates. She makes a note to talk to the school's reading specialist to see if she has suggestions for sight-word instruction and practice that will be useful for working with her bilingual students. Miss Garcia also notes that many of the children enjoy humor (like Frank) and animals (like Noemi) so she decides to create a display with funny animal books and poems to build on her students' interests. Miss Garcia reflects on

Student	Anecdotal notes	**Analysis and insights** (strengths marked with *)	Follow-up
Noemi	Oct. 3–independent reading time Noemi quickly went to the classroom library and chose the book I read during read-aloud this morning (*What Do You Do with a Tail Like This?* by Jenkins and Page). She demonstrated appropriate book-handling skills and looked at the book, page-by-page for about 5 minutes. She smiled and giggled for some of the pages. When I asked her to show me what she was doing, she said, "Reading!" When I asked if she liked the book, she said, "Yes! I love *animales!*" When I asked her to point to a word, she pointed to *What* at the top of the page. When I asked her what the word was, she said, "*The*?" I asked her to show me other words, and she pointed to several words, but when I asked her what the words were, she shrugged her shoulders. When I asked her to point to what we read, she pointed to the words (not the pictures).	Noemi usually choses to read the books I have shared during read-alouds* Noemi has appropriate book-handling skills* Noemi enjoys independent reading time and is able to engage with a book for 5 minutes* Noemi understands that we read the words (not the pictures), and she has the concept of word* Noemi "loves" this book and animals* Noemi was not able to read the words she pointed out.	Display previous read-aloud books so Noemi can find them easily. Suggest other animal books that Noemi may enjoy as well as bilingual concept books. Read a predictable book with a repeating pattern for read-aloud and see if Noemi is able to identify the words that are repeated. Observe her in the Words Center and during shared reading and guided reading to see if she is able to identify the sight words we are learning.
Frank	Oct. 3–Shared reading of a chart poem, *I can . . .* Frank was attentive and engaged. He read along for the repeated parts, especially, "I can" at the beginning of each line. He volunteered to use the pointer to read along with a line, and with my help he was able to show 1:1 correspondence as we read the line together. Frank smiled, and laughed when we read the line, "I can even get in trouble some of the time!" When asked, Frank was able to point to the words *I can* but not *run and play*.	Frank enjoys shared reading and was attentive and engaged* Frank read the repeated part of each line* Frank was able to use the pointer for 1:1 correspondence with my help* Frank understood the humor of the poem* Frank was able to point to the words *I can* at the beginning of each line of the poem* Frank was not able to identify other words in the poem such as *run and play*.	Share humorous books and poems with Frank. Continue to provide shared-reading experiences with repeated phrases. See if Frank is able to identify words in longer repeated phrases. Work on 1:1 correspondence with Frank during guided reading.

FIGURE 8.1. Notebook page for Noemi and Frank from October 3.

her approach to shared reading and wonders if it could be more effective, so she decides to review some of her professional books to see if there are ways she can improve her practice, especially to support her bilingual learners.

Miss Garcia believes that *Kidwatching* is a **valuable** process that allows her to make her students' literacy behaviors **visible** so she can learn about their strengths and passions. The insights she gains help her identify next steps for teaching to support her students' ongoing literacy development.

How *Portfolios* Can Help You Identify and Understand Your Students' Strengths

Portfolios are collections of student work that help teachers make connections among assessment, curriculum, and student learning (Asp, 2000; Cohen & Wiener, 2003). They provide a record of a student's ongoing literacy development over time and operate from an asset-based perspective that invites students, teachers, and families to honor, celebrate, and document a student's learning across the school year. Portfolios align with constructivist views of education wherein educators believe "all students are capable of succeeding in schools when teachers can find ways to build on knowledge students bring from home" (Kim & Yazdian, 2014, p. 221). Furthermore, portfolios offer a meaningful way to assess linguistically diverse students that does not view their linguistic and cultural differences as deficits; rather, portfolios show what students **can do** and the **progress they are making.**

A portfolio contains samples of the child's work to demonstrate their learning processes as well as to show finished products. Through guided self-evaluation and reflection, students can learn to select meaningful pieces to add to their portfolio, reflect on their growth, identify their strengths, and set goals for the future. Teachers can then use insights gained from portfolios to plan and implement instruction that celebrates and builds on students' strengths. Kim and Yazdian (2014) argued that "portfolio assessment provides rich contexts for teachers to transform their teaching to meet the needs of individual students (p. 223). Portfolios also serve as a powerful communication tool so students and teachers can share literacy learning progress with parents and other family members.

Paper portfolios were commonly used in the 1990s, and some teachers still use them today; however, more recently, digital portfolios have increased in popularity with tools such as Google Drive or Seesaw. Regardless of the format used, portfolios are a useful student-centered approach to assessment that values each learner and the strengths they possess.

ASSESSMENT STRATEGY 8.2.
Portfolios

Purpose

The purpose of the *Portfolios* assessment strategy is to build a representative sample of student work to demonstrate performance and progress over time. The portfolio is a student-centered approach to assessment that allows students and teachers to select samples of each student's work that reflect their strengths and progress and promote student self-evaluation and goal setting. The portfolio can also be used as a tool for communicating with parents and families about students' literacy processes and progress. In addition, insights gained from portfolios can inform teachers' instruction.

Value

Portfolios offer an equitable approach to assessment that is designed to help you view every student as having valuable strengths that can inform and enhance their learning. While portfolios have a general format and process, the contents and the insights gained are focused on the individual student. Portfolios empower students to be self-directed learners who reflect on their work, understand their strengths, and set goals for continued growth. Portfolios also provide a useful way to communicate with families about children's literacy development and to ensure that instruction builds on student strengths.

Procedures

When you **prepare** to use portfolio assessment with your students, there are several decisions to make that are outlined below.

1. Decide on the focus of the portfolio. Consider if it will be a showcase portfolio that contains a student's "best work," a weekly sample to show development, video clips of literacy tasks being completed, both student- and teacher-selected pieces, writing samples with drafts included, a collection of artifacts to show the student's accomplishments aligned to specific standards, or something else.
2. Once you have determined the focus of the portfolio, consider how you will organize and store them. Two basic options are paper portfolios or digital portfolios.
    - For paper portfolios, you can use large file folders, pocket folders, accordion files, three-ring binders, large "envelopes" created by folding and stapling sheets of chart paper or bulletin board paper, or even shopping bags. Depending on the size and number of portfolios, designate a plan for storage such as a milk crate, drawer, or large box.
    - For digital portfolios, the easiest method is to create a Google Folder named "Student Portfolios" (add the class or year to the folder name) and save it in your Google Drive. Create a subfolder for each student, and save it with the student's name. You may wish to use other digital tools such as Seesaw or Dropbox.
    - Determine how student work samples will be selected for the portfolio and reviewed and shared. Some questions and suggestions you can use to guide your decision making are provided in Figure 8.2.
3. Once you have made all of these decisions, you are ready to implement portfolio assessment in your classroom, but be prepared to make adjustments to ensure that the approach is working for you, your students, and their families. To learn more about portfolio assessment, see how Mrs. Ahmad uses them in her fourth-grade classroom in the implementation example that follows.

Considerations	Suggestions for getting started
Who selects work samples?	While the goal is for students to take ownership of the portfolio plan, at least initially, the teacher and student work together to select samples for the portfolio to ensure that representative work is included.
How often are work samples added to the portfolio?	Once a week is a good starting place to ensure that the process is manageable and you have enough pieces to show growth and change over time. We recommend adding one to three new pieces each week. Remember those pieces may be finished, in process, and video and audio files may also be selected to demonstrate student performance on a specific task, such as reading aloud, explaining a skill, discussing a text, or reading an authored piece aloud.
How and how often do teacher and student review the portfolio?	If you are able to review portfolios with an average of two students each day, this means you should be able to review each child's portfolio about twice a month. Most teachers prefer to set aside time in their calendars for portfolio review to ensure that they and their students are prepared to have meaningful discussions around the portfolio.
How is student self-evaluation addressed?	We recommend using a portfolio discussion template to ensure that student self-evaluation is addressed. See Form 8.1.
How is student goal setting included?	We recommend using a portfolio discussion template to ensure that student goal setting is included. See Form 8.1.
How and how often are portfolios shared with and reviewed by families?	We recommend using already-scheduled conferences in the fall to kick off the portfolio assessment process with families. After that, we recommend connecting with families monthly to share and seek their input on student portfolios.
How does the teacher reflect on portfolios to determine specific ways to leverage each student's strengths and to enhance teaching and learning overall?	We recommend using a set of reflection questions to guide your process initially. See Form 8.2 for suggested reflection questions.

FIGURE 8.2. Considerations for selecting, reviewing, and sharing portfolios.

Collecting, Analyzing, and Using Data

The pieces that are added to the portfolio comprise the main data and reflect the student's work over time. The Portfolio Discussion Template (Form 8.1) is a way to collect and analyze data. Teacher Reflection Questions for Using Insights from Portfolio Assessment (Form 8.2) is another tool to help the teacher use the data to reflect on and enhance their teaching to improve student learning.

Making Students and Teachers Visible

Portfolio assessment puts the focus squarely on each individual student and their learning and development over time. The student takes the lead in selecting pieces to add to the portfolio, providing a rationale for why they selected each piece, reflecting on their progress and strengths, sharing the portfolio with their teacher and families, and setting their own goals. Through the portfolio assessment process, students make their skills, strengths, thoughts, insights, and goals visible. Teachers are also highly visible throughout the portfolio assessment process. They must create literacy-rich opportunities for students to demonstrate their literacy skills, processes, and development. Teachers' rich knowledge of their students and the curriculum as well as literacy and general development are clearly visible as they provide invitations and support for students to take ownership of their learning through portfolio assessment.

Implementation Example

Mrs. Ahmad has been teaching fourth grade for 5 years at Copley Elementary School. She has 23 students in classroom 4-A this year. She has used portfolios for most of her teaching career, but she has recently shifted to digital portfolios from paper portfolios because she believes they are easier to store and share with families. She also likes that digital portfolios make it easy to include photos, video clips, and audio clips of students engaged in literacy tasks.

At the beginning of the school year, Mrs. Ahmad introduces her students to portfolio assessment. She explains that an artist has a portfolio to show the different types of art they have created, and when she was studying to be a teacher, she created a portfolio to show her development as a teacher. She asks if any of the students have seen scrapbooks or photo albums that capture important moments in someone's life. After several students share, she asks if some students collect mementoes from vacations, birthdays, celebrations, or accomplishments. Aliyah shares that she has a box with ribbons and medals from dance competitions, and Gabe nods and says he displays his baseball trophies, ribbons, and game balls on his dresser. Diamond says her mother takes her picture in the same place on the first and last day of school each year so they can see how much she has grown and changed. She explains that her mother prints out the pictures and keeps them in a photo album with a section for Diamond and her siblings Tiara and Terrence.

Mrs. Ahmad smiles and explains, "That's exactly what portfolios do. They provide evidence of what you can do, highlight and celebrate your strengths, and show how you have grown over time. Our portfolios will focus on your strengths and development as readers and writers this year."

Mrs. Ahmad's school uses Google Classroom so it is familiar to most of her students and their families. Her school provides a Chromebook for each student to use at school and to take home. She sets up a folder for each of her students in Google Drive, and she shares it with their family. When she shares the portfolio with families, she uses the note in Figure 8.3.

Mrs. Ahmad tells the students that they will be asked to add at least one thing to their portfolio each week. She shows them how to keep a list of possible pieces to include by using a Google Form (see Figure 8.4). She shows them that she does the same thing,

Dear 4-A Families:

I am sharing your child's digital portfolio. This will be an important tool for us in fourth grade. The portfolio will focus on your child's reading and writing strengths, development, and goals. I will share it with you regularly so you can see your child's progress and offer input. The portfolio is empty now, but we will soon begin adding files such as completed work, video clips, photos, and audio clips. We will also review and discuss the portfolio at conferences. I look forward to working with your child and to being partners to help them have a great year!

Sincerely,
Mrs. Ahmad

FIGURE 8.3. Portfolio introduction note for families.

but her Google Form has a space for each of her student's names so she can keep track of what she would like to add to the portfolio for each of her students.

She reminds the students that they may want to include written work (that they can take a photo of or scan and upload to their digital portfolio) or e-files from assignments they complete on their Chromebooks. Her students also know how to take photos and videos with their Chromebooks so they often take pictures of their artwork or completed projects and routinely create video recordings of their own oral reading or explanation of a learning task they have completed.

She sets aside 5 minutes every afternoon for students to think about the work they did that day and encourages them to make notes on the Google Form for any pieces they may want to add to their portfolios. Mrs. Ahmad has created a schedule so that she can review the portfolio every other week with each student. Since she has 23 students, that means she meets with two or three students daily. Each of these portfolio discussions lasts about 7–10 minutes, and she generally schedules them during independent- or

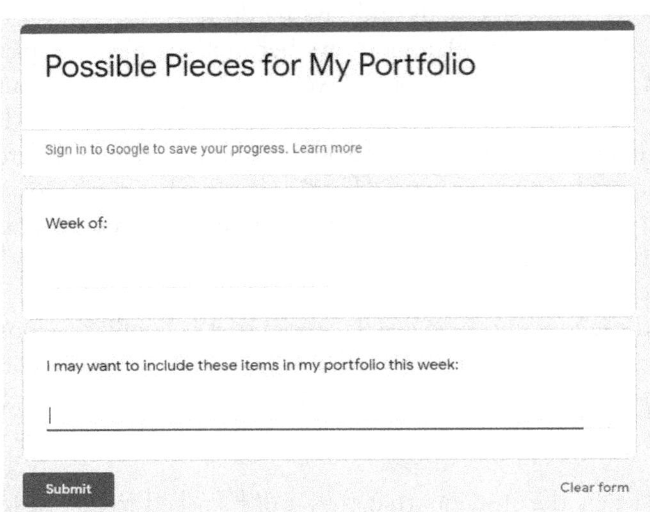
Possible Pieces for My Portfolio

Sign in to Google to save your progress. Learn more

Week of:

I may want to include these items in my portfolio this week:

Submit

Clear form

FIGURE 8.4. Google Form for possible pieces to add to portfolio.

partner-reading time. During these discussions, she and the students review their lists of possible pieces to include and they each select one (or possibly two) from each week. See Figure 8.5 for an example of how she completed the template when conferencing with Pen, a student in her classroom who uses the pronouns *they* and *them*.

Families have access to their child's digital portfolio at all times, but Mrs. Ahmad schedules conferences with them four times each year to discuss the portfolios as part of a three-way conference with the student, their family, and herself. The conferences may be done in person, but increasingly more families are preferring to meet via Zoom or on Google Meet. Mrs. Ahmad tries to be as flexible as possible so that all families are able to attend these portfolio conferences. She asks the student to "take the lead" and guide their family through the portfolio discussing the pieces, why they were selected, the strengths they demonstrate, and goals on which they have been working. Mrs. Ahmad also invites family members to ask questions, celebrate the student's work, and discuss the importance of the student's strengths. The conferences usually last about 20 minutes. To prepare students for the three-way conference, Mrs. Ahmad uses these prompts:

- Remember, we are focusing on the portfolio from (insert date) until today.
- Choose at least one piece to share from your portfolio from near the beginning, from the middle, and from the end of the time frame.
- Be sure to tell why you selected each piece.
- Share some things you are proud of from these pieces.
- Share a couple of your strengths.
- Discuss at least one goal you set and how it's going.
- Invite your family to ask questions or share reactions with you.

On a Tuesday evening, Mrs. Ahmad had a three-way conference with Pen and their mother, stepfather, and grandmother using Google Meets. Mrs. Ahmad shares her screen so she can access the files as Pen talks about the pieces in their portfolio. Pen was excited to share the things they had added to the portfolio since their last conference. Pen discussed their reading log and talked about how they enjoy reading and exploring new genres. Pen explained that their interest in reading and their reading habit are strengths they are proud of. Pen's mother smiled and said, "Yes, my little bookworm!" Pen then shared a goal they set to read more nonfiction so they could finish a report on birds of prey. Pen's stepfather asked, "Do they have to be books or can we search on the Internet?" Pen responded, "Pops, we can use the Internet. Will you help me find some good sites?" "Sure, Pen, we can start tonight." The conference continued with Pen taking the lead and finally asking, "Mama, Pops, and Grandma, do you have anything you want to share about my portfolio?" Pen's mother smiled, and responded, "You are growing so much as a reader, Pen! I am so proud of you, and your portfolio is wonderful." Pen's grandmother nodded and chimed in, "Yes, Pen, I loved seeing your portfolio." Pen's stepfather commented, "I want to read your report on birds of prey so we can see what information we need to search for on the Internet." Mrs. Ahmad closed the conference by saying, "Thank you, Pen, for sharing your portfolio with us, and thank you to your mom, stepfather, and grandmother for joining us. Pen, you have many strengths, and I am excited to keep working with you so you can continue to grow as a reader and writer. Thanks and good night, all!"

Student: Pen **Date:** March 19

Prompts (student-selected pieces)	Notes
What piece do you want to add to your portfolio from the week of ______? • Tell me about it. • Why did you select it? • What does it show about you as a literacy learner? • What does it show about your strengths?	**Last week:** Reading log because I finished a book and started one from a different genre. I'm trying to read more and to read from different genres, like biography, nonfiction, mystery, and poetry. I'm really starting to like lots of different kinds of books. My mom said I'm becoming a bookworm! **This week:** Oral reading video because I've been working on my expression and phrasing. I think my fluency has gotten better, and I am more confident when we do partner reading.
Prompts (teacher-selected pieces)	**Notes**
I would like to add this to your portfolio because: • What do you think it shows about you as a literacy learner? • What does it show about your strengths?	**Last Week:** The new ending you wrote for *The One and Only Ivan* (Applegate, 2012) because it shows you understand plot, character, and setting and how they interact in a story. This piece shows you understand how a story is constructed and you used your knowledge and creativity. **This week:** Your research project on birds of prey. Your notes show that you're able to read and comprehend informational texts, summarize key ideas, and organize information.
Prompts for portfolio review	**Notes**
As you look at your portfolio: • What do you notice? • What makes you proud?	I did lots of reading and writing last week! I can concentrate longer when I read. I am proud of all the reading and writing I'm doing, and I think I'm getting stronger as a reader and writer too.
Goal setting	**Notes**
Based on this portfolio review: • What goal do you want to set for yourself? • How can I help you reach that goal?	I want to read more information books and online sources about birds so I can finish my research project and share it with others. You can give class time for our projects and conference with me to give me feedback when I'm stuck.

FIGURE 8.5. Example of a portfolio discussion template for Pen.

Mrs. Ahmad reflects on her teaching and her students' work, progress, strengths, and struggles on a daily basis as part of her work as a teacher. However, about once a month, she asks herself the questions from Form 8.2 to ensure that she is making specific connections from her reflections to her practice. (See Figure 8.6 for her completed form.)

Mrs. Ahmad is pleased with how her approach to portfolio assessment is working, but she is always thinking of ways she can improve her practice. She and her teammates in fourth grade have been talking to the third-grade and fifth-grade teachers to explore the idea of multiyear portfolios. She is grateful that she has such collaborative colleagues who freely share ideas, help her reflect and grow, and support each other. She believes portfolios have significant **value** because they make **visible** what her students know and can do, so she hopes her colleagues will join her in implementing them in their classrooms.

How Using the *Can You Help Me Understand?* Assessment Strategy Can Reveal Your Students' Strengths

Sometimes when assessing a student's oral reading, comprehension, or other aspect of their reading performance, you may wonder, "Why did they do that?" or "What were they thinking when they did that?" Instead of wondering or assuming they do not know or cannot do something, you can use the *Can You Help Me Understand?* assessment strategy to learn why students did what they did or answered in a certain way. Rather than questioning the student to determine what they know, which is a traditional approach to questioning, this assessment strategy positions the student as the expert and the teacher as the learner and invites students to make their thought processes, knowledge, and strategies visible to you. By sending the message that you value the student's insights and understanding of their own learning processes, you are demonstrating that you see them as competent, believe in their genius, and want to learn from them so you can support their learning and growth. This assessment strategy also offers an opportunity for students to develop their metacognition (i.e., thinking about their own thinking so they can become more strategic and intentional readers). Through using the *Can You Help Me Understand?* assessment strategy, you will be able to get a glimpse into students' heads and understand the strengths they possess that they use when reading. You can then use these insights to identify ways you can build your instruction on the strengths the students bring to their reading and learning. While we are presenting this as a separate strategy, it is really an add-on that can be used with other assessments and instructional activities you already use in your classroom.

ASSESSMENT STRATEGY 8.3.
Can You Help Me Understand?

Purpose

The *Can You Help Me Understand?* assessment strategy offers an approach to assessment that you can use with a student after they have completed a task or while they are engaged in it. In fact, you can add *Can You Help Me Understand?* to almost any other assessment

Reflection question	Responses
As I look at my students' portfolios, what strengths do I see? • What insights can I gain about my teaching and student learning opportunities in my classroom?	My students are so interested in reading and sharing what they are reading. They really have formed a literacy community. They recommend books to one another, and students like Pen are reading more widely because their peers have recommended books and new genres to them. I am glad that the time for partner reading, independent reading, and book clubs has been productive. I need to make sure that my classroom library is highlighting new books and I'm doing book talks to introduce new authors and genres such as historical fiction and autobiography.
What am I doing to use students' strengths to improve learning? • What is working well? • What improvements can I make?	Many of my students have strong interests and I am providing opportunities for them to read about and do research reports on those topics. They are very motivated to do this, and books, magazines, and websites I've provided have offered them choice in what to read, and extra visits to the library have bene helpful too. I need to provide more instruction on how to summarize important information from the nonfiction sources they are reading. I can do a think-aloud to model this.
As I reflect on my students' strengths, what aspects of my teaching do I think are supporting their learning?	Choice is important plus lots of opportunities for self-directed learning.
What advice did students share about how I can help them reach their goals? • What action can I take to address their advice?	Students suggested more time working with me for feedback. I need to look at my conferencing schedule and see if I can find snippets of time to do more conferencing with students who want it. I also need to look at how I can scale up peer conferencing so they can learn from and with one another.
What do I see as my strengths in literacy teaching?	I feel like the element of choice and the many opportunities for students to take ownership of their learning are strengths for how I teach.
What goal do I want to set to improve my literacy teaching?	I need to do more modeling and thinking aloud to help students understand complex processes such as summarizing.

FIGURE 8.6. Example of teacher reflection questions for using insights from portfolio assessments.

strategy you use in your classroom. In *Can You Help Me Understand?* the student is positioned as the expert (i.e., the teacher) about their reading and learning processes, and the teacher is positioned as the learner who is seeking to understand the student and their strengths. By using a few inviting questions, you can gain insight into the student's thinking, strategy use, and knowledge. You can then use these insights to provide personally relevant instruction to build on students' strengths to advance their literacy learning.

Value

The *Can You Help Me Understand?* assessment strategy offers value in several areas. First, you can use it as a quick add-on to other assessment strategies so you can gain understanding of a student's thinking and strengths. Second, and most importantly, it situates the student as an expert on their own learning and reading, which demonstrates respect for and belief in the individual learner as a competent person who brings strengths to their learning. Third, it allows the teacher to gain access into the in-the-head processes that the student uses when reading or completing other literacy tasks. Fourth, it offers an invitation for students to develop metacognitive awareness about their own thinking and problem solving. Finally, it provides useful information about how to support the student's reading development.

Procedures

1. To **prepare** for this assessment strategy, it is important to consider the inviting questions you will use. The purpose of the inviting questions is to ask students to share (or teach us) about how they read a text, completed an assignment, or used problem solving or strategies to engage in a literacy task. In addition, it is essential to demonstrate a genuine interest in understanding the student's reading.
2. We recommend the following questions as a good starting place, but you may find that you wish to modify these questions to meet your specific needs better.
   - Can you help me understand what you did here?
   - Can you help me understand why you did that?
   - Can you help me understand your thinking here?
   - Can you help me understand what strategy you used here and why?
   - Can you help me understand what I can do to support you as a reader?
3. When you are working with a student or you are reviewing a student's completed or in-process work, if you wonder, "Why did they do this?" or "What were they thinking here?" you will be ready to implement the *Can You Help Me Understand?* assessment strategy.
4. While you will not want or be able to create a specific schedule for when or how often to use this assessment strategy, it is so helpful for developing a clear understanding of students' processes, skills, strategies, and strengths, you will want to use it often in combination with other assessment strategies. For example, you may want to use

it anytime you are doing *Running Records* (Assessment Strategy 6.2) or *Oral Reading Analysis* (Assessment Strategy 6.3) and something the student does (or does not do) confuses or intrigues you.

5. You will simply ask the inviting questions, listen carefully, and provide follow-up prompts to gather more information as needed. Three follow-up prompts are provided below.
   - Can you tell me more?
   - Can you show me?
   - Is there anything else you want me to understand?
6. You can record your notes in conjunction with other record-keeping systems you already use in your classroom, such as on *Running Records* (Assessment Strategy 6.2), *Oral Reading Analysis* (Assessment Strategy 6.3), or anecdotal records used for *Kidwatching* (Assessment Strategy 8.1).

Collecting, Analyzing, and Using Data

You will collect data by taking notes using the record-keeping system already in place for the main assessment strategy. Carefully review the notes, record any insights or questions you have, and jot down a plan for how to use those insights or questions to improve your teaching and your student's learning. You may wish to write the following information (Form 8.3) on the record-keeping tool you are using.

Making Students and Teachers Visible

This approach to assessment positions the student as the expert on their own learning and invites them to make their knowledge, skills, strategies, and strengths visible to their teacher through a series of inviting questions. Through this process, teachers get access to student thinking that is normally not visible. Teachers are also visible in this approach to assessment because they must identify their points of confusion and wonder related to their students' reading.

Implementation Example

In Assessment Strategy 6.3 (*Oral Reading Analysis*), Mr. Rivera listens to his third-grade student, Sophia, read from an informational book about birds. He notes that she methodically chunks multisyllabic words such as *re/lax/ing, use/less,* and *help/less/ly* accurately but very slowly and deliberately. Afterward when he is reading his notes, he wonders, "Why did Sophia read those words so slowly and methodically?" He remembers that she didn't do this when reading similar multisyllabic words the previous day during guided reading. He decides to use *Can You Help Me Understand?* to learn more about Sophia's approach to reading multisyllabic words. The next morning, he stops by Sophia's seat while she is working independently and says, "Sophia, can you help me understand something?" She smiles, and responds, "Sure." Their conversation and his notes (Figure 8.7) follow.

MR. RIVERA: Sophia, when you read with me earlier today, you read the words *relaxing, useless,* and *helplessly* really slowly. Do you remember that?

SOPHIA: Yeah, I do.

MR. RIVERA: Can you help me understand what you were doing when you read those words?

SOPHIA: I was chunking them—like you showed us.

MR. RIVERA: Can you help me understand why you did it slowly?

SOPHIA: You showed us that way. So I did it that way.

MR. RIVERA: Can you tell me more?

SOPHIA: You are a good reader, so I did it like you showed us.

MR. RIVERA: Sophia, you are such a serious student, but I think I did something to confuse you! I wanted you to know how to chunk the long words so they are easier to read, but I didn't show you how to put the word together and read it all together.

SOPHIA: I just thought we were supposed to read the chunks. Like you did.

MR. RIVERA: Can you show me how to read those words?

SOPHIA: Uh huh. (*Mr. Rivera writes the words on a piece of paper and shows it to Sophia. She then reads the words fluently.*) Relaxing, useless, helplessly.

MR. RIVERA: Thanks for helping me understand what you did and why. Is there anything else you want to help me understand?

SOPHIA: Hmmm. Yeah. When I see a long word, I look ahead and read it in my head first. Is that okay? My big sister showed me.

MR. RIVERA: That's definitely okay. That shows that you are developing and using strategies to improve your accuracy and fluency. Is there anything you want me to understand about how I can help you with your reading?

SOPHIA: Talking like this helps.

MR. RIVERA: Very good. Sophia, I'll make sure we talk like this about your reading often. Thank you!

During their conversation and immediately afterward, Mr. Rivera records the data on the back of the record sheet for the *Oral Reading Analysis* (Assessment Strategy 6.3) he completed for Sophia the previous day. His notes are provided below in Figure 8.7.

After school, Mr. Rivera reviews his notes, and focuses his attention on the "What I plan to do . . ." column. He makes notes in his lesson plans to incorporate these ideas into his teaching over the next few days.

Mr. Rivera describes the *Can You Help Me Understand?* assessment strategy as the most **valuable** assessment strategy in his toolkit because it allows him to fill in gaps in his understanding of his students as reader and learners. By using this assessment strategy, he is able to make his students' literacy skills, strategies, and behaviors **visible** so he can plan appropriate instruction that will support their development and progress.

What I asked	What student said	What student showed me	My insights	I plan to . . .
Why did you read the words so slowly and chunk by chunk?	Because you are a good reader and showed us how to do it.	When I asked her to read the words *relaxing, useless,* and *helplessly,* she did so fluently.	I need to be careful about how I model skills. Sophia sees me as a good reader, and her sister too. Am I providing enough opportunities for her to see her own reading strengths?	Ask Sophia if she will demonstrate for her guided-reading group how to chunk and then blend multisyllabic words. In our next portfolio review, discuss reading strengths with Sophia, including her use of strategies and reading role models.
What else do you want me to understand?	I look ahead if there are long words and read them in my head first. My big sister showed me.	She is strategic when she reads long words, and her sister is a resource for her reading.	Sophia understands reading is a strategic process, and sees her sister as a role model for reading.	Discuss what other strategies Sophia uses when reading multisyllabic words or encounters challenging text. Learn more about her reading role models.
What can I do to help you as a reader?	Talk like this.	These conversations are helpful to her too.	By having this conversation, I learned a lot about Sophia's reading.	Make sure I'm having conversations like this with Sophia regularly.

FIGURE 8.7. Example of recorded data for *Can You Help Me Understand?*

How the *Literacy Provision Inventory* Can Help You Learn about Students' Strengths

Interest inventories have often been used in education, but they typically just focus on students' hobbies and favorite things, and while this can be somewhat helpful, in the *Literacy Provision Inventory* we instead offer an equity-based approach that focuses on the provisions (i.e., resources or strengths) that students bring to their literacy learning. In our work on readers' rights (Bass et al., 2008) we discussed how all students bring three types of provisions to their literacy learning: literacy knowledge provisions, cultural provisions, and social provisions. Literacy knowledge provisions are the in-school and out-of-school knowledge, skills, and strategies that students have. In addition, students have cultural provisions they bring to school in the form of "shared knowledge, customs, emotions, rituals, traditions, values, and norms" (Ogbu, 1988, p. 11) that they acquire through their daily lives in their homes and communities. Finally, social provisions are the ways students interact with others in routines and contexts they encounter in and out of school (Bass et al., 2008, p. 50). By learning about these provisions and using them as the basis for instruction, we can plan and provide culturally relevant instruction that honors students for who they are and builds on their many strengths.

ASSESSMENT STRATEGY 8.4.
Literacy Provision Inventory

Purpose

The *Literacy Provision Inventory* allows you to gather information about each student's literacy provisions—literacy knowledge, cultural, and social. This assessment strategy comprises a series of questions to use as an interview, and it also provides an opportunity to go back periodically to have conversations with each student to add any new information. This assessment strategy also helps the teacher identify key insights so they can plan instruction that builds on the student's literacy provisions.

Value

This assessment operates from an asset-based lens wherein all students are viewed as having strengths (or provisions) in the areas of literacy knowledge, cultural provisions, and social provisions. It provides an easy-to-implement assessment for gathering information about your students' strengths and backgrounds so you can approach your teaching from an equity-minded perspective that builds on their provisions.

Procedures

1. In the first few weeks of the school year, invite each student to meet with you to complete the *Literacy Provisions Inventory*. Because it will take 10–15 minutes per student, you will want to **prepare** a schedule to ensure that you are able to complete several interviews each day. At the end of the quarter or semester, you will want to invite each student to do an update interview using the *Literacy Provisions Inventory*.
2. Using the questions and record sheet in Form 8.4, conduct the *Literacy Provisions Inventory* as an interview. You can use Form 8.4 to take notes, or you can type the responses into a document on your computer or tablet.
3. While interviewing the student, be sure to sit with them in a comfortable setting such as at a table in a quiet part of the classroom.
4. After the interview, thank the student for their time and for sharing this important information with you. Let them know that you will be using what you learned from them to help you teach and support them in your classroom.

Collecting, Analyzing, and Using Data

You will **collect** data by filling out the record sheet in Form 8.4 by hand or by typing your notes into your laptop or tablet while conducting the interview. Immediately after the interview, review your notes and fill in any additional information, including your insights and next steps. To **analyze** the data, review each student's interview individually to identify strengths you want to leverage, follow-up questions you want to ask, and key insights you want to remember. Once you have conducted all the *Literacy Provision Inventory* assessments for your class, **use** the data to identify patterns across student interviews to determine strategies, opportunities, curricular content, or lessons you want to implement for groups of students.

Making Students and Teachers Visible

In the *Literacy Provision Inventory* assessment, students are interviewed to learn about their strengths (provisions) in their own words. In short, students tell their own stories and make themselves visible to their teachers. Teachers build on trusting, respectful relationships they establish with their students by engaging in conversations about their literacy provisions. In doing so, teachers make their commitment to equity-focused instruction visible to their students.

Implementation Example

Mrs. O'Malley is a fifth-grade teacher. Simon is a student in her class. Toward the end of the first week of school, she meets with Simon at a table in a quiet corner of the classroom to do the *Literacy Provisions Inventory*. She tells him, "Simon, I am so glad to have you in our class. I want to get to know you better so I can be sure to teach and support you in ways that will be most helpful for you. Just like you bring your supplies to school in your backpack each day, I also believe that you have an imaginary backpack that represents all of the knowledge, resources, and strengths you have that help you learn and grow. I am going to interview you so I can learn more about what is in your imaginary backpack. Does that make sense?" Simon shrugs his shoulders, and he responds, "I dunno."

Mrs. O'Malley smiles and continues, "The kinds of things in your imaginary backpack are the knowledge you have about reading and writing, the strengths you have developed from being part of your family and community, and the ways you have learned to work with and use your communication and collaboration skills. There are no wrong answers since you will be teaching me about who you are so I can do a better job of teaching you, building on your strengths, and making sure our curriculum is meaningful to you. Does that sound okay?"

Simon smiles, and says, "I guess so." Mrs. O'Malley explains, "I'll be taking notes so I can remember what you tell me." Simon nods in agreement and says, "Um-hmm." Mrs. O'Malley uses the questions from Form 8.4 to guide the interview with Simon. She types notes into an electronic version of Form 8.4 because she feels she can type faster and capture more of what each student says with greater accuracy.

During the interview, Mrs. O'Malley uses follow-up prompts such as, "Can you please tell me more?" or "Can you give me an example?" because Simon is soft-spoken and tends to share short responses. These prompts result in him sharing more and ensure that she gets to know him better and is able to collect useful data.

Shortly after the interview is concluded, she reviews her notes and makes revisions and additions to make sure that she captured as much of what Simon shared as possible (see Figure 8.8).

Student name (preferred): Simon **Date:** Sept. 12

Background information
Tell me about your family:
Who is in your family? My mom and dad, two big brothers, and my little sister. I have two grandmas and a grandpa, too, and lots of aunties and uncles and cousins.
Who lives with you? My mom and dad, two brothers, little sister, and our two cats, Sasha and Daisy.
What language do you speak at home? English, but my grandma speaks German and English too.

Tell me about your favorite . . .	
School subject: math	Sport or game: soccer and Minecraft and Fortnite
Food: pizza and candy!	Book or author: Trapped in a Video Game books
Animal: cats	Famous person: Christiano Ronaldo
Color: orange	Place: my bed because my house is crowded
TV show /video/movie: ESPN soccer	Thing to do in your free time: soccer, video games
Song or type of music: country	Memory: when my soccer team won a tournament

Literacy knowledge questions	**Literacy knowledge responses**
Tell me about your reading:	Reading is okay. I am a pretty good reader. I don't read that much except at school.
What is easy for you?	Short books are easy for me.
What is harder for you?	Long books and books with lots of big words are hard for me. Sometimes it's hard to concentrate on my reading.
What do you enjoy reading? Why?	Books about soccer and sports and video games because they are interesting. I can learn things to get better at playing sports and video games too.
What do you not like to read? Why?	I don't like to read long books or books that tell stories about the olden days. They are boring.
Tell me about your writing:	I am an okay writer. I like writing about soccer and video games, but I don't like writing stories.
What is easy for you?	Writing in my journal is easy because it's free choice.
What is harder for you?	Writing stories and research reports is hard for me.
What do you enjoy writing? Why?	I enjoy writing in my journal because I can write about anything I want.
What do you not like to write? Why?	I don't like to write things that are assigned because I don't get to choose what to write about.
What do you do when you get stuck reading hard words?	I look for parts I know and I try to figure out what starts with the first letter and would make sense.
What do you do when you do not understand something you are reading?	Sometimes I skip a word if I can't figure it out. If I don't understand I usually read it again. If I'm at home, I ask my mom sometimes. Sometimes I just skip it or stop reading.

(continued)

FIGURE 8.8. Example of a *Literacy Provision Inventory.*

Literacy knowledge questions	Literacy knowledge responses
What are you proud of about your reading and writing?	I can read chapter books now and I used to not be able to do that.
What do you want to work on with your reading and writing?	I want to be able to read big chapter books like my big brothers.
Insights about literacy knowledge: *Simon is interested in sports (mainly soccer) and video games, and he reads and writes about those topics. He demonstrates awareness of his interests and aspects of reading and writing that are easy and hard. He seems to read and write mainly for school and does not seem to enjoy reading and writing outside of school. He is aware of strategies he uses to figure out unknown words, but he only rereads or asks his mom if he doesn't understand something he is reading. Do further strategy work for monitoring and fixing up comprehension problems.*	
Cultural provisions questions	**Cultural provisions responses**
What things do you do together with your family?	We go fishing and watch movies together. We go to visit my grandparents, aunties, uncles, and cousins for cookouts and for birthdays.
What things do you do to help at home?	I clean my room and set the table. I help clear the dishes and put them in the dishwasher. When I'm older I can take out the garbage and mow the grass, but my older brothers do those things now.
Do you use reading and writing at home? If so, how?	I read and write at home for homework.
How do you spend time on the weekend?	Mostly I play soccer, go fishing, play with my cats, and play video games. Sometimes we visit family and play outside and have a cookout. My cousin Charlie and I like to go fishing and exploring in the woods.
In your family, what are you the best at?	I am the best at playing Fortnite. I am probably the best of all my friends too.
What things are your family members best at?	My dad is the best singer, and he plays guitar too. My mom is the best dancer, my brother Peter is the best at basketball, and Henry is the best at eating! My little sister Lucy is the best at piano because she takes piano lessons.
If someone just moved to your neighborhood, what would you want them to see or do and why?	I would want them to go fishing down at the river. It's peaceful and you can swim and canoe too. You can go exploring in the woods too. It's so much fun! My dad has a four-wheeler and that's a blast when he takes us for rides!
What are special things your family does to celebrate birthdays, holidays, or other important times?	We have cookouts to celebrate birthdays. All of my cousins play together and it's lots of fun. Sometimes my dad and uncles play music and sing, and my mom tries to teach us line dances.
Insights about cultural provisions: *Simon has an extended family that lives nearby, and they enjoy celebrating birthdays and having cookouts. Simon and his family enjoy fishing and being outdoors, and he enjoys spending time with his cousins. Music seems to be important in Simon's family, and he enjoys country music. Simon seems proud of his skill playing* Fortnite.	

(continued)

FIGURE 8.8. *(continued)*

Social provision questions	Social provisions responses
Tell me about your friends:	My best friends are Danny, Hector, Jake, Walter, and my cousin Charlie. We play soccer and video games together. Sometimes we go fishing, and we like to explore the woods and look for treasures. Sometimes my dad or my friends' dads will take us for rides on four-wheelers.
If I asked your friend to tell me about you, what would they say?	They would say I'm good at Fortnite, and I go crazy when I play video games. They would say I'm funny and nice and that I love my cats.
If you are working on a team, in a group, or with a partner, what are you best at?	I'm good at soccer, and I am a captain on my team. I'm good at encouraging the other players, and I can lead practice drills.
Do you prefer to work alone, with a partner, or in a group? Tell me why.	I like to work with a partner or in a group because reading and writing at school by myself is boring.
What do teachers do that make learning hard or frustrating for you?	When teachers make us read or write long things by ourselves, it's hard.
What do teachers do that make learning enjoyable for you?	When teachers let us choose and work with a partner I can choose or in a group I like that.

Insights about social provisions: *Simon has lots of friends and cousins, and they enjoy playing soccer and video games as well as fishing, canoeing, and exploring in the woods. Simon likes working with partners and in groups, and he likes when teachers let him have choice in his learning and when determining partners. He is on a soccer team and is a captain, which shows that he has leadership skills.*

Follow-up questions to ask:

Has Simon read books about outdoor adventure, fishing, four-wheelers, and other areas of interest?

If Simon could choose what to read and what to write, what would he select?

How does Simon use reading and writing inFortnite? For his other hobbies?

Strengths to leverage:

- *Lots of interests that can be linked to reading, writing, and the curriculum.*
- *Likes choice for reading, writing, and assignments.*
- *Is a leader in soccer. Give him chances to be a group leader for projects and activities in the classroom.*
- *Has lots of friends.*
- *Is very social and works well with others.*
- *He has a large and close family.*
- *He enjoys the outdoors and may be able to share his knowledge about plants, animals, nature, etc.*

(continued)

FIGURE 8.8. *(continued)*

Instructional ideas to implement: • *Locate books on topics that Simon is interested in and have him choose one to read.* • *Ask Simon to be a group leader for a book club with several of his friends, and have them choose the book they will read and discuss.* • *Regularly provide free choice for reading and writing assignments and monitor Simon's engagement and growth.* • *Give Simon the opportunity to choose his partner for in-class activities and projects.* • *Find ways for Simon to share his knowledge of the outdoors/nature in upcoming science units.*
Ideas for grouping and curriculum development: • *Many of the students reported liking to work with partners and in groups. Provide more opportunities for book clubs, partner reading, and writing workshop so students can work collaboratively.* • *Look for ways to incorporate outdoor education into the curriculum since so many of the students enjoy fishing, camping, and outdoor activities.* • *Provide opportunities for students to choose their reading and writing materials and assignments to foster engagement and build ownership.* • *Consider ways to get more students to share their strengths and areas of expertise. This could be a great way to build leadership skills too.*

FIGURE 8.8. *(continued)*

Mrs. O'Malley finds the *Literacy Provisions Inventory* to be a **valuable** assessment tool for making her students' strengths, assets, and backgrounds **visible.** By doing so, she is able to leverage the unique and important provisions each of her students brings to their learning.

How the *Photo Elicitation Interview* Can Help You Learn about Students' Out-of-School Literacy Use— and Their Points of Pride, Strengths, and Interests

The old adage "a picture is worth a thousand words" is true in many ways, including in assessment. The *Photo Elicitation Interview* has been used for a number of years as a research tool, and more recently, it has been used with young children (Pyle, 2012). In research, the goal of the photo elicitation interview is to understand the topic under study through the eyes of the participant who chooses what to photograph and how to explain the photo to the researcher. In assessment, the photo elicitation interview invites students to take photos of ways they use reading and writing outside of school, things they are proud of, things they are good at, and things that are interesting and/or important to them. These photos can then be used to encourage meaningful discussions so a teacher can get to know their students and their strengths, interests, and ways of using literacy outside of school. By carefully choosing prompts that will make visible students' strengths, passions, and genius, teachers can tailor the assessment to gather the types of information about their students that will be most helpful to guiding their instruction toward equity and relevance for all their students. A photo elicitation interview works well with all students but provides useful support for students who are newer to learning English or those who are shy because the photos serve as a stimulus for the student to share and the teacher to ask questions, pose ideas, or make clarifications.

ASSESSMENT STRATEGY 8.5.
Photo Elicitation Interview

Purpose

The *Photo Elicitation Interview* (PEI) provides a structure for students to make visible their out-of-school uses of reading and writing as well as their personal points of pride, interests, and strengths. Through a series of open-ended prompts, students take and share photographs that become the stimulus for a student-centered interview with their teacher. Teachers can then use what they learn about their students to plan and implement culturally responsive instruction that builds on their students' strengths, passions, and genius.

Value

PEI offers a student-centered approach to assessment wherein students make themselves visible as literate individuals who are competent and endowed with important strengths and interesting passions. Through photos students take themselves, teachers can learn about their students through their own eyes.

Procedures

1. To **prepare** for PEI, show students how to use their school-issued Chromebook or iPad to take photographs. If the school does not issue each student technology, create a check-out schedule for students to sign up to use the technology that is available in the classroom or school.
2. Tell students that you want them to take photos that show the following things:
   - How they use reading and writing outside of school.
   - Something they are proud of.
   - Something they are good at.
   - Something they think is interesting and/or important.
3. Ask students to identify one or two photos for each of the four areas listed above.
4. Invite students—one at a time—to meet with you in a quiet area of the classroom. Use the template in Form 8.5 to guide the PEI interview.

Collecting, Analyzing, and Using Data

To **collect** data, write notes about what students discuss for each of the photos they share in the "Notes on student discussion of photos" column in Form 8.5. After the interview, fill in the right-hand column, "Insights and next steps." To **analyze** the data, focus on what you learned about the student's out-of-school literacy uses, points of pride, strengths, and interests by asking yourself these questions:

- What did I learn about this student in this area?
- How can that new learning help me be a better teacher for the student?
- How can I connect their out-of-school literacy uses with what we do in school?
- How can I build on their points of pride in the curriculum and in my instruction?
- How can I celebrate and build on their strengths in the curriculum and in my instruction?
- How can I address their interests and the things they find important in the curriculum and in my instruction?

Finally, fill in the "Important things I learned about the student" section at the bottom of the template. Consider anything new you learned about the student and how to **use** the data to get to know and understand them better. These things may (or may not) relate directly to literacy and school. While PEI is designed to develop an understanding of an individual student, you may also wish to look across your notes to identify things about which multiple students are interested or where there are other commonalities that you can use for instructional and curricular planning.

Making Students and Teachers Visible

Photo elicitation interviews are all about students making themselves visible as learners and as individuals through the photos they take and discuss. Because students not only take the photos and choose which ones to share, but also explain each photo, PEI provides multiple ways for students to be visible and central in this assessment. Teachers' knowledge of their students is supported and built through PEI, which also leverages their expertise in curricular and instructional planning.

Implementation Example

Mr. Dixon is a fourth-grade teacher at Central Elementary School who has over 10 years of teaching experience. Ebony is a student in his class. He knows that she lives with her mother, younger brother, and grandmother, who speaks Polish. As a 1:1 school, all third-, fourth-, and fifth-grade students have school-issued Chromebooks, so Mr. Dixon has already shown the students how to take photos with their laptops and to save them in a folder for PEI photos. One afternoon in early September, he tells the students that he wants to get to know them so he can make sure his instruction is effective and the curriculum as meaningful and builds on their strengths and interests. He tells them that they will take photos to answer four specific questions, and then he will meet with each of them individually so they can describe one or two of their photos for each question.

To help with their planning, he a distributes a paper copy of the chart in Form 8.6. He provides time for them to ask about the questions to make sure they understand what they are being asked to do.

Mr. Dixon assigns a specific day the next week for each student to be ready to share their photos with him for PEI. Since he has 25 students in his class, he schedules PEI with five students each day for a week. He puts the PEI assessment time on the class schedule so he will have sufficient time to meet with each student for 10–15 minutes. During this time, the other students will be doing independent work, self-selected reading, partner reading, and project work, so they are engaged in learning activities that they can do without his assistance and he can focus entirely on each student with whom he is doing PEI.

On Tuesday morning, Mr. Dixon is scheduled to meet with Ebony, Araceli, Justin, and Zhen. He invites Ebony to a table in the corner of the classroom and reminds her to bring the chart (Form 8.6) and her Chromebook. He asks her to sit next to him so they can look at her computer screen together to see the photos.

MR. DIXON: Ebony, I'm looking forward to seeing your photos and learning about them. Can you show me a photo of how you use reading and writing outside of school?

EBONY: Yes. I have two. Can I show you both?

MR. DIXON: Of course! Can you show me the first one you want to share?

EBONY: Okay. This picture is my Girl Scout handbook and my badges.

MR. DIXON: Can you tell me more about the picture?

EBONY: I am a Girl Scout, and we do lots of things and earn badges. We read the handbook and keep track of what we do for each badge. We go camping and do projects to help people and pick up garbage. Stuff like that.

MR. DIXON: Can you tell me more?

EBONY: We are working on two badges now—first aid and simple meals. It's so we'll be ready for a camp-out soon. My mom is the Scout Leader, so I get to help out a lot.

MR. DIXON: That sounds really interesting, Ebony. Can you tell me about your other photo?

EBONY: It's a picture of my favorite cookbook. I like to bake with my grandma. We look for recipes in her cookbooks. They are in Polish so I can only read some of the words. Sometimes the recipes are just in my grandma's head and she tells them to me. We bake cookies the most, but sometimes we bake bread and muffins. Sometimes we even make a cake.

MR. DIXON: What a delicious way to use reading, Ebony! What is your favorite thing to bake?

EBONY: Probably chocolate chip cookies or chocolate cake with chocolate frosting!

MR. DIXON: Ebony, can you please show me a photo of something that makes you proud?

EBONY: This is a picture of the birthday cake we made for Jacob's birthday. He's my little brother. I even decorated it myself. I'm only 10, but I am the second best baker in my family!

MR. DIXON: Who is the best?

EBONY: My grandma!

MR. DIXON: Ebony, can you tell me about the photo that shows something you are good at?

EBONY: I was going to show you a picture of something else I baked, but I decided to show you a picture of my soccer team. I'm the goalie. I can usually block shots and keep the other team from scoring. I am also helping my little brother who wants to be a goalie.

MR. DIXON: What does it take to be a good goalie?

EBONY: I have to pay attention and be really focused. I have to know the rules good and be ready if the other team kicks the ball at the goal.

MR. DIXON: Ebony, what photo did you bring to show something interesting or important?

EBONY: I brought two for this question. Is that still okay?

MR. DIXON: Absolutely! Go ahead and share the first one.

EBONY: Okay. This is a picture of my Awana book and my Bible. These are important to me because my family goes to church together, and I go to Awanas on Wednesday night. I am learning about the Bible and to be a good person.

MR. DIXON: Thanks for sharing that, Ebony. What is your second photo?

EBONY: This is for the Olympics. I'm interested in soccer and track, but I want to learn about other sports. I can't wait to watch it on TV in the summer.

MR. DIXON: Ebony, thank you so much for sharing your photos with me. I learned a lot about you!

See Figure 8.9 to see how Mr. Dixon filled out the PEI template.

Mr. Dixon continues meeting with the other four students assigned to Tuesday. He believes the real **value** of PEI is that it allows him to learn a great deal about each of his students as they make their uses of literacy, interests, and strengths **visible.** For each of his students, he identifies at least one "next step" that he can implement immediately so he is able to put his new learning from PEI into action right away. He also combines notes about connections he can make to the existing curriculum as well as new lessons and units he can create. Mr. Dixon plans to meet with students for PEI four times during the year to ensure that he continues to build his knowledge of his students and their strengths and interests.

Conclusion

Instruction that is equitable and personally meaningful must be built on a teacher's knowledge of their students. Many traditional approaches to assessment focus on identifying what students don't know or can't do, and that approach only tells part of the story. Identifying students' strengths honors the genius and dignity that are inherent in each student. Once teachers have a sense of their students' strengths, they can plan and implement instruction that builds on those strengths, which provides equitable access to meaningful and relevant instruction for all students.

Student: Ebony **Date:** September 21

Prompt	Notes on student discussion of photos	Insights and next steps
Can you tell me about the photo(s) you took about how you use reading and writing outside of school?	*Girl Scouts: upcoming camping trip, working on badges for first aid and simple meals.* *Baking: with Grandma, uses recipes that are in Polish.*	*First aid unit in health class connects with first aid badge. Maybe Ebony can share what she has done to earn her badge. See if there are other Scouts in the room who could share too.* *Are there other badges that connect with curriculum?* *How much Polish does Ebony know? Are there any English-Polish cognates ?* *Connect recipes with fractions for math. Possible science connections for states of matter, following instructions/directions.*
Can you tell me about the photo(s) you took of something you are proud of?	*Chocolate birthday cake she baked and decorated for her brother.*	*She is confident as a baker. She stressed that she decorated it by herself. She seems to have a special relationship with her grandmother.* *How can I build on her confident and independent attitude in class?*
Can you tell me about the photo(s) you took of something you are good at?	*Soccer—she's the goalie, and she is helping her younger brother who wants to be a goalie.*	*She has a good attention span and is very focused. I've seen this in school too. She is helping her brother and may enjoy helping others in the classroom too, especially in areas where she is confident.*
Can you tell me about the photo(s) you took of something you find interesting and/or important?	*Awanas book and Bible—she's a Christian and her family attends church together.* *Olympics—especially soccer and track, but she wants to learn about other sports*	*She attends Awanas every Wednesday. I wonder how many other students in our class do as well. I don't know the program and if there are connections I could make to the curriculum. I will check online to see if I can get some information.* *There are some great biographies of Olympic heroes in the library. I will share them with Ebony. I'll mention this to Mrs. Gibson, our PE teacher, to see if she will be teaching about the Olympics this year.*

Important things I learned about the student: *Ebony has a lot of interests and strengths! She seems to know what she is good at, and she is confident in those abilities. She is focused and likes to be independent. She is a "joiner" who belongs to Girl Scouts, a soccer team, and Awanas. She knows some Polish from her grandmother.*

FIGURE 8.9. Example of a *Photo Elicitation Interview.*

FORM 8.1

Portfolio Discussion Template

Student: ______________________________ **Date:** ________________

Prompts (student-selected pieces)	**Notes**
What piece do you want to add to your portfolio? • Tell me about it. • Why did you select it? • What does it show about you as a literacy learner? • What does it show about your strengths?	
Prompts (teacher-selected pieces)	**Notes**
I would like to add this to your portfolio because: • What do you think it shows about you as a literacy learner? • What does it show about your strengths?	
Prompts for portfolio review	**Notes**
As you look at your portfolio: • What do you notice? • What makes you proud?	
Goal setting	**Notes**
Based on this portfolio review: • What goal do you want to set for yourself? • How can I help you reach that goal?	

FORM 8.2

Teacher Reflection Questions for Using Insights from Portfolio Assessment

Reflection question	Responses
As I look at my students' portfolios, what strengths do I see? • What insights can I gain about my teaching and student learning opportunities in my classroom?	
What am I doing to use students' strengths to improve learning? • What is working well? • What improvements can I make?	
As I reflect on my students' strengths, what aspects of my teaching do I think are supporting their learning?	
What advice did students share about how I can help them reach their goals? • What action can I take to address their advice?	
What do I see as my strengths in literacy teaching?	
What goal do I want to set to improve my literacy teaching?	

FORM 8.3

Recording Data for *Can You Help Me Understand?*

What I asked	What student said	What student showed me	My insights	I plan to . . .

FORM 8.4

Literacy Provision Inventory

(LITERACY KNOWLEDGE, CULTURAL, AND SOCIAL PROVISIONS)

Student name (preferred): ______________________ **Date:** ____________

Background information	
Tell me about your family: Who is in your family? Who lives with you? What language do you speak at home?	
Tell me about your favorite . . .	
School subject:	Sport or game:
Food:	Book or author:
Animal:	Famous person:
Color:	Place:
TV show/video/movie:	Thing to do in your free time:
Song or type of music:	Memory:
Literacy knowledge questions	**Literacy knowledge responses**
Tell me about your reading: What is easy for you? What is harder for you? What do you enjoy reading? Why? What do you not like to read? Why?	

(continued)

Literacy Provision Inventory *(page 2 of 5)*

Literacy knowledge questions	Literacy knowledge responses
Tell me about your writing: What is easy for you? What is harder for you? What do you enjoy writing? Why? What do you not like to write? Why?	
What do you do when you get stuck reading hard words? What do you do when you do not understand something you are reading?	
What are you proud of about your reading and writing? What do you want to work on with your reading and writing?	
Insights about literacy knowledge:	

(continued)

Literacy Provision Inventory *(page 3 of 5)*

Cultural provisions questions	Cultural provisions responses
What things do you do together with your family? What things do you do to help at home? Do you use reading and writing at home? If so, how? How do you spend time on the weekend?	
In your family, what are you the best at? What things are your family members best at?	
If someone just moved to your neighborhood, what would you want them to see or do and why?	
What are special things your family does to celebrate birthdays, holidays, or other important times?	
Insights about cultural provisions:	

(continued)

Social provisions questions	Social provisions responses
Tell me about your friends:	
If I asked your friend to tell me about you, what would they say?	
If you are working on a team, in a group, or with a partner, what are you best at?	
Do you prefer to work alone, with a partner, or in a group? Tell me why.	
What do teachers do that make learning hard or frustrating for you?	
What do teachers do that make learning enjoyable for you?	
Insights about social provisions:	
Follow-up questions to ask:	

(continued)

Strengths to leverage:
Instructional ideas to implement:
Ideas for grouping and curriculum development:

FORM 8.5

Photo Elicitation Interview Template

Student: ______________________________ **Date:** ______________

Prompt	Notes on student discussion of photos	Insights and next steps
Can you tell me about the photo(s) you took about how you use reading and writing outside of school?		
Can you tell me about the photo(s) you took of something you are proud of?		
Can you tell me about the photo(s) you took of something you are good at?		
Can you tell me about the photo(s) you took of something you find interesting and/or important?		
Important things I learned about the student:		

FORM 8.6

Planning for PEI

Question	Ideas for photos	Photos I took	Photos I will share with my teacher
How do you use reading and writing outside of school?			
What is something that makes you feel proud?			
What are you good at doing?			
What is something interesting or important to you?			

9

Literacy Assessment as Oeuvre

Teachers and Students Building a Visible Body of Work

In Chapter 1, we introduced you to our assessment goals that offer an alternative to current assessment practices that are failing our students and teachers. Failing practices include overreliance on high-stakes and state testing programs that mark student success solely with test scores. Frequently these practices press teachers to "march through a curriculum that is fixated on raising test scores" (p. 1). In this book, we offer 28 assessment strategies that are designed to do just the opposite, placing emphasis on teachers' decision making and students as individuals with strengths and needs that often go unrecognized. The assessments in this book are grounded in equity principles, making visible students' lived experiences, their cultural and linguistic histories, their beliefs about themselves as readers, and their strengths and needs in ways that provide direction for instruction that is responsive and supportive of all students.

We have learned from teachers that they value differentiated and responsive instruction to support equity practices, yet they often tell us that they don't have the resources, such as literacy assessments that vary in purpose and outcomes, to guide such instruction. As we demonstrated with every assessment strategy in this book, the assessments we offer make visible a wide range of students' attributes and needs. Further, they are doable, practical, and already embedded in common literacy instructional elements (e.g., conferencing with students, questioning text comprehension, identifying phonics and decoding skills and strategies, identifying strengths, collecting data in portfolios). Although embedded in common instructional practices, our assessment strategies, in many ways, push thinking beyond what is typical, providing explicit directions for instruction that is student specific and responsive to differences among our students.

The assessments in this book will make a difference for you and your students. You will have ownership of the assessments you use, the data you collect, and the interpretations you make of your students' learning and attributes. And, you will have the data you need to provide instruction that is responsive and supportive for every student in your classroom. As you work with your students to complete assessments described in this book, you can make the complexity of their literacy visible.

Through these assessments, you can help your students build a "body of work" that we like to think of as their "literacy oeuvre." In general, the term *oeuvre* refers to a substantial body of work that represents an artist's creative expressions. Those outward expressions are considered the externalization of the artist's mental and creative efforts. Our conceptualization of *literacy oeuvre* emphasizes two critical aspects of the assessment approach we promote in this book. Both are essential if we expect to implement equity-based assessments and instruction that make visible students' expressions of beliefs, interests, histories, and goals.

First, the approach in this book combats a narrow view of assessment because we have focused on documenting the complexity of students' literacy. A student's *literacy oeuvre* represents the student's mental and creative efforts, so they are personal and reflect the dignity inherent in each student. Considering students' literacy expressions as their *literacy oeuvre* emphasizes the personal, generative, and developmental nature of these expressions and the fact that they are not fixed but are changing in response to new learnings within the sociocultural context of their lives.

Second, a student's *literacy oeuvre* develops across time, and to ensure a complete and accurate view of the depth, breadth, and progression of the student's literacy work, the totality of the work must be considered. Unlike the artist where an accurate appraisal of their work stems from a view of the totality of that work, often judgments about a student's literacy knowledge are based on minimal or incomplete information. To get an accurate view of a students' literacy expressions, care must be taken to gather evidence of the student's work across time, using multiple measures to gather data about students reading for a variety of purposes in different types of texts. Thus, students are building a body of work, a *literacy oeuvre,* that makes visible their knowledge, identities, agency, literacy development, strengths, and needs.

By using these multiple assessments with their students over time, teachers create their own *teaching oeuvre,* or body of work, that makes visible their professional growth and expressions of understanding about their students' literacy from collecting, analyzing, and using the multiple forms of data. A *teacher's oeuvre* makes visible how they build understandings of their students as literate beings as well as their professional growth related to teaching, learning, and literacy itself.

In the remainder of this chapter, we share frequently asked questions posed by teachers with whom we have worked, and we provide our suggestions for implementing our assessment strategies.

Frequently Asked Questions

How does this approach to literacy assessment work in a classroom over a school year?

Let's look at how Mrs. Dunn-Collier, a second-grade teacher, implements this approach to assessment in her classroom with her 22 students. She describes assessment in her classroom as ongoing and intertwined with her instruction. In fact, she implements many of the assessments and collects assessment data as part of her daily instruction. Doing so allows her to be efficient with her time because as is true with all teachers, she is busy at school and in her personal life too.

In the beginning of the year, Mrs. Dunn-Collier focuses on getting to know her students and their families because she knows that these relationships will be foundational for teaching and learning in her classroom. Early in the school year, she begins to conduct her *Initial Student Conversations* (Assessment Strategy 2.2) as well as her *Initial Parent Conversations* (Assessment Strategy 2.1). The information she learns from these assessments helps her plan to implement *Celebrating Identities with Students and Their Families* (Assessment Strategy 2.3). Mrs. Dunn-Collier uses *Kidwatching* (Assessment Strategy 8.1) daily to focus on several students to gather data and gain insights about her students' reading behaviors. She collects data about her students' constrained skills through a variety of assessments, such as *Running Records* (Assessment Strategy 6.2) and the *Developmental Spelling Assessment* (Assessment Strategy 6.5). She assesses their comprehension through *Retellings* (Assessment Strategy 5.1) and *Questioning of Text Comprehension* (Assessment Strategy 5.3) and uses *Semantic Word Sorts* (Assessment Strategy 5.4) as part of her daily small-group reading instruction. She often likes to link *Running Records* with a comprehension assessment such as *Retellings* or *Questioning of Text Comprehension* because that allows her to gather more data in an efficient manner. As the year progresses, Mrs. Dunn-Collier and her students implement *Portfolios* (Assessment Strategy 8.2), *Student Self-Assessment* (Assessment Strategy 7.3), and *Goal Setting* (Assessment Strategy 7.4), among other assessments that inform her instruction.

As Mrs. Dunn-Collier plans her instruction, she considers the assessment data she already has to inform her planning as well as the questions she has that assessment can help her answer. She often jokes that she does her lesson planning "in pencil" because she is always adjusting her plans as she gathers more data about students and gains greater insights into what instruction is needed to leverage her students' strengths while addressing their needs. Because this approach to assessment is ongoing and focuses on students' literacy oeuvres, which represent their growth over time, Mrs. Dunn-Collier reports that she spends a few minutes daily reviewing her students' literacy assessment data. This process is central to her effectiveness as a teacher. She knows that as the school year gets busy, it can be tempting to reduce her focus on literacy assessment and reviewing each student's growth over time, but she reminds herself that even once she knows her students and their interests, literacy strengths, and areas for growth well, there is still so much more to learn and address in her literacy instruction.

To support the ongoing nature of this approach to literacy assessment, Mrs. Dunn-Collier has tried several ways to organize her assessment data over the years, and she has settled on using individual student folders and a class digest. She has an individual folder for each student, and she notes it can be a paper folder or an electronic folder, but she prefers hard copy folders that she stores in hanging files in a box she keeps on a table behind her desk. Within each individual student folder, she places the assessment record sheets and notes she has for that student. She has a coversheet for each student folder that serves as a running summary where she records the date and brief comments, questions, or next steps that she wants to remember and follow up on for that student. See Figure 9.1 for a sample of a summary sheet from the individual student folder for Antonio from the first month of school.

Mrs. Dunn-Collier also has a class folder that contains the class digest where she keeps an ongoing record of high-level reflections, observations, questions, and next steps

Date	Assessment	Finding, big idea, next step, question
9/3	Initial Student Conversation (2.2)	Shy! How can I get him to open up?
9/7	Running Record (6.2)	Great accuracy but very choppy.
9/7	Student Retelling (5.1)	Got main idea.
9/10	Developmental Spelling Assessment (6.5)	Transitional speller. How is his spelling in other contexts?
9/15	Running Record (6.2)	Fluency needs work. Assess again next week.
9/15	Questioning of Text Comprehension (5.3)	Good lower-level comprehension, but need to work on higher-level comprehension.
9/17	Kidwatching (8.1)	Hard time sticking with a book. Was it the book or the task of independent reading?
9/24	Initial Parent Conversation (2.1)	Spanish is primary language, but English is also spoken at home.
9/30	Celebrating Identities with Students and Their Families (2.3)	Family shared freely and enthusiastically.

FIGURE 9.1. Summary sheet for Antonio for September.

for the class, with a focus on groups of students who have similar strengths, needs, and interests. She finds that the class digest helps her remember the big ideas that she needs to follow up on in her planning, assessment, and teaching. See Figure 9.2 for a sample class digest from the first month of school.

When explaining her overall approach to organizing all the assessment data she collects, analyzes, and uses in her teaching, Mrs. Dunn-Collier calls it a layered approach. She focuses primarily on the individual student folders she has for each of her students, but as a teacher with 22 students in her classroom, she uses the class digest to identify groups of students who have similar strengths, needs, and interests to inform her instructional planning as well as grouping strategies. She reports that her goal is for this organizational approach to be informative yet still manageable with the many other demands on her time and attention. She explains that this organizational approach works for her, but she urges other teachers to tweak it to meet their needs or to develop their own ideas of what will work best in their classrooms.

In my school, I'm required to give assessments like DIBELS, 1-minute fluency probes, and required tests. Is there a way I can make those assessments more meaningful and useful?

We urge you to become an advocate for assessment practices that are equitable, humanistic, and student-centered because as a professional you have a great deal to offer to the conversation and decision-making processes associated with literacy assessment. Talk

Date	Assessment	Next step or question
9/3	Initial Student Conversations (2.2)	Follow up with Luis, Esmerelda, Bethany, and Michael who were very quiet and hardly responded. How can I make them more comfortable?
9/7	Running Records (6.2) Student Retellings (5.1)	Form initial groups for small-group instruction.
9/10	Developmental Spelling Assessment (6.5)	Need to cross-check with spelling from authentic texts students write.
9/15	Running Records (6.2) Questioning of Text Comprehension (5.3)	Look at small groups and adjust.
9/17	Kidwatching (8.1)	Need to make a schedule to observe these students more often when engaged in independent reading: Jasmine, Emory, Shanika, Matthew, and Kyung.
9/24	Initial Parent Conversation (2.1)	Offer an interpreter rather than asking families if they want one.
9/20	Celebrating Identities with Students and Their Families (2.3)	Need to break the class into smaller groups next time. Need more helpers to record data so I can capture more information.

FIGURE 9.2. Summary sheet for Mrs. Dunn-Collier's class for September.

with your colleagues, your principal, and district administrators about professional development and opportunities for teachers to make visible their knowledge of reading, development, and their students through literacy assessment. However, we do understand that even with your advocacy efforts, you may still have required assessments that all teachers in your grade level, school, district, or state must administer. Let's look at examples of how some teachers have used assessment strategies from this book as tools to make some of the required assessments they must administer more meaningful and useful.

Miss Mitchell teaches first grade, and she is required to give the DIBELS to all her students each quarter. She finds some of the assessment data useful, but she often wonders why students answered as they did and what they were thinking. DIBELS doesn't allow her to ask such questions during the assessment, so she uses *Can You Help Me Understand?* (Assessment Strategy 8.3) to go back after completing and scoring the DIBELS to learn more about a student's understandings, misconceptions, thought processes, and strategies. She uses this approach on an as-needed basis when she truly has questions about a student's performance or responses. Miss Mitchell has had many "*a-ha* moments" when using this approach, and she uses those insights to help her plan appropriate instruction to help her students progress in their acquisition of constrained skills.

Mrs. McKeown is a fifth-grade teacher, and she is required to give end-of-unit tests each quarter in reading. She is concerned that the testing takes a great deal of time, and it offers very little useful information other than how many items students got correct, and how many they missed. She also uses *Can You Help Me Understand?* to figure out why students responded to questions as they did, what they were thinking, and how they understood and approached specific items. She makes notes to score and report data before she uses *Can You Help Me Understand?* with specific students whose responses or scores puzzled her. She doesn't use this assessment strategy with each student on each end-of-unit test; rather, she uses it on an as-needed basis to help her fill in gaps and understand those students' reading, thinking, and strategies better. Mrs. McKeown believes the required end-of-unit tests do not provide her with useful information about the students' comprehension. Because she has already taught her students how to do a think-aloud, she sometimes follows up using *Think-Alouds* (Assessment Strategy 5.2) when she really wants to delve into some of her students' thinking and the strategies they use to comprehend. She also uses *Conferencing with Retrospective Miscue Analysis* (Assessment Strategy 3.2) to engage students in their self-evaluation of oral reading miscues and their use of fix-up strategies that support their reading and comprehension.

Mr. Nyant teaches second grade, and his district requires him to administer 1-minute fluency probes to each of his students every month. The focus of this assessment is accuracy and rate, and those are the data points he has to report to the school office for each student. He believes that the assessment could be more helpful and informative if it also addressed error analysis and prosody, so he adds an *Oral Reading Analysis* (Assessment Strategy 6.3) so he can do error analysis, assess self-correction, and gather data on students' prosody, reading behaviors, and use of strategies. While he only turns in the required scores for accuracy and rate, Mr. Nyant believes that he gains greater insights by expanding the required 1-minute fluency probes by using oral reading analysis. He also uses *Goal Setting* (Assessment Strategy 7.4) when he discusses the results with each student and works with them to set goals for their oral reading that he then follows up on with them throughout the month before the next 1-minute fluency probe and oral reading analysis is administered.

Because required assessments generally have specific administration rules, you will need to follow those rules and report scores as required. You will also want to check with the person who oversees the testing to make sure that what you are adding does not negate or invalidate the required assessment process.

How do I get started with the empowering approach to reading assessment promoted in this book?

Start small and start in a way that makes sense and is manageable for you! We recommend that you select a couple of assessment strategies from the book that you think would be helpful for your teaching and your students' learning. Let's look at how Ms. Gordinski, a kindergarten teacher, started implementation in her classroom last year.

Ms. Gordinski selected two assessment strategies that she thought would work well in her kindergarten classroom as part of her daily instruction. She decided to start with

What Can You Show Us? (Assessment Strategy 6.1) and *Kidwatching* (Assessment Strategy 8.1). She implemented *What Can You Show Us?* first because she already used daily read-alouds, shared reading, and small-group reading instruction in her classroom, and she thought that this assessment strategy would help her gather useful data and insights within the daily reading instruction and activities in her classroom. Since she did not want to be overwhelmed, she decided to try the assessment strategy a couple of times without recording any data or notes so she could just get comfortable with the process. After a couple of days, she started taking notes and quickly felt comfortable doing so. Mrs. Gordinski realized that the more she implemented *What Can You Show Us?*, the easier it got and the more data she was able to collect about her students' constrained skills and other aspects of reading.

From that experience, Mrs. Gordinski realized the importance of trying out a new assessment strategy first before implementing it fully. She then began using *Kidwatching* with three students so she could get comfortable with the process, such as how to record notes, and how to manage it within her classroom and schedule. Within about a week, she was ready to develop a schedule to use *Kidwatching* with more of her students, and within in a month, she was implementing it fully with her entire class.

Mrs. Gordinski began to feel like she had a much better understanding of her students' reading development because of these assessment strategies. She commented to a teaching colleague, "I feel like I have learned so much and become so much more knowledgeable about my students' reading just from using these two assessment strategies. I also realized that for this assessment to be useful, I have to bring my knowledge and understanding of reading and my students to the table." Because she felt confident with these two assessments, she began to consider what additional assessment strategy to add to her classroom next.

I really like the assessments in this book, but I am overwhelmed already by all I have to do. How can I make this assessment approach manageable within my busy schedule?

Just like Mrs. Gordinski in the previous example, we recommend that you start small with one assessment, or maybe two, and get comfortable with them in your own time frame. We suggest you embed the assessments into your daily literacy instruction so that the assessments are tools to support your instruction, not something to add to your workload.

Let's look at an example from Mr. Miller, a third-grade teacher, who has been implementing reading conferences in his classroom for several years. He decided to add *Goal Setting* (Assessment Strategy 7.4) to his conferences because he wanted to support his students' agency development. To get started, he planned for 2–3 extra minutes for each conference, so he could discuss goal setting with each student. To collect data, he simply made a note about the goals at the bottom of the conference record sheet he already used. He got the benefits of adding the *Goal Setting* assessment, but he did it in a way that was easy and efficient for him.

Several months after he added goal setting to his classroom, Mr. Miller decided to use the *Photo Elicitation Interview* (Assessment Strategy 8.5) with two students who were relatively new to his classroom. He wanted to get to know them better by gaining insights into how they use literacy outside of school, their strengths, and their interests. Rather than feeling pressured to use the assessment with all of his students, he decided to use it in a way that helped him reach his goal of getting to know the two new students in his classroom.

If you are thinking about using one of the assessments in this book, we urge you to choose one that will answer a question that has you puzzled or one that will help your instruction. For example, if you want to know more about the strategies your students use, and what they are thinking when they make and correct miscues in their oral reading, we recommend that you use *Conferencing with Retrospective Miscue Analysis* (Assessment Strategy 3.2), or if you want to know more about your students' understanding of high-frequency, useful vocabulary, you may want to try the *Vocabulary Knowledge Assessment* (Assessment Strategy 4.1). For additional suggestions on how to implement the assessments and approach in this book—in ways that are both manageable and efficient—see our responses to the next two questions.

Should I add these assessments to what I've always done, or should I use them instead?

We offer two answers to this question—*replacement* and *addition/transformation*. There are only so many hours in a school day, and when you add new assessment strategies to your teaching, you need to consider how to do that in a manageable day. While assessment is essential for effective teaching and learning, you want to make sure you are not spending so much time and effort on assessment, that it limits the time for instruction, guided practice, and application. Therefore, we generally urge teachers to consider the *replacement* option, meaning that instead of doing a worksheet with comprehension questions to assess a student's comprehension, you replace it with a new assessment strategy that also focuses on comprehension, such as *Retellings* (Assessment Strategy 5.1), but allows you to gather more useful data and gain a deeper understanding of your students' comprehension skills and processes. Or, rather than having students write definitions for new vocabulary words or doing a matching or fill-in-the blank worksheet, use *Language Detective* (Assessment Strategy 4.1) to gain a deeper understanding of students' vocabulary knowledge and comprehension. When making a decision about replacing a traditional assessment with one from this book, consider which assessment will provide you with the authentic data you need to plan instruction to support all of your students.

The *addition/transformation* option is the other way to incorporate new assessment strategies into your teaching. This option makes the most sense when you are using an assessment that is valuable to you or is required by your school or district, but you want to extend or enhance it to make it more valuable. For example, you may already be using an interest inventory to learn about your students' likes, dislikes, and hobbies, but you may feel that assessment only gives you basic information. You may decide to add another assessment strategy such as the *Photo Elicitation Interview* (Assessment Strategy 8.5) to extend and enhance the interest inventory. Or you may decide to merge items from the interest inventory you already use in your classroom with the *Literacy Provision Inventory* (Assessment Strategy 8.4) to transform them into something new that meets your needs and will support teaching and learning in your classroom. The best advice we can offer is to trust yourself as a professional, be confident and comfortable to try new things, refine them to fit your context, and give up those assessment strategies and practices that do not work or are not useful.

How do I explain this approach to reading assessment to others?

This empowering approach to assessment is definitely different from what many educators, parents, and even students are used to. Therefore, it is a good idea to explain not only what you are doing with reading assessment but also why. In this section, we present examples of what Mr. Sandoval, a fourth-grade teacher shared with his students, their parents/families, his principal, and his colleagues. We think these examples will be helpful as you think about how to discuss this approach to reading assessment with the key partners in your assessment process.

Students: "I believe in you, and my job as a teacher is to help you be successful. One of my main goals this year is to help each of you become an effective and engaged reader. To do that, I will work with you to use assessment to learn about your interests, goals, strengths, areas for growth, skills, and strategies. What I learn from these assessments will help me teach and support you better. We will not use tests and quizzes like those that you might have used in the past. We will use conferences, discussions, observations, reading together, and work samples as assessments that will support your learning and help me be a better teacher for you."

Parents/families: "I am committed to helping your child grow as an effective and engaged reader this year. To do that, we will use assessments to inform and guide my instruction. To be an effective teacher for your child, I must understand your child's interests, goals, strengths, areas for growth, skills, and strategies, and the assessments we use in our classroom will do just that. By conferencing with your child, observing their reading, reviewing their work samples, reading with them, and having regular discussions about their skills and strategies, I will be able to get to know your child as a reader and support their development. We will not use traditional tests and quizzes like those that you might have experienced in the past because those assessments only provide a snapshot of who your student is as a reader. The assessments we will use provide lots of information and helpful details, like a movie, so I can really get to know your child and their reading, and they will help me provide effective instruction for your child."

Principal: "I have been working hard to grow as a teacher of reading, and I am using an approach to assessment that allows me to learn more about my students so I can teach them more effectively. I am committed to equity, and this approach to assessment supports maximum growth and progress for every single one of my students. I do not plan to use traditional tests, quizzes, and worksheets to assess student learning in reading this year. Instead, I plan to use conferences, focused observations, work samples, reading with children, and discussions about skills and strategies to assess students' reading and to inform my instructional planning. Since this approach is different from what most people are used to, I will explain it to parents as well as students. I believe this approach to assessment also helps me to grow as a professional and to improve as a teacher, so I would love to have you visit our classroom to see this approach in action."

Colleagues in general situations: "I am using a new empowering approach to reading assessment that focuses on equity and is based on the professional expertise of the teacher. In this approach, assessment is an integral part of instruction, not something that happens after teaching is completed. By using conferences, kidwatching, work samples, reading with children, and discussions about their skills and strategies, I learn more than from tests, quizzes, and worksheets. Through this approach to assessment, I have learned so much about my students as individuals and readers. I have also become more confident and knowledgeable about how to support each of my students' reading growth. I would love to share this approach with you to see if you might want to work together to implement it in our classrooms."

Colleagues at schoolwide data meetings: "The assessments I am implementing provide explicit data sets that go beyond the test scores of the progress monitoring assessments we are using. I implement student portfolios where, for example, I keep student work samples, oral reading and comprehension data, and performance on decoding assessments. When I bring a student's portfolio to our team meetings, I can share (1) explicit examples of students' performance and what I noted as strengths and needs, (2) records of each student's progress over time, with recommendations for adjustments that might be needed, and (3) how students are evaluating and responding to their own performance. These specific data sets will be extremely useful as we plan schoolwide instruction that is appropriate and responsive to our individual students. These explicit data sets, that go beyond test scores and general observations, can support confidence in our instruction."

Final Thoughts

As you and your students implement the assessments in this book and build your students' literacy oeuvres, we believe you will see how this approach can transform assessment into a powerful tool that is humanizing, empowering, and focused on equity. Throughout the chapters in this book, you have seen multiple examples of how this assessment approach is framed around four guiding principles:

1. Reading assessment must occur through an equity mindset.
2. Reading assessment must ensure the visibility of teachers and students in the assessment process.
3. Reading assessment must be embedded in daily instructional and learning activities.
4. Reading assessment must account for reading's complexity.

Because one of these key principles focuses on the visibility of teachers, it is essential that you consider how this approach fits into your classroom, leverages your professional expertise, and meets the needs of every single student in your classroom.

References

Afflerbach, P., Cho, B.-Y., Crassas, M. E., & Kim, J.-Y. (2019). Best practices in reading assessment. In L. M. Morrow & L. B. Gambrell (Eds.), *Best practices in literacy instruction* (6th ed., pp. 309–333). New York: Guilford Press.

Alexander, P. A. (2020). What research has revealed about readers' struggles with comprehension in the digital age: Moving beyond the phonics versus whole language debate. *Reading Research Quarterly, 55*(1) 89–97.

Almasi, J., & Hurt, S. (2019). Best practices in narrative text comprehension. In L. M. Morrow & L. B. Gambrell (Eds.), *Best practices in literacy instruction* (6th ed., pp. 221–249). New York: Guilford Press.

Alsup, J. (2005). *Teacher identity discourses: Negotiating personal and professional spaces*. New York: Routledge.

Anti-Defamation League. (2019). Moving from safe classrooms to brave classrooms. Retrieved from *www.adl.org/education/resources/tools-and-strategies/moving-from-safe-classrooms-to-brave-classrooms*.

Aroa, B., & Clemens, K. (2013). From safe spaces to brave spaces: A new way to frame dialogue around diversity and social justice. In L. Landreman (Ed.), *The art of effective facilitation* (pp. 135–150). Sterling, VA: Stylus.

Asan, A. (2007). Concept mapping in science class: A case study of fifth grade students. *Journal of Education Technology*, 186–195.

Asp, E. (2000). Assessment in education: Where have we been? Where are we headed? In R. S. Brand (Ed.), *Education in a new era* (pp. 123–157). Alexandria, VA: Association for Supervision and Curriculum Development.

Aspen Education & Society Program and the Council of Chief State School Officers. (2017). Leading for equity: Opportunities for State Education Chiefs. Washington, DC.

Bandura, A. (1977). Self-efficacy: Toward a unifying theory of behavioral change. *Psychological Review, 84*(2), 191–215.

Bandura, A. (2001). Social cognitive theory: An agentic perspective. *Annual Review of Psychology, 52*, 1–26.

Bandura, A. (2008). Reconstrual of "free will" from the agentive perspective of social cognitive theory. In J. Baer, J. C. Kauffman, & R. F. Baumeister (Eds.), *Are we free?: Psychology and free will* (pp. 86–127). New York: Oxford University Press.

Bandura, A. (2012). On the functional properties of perceived self-efficacy revisited. *Journal of Management, 38*(1), 9–44.

Bass, J., Dasinger, S., Elish-Piper, L., Matthews, M. W., & Risko, V. (2008). *Declaration of readers' rights: Renewing our commitment to students*. Boston: Pearson.

Bear, D. R., Invernizzi, M., Templeton, S., & Johnston, F. (2008). *Words their way* (4th ed.). Upper Saddle River, NJ: Pearson.

Beck, I. L., McKeown, M. G., & Kucan, L. (2013). *Bringing words to life: Robust vocabulary instruction* (2nd ed.). New York: Guilford Press.

Brady, M. (2012). JoLLE Forum: The testing juggernaut. *Journal of Language and Literacy Education, 8*(2), 1–6.

Bransford, J. D., Brown, A. L., & Cocking, R. R. (2000). *How people learn: Brain, mind, experience, and school: Expanded edition*. Washington, DC: National Academies Press.

Brigham, C. C. (1923). *A study of American intelligence*. Princeton, NJ: Princeton University Press.

Broadfoot, P. (2020). Editorial, dynamic versus arbitrary standards: Recognizing the human factor in assessment. *Assessment in Education*, 9(2), 157–159.

Brown, S. (2011). Becoming literate: Looking across curricular structures at situated identities. *Early Childhood Education Journal, 39*(4), 257–265.

Cabral-Márquez, C. (2015). Helping students set and attain personal reading goals. *The Reading Teacher, 68*(6), 464–472.

Calkins, L. (2003). *The nuts and bolts of teaching writing*. Portsmouth, NH: Heinemann.

Campano, G., & Carpenter, M. (2005). The second class: Providing space in the margins. *Language Arts, 82*(3), 186–194.

Cantor, P. Osher, D., Berg, J., Steyer, L., & Rose, T. (2019). Malleability, plasticity, and individually: How children learn and develop in context. *Applied Developmental Science, 23*(4), 307–337.

Cazden, C. B. (1988). *Classroom discourse*. Portsmouth, NH: Heinemann.

Clay, M. M. (1982). *Observing young readers: Selected papers*. Exeter, NH: Heinemann.

Clay, M. M. (2000). *Running records for classroom teachers*. Auckland, New Zealand: Global Education Systems.

Clay, M. M. (2001). *Change over time in children's literacy development*. Portsmouth, NH: Heinemann.

Clay, M. M. (2005). *Literacy lessons designed for individuals: Part two teaching procedures*. Portsmouth, NH: Heinemann.

Clay, M. M. (2015). *Change over time updated*. Portsmouth, NH: Heinemann.

Clay, M. M. (2019). *An observation survey of early literacy achievement* (4th ed). Auckland, New Zealand: Marie Clay Literacy Trust.

Cobb, C., & Blachowicz, C. (2014). *No more "look up the list" vocabulary instruction*. Portsmouth, NH: Heinemann.

Cobb, F., & Krownapple, J. (2019). *Belonging through a culture of dignity: The keys to successful equity implementation*. San Diego, CA: Mimi & Todd Press.

Cohen, J. H., & Wiener, R. B. (2003). *Literacy portfolios: Improving assessments, teaching and learning* (2nd ed.). Upper Saddle River, NJ: Pearson.

Council of Chief State School Officers. (2017). *Leading for equity: Opportunities for state education chiefs*. Washington, DC: Author.

Dalton, B., Robinson, K. H., Lovvorn, J. F., Smith, B. E., Alvey, T., Mo, E., et al. (2015). Fifth-grade students' digital retellings and the common core: Modal use and design intentionality. *The Elementary School Journal, 115*(4), 548–569.

Daniel, S., Jiménez, R., Pray, L., & Pacheco, M. (2017). Scaffolding to make translanguaging a classroom norm. *TESOL Journal*, 1–14.

Darling-Hammond, L. (2010). *The flat world and education: How America's commitment to education will determine our future*. New York: Teachers College Press.

Darling-Hammond, L. (2021, April 5). Accelerating learning as we build back better. Editors' Pick, *Forbes*. Retrieved from *www.forbes.com/sites/lindadarlinghammond/2021/04/05/accelerating-learning-as-we-build-back-better/?sh=5fd0751a6722*.

Davis, A. (1998). *The limits of educational assessment*. Oxford, UK: Blackwell.

Delgado, R., & Stefancisc, J. (2017). *Critical race theory: An introduction* (3rd ed). New York University Press.

Dennis, D. V. (2017). Learning from the past: What ESSA has the chance to get right. *The Reading Teacher, 70*(4), 395–400

diSessa, A. A. (2018). A friendly introduction to "knowledge in bits and pieces": Modeling types of knowledge and their roles in learning. In G. Kaiser et al. (Eds,), *Invited lectures from the 13th International Congress on Mathematical Education*. Cham, Switzerland: Springer.

Duke, N. K. (2020). When young readers get stuck. *Educational Leadership, 78*(3), 26–33.

Dyson, A. H. (1990). Weaving possibilities: Rethinking metaphors for early literacy development. *The Reading Teacher, 44*(3), 202–213.

Elkonin, D. (1971). Development of speech. In A. V. Zaporozhets & D. B. Elkonin (Eds.) *The psychology of preschool children*. Cambridge, MA: MIT Press.

Enright, K. A., Wong, J. W., & Sanchez, S. L. (2021). *Journal of Literacy Research, 53*(4), 437–467.

Esteban-Guitart, M., & Moll, L. C. (2014). Funds of identity: A new concept based on the funds of knowledge approach. *Culture and Psychology: 25 Constructive Years, 20*(1), 31–48.

Fountas, I. C., & Pinnell, G. S. (2006). *Teaching for comprehension and fluency: Thinking, talking, and writing about reading, K–8*. Portsmouth, NH: Heinemann.

Freire, P. (2005). *Pedagogy of the oppressed* (30th anniversary ed.) (M. B. Ramos, Trans.). New York: Continuum.

Ganske, K. (1999). The developmental spelling analysis: A measure of orthographic analysis. *Educational Assessment, 6*, 41–70.

Ganske, K. (2018). *Word sorts and more: Sound, pattern, and meaning exploration, K–3* (2nd ed.). New York: Guilford Press.

Ganske, K. (2019). Best practices in vocabulary instruction. In L. M. Morrow & L. B. Gambrell (Eds.), *Best practices in literacy instruction* (6th ed., pp. 199–220). New York: Guilford Press.

Gates, M. (2019, November 12). A civil rights challenge to standardized testing in college admissions. Harvard Civil Right—*Civil Liberties Law Review. Amicus blog*. Retrieved from *https://harvardcrcl.org/a-civil-rights-challenge-to-standardized-testing-in-college-admissions*.

Gee, J. P. (2013). Reading as situated language: A sociocognitive perspective. In D. E. Alvermann, N. J. Unrau, & R. B. Ruddell (Eds.), *Theoretical models and processes of reading* (6th ed., pp. 136–151). Newark, DE: International Reading Association.

Gentry, R. (1981). Learning to spell developmentally. *The Reading Teacher, 34*, 378–381.

Gershoff, E. T., & Aber, J. L. (2006). Neighborhood and schools: Contexts and consequences for the mental health and risk behaviors of children and youth. In L. Balter & C. S. Tamis-LeMonda (Eds.), *Child psychology: A handbook of contemporary issues* (pp. 611–645). New York: Psychology Press.

Gerzon, N., & Jones, B. (2020, July). Leading formative assessment in Dallas: Toward student agency and academic achievement. Retrieved from *www.wested.org/making-a-difference/formative-assessment-ben-milam*.

Gilchrist, T. (2018, October 13). *What is agency? Should it be measured?* Tanya Gilchrist. *www.tanyagilchrist.com*.

González, N., Moll, L. C., & Amanti, C. (2005). *Funds of knowledge: Theorizing practices in households, communities, and classrooms*. Mahwah, NJ: Erlbaum.

Goodman, Y. M., & Marek, A. M. (1996). *Retrospective miscue analysis: Revaluing readers and reading.* Somers, NY: Richard C. Owen.

Goodman, Y. M., Watson, D. J., & Burke, C. L. (2005). *Reading miscue inventory: From evaluation to instruction* (2nd ed.). Katonah, NY: Richard C. Owen.

Gowin, D. B., & Alvarez, M. C. (2005). *The art of educating with V diagrams.* New York: Cambridge University Press.

Griffith, R., & Lacina, J. (2018). Building on strengths. *The Reading Teacher, 71*(5), 513–514.

Halliday, M. A. (1993). Towards a language-based theory of learning. *Linguistics and education, 5*(2), 93–116.

Halliday, M. A. K. (1975). *Learning how to mean.* New York: Edward Arnold.

Halliday, M. A. K. (2004). Introduction: How big is a language? On the power of language. In J. Webster (Ed.), In *The collected works of M. A. K. Halliday. Vol. 5. The language of science* (pp. XII–XXIV). Halliday, London: Continuum.

Hammond, Z. L. (2015). *Culturally responsive teaching and the brain: Promoting authentic engagement and rigor among culturally and linguistically diverse students.* Thousand Oaks, CA: Corwin.

Hamre, B., & Pianta, R. (2001) Early teacher-child relationships and the trajectory of children's school outcomes through eighth grade. *Child Development, 72*(2), 625–638.

Hudson, R. F., Lane, H. B., & Pullen, P. C. (2005). Reading fluency assessment and instruction: What, why, and how? *The Reading Teacher, 58*(8), 702–714.

Hughes, J. N., Cavell, T. A., & Wilson, V. L. (2001). Further support of the developmental significance of the teacher–student relationship. *Journal of School Psychology, 39*(4), 289–302.

Iddings, A. C. D., Risko, V. J., & Rampulla, M. P. (2009). When you don't speak their language: Guiding English-language learners through conversations about text. *The Reading Teacher, 63*(1), 52–61.

International Literacy Association. (2019a). *Children experiencing reading difficulties: What we know and what we can do.* [Literacy leadership brief]. Newark, DE: Author.

International Literacy Association. (2019b). *Right to policies that ensure equitable literacy instruction* [Research brief]. Newark, DE: Author.

International Reading Association. (2013). *Formative assessment.* [Position statement]. Newark, DE: Author.

International Reading Association. (2014). *Using high-stakes assessments for grade retention and graduation decisions* [Position statement]. Newark, DE: Author.

Irwin, P. A., & Mitchell, J. N. (1988). Using retellings to make instructional decisions. In S. M. Glazer, L. Searfoss, & M. Gentile (Eds.), *Reexamining reading diagnosis: New trends and procedures* (pp. 128–149). Newark, DE: International Reading Association.

Ivey, G., & Johnston, P. H. (2017). Emergent adolescence in engaged reading communities. *Language Arts,* 94(3), 159–169.

Jiménez, R. T., David, S., Pacheco, M., Risko, V. J., Pray, L., Fagan, K., et al. (2015). Using translation to drive conceptual development for students becoming literate in English as an additional language. *Research in the Teaching of English,* 49(3), 248–271.

Johns, J. L., Lenski, S. D., & Elish-Piper, L. (2002). *Teaching beginning readers: Linking assessment and instruction* (2nd ed). Dubuque, IA: Kendall Hunt.

Johnston, P. (2005). Literacy assessment and the future. *The Reading Teacher, 58*(7), 684–686.

Johnston, P., & Costello, P. (2005). Principles for literacy assessment. *Reading Research Quarterly,* 40(2), 256–267.

Johnston, P. H. (1997). *Knowing literacy: Constructive literacy assessment.* Portland, ME: Stenhouse.

Johnston, P. H. (2000). *Running records: A self-tutoring guide.* York, ME: Stenhouse.

Johnston, P. H. (2003). Assessment conversations. *The Reading Teacher, 57*(1), 90–92.

Johnston, P. H. (2004). *Choice words: How our language affects children's learning.* Portland, ME: Stenhouse.

Johnston, P. H., Champeau, K., Hartwig, A., Helmer, S., Komar, M., Krueger, T., et al. (2020). *Engaging literate minds: Developing children's social, emotional, and intellectual lives, K–3*. Portsmouth, NH: Stenhouse.

Kaufman, D. (2000). *Conferences and conversation: Listening to the literate classroom*. Portsmouth, NH: Heinemann.

Kim, Y., & Yazdian, L. S. (2014). Portfolio assessment and quality teaching. *Theory Into Practice, 53*(3), 220–227.

Kim, K. H., & Zabelina, D. (2015). Cultural bias in assessment: Can creativity assessment help? *The International Journal of Critical Pedagogy*, 6(2), 129–147.

Knoester, J., & Au, W. (2017). Standardized testing and school segregation: Like tinder for fire? *Race Ethnicity and Education, 20*(1), 1–14.

Koretz, D. (2017). *The testing charade: Pretending to make schools better*. University of Chicago Press.

Krueger, W. K. (2020). *This Tender Land*. New York: Atria Books.

Kuby, C. R. (2010). Kidwatching with a critical eye: The power of observation and reflexive practice. *Talking Points, 22*(2), 22–28.

Kusimo, P., Ritter, M. G., Busich, K., Ferguson, C., Trumbull, E., & Solano-Flores, G. (2000). Making assessment work for everyone: How to build on student strengths. Retrieved from *www.wested.org/wp-content/uploads/2016/11/137157875720130617_REL0001_Making_Assess-3.pdf.*

Ladson-Billings, G. (2014). Culturally relevant pedagogy 2.0: a.k.a. the remix. *Harvard Educational Review, 84*(1), 74–135.

Lake, R. (2012). *Dear Nel: Opening the circle of care* (Letters to Nel Noddings). New York: Teachers College Press.

Leap Innovations. (n.d.). Student agency rubric. Retrieved from *www.leapinnovations.org/wp-content/uploads/2019/06/Student-Agency-Rubric.pdf.*

Lenz, L. (2016, September 11). A strengths-based approach to teaching English learners [blog]. Retrieved from *www.cultofpedagogy.com/strength-based-teacing-esl.*

Lipson, M. Y., & Wixson, K. K. (2013). *Assessment of reading and writing difficulty* (5th ed.). Boston: Pearson.

Maitra, D. (2017). Funds of knowledge: An underrated tool for school literacy and student engagement. *International Journal of Society, Culture & Language*, 5(1), 94–102.

Martens, P., & Adamson, S. (2001). Inventing literate identities: The influence of texts and contexts. *Literacy Teaching and Learning*, 5(2), 27–50.

Martinez, R. A. (2018). Beyond the English learner label: Recognizing the richness of bi/multilingual students' linguistic repertoires. *The Reading Teacher, 71*(5), 515–522.

McCarthey, S. J. (2001). Identity construction in elementary readers and writers. *Reading Research Quarterly, 36*(2), 122–151.

McNeill, E. (2020). *Immigration stories in the emergent bilingual classroom: Revealing funds of knowledge and brave spaces through literacy curriculum* [Doctoral Dissertation Indiana University]. IU Scholarworks. *http://hdl.handle.net/2022/26379.*

Mehan, H. (1979). *Learning lessons: Social organization in the classroom*. Cambridge, MA: Harvard University Press.

Mercer, N., & Hodgkinson, S. (Eds.) (2008). *Exploring talk in school*. Thousand Oaks, CA: Sage.

Milner, H. R. (2018). Confronting inequity/assessment for equity. *Educational Leadership, 75*(5), 88–89.

Moje, E. B. (2004). Powerful spaces: Tracing the out-of-school literacy spaces of Latino/a youth. In K. Leander & M. Sheehy (Eds.), *Spatializing literacy research and practice* (pp. 15–38). New York: Peter Lang.

Moll, L. (2015). Tapping into the "hidden" home and community resources of students. *Kappa Delta Pi Record, 51*(3), 114–117.

Morrell, E. (2020, August 4). Literacy teaching in turbulent times (Ernest Morrell & Nell K. Duke). Available at *Literacyworldwide.org/Digital events.*

Morrell, E., & Morrell, J. (2018, November). "Kidwatching": Discovering every child's genius. Retrieved from *https://iei.nd.edu/initiatives/notre-dame-center-for-literacy-education/news/Kidwatching-discovering-every-childs.*

Morrow, L. M. (1986). Effects of structural guidance in story retelling on children's dictation of original stories. *Journal of Reading Behavior, 18*(2), 135–152.

Morrow, L. M. (2020). *Literacy development in the early years: Helping children read and write* (9th ed.). Hoboken, NJ: Pearson.

Morrow, L. M., Dougherty, S. M., & Tracey, D. H. (2019). Best practices in early literacy: Preschool, kindergarten, and first grade. In L. M. Morrow & L. B. Gambrell (Eds.), *Best practices in literacy instruction* (6th ed., pp. 75–103). New York: Guilford Press.

Murray, C., & Malmgren, K. (2005). Implementing student-teacher relationship program in a high-poverty urban school: Effects on social, emotional, and academic adjustment and lessons learned. *Journal of School Psychology, 43*(2), 137–152.

Neuman, S. B., & Wright, T. S. (2013). *All about words: Increasing vocabulary in the common core classroom, PreK–2.* New York: Teachers College Press.

Nieto, S., & Bode, P. (2018). *Affirming diversity: The sociopolitical context of multicultural education* (7th ed.). Boston: Pearson.

Noddings, N. (2005). *The challenge to care in schools: An alternative approach to education* (2nd ed.) New York: Teachers College Press.

Noddings, N. (2013). *Caring: A relational approach to ethics and moral education* (2nd ed.). Berkeley: University of California Press.

Ogbu, J. (1988). Cultural diversity and human development. In D. T. Slaughter (Ed.), *Black children and poverty: A developmental perspective* (pp. 11–28). San Francisco: Jossey-Bass.

Olshavsky, J. E. (1977). Reading as problem-solving: An investigation of strategies. *Reading Research Quarterly, 12*(4), 654–674.

Orellana, M. F., & Garcia, O. (2014). Conversation currents: Language brokering and translanguaging in school. *Language Arts, 91*(5), 386–392.

Owocki, G., & Goodman, Y. (2002). *Kidwatching: Documenting children's literacy development.* Portsmouth, NH: Heinemann.

Pacheco, M. B., Daniel, S. M., & Pray, L. C. (2017). Scaffolding practice: Supporting emerging bilinguals' academic language use in two classroom communities. *Language Arts, 95*(2), 63–76.

Pacheco, M. B., Daniel, S. M., Pray, L. C., & Jimenez, R. T. (2019). Translingual practice. strategic participation, and meaning-making. *Journal of Literacy Research, 51*(1), 75–99.

Paechter, C., & Clark, S. (2007). Who are tomboys and how do we recognise them? *Women's Studies International Forum, 30*(4), 342–354.

Paris, S. G. (2005). Reinterpreting the development of reading skills. *Reading Research Quarterly, 40*(2), 184–202.

Pearson, P. D., & Cervetti, G. N. (2017). The roots of reading comprehension instruction. In S. E. Israel (Ed.), *Handbook of research on reading comprehension* (2nd ed., pp. 12–56). New York: Guilford Press.

Penul, W. R., & Watkins, D. A. (2019). Assessment to promote equity and epistemic justice: A use-case-of a research-practice partnership in science education. *The Annals of the American Academy, 683*(1), 201–216.

Perfetti, C. A., & Dunlap, S. (2008). Learning to read: General principles and writing system variation. In K. Koda & A. M. Zehler (Eds.), *Learning to read across languages: Crosslinguistic relationships in first- and second-language literacy development* (pp. 13–38). New York: Routledge.

Pluralism Project. (n.d.). Many local traditions. The Pluralism Project Harvard University. Retrieved from *https://pluralism.org/files/pluralism/files/many_local_traditions.pdf.*

Puzio, K., Keyes, C. S., & Jimenez, R. T. (2016). It sounds more like a gangbanger: Using collaborative translation to understand literary concepts. *Language Arts,* 93(6), 444–456.

Pyle, A. (2012). Engaging young children in research through photo elicitation. *Early Childhood Development and Care, 183*(11), 1544–1558.

Raburu, P. A. (2015). The self- who am I?: Children's identity and development through early childhood education. *Journal of Educational and Social Research,* 5(1), 95–102.

RAND Reading Study Group. (2002). *Reading for understanding: Toward an R & D program in reading comprehension*. Santa Monica, CA: RAND.

Rasinski, T. V., Reutzel, D. R., Chard, D., & Linan-Thompson, S. (2011). Reading fluency. In M. L. Kamil, P. D. Pearson, E. B. Moje, & P. P. Afflerbach (Eds.), *Handbook of reading research* (4th ed., pp. 286–319). New York: Routledge.

Razfar, A., & Gutierrez, K. D. (2013). Re-conceptualizing early childhood literacy: The sociocultural influence and new directions in digital and hybrid mediation. In J. Larson & J. Marsh (Eds.), *The Sage handbook of early childhood literacy,* (2nd ed., pp. 52–79). Los Angeles, CA: Sage.

Reyes, I., Iddings, A. C. D., & Feller, N. (2015). Building relationships with diverse students and families: A funds of knowledge perspective. *Journal of Early Childhood Literacy,* 16(1), 8–33.

Richgels, D. J., Poremba, K. J., & McGee, L. M. (1996). Kindergarteners talk about print: Phonemic awareness in meaningful contexts. *The Reading Teacher,* 49, 632–642.

Risko, V. J., & Walker-Dalhouse, D. (2012). *Be that teacher! Breaking the cycle for struggling readers.* New York: Teachers College Press.

Ritchhart, R., & Church, M. (2020). *The power of making thinking visible: Practices to engage and empower all learners*. Hoboken, NJ: Jossey-Bass.

Rosenblatt, L. M. (2013). The transactional theory of reading and writing, In D. E. Alvermann, N. J. Unrau, & R. B. Ruddell (Eds.), *Theoretical models and processes of reading* (6th ed., pp. 923–956). Newark, DE: International Reading Association.

Scanlon, D. M., & Anderson, K. L. (2020). Using context as an assist in word solving: The contributions of 25 years of research on the Interactive Strategies Approach. *Reading Research Quarterly,* 55(S1), 510–534.

Schunk, D. H. (2001). *Self-regulation through goal setting.* Greenborough, MN: Eric Clearinghouse on Counseling and Student Services. (ERIC Document Reproduction Service Report No. ED452671)

Schunk, D. H. (2003). Self-efficacy for reading and writing: Influence of modeling goal setting, and self-evaluation. *Reading & Writing Quarterly,* 19(2), 159–172.

Seban, D., & Tavsanli, O. F. (2015). Children's sense of being a writer: Identity construction in a second grade writers' workshop. *International Electronic Journal of Elementary Education, 7* (2), 217–234.

Shepard, L. A., Penul, W. R., & Davidson, K. L. (2017). Design principles for new systems of assessment. *Phi Delta Kappan,* 98(6), 47–52.

Siraj-Blatchford, J. (2009). Editorial: Education for sustainable development in early childhood. *International Journal of Early Childhood, 41*(2), 9–22.

Soares, J. A. (2020, June 22). Dismantling white supremacy includes ending racist tests like the SAT and ACT. Teachers College Press Blog. Retrieved from *www.tcpress.com/blog/dismantling-white-supremacy-includes-racist-tests-sat-act.*

Sroufe, L. A., Egeland, B., Carlson, E. A., & Collins, W. A. (2005). *The development of the person: The Minnesota study of risk and adaptation from birth to adulthood.* New York: Guilford Press.

Stahl, K. A. D., & Bravo, M. A. (2010). Contemporary classroom vocabulary assessment for content areas. *The Reading Teacher,* 63(7), 566–578.

Stanovich, K. E. (1986). Matthew effects in reading: Some consequences of individual differences in the acquisition of literacy. *Reading Research Quarterly, 22*(4), 360–407.

Sternberg, R. J. (1988). Applying cognitive theory to the testing and teaching of intelligence. *Applied Cognitive Psychology, 2*(4), 231–255.

Sternberg, R. J. (2000). The theory of successful intelligence. *Gifted Education International, 15*(1), 4–21.

Sternberg, R. J., & Grigorenko, E. L. (2000). *Teaching for successful intelligence.* Arlington Heights, IL: Skylight.

Teale, W. H., Paciga. K. A., & Hoffman, J. L. (2007). Beginning reading instruction in urban schools: The curriculum gap ensures a continuing achievement gap. *The Reading Teacher, 61*(4), 344–348.

Tomasello, M. (2003) *Constructing language: A usage-based theory of language.* Cambridge, MA: Harvard University Press.

Tomasello, M., Carpenter, M., Call, J., Behne, T., & Moll, H. (2005). Understanding and sharing intentionality: The origins of cultural cognition. *Behavioral and Brain Sciences, 28*(5), 675–735.

Tudge, J. (2008). *The everyday lives of young children: Culture, class, and child rearing in diverse societies.* New York: Cambridge University Press.

UNESCO. (2020, May 9). *While the COVID crisis increases inequalities, UNESCO recalls that reading is the basis of development.* Paris: UNESCO.

Valencia, S. W., Wixson, K. K., & Pearson, P. D. (2014). Putting text complexity in context: Refocusing on comprehension of complex text. *The Elementary School Journal, 115*(2), 270–289.

Valenzuela, A. (1999). *Subtractive schooling: U.S.-Mexican youth and the politics of caring.* Albany: State University of New York Press.

van der Putten, S. A. (2017). Are motivational theories too general to be applied in education? *SFU Ed Review*, Special Edition, pp. 1–12.

Vasquez, V. (2010). *Getting beyond "I like the book": Creating space for critical literacy in K–6 classrooms* (2nd ed.). Newark, DE: International Reading Association.

Vaughn, M., Premo, J., Sotirovska, V. V., Erickson, D. (2019). Evaluating agency in literacy using the Student Agency Profile. *The Reading Teacher, 73*(4), 427–441.

Victoria Department of Education and Early Childhood Development. (2012). Department of Education and Early Childhood Development Annual Report 2011–2012. Retrieved from *www.education.vic.gov.au/Documents/about/department/201112deecdannualreport.pdf.*

Vygotsky, L. S. (1978). *Mind in society: The development of higher mental process.* Cambridge, MA: Harvard University Press.

Walsh, R. (2016, December 18). Beyond grades: How am I doing? Retrieved from *https://russonreading.blogspot.com/search?q=What+am+i+doing.*

Werblow, J., Duesbery, L., & Koulidobrova, H. (2020). Shifting the perspective: The case for dual language programs as the gold standard for achieving educational equity in schools. *Literacy Today, 37*(3) 23–24.

West, J. (2002). Motivation and access to help: The influence of status on one child's motivation for literacy learning. *Reading & Writing Quarterly: Overcoming Learning Difficulties, 18*(3), 205–229.

Wilhelm, J. D. (2001). *Improving comprehension with think-aloud strategies.* New York: Scholastic.

Wilson, P., & Long, I. (2018). *The big book of blob trees* (2nd ed.). New York: Routledge.

Wortham, S. E. F. (2010). Listening for identity beyond the speech event. *Teachers College Record, 112*, 2848–2871.

Zeiser, K., Scholz, C., & Cirks, V. (Oct. 2018). *Maximizing student agency: Implementing and measuring student-centered learning practices.* Washington, DC: American Institutes for Research.

Children's Literature Cited

Becker, A. (2013). *Journey*. New York: Random House.

Brucbac, J., & Ross, G. *The story of the Milky Way: A Cherokee tale*. New York: Houghton Mifflin.

Byers, G. (2020). *I am enough*. New York: Balzar & Bray, Harper Collins.

Curtis, C. P. (1998). *Bud, not Buddy*. New York: Penguin Random House.

Delacre, L. (2016). *Áolinguito, de la A A La Z! Descubriendo el bosque nublado / Olinguito, from A to Z! Unveiling the cloud forest* (English and Spanish Edition). San Francisco: Children's Book Press.

Fradin, J. B., & Fradin, D. B. (2011). *Tornado! The story behind these twisting, turning, spinning, and spiraling storms*. Washington, DC: National Geographic Partners.

Havill, J. (1989). *Jamaica tag-along*. New York: Houghton Mifflin Harcourt.

Kinney, J. (2007). *Diary of a wimpy kid*. New York: Amulet Books.

Kline, S. (1988). *Horrible Harry in room 2B*. New York: Scholastic.

Lawson, J. A. (2016). *Sidewalk flowers*. Toronto: Groundwood Books/House of Anansi Press.

Lee, J. (2015). *Pool*. San Francisco: Chronicle Books.

Oughton, J. (1966). *How the stars fell into the sky: A Navajo legend*. New York: Sandpiper Houghton Mifflin.

Quite an adventure. Selected from *The Project Gutenberg EBook of Our Story*. Book released August 20, 2016. [Ebook #53860]

Wiesner, D. (1998). *Tuesday*. New York: Clarion Books.

Wiles, D. (2001). *Freedom summer*. New York: Aladdin Paperbacks.

Index

Note. *f* or *t* following a page number indicates a figure or a table.

D

E

F

G

H

I

K

L

M

N

O

V

W